The Tidelands Oil Controversy

A Legal and Historical Analysis

ERNEST R. BARTLEY

The Tidelands Oil Controversy

A Legal and Historical Analysis

AUSTIN : 1953
UNIVERSITY OF TEXAS PRESS

UNIVERSITY OF TEXAS PRESS
Austin 12

THOMAS NELSON AND SONS LTD

Parkside Works Edinburgh 9
3 Henrietta Street London WC2
312 Flinders Street Melbourne C1
5 Parker's Buildings   Burg Street   Cape Town

Thomas Nelson and Sons (Canada) Ltd
91–93 Wellington Street West   Toronto 1

Société Française d'Editions Nelson
25 rue Henri Barbusse Vᵉ

To My Wife
Ruth Arline
who had patience

Preface

THE FACT THAT the American scheme of government divides power between state and nation gives rise to many controversies over the extent of authority each level of government should exercise. This book is a legal and historical analysis of one such dispute. The issue of control and ownership of offshore lands has only recently been brought to a head with the decisions of the Supreme Court in *United States* v. *California, United States* v. *Texas,* and *United States* v. *Louisiana.* Here, in one small instance among the numerous clashes of state and national interests, may be found international law, American constitutional law, the machinations of pressure groups, the workings of Congress, and a new, eventful chapter in the history of the Supreme Court of the United States as the "umpire" of the American federal system.

The writer of a work of this nature is in the debt of many persons. Senators Spessard Holland and George Smathers of Florida, Senator Eugene Millikin of Colorado, former Senator Claude Pepper of Florida, and former Congressman Sam Hobbs of Alabama very kindly provided copies of various Congressional hearings and reports. The late Harold L. Ickes, former Secretary of the Interior, took time from his extraordinarily crowded schedule to write lengthy letters in answer to the questions which I posed to him. Although Mr. Ickes' views and mine were seldom in agreement, he gave me information I could not have obtained otherwise and allowed me to quote from his letters. I would single out, too, four other persons who provided materials not available from other sources. Mr. William W. Clary, formerly special assistant to the attorney general of California and member of the law firm of O'Melveny and Myers, gave aid on the California side of the problem. Senator Price Daniel of Texas, attorney general of that state during most of the period of the controversy, made available all briefs and materials relating to the Texas situation. Mr. Cullen Liskow, of Lake Charles, Louisiana, performed a similar function for that state. Finally, Congressman W. R. Poage of Texas expedited the obtaining of materials stating the position of the United States and offered many helpful suggestions.

Professor Manning J. Dauer and Mr. Robert Fuquay of the University of Florida and Professor Charles T. McCormick of the University of Texas School of Law read the manuscript in great detail, thereby decreasing the percentage of errors inevitable in a work of this kind. I would acknowledge aid extended in the formative period of this study by Professors Eric Bellquist and Dwight Waldo of the University of California. My mentor and friend, Professor David B. Fellman of the University of Wisconsin, has provided needed encouragement. Mr. Dwynal Pettengill performed the laborious task of checking citations.

For errors of fact or interpretation, I alone must assume responsibility.

ERNEST R. BARTLEY

Gainesville, Florida
1 February 1953

Contents

Preface vii

1. The Problem 3

2. The Territorial Concept of the Marginal Sea . . 7

3. Claims of the Original States to Submerged Lands . 27

4. Claims of Later States to Submerged Lands . . 43

5. California's Claims to Submerged Lands . . . 59

6. Texas' Claims to Submerged Lands 79

7. Congressional Policy on Submerged Lands Prior to World War II 95

8. Executive Policy on Submerged Lands Prior to *United States* v. *California* 122

9. The Quitclaim Attempt in 1945 144

10. *United States* v. *California* 159

11. The Immediate Aftermath of *United States* v. *California* 182

12. *United States* v. *Louisiana* and *United States* v. *Texas* 195

13. Quitclaim or Federal Control?   213

14. The New Doctrine of Paramount Powers   .   .   .   247

15. Conclusions   274

Appendix: Congressional Hearings on Control of Sub-
    merged Lands in the Marginal Sea   .   .   .   283

Table of Cases   287

Index   299

Scarcely any political question
arises in the United States
that is not resolved,
sooner or later,
into a judicial question

ALEXIS DE TOCQUEVILLE

The Tidelands Oil Controversy

A Legal and Historical Analysis

1 .

The Problem

Fundamental to the American political system is the principle of federalism. The division of governmental powers between state and nation through the medium of a written document is one of the most important realities of American constitutional existence. It was Woodrow Wilson who wrote that every great internal crisis in the course of the nation's history has turned on an issue of opposed state and national rights.[1] Reflection supports the sageness of the observation. American federalism has not been a matter of theoretically defined relationships of nation to state, relationships to which lip service has been paid while in practice the divisions of power have been ignored. Federalism has been a practical force in the American society.

Controversy over the proper limits of state and national powers has been constant from 1789 to the present. The disputes have been basic and fundamental, even involving a resort to armed force when the flames of secession and slavery tore at the bonds of union with terrible fury. The arguments over the appropriate provinces of the state and national governments continue unabated today. In 1948 a consequential segment of the Democratic party "seceded" over questions of opposed state and national rights. In 1952 the Democratic party very nearly split again on the issue. The campaign was fought, to some degree, with a recognition on the part of Governor Stevenson and General Eisenhower that the people did, indeed, feel deeply about the matter. Advocates of the states' rights point of view are not found alone in the South; vocal expression opposing the "domination of Washington bu-

[1] Woodrow Wilson, *Constitutional Government in the United States* (New York, Columbia University Press, 1921), 174–75.

3

reaucrats" occurs in all sections of the nation.[2] On the other hand, supporters of "big government" and the welfare state have been as ardent in the exposition of their political and economic doctrines as their opposites, the "states' righters." Yet, with all the controversy, none but a few theoreticians would deny the statement of the late Justice Murphy that "we derive much of our strength as a nation from our dual system of federal government."[3]

It was on 23 June 1947 that the United States Supreme Court, in a memorable opinion, wrote another chapter in the extensive and apparently unending dispute over national as opposed to state authority. In *United States* v. *California,* the court held that "California is not the owner of the three-mile marginal belt along its coast, and that the Federal Government rather than the state has paramount rights in and power over that belt, an incident to which is full dominion over the resources of the soil under that water area, including oil."[4] This precedent-making ruling was to be followed, three years later, by two more judgments, which substituted, in effect, the name of Texas[5] and the name of Louisiana[6] for that of California in the earlier decision. Landmark cases in the history of national-state relations had been decided.

The United States Supreme Court had reversed, on the face of it, a trend of over 150 years during which the states had exercised both jurisdiction and ownership over the beds of their navigable waters; for, surprisingly, the issue of which authority, state or nation, should control the submerged lands is less than twenty years old. Until the late 1930's there appeared to be little, if any, doubt that these areas were not only under the primary control of the littoral states but were actually a part of them, subject only to the exercise of those powers specifically granted to the national government by the Constitution.

[2] Typical of such expressions is that of the Indiana Legislature in 1945. In January of that year, the Legislature adopted House Concurrent Resolution 2, which declared: "Indiana needs no guardian and intends to have none. . . . We are fed up with subsidies, doles, and paternalism. We are no one's step-child. We have grown up. We serve notice that we will resist Washington, D.C. adopting us. . . . [We will] fetch our county courthouse and city halls back from Pennsylvania Avenue . . . [and] restore the American Republic and our forty-eight states to the foundations built by our fathers."

In January 1951, a resolution was introduced in the Nebraska Legislature asserting that the development of natural resources "is a function of the State and subject to the control and regulation of the State." Its supporters called it a "states rights bill, pure and simple." *Omaha World Herald,* 6 February 1951.

[3] *Pacific Coast Dairy* v. *Department of Agriculture,* 318 U.S. 285, 304 (1943).

[4] 332 U.S. 19, 38.

[5] *United States* v. *Texas,* 339 U.S. 707, 719–20.

[6] *United States* v. *Louisiana,* 339 U.S. 699, 705–706.

It came as a considerable shock to the officials of coastal states to find that they did not have the authority over the area from low-water mark to the three-mile limit which they had assumed. The coastal states for nearly 150 years had utilized and controlled the marginal-sea area as though they owned it—which in fact they thought they did. They had regulated the fisheries in the area, applying state laws to vessels licensed under national statutes and operated by out-of-state persons. They had prescribed the size of fish that might be taken, had directed the manner in which fish might be caught, and had even exercised successful though indirect control over the activities of floating canneries operating outside the three-mile limit. Oysters, shrimp, and sponges had been subjected to similar controls. The states had granted or leased areas in the marginal sea to private persons and corporations and to the national government itself. The purposes of these state grants were many and varied. Long before any person dreamed of black gold, the process of land reclamation and harbor development, on land granted or leased by the states, had begun. Breakwaters had been built and harbors dredged from below low-water mark and converted to useful commercial purposes. Later, with visions of wealth from petroleum royalties spurring them to action, the states of California, Texas, Louisiana, and, to a lesser extent, others, had leased the offshore lands for oil production. Immensely valuable property rights had been established in the marginal-sea areas, rights dependent upon grant or lease by a state made upon the unchallenged assumption that the state "owned" the area it purported to grant or lease.

Considered in a very narrow and technical sense, the Supreme Court had determined that it no longer lay within the power of the states of California, Texas, and Louisiana to lease the submerged lands in the open sea beyond the low-water mark for the purpose of oil production. It will be demonstrated, however, that the effect of these three cases will be felt far beyond the apparently circumscribed opinions of the majority of the court. A direct clash of interests between the states and the national government resulted in a decision which broadened, as have many decisions of the high tribunal in the past, the power and authority of the federal government.

There have been varying and frequently diametrically opposed interpretations of these important cases. Much of the misunderstanding and genuine apprehension presently felt by public-spirited citizens throughout the nation is a result of a lack of proper information on the issues which are involved. Both sides have hurled unfounded charges and have misused legal concepts, and the net result of all the sound and fury has been further confusion. It is therefore proposed to examine extensively the history and legal background of *United States* v. *California, United States* v. *Texas,* and *United States* v. *Louisiana* and from these materials to draw certain conclusions in regard to the future status of the disputed submerged areas and to show the impact of the decisions upon the American federal system.

This dispute could arise only in a federal system. Few controversies of the day have presented with greater clarity the issue of opposed state and national power. Compared with the specter of an international atomic conflagration or the immediate problem of a possibly disastrous inflation in the domestic economy of the United States, the controversy over the submerged lands appears at first blush a very minor thing, to be dismissed lightly. Yet the dispute will be recorded by legal historians as a significant milestone in the development of the powers of the national government. The judicial opinions may well serve as precedent for an expansion of national power but dimly foreseen at the present time. The minor seed of what is popularly known as the "tidelands oil controversy"[7] may bear important fruit in the bitter domestic struggle over national authority as against states' rights.

[7] Technically, the argument can be advanced that the term "tidelands" embraces only the strip of land between high- and low-water marks. *Borax Consolidated* v. *Los Angeles,* 296 U.S. 10 (1935), so held. On the other hand, the California Supreme Court has construed the word broadly and applied it to lands permanently submerged by tidal waters. *San Pedro, etc., R. Co.* v. *Hamilton,* 161 Cal. 610, 614 (1911). Journalistic usage, moreover, has given to the word a meaning inclusive of the area from high-water mark out to at least the three-mile limit. The writer has chosen the title that he has for this work because the dispute has been so denominated in the public mind.

2 ·

The Territorial Concept of the Marginal Sea

The controversy over control of the submerged lands off the coasts of California, Louisiana, and Texas was immediately prompted by the presence of immensely valuable petroleum deposits. The dispute is a recent one, but it is important to remember that this is only one in a long series of contests, dating back for centuries, which have been waged for the purpose of gaining or maintaining dominion over the seas adjacent to a nation's coasts. The roots of the decisions of the United States Supreme Court in the submerged lands cases are buried deep in the musty records of the past.

In Roman law, the sea was considered as being open to all persons (*res communes*) and therefore incapable of appropriation and ownership (*res nullius*).[1] No substantial modification of this doctrine can be noted until the rise of the great maritime nations of the Middle Ages. By the beginning of the seventeenth century, Venice had laid claim to ownership of the Adriatic. Genoa asserted proprietorship of the Ligurian Sea. Denmark and Sweden shared, not without argument, pretensions in the Baltic, while France and England made extravagant claims to the seas off their coasts.[2] In the meantime, Spain and Portugal had proceeded, through the Treaty of Tordesillas in 1494, to divide the oceans and territories of the New World between them. Spain asserted dominion over, and exclusive rights to navigate, the Pacific, the

[1] Percy Thomas Fenn, "Justinian and the Freedom of the Sea," 19 *American Journal of International Law* (1925), 716, 721.
[2] William E. Hall, *A Treatise on International Law,* ed. A. Pearce Higgins (7th ed., London, Clarendon Press, 1917), 144–45; Charles G. Fenwick, *International Law* (3d ed., New York, Appleton-Century-Crofts, 1948), 417.

Gulf of Mexico, and the western Atlantic. Portugal's claims extended
to the Atlantic south of Morocco and covered the Indian Ocean.[3]

England and Holland, however, were unwilling to accept such a
division and answered the Iberian decrees with deadly, efficient forays
by Drake and Cavendish and with a blunt refusal to cease trade with
the Orient. England thus argued by force the freedom of the seas where
it served her purposes, but at the same time she held on to her claims
of dominion over portions of the North Sea, the Bay of Biscay, and
the Atlantic from Cape Finisterre, Spain, to Stadland, in Norway.[4]

Thus history prepared a setting for the writings of Grotius and Selden. In 1609, Grotius urged the acceptance of the old Roman law
principle in his *Mare liberum*, elaborating and qualifying his concepts
in 1625 in his *De jure belli ac pacis*. To Grotius the open sea was *res
communes*. The ability to exercise dominion over any part of it was
dependent upon physical power to control. Grotius' interpretation of
the open sea as *res communes* bolstered the assertions of the Dutch that
they had the right to navigate the Indian Ocean, an area claimed exclusively by Portugal.[5]

Selden, at the instigation of the Crown, replied to Grotius in 1635.
Mare clausum defended at length the official British attitude toward
dominion and control of the seas adjacent to English coasts. Selden's
task was a most difficult one, for he was faced with the necessity of being an advocate for a fundamentally inconsistent position. In some
areas of the world, England chose to utilize the principle of the non-
appropriability of the open sea; yet near her own shores, she asserted
outright and complete dominion. Selden attempted to rationalize this
contradictory situation by basing English assertions of proprietary rights
on the long practice of English dominion over the seas adjacent to the
coast. The Spanish and Portuguese, he contended, could point to no
such lengthy practice as a basis for their claims. To this was added a
very practical consideration: namely, that England alone had the naval

[3] Thomas Wemyss Fulton, *The Sovereignty of the Sea* (London, W. Black-
wood & Sons, 1911), 4–5; Fenwick, *op. cit.*, 417–18.

[4] Hall, *op. cit.*, 149. Hall tells of Queen Elizabeth's reaction to the request of
the Spanish minister to the English Court in regard to the presence of English
vessels in Spanish-proscribed waters. Without regard to her own inconsistent
position in claiming certain sea areas as "territory" of England, she refused to
admit that English ships could in any way be prohibited from entering the waters
covered by the Spanish edict. See also Fulton, *op. cit.*, 18.

[5] Spanish claims were defended by Gentili in his *Hispanicae advocationis libri
duo*, published posthumously in 1613.

might to make good her claims. This factor was of major importance, for the Spanish Armada had been defeated in 1588.[6]

Gradually the claims to various seas began to disappear, and by the beginning of the nineteenth century Hall summed up the situation as follows:

> Down to the beginning of the nineteenth century, then, the course of opinion and practice with respect to the sea had been as follows. Originally it was taken for granted that the sea could be appropriated. It was effectively appropriated in some instances; and in others extravagant pretensions were put forward, supported by wholly insufficient acts. Gradually, as appropriation of the larger areas was found to be generally unreal, to be burdensome to strangers, and to be unattended by compensating advantages, a disinclination to submit to it arose, . . . the larger claims disappeared, and only those continued at last to be recognised which affected waters the possession of which was supposed to be necessary to the safety of a state, or which were thought to be within its power to command. . . . The true key to the development of the law is to be sought in the principle that maritime occupation must be effective in order to be valid.[7]

As the more grandiose claims began to die, there appeared a new doctrine for the measurement of a nation's dominion in the coastal sea, first stated in 1702 by Bynkershoek. Effectiveness of occupation and control of the sea was the basis of his position, expressed in the famous *generaliter dicendum esset, potestatem terrae finiri, ubi finitur armorum vis.* The sea, to the distance that a cannon shot could reach and thereby control, might be appropriated. Galiani, an Italian jurist, proposed a fixed range for cannon of three miles,[8] a position subsequently adopted by many other writers on international law.

But sharp and extended controversy arose immediately concerning the character of this three-mile belt, as well as the purposes to which it might be put by a littoral nation. Was the marginal sea[9] the "prop-

[6] Fulton, *op. cit.,* 338, 369–70. Sir John Burroughs takes this position in *The Soveraignty of the British Seas* (London, 1651).   [7] *Op. cit.,* 154–55.

[8] *De' Doveri de' principi neutrali* (1782), cited in Fulton, *op. cit.,* 563. There are those who believe that the cannon-shot rule was the product of the fertile mind of Grotius and that Bynkershoek did not invent it. Further, there are those who argue that Galiani was a poor artilleryman, for, they maintain, guns at that time did not have the range ascribed to them. The writer sees no need to enter into this controversy. Those interested will find an excellent summary in M. W. Mouton, *The Continental Shelf* (The Hague, Martinus Nijhoff, 1952), 193–200.

[9] This term will be used generally to denote that part of the sea within three nautical miles of the shores of a nation, measured outward from low-water mark

erty" of the littoral state, or did the littoral power merely have certain rights, jurisdiction, and duties in the area? The development of this question in English practice and international law was to be of vital consequence many years later when control of oil production in the marginal seas of the United States was to be disputed.

English writers and courts have generally upheld the sovereignty and jurisdiction of the British Crown over the marginal sea; and the majority, since the time of Lord Chief Justice Hale, have based their views upon the concept of the three-mile zone as the "property" of the King. Thomas Digges, sixteenth-century commentator, believed that the kings of England from ancient times "haue in the right of theire crowne helde the seas abowte this Ilande"—a claim based on the "Common Lawe."[10] Reflecting the spirit of his times, Serjeant Robert Callis, in a lecture on the Statute of Sewers delivered at Gray's Inn in 1622, stated that in English common law the seas around the British Isles, together with any islands, belonged in property to the King.[11] Selden's *Mare clausum* expressed to those outside the realm the beliefs of Digges and Callis which had been pronounced for internal consumption.

Lord Chief Justice Hale, writing in 1667, took Selden's views as his point of departure. The eminent Justice believed that the King had both jurisdiction and property in the narrow seas adjoining the coasts of England. He expressed it thus:

> In this sea, the King of England hath a double right, viz, a right of jurisdiction which he ordinarily exerciseth by his admiral, and a right of propriety or ownership. The latter is that which I shall meddle with. The King's right of propriety or ownership in the sea and soil thereof is evidenced principally in these things that follow.[12]

Hale's exposition was one of internal law and he made no effort to set or determine the extreme outer boundaries of the King's jurisdiction. His doctrine is the one which appears to have most greatly influenced English thinking.[13]

---

or from the seaward limit of a bay, river mouth, or other inland water. The writer bases this definition upon "Research in International Law," 23 *American Journal of International Law* (Special Supplement, 1929), 250.

[10] "Arguments prooving the Queenes Ma^tles propertye in the Sea Landes, and salt shores thereof," reprinted in Stuart A. Moore, *A History of the Foreshore and the Law Relating Thereto* (3d ed., London, Stevens and Haynes, 1888), 187, 203.

[11] Percy Thomas Fenn, *The Origin of the Right of Fishery in Territorial Waters* (Cambridge, Harvard University Press, 1926), 178–79.

[12] "De jure maris," reprinted in Stuart A. Moore, *op. cit.*, 370 ff.

[13] For a very complete list of English writers to 1776 who followed, in the

Later English writers have followed similar patterns. Thus Joseph Angell, in an American work dealing largely with the English common law, says:

In this respect, it will appear, that the Roman law has been very much surpassed, by the common law of England. For although, as will presently be shewn, the sea, &c. according to the provisions of the common law, are as public and common, as they were among the Romans; yet it is not only the policy of the common law to assign everything capable of occupancy and susceptible of ownership a legal and certain proprietor—but also to make those things which by their nature cannot be *exclusively* occupied and enjoyed, the property of the sovereign. . . .

To the King, therefore, is not only assigned the sovereign dominion over the sea adjoining the coasts, and over the arms of the sea; but in him is also vested the *right of property* in the *soil thereof*.[14]

One could cite numbers of other authors to a similar effect.[15] In the twentieth century, Sir Cecil Hurst, former president of the Permanent Court of International Justice, wrote that the rights of the British Crown were actually established long before the three-mile limit was conceived but that these rights, which he labels as "property rights," do not now extend beyond the three-mile zone.[16]

A study of British cases merely confirms the pattern which has been outlined. First of all one sees a tendency to deem the Crown owner of wide sea areas. The expanse is gradually contracted until, with very few exceptions, English cases hold the King to be the owner, with qualified proprietary rights, of the zone previously defined as the marginal sea.

Three very early cases give clues to the course common-law practice

------

main, Hale's ideas see Appendices A to I, "Brief for the State of California in Opposition to Motion for Judgment," No. 12 Original, October Term 1946, pp. 47–50.

[14] Joseph Angell, *Right of Property in Tidewaters* (Boston, C. C. Little & J. Brown, 1826), 17–18. A second edition of this work appeared in 1847.

[15] See, e.g., Joseph Chitty, *A Treatise on the Law of the Prerogatives of the Crown* (London, 1820), 173: "Under this head it may also be mentioned, that the King possesses the sovereign dominion in all the narrow sea, that is, the seas which adjoin the coasts of England, and other seas within his dominions."

In England from the time of Lord Hale it has been treated as settled that the title to the soil of the sea, or of the arms of the sea, below ordinary high-water mark, is in the King. William E. Hall, *The Rights of the Crown in the Sea-Shores of the Realm*, first published in 1830, reprinted in Stuart A. Moore, *op. cit.*, 667 ff.

[16] Sir Cecil Hurst, "Whose is the Bed of the Sea?" 4 *British Yearbook of International Law* (1923), 34.

was later to take. *Johnson* v. *Barret* held that the soil between high-
and low-water marks belonged to the King,[17] while in the *Case of the
Royal Fishery of Banne* the Crown's ownership of the bed of the sea
was relied upon as a basis for holding that the King owned the beds of
navigable rivers insofar as the beds of those rivers were subject to the
ebb and flow of the tide.[18] The holding in *Bulstrode* v. *Hall and
Stephens* is to similar effect.[19] These cases appear to have been based
upon the concept of extending Crown ownership inward rather than
outward from the low-water mark. The King's ownership below low-
water mark was apparently admitted by all parties without argument
in these early decisions.

After 1760, the British courts took judicial cognizance of the "cannon shot" rule, though it appears that such action was fairly well confined to neutral waters in time of war.[20] Thus, in that year, the High
Court of the Admiralty held that a French vessel captured by a British
man-of-war in a Spanish harbor was not a valid prize because it was
taken within reach of Spanish guns.[21] Lord Stowell elaborated this
rule in two further cases. In the first he spoke of "waters belonging to
Prussia" in invalidating a capture of Dutch ships by an English vessel
in neutral Prussian waters.[22] In *The Anna*, five years later, he repeated
the doctrine in the case of the capture of an American ship by a British
naval vessel off some mud islands located within three miles of the
Mississippi delta.[23] At that date Louisiana was a territory of the United
States, a neutral country.

The most definite pronouncements of English courts concerning the
King's rights to jurisdiction and property in the marginal sea, however,
occur some years after 1776. This date is important, for it has been held
that when the American Revolution took place the thirteen original

[17] 82 Eng. Rep. 887 (1646).
[18] 80 Eng. Rep. 540, Davis 55 (1674).
[19] 82 Eng. Rep. 1024, 1 Sid. 148 (1674).
[20] Comment, "Conflicting State and Federal Claims of Title in Submerged
Lands of the Continental Shelf," 56 *Yale Law Journal* (1947), 360.
[21] *The De Fortuyn*, Marsden's *Admiralty Cases* 175 (1760).
[22] *The Twee Gebroeders*, 165 Eng. Rep. 422, 3 C. Rob. 162 (1800).
[23] 165 Eng. Rep. 809, 5 C. Rob. 373 (1805). *Rex* v. *Forty-nine Casks of
Brandy*, 166 Eng. Rep. 401, 413 (1836), supports this view of the three-mile belt
as no more than a neutral zone: "As between nation and nation, the territorial
right may, by a sort of tacit understanding, be extended to three miles; but that
rests upon different principles, viz. that their own subjects shall not be disturbed
in their fishing, and particularly in their coasting trade and communications
between place and place during war; they would be exposed to danger if hostilities were allowed to be carried on between belligerents nearer to the shore
than three miles."

states succeeded to the rights and prerogatives of the British Crown.[24] The determination of exactly what these rights were, before and after 1776, therefore bears a definite relationship to the issues which faced the United States Supreme Court in 1947 and 1950 over control of oil production in the submerged lands. In the 1947 case, California contended that the thirteen original states held, as a former Crown prerogative, both jurisdiction and property in the marginal sea. The Department of Justice, on the other hand, argued that no proprietary or territorial concept of the marginal sea existed in 1776. It is significant to note that there are only three cases[25] in which there is evidence that, prior to 1776, British courts believed that the King held property rights in the marginal sea.

Yet the Crown did hold some rights, whatever their content. Along with this slowly developing concept of property rights in the marginal sea, there grew a theory that Crown rights were held subject to certain public trusts. The Magna Carta had forbidden the King to grant exclusive fishing rights in tidal waters, a power he had exercised prior to 1215.[26] Thus in *Blundell* v. *Catterall,* Lord Justice Holroyd declared:

> By the common law, though the shore, that is to say the soil betwixt the ordinary flux and reflux of the tide, as well as the sea itself, belongs to the King; yet it is true that the same are also *prima facie publici juris,* or clothed with a public interest. But this *jus publicum* appears from Lord Hale to be the public right in all the King's subjects, of navigation . . . and also the liberty of fishing in the sea. . . .[27]

To similar effect is a statement in *Benest* v. *Pipon:*

> The sea is the property of the King, and so is the land beneath it, except such part of that land as is capable of being usefully occupied without prejudice to navigation, and of which a subject has either had a grant from the King, or has exclusively used for so long a time as to confer on him a title by prescription. . . . This is the law of England . . . derived from a universal principle of convenience and justice.[28]

It thus appears that the public could not be denied a right of fishery or navigation, though grants of other perquisites below low-water mark

---

[24] *Martin* v. *Waddell,* 16 Pet. 345, 367 (1842).
[25] See footnotes 17, 18, and 19 of this chapter.
[26] *Gann* v. *Free Fishers of Whitstable,* 11 Eng. Rep. 1305, 1312 (1865). Legally, at this period, a grant of exclusive fishing rights was known as a "several fishery."
[27] 106 Eng. Rep. 1190, 1201, 5 B. & Ald. 268, 298 (1821).
[28] 12 Eng. Rep. 243, 246–47 (1829).

were within the power of the Crown.[29] With the exception of the rights of public navigation and fishery, however, decisions subsequent to 1776 evidence that the British Crown held title in property to lands below low-water mark.[30]

The three-mile limit as an exterior boundary to Crown prerogatives appears in the language of British courts in the middle of the nineteenth century. Lord Watson, in *Lord Advocate* v. *Wemyss,* expressed the prevailing view when he said: "I see no reason to doubt that, by the law of Scotland, the solum underlying the water of the ocean, whether within the narrow seas, or from the coast outward to the three mile limit, and also the minerals under it, are vested in the Crown."[31]

[29] *Free Fishers of Whitstable* v. *Gann,* 144 Eng. Rep. 1003, 1008 (1865); *Murphy* v. *Ryan,* Ir. R. 2 C. L. 143, 149 (1868); *Attorney General* v. *Parmenter,* 147 Eng. Rep. 345, 352 (1811). In the case of *Lord Fitzhardinge* v. *Purcell* [1908] 2 Ch. 139, 166–67, there is a concise statement of the whole doctrine: "Clearly the bed of the sea, at any rate for some distance below low-water mark, and the beds of tidal navigable rivers, are prima facie vested in the Crown, and there seems to be no good reason why the ownership thereof by the Crown should not also, subject to the rights of the public, be a beneficial ownership. The bed of the sea, so far as it is vested in the Crown, and a fortiori the beds of tidal navigable rivers, can be granted by the Crown to the subject. There are many several fisheries which extend below low-water mark or exist in the beds of navigable rivers. The whole doctrine of 'incrementa maris' seems to depend on the beneficial ownership of the Crown in the bed of the sea, which in the older authorities is sometimes referred to as the King's royal waste. It is true that no grant by the Crown of part of the bed of the sea or the bed of a tidal navigable river can or ever could operate to extinguish or curtail the public right of navigation and rights ancillary thereto. . . . It is also true that no such grant can, since Magna Carta, operate to the detriment of the public right of fishing. But, subject to this, there seems no good reason to suppose that the Crown's ownership of the bed of the sea and the beds of tidal navigable rivers is not a beneficial ownership capable of being granted to a subject. . . . This beneficial ownership of the Crown, or the Crown's grantee, can only, I think, be considered to be limited by well-known and clearly defined rights on the part of the public." It appears that the Crown has the power to grant mineral rights within the three-mile zone, so long as the public rights of navigation and fishery are not interfered with. Halsbury's *Laws of England* (2d ed., London, 1932), VI, 732, §988.

[30] *Free Fishers of Whitstable* v. *Gann,* 144 Eng. Rep. 1003, 1011 (1865): "The soil of the sea-shore to the extent of three miles from the beach is vested in the Crown. . . ."

Attorney General v. *Chambers,* 43 Eng. Rep. 486, 489 (1854): "The Crown is clearly . . . entitled to the 'littus maris' as well as to the soil of the sea itself adjoining the coasts of England."

Attorney General v. *Hanmer,* 4 Jur. N.S. 751, 753 (1858): "Lord Hale says that the main sea is the waste and demesne of the kings of England, and the king is the owner of that great waste the sea."

See also *King* v. *Smith,* 2 Doug. 441 (1780).

[31] [1900] A.C. 48, 66. To the same effect see *Lord Advocate* v. *Clyde Trustees,* 19 Rettie 174, 177, 183 (Court of Sessions, 1891); *The Leda,* Swa. Adm. 40,

Further evidence for the extension and growth of this territorial doctrine in British law is found in the Cornwall Arbitration case of 1858. This was a proceeding between the Queen and the Prince of Wales, who was also duke of Cornwall. At issue were the mineral rights to lands underlying the sea in the duchy of Cornwall, both above and below low-water mark. While this was not a judicial controversy, the arbitrator in the case held the mineral rights below low-water mark vested in the Queen, even though the Duke had been the first occupant. The argument was that the bed of the sea below low-water mark belonged in property to the Crown, and the arbitrator so held. Parliament ratified this decision by passing the Cornwall Submarine Mines Act.[32]

Only one important British case appears to be in contraposition to the accepted line of decisions, the case of *Queen* v. *Keyn*.[33] Keyn was indicted in the Central Criminal Court for manslaughter, he being a foreigner in command of a ship passing within the English three-mile zone bound on a voyage to a foreign port. Within that zone his ship collided with a British ship, and as a result a passenger of the English vessel was drowned. It was admitted that under British law his actions constituted manslaughter. The question was, however, whether the Central Criminal Court had jurisdiction over Keyn under these circumstances.

The opinion is extremely lengthy and involved, filling 180 pages, with each of the thirteen judges stating his views. Legal experts have

---

42 (1856); *General Iron Screw Collier Co.* v. *Schurmans,* 70 Eng. Rep. 712, 717 (1860).

[32] The history of the Cornwall Arbitration is treated more completely in Hurst, *loc. cit.,* 34–35; and "Supplemental Memorandum by the Committee on Law and Legislation of the American Association of Port Authorities," *Hearings* before the Senate Committee on Public Lands and Surveys on S.J. Res. 83 and 92, 76th Cong., 1st sess. (1939), 243–44. These hearings will hereinafter be cited as *Hearings* on S.J. Res. 83 and 92 (1939). The Port Authority brief made the point that the Cornwall controversy was concerned with the extent to which the Duke of Cornwall had appropriated the lands and not with any question of whether or not the lands were ownerless.
The act of Parliament of 1858, 21–22 Vict., c. 109, reads in part as follows: ". . . first, that the Right to all Mines and Minerals lying under the Seashore between High and Low Water Marks within the said County of Cornwall, and under Estuaries and tidal Rivers and other Places even below Low Water Mark, being in and Part of said County, is vested in his Royal Highness as part of the Soil and territorial possessions of the Duchy of Cornwall; secondly, that the Right to all Mines and Minerals lying below Low-water Mark under the open Sea, adjacent to but not being part of the County of Cornwall, is vested in Her Majesty the Queen in right of her Crown. . . ."
[33] L.R. 2 Exch. Div. 63 (1876). This case is often referred to, especially in the literature of international law, as the *Franconia* decision.

disputed among themselves the issue of exactly what points the majority agreed upon, but it can be said at least that Keyn won his case on a 7–6 division. Of the seven majority judges, five held that the Central Criminal Court had no jurisdiction in the absence of parliamentary legislation to that effect, while two went further, reasoning that the power of a nation over its three-mile zone in international law is present only for certain limited purposes. To extend the criminal law of England to apply to foreigners in this zone, these two felt, would be inconsistent with this limited jurisdiction, even should Parliament act to that end. The six dissenting judges, among them Lord Coleridge, held that English criminal law did extend over the three-mile zone because that area was part of the territory of England.

The conclusions of the majority can be partially expressed in a statement by Sir R. Phillimore:

The sound conclusions which result from the investigation of the authorities which have been referred to appear to me to be these:—

The concensus of civilized independent states has recognized a maritime extension of frontier to the distance of three miles from low-water mark, because such a frontier or belt of water is necessary for the defense and security of the adjacent state.

It is for these particular objects that a dominion has been created over this portion of the high sea.

This proposition is materially different from the proposition contended for, namely, that it is competent to a state to exercise within these waters the same rights of jurisdiction and property which appertain to it in respect to its land and its ports.[34]

Yet the dissenters were able to cite the very cases which have been previously considered here as authority for a belief that "English judges have held repeatedly that these coast waters are portions of the realm."[35]

It is difficult to see how the case may be read as a repudiation of the territorial concept of the marginal sea in British legal thought. The majority were concerned with statutory construction, though there was confusion on the question of whether or not the three-mile zone was property. This confusion the Parliament promptly cleared up with its

[34] *Ibid.*, 81. Although Crown rights of property were not an issue in *Attorney General for British Columbia* v. *Attorney General for Canada,* [1914] A.C. 153, Lord Haldane did say that the character of the three-mile zone was in question, a view which lends support to the statement of Phillimore in *Queen* v. *Keyn.*
[35] L.R. 2 Exch. Div. 63, 155 (1876).

Territorial Waters Jurisdiction Act,[36] which, in effect, overruled the majority in *Queen* v. *Keyn*. Further, again let it be noted, the territorial concept was specifically rejected by only two of the majority judges.

The edge which the case might have had was further dulled by the decision in *Secretary of State for India* v. *Chelikani Rama Rao* in 1916.[37] Here the Judicial Committee of the Privy Council held that the islands formed at the mouth of the Godavari River within the three-mile limit belonged in property to the Crown. Lord Shaw of Dumferline said:

> The case is not complicated by any point as to geographical location, or by the question whether a limit from shore seawards should be beyond three miles, should be the extreme range of cannon fire, or should even be more if the locus be claimed to be intra fauces terrae—no such questions arise here. The point is geographically within even three miles of British territory: at that point islands have arisen from the sea. Are these islands no man's land? The answer is they are not; they belong in property to the British Crown.[38]

Lord Shaw admitted that doubt had been cast on this concept of property in the three-mile zone by *Queen* v. *Keyn,* but he went on to point out that that case had reference on its merits solely to the limits of admiralty jurisdiction and was a divided opinion with the majority merely finding that the King's admiral had never had such jurisdiction. Citing cases, he then summed up: "Their Lordships do not doubt that the general law, as already stated, is supported by the preponderating considerations of practical convenience, and that, upon the particular case in hand, the ownership of the islands formed in the sea in the estuary or mouth of the Godavari River is in the British Crown."[39]

One might think that a possible clue to British thought on the territorial character of the marginal sea could be found in the charter grants to the colonies in the New World, but actually few such conclusions

---

[36] 41–42 Vict., c. 73 (1878). The language of the act declares future policy and states that past policy, that is, the decision in the *Franconia* case, was incorrect.   [37] 43 Indian App. 192.   [38] *Ibid.,* 199.

[39] *Ibid.,* 203. Justice Black, in *United States* v. *California,* 332 U.S. 19, 33, cited *Queen* v. *Keyn* as proving that there was "considerable doubt" about a territorial concept in the marginal-sea area as late as 1876. In the light of prior decisions and later comment, as evidenced in *Secretary of State for India* v. *Chelikani Rama Rao,* it is most difficult to see how Black arrived at such a conclusion, or why he was willing to base all his reasoning on the point on *Queen* v. *Keyn,* a case which constituted an exception to the generally established principles of English law and which had been repudiated by the British Parliament.

can be drawn. It is true that grants were made of marine and other
lands as well as of the seas "thereunto adjoining"[40] but it does not appear that the Crown was in any way conscious that these were territorial grants in the marginal sea. They appear to be rather guarantees
of fishing rights, for many colonies depended in some measure on this
industry for livelihood.[41] Even the interpretations of American courts
concerning the effect of the charter grants, while holding that the
Crown was the source of such legal title as existed,[42] still subjected the
grants to the doctrine that the rights were granted "as far as by the law
of nations, one government is conceded to hold an exclusive right to
the sea-coasts and other shore and arms of the sea, where the sea ebbs
and flows."[43] It would appear clear that at the time these grants were
made, the British doctrine of a right to property in the marginal sea
was still in the developmental stage, though certainly elements of a
proprietary concept were present.

From this brief discussion of English cases, writers, and charters, it
would appear that English writers before 1776 did contend that the
King held some portion of the adjacent seas as property, but the extent
of those areas was relatively undetermined. British cases prior to 1776
intimate that the Crown held in property an area, undefined in extent,

[40] Grant of Queen Elizabeth to Sir Walter Raleigh of 25 March 1584. Benjamin
P. Poore, *The Federal and State Constitutions, Colonial Charters, and Other
Organic Laws of the United States* (2d ed., Washington, Government Printing
Office, 1878), II, 1379–82. To similar effect see grants by James I of 1609, 1611,
and 1620 and grants of later sovereigns. *Ibid.*, 921–31, 933–35, 947.

[41] Thus the grant of 3 November 1620 of James I to the Plymouth Company
included the "Seas, Waters, Fishings." *Ibid.*, 921–31. Discussing the effect of this
grant, Chief Justice Shaw said in *Barker* v. *Bates,* 13 Pick. 255, 259 (Mass.
1832): "In that [grant] of James I, of November 1620, to the council of Plymouth, upon the basis of which most of the others were framed, there is granted
not only the soil described, but also all havens, ports, rivers, waters, fishings,
mines and minerals, as well royal as other mines &c., and all and singular other
commodities, jurisdictions, *royalties,* privileges, franchises and preëminencies,
both within the said tract of land upon the main, and also within the islands and
seas adjoining."

[42] *Commonwealth* v. *Roxbury,* 9 Gray 451, 478 (Mass. 1857), is illustrative
of this type of case. There Chief Justice Shaw said: "At the time of the settlement of Massachusetts and the other English colonies in America, the only
source of title to the vacant and unsettled lands of this portion of the continent,
claimed by the crown of England by right of discovery, was a grant from the
king. It was not merely the only source of legal title to the soil, but the only
source of authority for exercising limited powers of government, in and over the
lands thus granted." In *Tinicum Fishing Co.* v. *Hartley,* 61 Pa. 21 (1869), and
Armour & Co. v. *Newport,* 110 Atl. 645 (R.I. 1920), American courts held that
certain grants of the Crown in Rhode Island and Pennsylvania did not effect a
transfer of submerged soil under certain rivers and below high-water mark.

[43] *Weston* v. *Sampson,* 8 Cush. 347, 353 (Mass. 1851).

below low-water mark. There is little evidence in charters granted by the Crown during the Colonial period to support the view that the Crown granted property rights in submerged lands below low-water mark.

British cases after 1776 adopted the concept of the three-mile limit first in connection with protection of neutral waters and then, by the end of the nineteenth century, had translated this three-mile idea into a concrete doctrine of Crown ownership, subject to the public rights of navigation and fishery. Although there appears to be no case authority which can be utilized definitely as a basis for Crown ownership prior to that date, the writings of publicists would lend credence to the argument that the concept had its birth before 1776.

While the British courts and writers were developing their ideas of a territorial three-mile zone, what was the situation in international law? Two questions are pertinent: (1) What is the extent of the marginal sea under international law and practice? and (2) Is there a generally accepted rule of international law to the effect that a maritime nation owns a belt of land below low-water mark?

The minimum extent of jurisdiction which any maritime nation claims over the marginal sea at the present time is three nautical miles.[44] This minimum zone is subject to a "well-established servitude," under which ships of every nation have the right of innocent passage through the territorial waters.[45] The maximum limit of this jurisdiction appears to be in serious doubt. George Grafton Wilson points out that of nearly fifty text writers who made statements on the matter before 1900, nineteen approved a cannon-shot limit; six, a fifty-mile limit or greater; five, a three-mile limit; and the others approved limits based on navigable depth of waters, tides, coast-line sinuosity, effective control, and similar criteria.[46]

In the time of Bynkershoek, the range of artillery fire was roughly three nautical miles. If the effective range of artillery be a criterion of minimum distance, then there are grounds for arguing that as the

[44] Philip Caryl Jessup, *The Law of Territorial Waters and Maritime Jurisdiction* (New York, G. A. Jennings Co., 1927), 18–49.

[45] Fenwick, *op. cit.*, 394. The right of innocent passage is subject to the observance of such special regulations as quarantine and customs controls.

[46] George Grafton Wilson, *Handbook of International Law* (3d ed., St. Paul, West Publishing Co., 1939), 100–101. A four-mile limit was used as a basis for decision in *United Kingdom* v. *Norway* (the *Norwegian Fisheries* case), International Court of Justice, 18 December 1951.

range of ordnance increases, the extent of the marginal sea which a maritime state may control becomes correspondingly greater. Although this has never been an issue, there are dicta in lower United States court decisions to support the view.[47] Wilson notes that there have been efforts to secure an extension of the zone, though the expressions have been based primarily on expediency and certainly less on the increased range of cannon.[48]

The nations themselves have come to no agreement on the outer extent of the marginal sea. The lack of uniformity was emphasized by the replies of various governments to a questionnaire on territorial waters prepared by a subcommittee of the Committee of Experts for the Progressive Codification of International Law which had been appointed by the League of Nations. While most of the nations were willing to admit a three-mile customs jurisdiction, Portugal, Norway, and

---

[47] *United States* v. *Smiley,* 27 Fed. Cases 1132, 1134 (1864): "This limitation of a marine league was adopted because it was formerly supposed that a cannon-shot would only reach to that extent. It is essential that the absolute domain of a country should extend into the sea so far as necessary for the protection of its inhabitants against injury from combating belligerents while the country itself is neutral. Since the improvement of modern times in ordnance, the distance of a marine league, which is little short of three English miles, may, perhaps, have to be extended so as to equal the reach of the projecting power of modern artillery."

Middleton v. *La Compagnie Generale Transatlantique,* 100 F. 866, 867 (1900): "Appellant's contention is based upon the old rule which limited jurisdiction over the waters of the ocean to a strip extending one marine league from shore, and considered inland waters a part of the main sea, when enclosed by headlands more than two marine leagues across. These arbitrary distances were fixed upon at a period when it was assumed that a marine league was the effective range of a heavy gun, and it may well be doubted whether they will not be extended by the courts to conform to changed conditions. Certainly it may be expected that every maritime nation will insist upon the control of its own coast waters to the extent to which it is able to dominate them from the shore. That question, however, need not be passed upon in this case."

[48] *Op. cit.,* 99–100. In 1894, the Institute of International Law recommended an extension to six miles with rights of neutrals to be stretched to artillery range during hostilities. Wilson notes that this declaration was more or less abortive in character, for since 1894 the tendency has been to stand generally by the three-mile definition. In 1928, the Institute reverted to the three-mile criterion. See Stefan Riesenfeld, *Protection of Coastal Fisheries under International Law* (New York, Columbia University Press, 1942), 108; Joseph A. Loret, "Louisiana's Twenty-Seven Mile Maritime Belt," 13 *Tulane Law Review* (1939), 252, 256.

Hall, *op. cit.,* 157, says of the problem: "It may be doubted . . . whether the three-mile limit has ever been unequivocally settled; but in any case, as it has been determined, if determined at all, upon an assumption which has ceased to hold good, it would be pedantry to adhere to the rule in its present form; and perhaps it may be said with propriety that a state has theoretically the right to extend its territorial waters from time to time with the increased range of guns."

Sweden wanted a wider zone for the protection of their fishery interests. Egypt, Estonia, Finland, Germany, and Greece accepted the three-mile definition of "sovereign rights" but wished a wider zone for other "administrative" purposes. Great Britain, Denmark, India, Eire, Japan, and New Zealand would not commit themselves to any policy. Four countries thought the whole question was so involved as to make mass agreement impossible.[49] Wilson notes that before World War I the Scandinavian countries claimed jurisdiction to four miles below low-water mark.[50]

Some countries frequently claim and exercise a wider jurisdiction. Thus the United States entered into a series of "rum treaties" designed to facilitate the enforcement of the Volstead Act. The one with Great Britain is illustrative. It declared that while "three marine miles" constituted the proper limits of territorial waters, Great Britain would not object to the boarding of British vessels by United States officials in search of illegal alcoholic beverages, provided such search was conducted within an hour's sailing time of the American coast.[51] It is important to note, however, that of the sixteen "rum treaties" entered into, in only six cases did the signatory nations agree that the three-mile limit constituted the extent of territorial jurisdiction for "ordinary" purposes.[52]

[49] William E. Masterson, "Territorial Waters and International Legislation," 8 *Oregon Law Review* (1929), 309, 324–36.

[50] *Op. cit.,* 101. The four-mile claim was used as a basis for decision in the *Norwegian Fisheries* case, International Court of Justice, 18 December 1951.

Whatever the extent of the marginal sea, the high seas are the common property of all the nations. Each nation may arrest its own subjects and seize their property without infringing the jurisdiction or interfering with the rights of any other country. *Francis* v. *Ocean Insurance Co.,* 6 Cow. 404 (N.Y. 1826).

[51] 43 U.S. Stat. 1761 (1924). See *Gillam* v. *United States,* 27 F. 2d 296, 299 (1924), for a typical statement upholding the right of Congress to enact legislation subjecting persons captured within the twelve-mile zone to the terms of the Volstead Act: "We think it equally clear that these statutes are valid, notwithstanding the fact that the territorial boundaries of the United States extend only to the 3-mile limit." Certiorari in the case was denied, 278 U.S. 635.

It should be noted that for certain purposes of admiralty jurisdiction the area *within* the three-mile limit is considered as a part of the high seas: e.g. *United States* v. *Smith,* Fed. Cases No. 16337 (1816), mutiny on a ship lying in the three-mile zone; *The Kaiser Wilhelm der Grosse,* 175 F. 215 (1909), civil suit for damages arising from the collision of two ships in the three-mile zone.

[52] Masterson, *loc. cit.,* 321. Belgium, Chile, Denmark, France, Greece, Italy, Norway, Poland, Spain, and Sweden refused to include the three-mile pledge. States including it were Cuba, Germany, Great Britain, Japan, the Netherlands, and Panama. Joseph Walter Bingham, *Report on the International Law of Pacific Coastal Fisheries* (Stanford University, California, Stanford University Press, 1938), 49 n.

Considering the disparity of present-day views upon the extent of territorial waters, the virtual impossibility of determining precisely what was the general practice of the law of nations in 1776 is not surprising. Mention has already been made of the fact that the British appear to have regarded the three-mile zone, at that date, as a sort of protective belt around neutral nations. Early practice in the United States seems to have been based on similar considerations.[53]

Yet for all the divergence of thought as to the extent of territorial waters, none would argue that territorial waters do not exist. There remains, however, the question of whether or not the area over which dominion is so exercised constitutes a part of the *territory* of the maritime state. It has been seen that the full-blown development of the territorial concept in Great Britain is of comparatively recent origin. In international law, it appears that early writers held to the territorial theory. In 1589, Gentili declared that "the adjacent part of a sea belongs to one's dominion, and the term 'territory' (*territorium*) is used both of land and water."[54] Even Grotius admitted in 1625 that "sovereignty over a part of the sea is acquired . . . in so far as those who sail over a part of the sea along the coast may be constrained from the land no less than if they should be on the land itself"[55]—an indication that perhaps this publicist was thinking in terms of a territorial concept.

Vattel regarded the area of the marginal sea "within reach of a cannon shot from the coast . . . as part of the national territory."[56] His *Le droit des gens,* published in 1758, greatly influenced later American publicists and legal thinkers. Fulton contended that the territorial concept was generally agreed upon in the latter half of the eighteenth century.[57] Hall maintained that "no serious question can arise as to the existence of property in marginal waters."[58] Many publicists have subscribed to the view that the littoral state has territorial sovereignty, including ownership, of the three-mile zone.[59]

---

[53] *Soult* v. *L'Africaine,* 22 Fed. Cases 805 (1804), says: "The single question for the consideration of the court is, whether this capture was made within the waters of the United States, or within a marine league of the coasts or shores thereof; it being within those limits only that this court can take cognizance of captures between belligerent powers."

[54] *De jure belli libri tres,* tr. John C. Rolfe (No. 16 in "Classics of International Law," Oxford, Clarendon Press, 1933), II, 384.

[55] *De jure belli ac pacis libri tres,* tr. Francis W. Kelsey (No. 3 in "Classics of International Law," Oxford, Clarendon Press, 1925), II, 214.

[56] *Le droit des gens,* tr. Charles G. Fenwick (No. 4 in "Classics of International Law," Washington, Carnegie Institution, 1916), III, 109.

[57] *Op. cit.,* 566.   [58] *Op. cit.,* 156.

[59] See, e.g., Paul Fauchille, *Traité de droit international public* (Paris,

The Grisbadarna Arbitration, before the Permanent Court of Arbitration in 1909, recognized the territorial concept of the marginal sea, for it was said in that proceeding in regard to a cession of territory that "the fundamental principles of the law of nations, both ancient and modern, in accordance with which, the maritime territory is an essential appurtenance of land territory, when it follows that at the time when, in 1658, the land territory called the Bohuslan was ceded to Sweden, the radius of maritime territory constituting an inseparable appurtenance of this land territory must have automatically formed a part of this cession."[60] Here is a bit of evidence which would point, by virtue of the date mentioned, to proof of the theory that the territorial concept is of long standing, perhaps antedating the American Revolution. Further credence is lent to this view when one reads in Mershon of a grant in 1662 by which Charles II of England sold the port of Dunkirk and its dependencies to France for five million francs. The transfer specifically included the ownership of the submerged lands in the English Channel off the coast of France adjoining Dunkirk.[61]

Early decisions of United States courts apparently accepted the territorial concept as a reflection of practice in international law. Thus Chief Justice John Marshall said in *Church* v. *Hubbart:* "The authority of a nation, within its own territory, is absolute and exclusive. The seizure of a vessel, within range of its cannon, by a foreign force, is an invasion of that *territory,* and is a hostile act which it is its duty to repel."[62] In 1812, Justice Story in the case of *The Ann* reiterated Marshall's statement, saying: "All the writers upon public law agree that every nation has exclusive jurisdiction to the distance of a cannon shot, or marine league, over the waters adjacent to its shores . . . and this doctrine has been recognized by the supreme court of the United States. . . . Indeed such waters are considered as a part of the territory of the sovereign."[63]

Rousseau & Co., 1925), I, 126–27; L. Oppenheim, *International Law* (5th ed., London, Longmans, Green & Co., 1935–37), I, 383; C. C. Hyde, *International Law, Chiefly as Interpreted and Applied by the United States* (Boston, Little, Brown & Co., 1922), I, 452, 751. Mouton, *op. cit.,* 215, says: ". . . it is a generally accepted rule of international law that the sea-bed and the subsoil under the territorial waters belong to the coastal state."

[60] J. B. Scott, *Hague Court Reports,* 121, 127.

[61] Stephen Lyon Mershon, *The Power of the Crown in the Valley of the Hudson* (Brattleboro, Vermont Printing Co., 1925), 13.

[62] 2 Cranch 187, 234 (1804). Italics added.

[63] Fed. Cases No. 397 (1812). In *The Apollon,* 9 Wheat. 362, 371 (1824), Story spoke of the "ordinary maritime jurisdiction" over waters within a cannon shot of the shores of the United States. In *The Marianna Flora,* 11 Wheat. 1, 42–

Justice Van Devanter, in a more recent decision, echoed the same basic philosophy when he said:

> Various meanings are sought to be attributed to the term "territory" in the phrase "the United States and all territory subject to the jurisdiction thereof." We are of the opinion that it means the regional areas—of land and adjacent waters—over which the United States claims and exercises dominion and control as a sovereign power. . . .
> It is now settled in the United States and recognized elsewhere that the territory subject to its jurisdiction includes the land areas under its dominion and control, the ports, harbors, bays and other enclosed arms of the sea along its coast and a marginal belt of the sea extending from the coast line outward a marine league, or three geographic miles.[64]

The United States assumed the existence of a territorial concept in the 1903 treaty with Panama, for Article II states:

> The Republic of Panama grants to the United States in perpetuity the use, occupation and control of a zone of land and land under water for the construction, maintenance, operation, sanitation and protection of said Canal of the width of ten miles extending to the distance of five miles on each side of the center line of the route of the Canal to be constructed; the said zone beginning in the Caribbean Sea three marine miles from mean low water mark and extending to and across the Isthmus of Panama into the Pacific Ocean to a distance of three marine miles from mean low water mark. . . .[65]

Certainly no differentiation is made here between dry land and submerged soils; there is obviously a belief in a concept of territory, territory which can be transferred from one owner to another.

Yet for all the apparent agreement expressed to this point in support of the territorial theory, it must be noted that there is a minority of publicists and jurists in international law who believe just as firmly that the

43 (1826), he rejected a contention that a ship at sea might "appropriate so much of the ocean as she may deem necessary for her protection, and prevent any nearer approach." He called this doctrine a "novel" one unsupported by authority.

64 *Cunard Steamship Co.* v. *Mellon*, 262 U.S. 100, 122 (1923). To the same effect see *Humboldt Manufacturers' Association* v. *Christopherson*, 73 F. 239 (1896); *United States* v. *Newark Meadows Improvement Co.*, 173 F. 426 (1909); *Dunham* v. *Lamphere*, 3 Gray 268 (Mass. 1856); *State ex rel. Luketa* v. *Pollock*, 136 Wash. 25 (1925); *State* v. *Ruvido*, 137 Me. 102 (1940).

65 W. M. Malloy, *Treaties, Conventions, International Acts, Protocols and Agreements of the United States* (Washington, Government Printing Office, 1910), II, 1350.

three-mile zone is not the territory of the maritime state whose shores it adjoins. The expressions of this latter group of writers find legal declaration in *Queen* v. *Keyn,* previously discussed. Hall quotes a number of authors who hold to the view that the sea is not susceptible to appropriation. Thus Ortolan says: "Ainsi, le droit qui existe sur la mer territoriale n'est pas un droit de propriété; on ne peut pas dire que l'état propriétaire des cotes soit propriétaire de cette mer. . . . En un mot, l'état a sur cet espace non la propriété, mais un droit d'empire; un pouvoir de législation, de surveillance et de juridiction."[66] Although Hall criticizes this view, he does not deny its existence. The United States, in its brief filed in support of its arguments in *United States* v. *California,* listed a number of writers, predominantly Continental, who have espoused similar views.[67]

One American state court decision and one lower federal court opinion are inconsistent with the theory of proprietary ownership in the marginal belt. The cases stand alone, for they have not been used as authority in later cases. In *Hogg* v. *Beerman,* the Ohio Supreme Court in a dictum stated that jurisdiction *only* was allowed to a distance of a marine league because the oceans, with their gulfs and bays, were incapable of appropriation by any nation. Only inland waters were deemed susceptible of being held by nations in the dual capacity of sovereigns and proprietors.[68] Five years later, the United States District Court for the District of South Carolina held, in the case of *The Hungaria,* that the territorial limits of federal court jurisdiction in civil admiralty cases did not run to the belt of water recognized by international law "for purposes of revenue and defense."[69] The court relied heavily on *Queen* v. *Keyn,* which had been decided only thirteen years before. These two decisions are not in accord with the majority of judicial expressions in the United States.

It thus appears that while in international law there is no settled rule on the extent of the marginal sea, no nation will permit a limit of

---

[66] Quoted in Hall, *op. cit.,* 156 n. In the same note are similar quotations from Heffter, Twiss, and Calvo. The last is quoted as saying: "Pour résoudre la question d'une manière à la fois rationnelle et pratique, il faut d'abord, ce nous semble, ne pas perdre de vue les états n'ont pas sur la mer territoriale un droit de propriété, mais seulement un droit de surveillance et de juridiction dans l'intérêt de leur défense propre ou de la protection de leurs intérêts fiscaux."
[67] "Brief for the United States in Support of Motion for Judgment," No. 12 Original, October Term 1946, p. 31. This brief will hereafter be cited as United States brief, *California* case. Listed are De Lapradelle, called by the United States the leading exponent of this school of thought, Von Liszt, Huger, and Carnazza-Ameri.   [68] 41 Ohio St. 91, 95 (1884).
[69] 41 F. 109, 110 (1889).

less than three miles. Further, the bulk of writing and legal decisions, with the exception of the minority views of certain Continental publicists, favors that consideration of the marginal sea which would allow it to be considered as the property of the littoral nation. It likewise appears that, in international law, the beginnings of a proprietary concept were present before the American Revolution.

The categorical statement of Mr. Justice Black that the territorial concept was but a "nebulous suggestion"[70] in 1776 is, at the very least, subject to argument. In English writing and practice and in international law as well, the territorial idea was certainly more than a "suggestion" at that date. The issue of whether or not jurisdiction and/or ownership passed from the Crown to the thirteen states individually in 1776 and the nature of that power forms the subject of the subsequent chapter.

[70] *United States* v. *California,* 332 U.S. 19, 32 (1947).

3·

Claims of the Original States
to Submerged Lands

English law and practice have greatly influenced the basic law of the United States in respect to submerged lands, for American law on the subject is derived from British usage.[1] American courts, directly or in dicta as the situation of a particular case may have demanded, have followed the British practice and have acknowledged that in England the King owned the soils under tidewaters.[2] This principle was extended to grant to the Crown similar rights in the American colonies before 1776.[3] Because of this admitted carry-over from British practice,

[1] Justice Gray, in *Shively* v. *Bowlby*, 152 U.S. 1, 14 (1894), said of English influence on the American law of submerged lands: "The common law of England upon this subject, at the time of the emigration of our ancestors, is the law of this country, except so far as it has been modified by the charters, constitutions, statutes or usages of the several Colonies and States, or by the Constitution and laws of the United States." See also *Cathcart* v. *Robinson*, 5 Pet. 264, 280 (1831).

[2] American decisions have taken over the basic concept of British practice, which holds, in effect, that the King is the proprietor of lands below high-water mark. In that capacity he can grant certain rights in these areas, but such grants are always limited by the right of the subjects to navigate on and fish in such waters. This right of the soil is entirely distinct from and subject to the greater public rights, but the existence of the *jus privatum* does not prejudice the *jus publicum*. *Shively* v. *Bowlby*, 152 U.S. 1, 11–14 (1894). To the same effect see *Browne* v. *Kennedy*, 5 Har. & J. 195 (Md. 1821); *State* v. *Black River Phosphate Co.*, 32 Fla. 82 (1893); *Furman* v. *City of New York*, 7 N.Y. Super. Ct. 16, 33 (1851).

[3] *Arnold* v. *Mundy*, 1 Halst. 1, 74 (N.J.L. 1821); *Martin* v. *Waddell*, 16 Pet. 367, 412 (1842); *Gough* v. *Bell*, 2 Zab. 441, 455 (N.J.L. 1850); *Commonwealth* v. *Alger*, 7 Cush. 53, 65 (Mass. 1851); *Weston* v. *Sampson*, 8 Cush. 347, 351–52 (Mass. 1851); *Commonwealth* v. *Roxbury*, 9 Gray 451, 482 (Mass. 1857);

it can be argued logically that the rights of the thirteen original states in the lands beneath navigable waters must have been those of British law in 1776.[4]

Since the King claimed the land by virtue of the right of discovery, grants from the Crown constituted the only source of legal title in the infant colonies in the seventeenth century. The theory, as settled by

---

People v. *N.Y. & Staten Island Ferry Co.,* 68 N.Y. 71, 76 (1876); *Weber* v. *Board of Harbor Commissioners,* 18 Wall. 57, 65 (1873); *Shively* v. *Bowlby,* 152 U.S. 1, 13 (1894); *Narragansett Real Estate Co.* v. *Mackenzie,* 82 Atl. 804, 810 (R.I. 1912).

[4] The thirteen original states have followed no uniform practice in regard to the power and extent of grants which the various state legislatures might make in the submerged lands. The theory was that the state legislatures had the same powers as the King, or the King together with Parliament, might have had. Thus it was held in New York that the legislature, as the representative of the people, could grant an exclusive privilege in the soils under navigable waters, even if that use were inconsistent with public rights. *People* v. *N.Y. & Staten Island Ferry Co.,* 68 N.Y. 71, 76 (1876); *Appelby* v. *City of New York,* 271 U.S. 364, 385, 399 (1926). In Pennsylvania the owner of the upland takes to high-water mark and has a qualified title to the area between high- and low-water marks, subject to the rights of navigation over it and improvement of it for purposes of navigation. *Wainwright* v. *McCullough,* 63 Pa. 66 (1869); *Zug* v. *Commonwealth,* 70 Pa. 138 (1871); *Philadelphia* v. *Scott,* 81 Pa. 80 (1876). In no case does the upland owner have title to land below low-water mark except through specific grant to that effect. In the absence of specific grant in Connecticut, the upland owner holds title only to high-water mark, with the incidental right to wharf out to navigable waters. *Simons* v. *French,* 25 Conn. 346 (1856). In Rhode Island the state holds absolute right to all overflowed lands bounding on salt water below high-water mark. *Narragansett Real Estate Co.* v. *Mackenzie,* 82 Atl. 804 (R.I. 1912); *New York, N.H. & H.R. Co.* v. *Morgan,* 56 Atl. 179 (R.I. 1903). A similar practice prevails in New Jersey. In *Stevens* v. *Paterson & Newark R. Co.,* 34 N.J.L. 532, 549 (1870), it is stated that "all navigable waters within the territorial limits of the state, and the soil under such waters, belong in actual propriety to the public; that the riparian owner, by the common law, has no peculiar rights in this public domain as incidents of his estate, and that the privileges he possesses by the local custom or by force of the wharf act, to acquire such rights, can, before possession has been taken, be regulated or revoked at the will of the legislature. The result is, that there is no legal obstacle to a grant by the legislature to the defendants, of that part of the property of the public which lies in front of the lands of the plaintiff, and which is below high water mark."

In order to encourage the building of wharves and similar structures for the benefit of commerce, the common-law rule that the sovereign owned to high-water mark was modified in Massachusetts. There a special law was enacted which granted to the upland owner a right out to low-water mark, or to a distance of one hundred rods where the tide ebbed and flowed for a distance of greater than that. *Commonwealth* v. *Charleston,* 1 Pick. 179 (Mass. 1822). Massachusetts is one of the few states where a grant of a several fishery originally emanating from the Crown was upheld. *Rogers* v. *Jones,* 1 Wend. 237 (1828).

judicial decisions, has been that the Indians found on the continent had no legal title to the soil but only a temporary right of occupancy.[5] This title of the King extended to the sea, as well as the land, and he held the same *publici juris* for the benefit of all his subjects.[6]

Did these rights, whatever they might have been, which had lodged with the Crown prior to independence, accrue to the central government under the Articles of Confederation, or did the rights remain with the individual states? There is much evidence to indicate that each of the thirteen states was an independent nation, capable of assuming within its borders what had formerly been Crown prerogatives. The Preliminary Articles of Peace, dated 30 November 1782, expressly list each state separately by name, as though each were a separate and sovereign entity.[7] Throughout this draft treaty one finds reference to various of the respective states.[8] In the Definitive Treaty of Peace, dated 3 September 1783, the states are once again listed separately and specifically.[9] H. R. G. Greaves says that each state retained "its sovereignty, freedom, and independence, and every power, justification, and right."[10] Representative Sam Hobbs, though testifying before the Senate Public Lands Committee in 1939 in favor of measures designed to declare the jurisdiction of the United States in the submerged lands in the three-mile zone, unwillingly admitted that upon the signing of the Treaty of Paris at the close of the American Revolution, each of the original thirteen states became an independent nation possessed of all the sovereign rights which had theretofore been possessed by the King.[11] One even finds statements in decisions of the Supreme Court to the effect that the jurisdiction of a state over the sea adjacent to its coast is that of an independent nation.[12] Such assertions, while dicta in the cases in which they were made, are indicative of a belief that the original thirteen states did not surrender their sovereignty to the imperfect central government under the Articles of Confederation. One does find a number of statements, which are not dicta, to the effect that the

[5] See, e.g., *Martin* v. *Waddell,* 16 Pet. 367, 409–10 (1842).

[6] *Commonwealth* v. *Roxbury,* 9 Gray 451, 478–83 (Mass. 1857).

[7] Hunter Miller, *Treaties and Other International Acts of the United States* (Washington, Government Printing Office, 1931), II, 96. Hereinafter cited as *Treaties of the United States.*

[8] *Ibid.* See especially Articles II and V.

[9] *Ibid.,* 152–53.

[10] H. R. G. Greaves, *Federal Union in Practice* (London, George Allen & Sons, 1940), 26–27.

[11] *Hearings* on S.J. Res. 83 and 92 (1939), 44.

[12] See, e.g., *Manchester* v. *Massachusetts,* 139 U.S. 240 (1891).

rights and properties of the Crown not theretofore granted, passed upon the declaration of independence to the thirteen original states as separate and distinct nations.[13]

This line of argument is opposed, however, by the decision in *United States* v. *Curtiss-Wright*.[14] In this case, Justice Sutherland took pains to demonstrate that certain powers of external sovereignty passed directly from the Crown to the "incipient Union" and had not become vested first of all in the states. He placed great stress on the oft-quoted statement by Rufus King in the Philadelphia Convention:

The states were not "sovereigns" in the sense contended for by some. They did not possess the peculiar features of sovereignty,—they could not make war, nor peace, nor alliances, nor treaties. Considering them as political beings, they were dumb, for they could not speak to any foreign sovereign whatever. They were deaf, for they could not hear any propositions from such sovereign. They had not even the organs or faculties of defence or offense, for they could not of themselves raise troops, or equip vessels, for war.[15]

The King utterance, however, is open to dispute, for the practical fact of the matter was that the states did perform many of these various "forbidden" acts. On historical grounds, it is easy to see after the briefest study of the government under the Articles that Sutherland's statement is open to serious question. The framers themselves viewed the Articles as a league of friendship. Randolph called the Congress of the Confederation a "mere diplomatic body."[16] Justice Iredell in *Penhallow* v. *Doane* stated that the Congress of the Confederation exercised powers with the "acquiescence" of the states.[17] Legal writers have attacked the soundness of Justice Sutherland's argument on this point.[18]

---

[13] *Martin* v. *Waddell*, 16 Pet. 367, 410 (1842); *Mumford* v. *Wardell*, 6 Wall. 423, 436 (1867); *County of St. Clair* v. *Lovingston*, 23 Wall. 46, 68 (1874); *Commonwealth* v. *Alger*, 7 Cush. 53, 82 (Mass. 1851); *People* v. *Trinity Church*, 22 N.Y. 44, 46 (1860); *Illinois Central R. Co.* v. *Illinois*, 146 U.S. 387, 456 (1892); *Massachusetts* v. *New York*, 271 U.S. 65, 85–86 (1926); *Appleby* v. *City of New York*, 271 U.S. 364, 381 (1926); *Shively* v. *Bowlby*, 152 U.S. 1, 14–16 (1894).

[14] 299 U.S. 304 (1936).

[15] 5 Elliott's *Debates* 212.

[16] *A Documentary History of the Constitution* (Washington, Government Printing Office, 1905), 137.

[17] 3 Dall. 54, 91 (1795). The writer is aware that Justice Sutherland put the statements of Justice Iredell to opposite use in the *Curtiss-Wright* decision.

[18] See, e.g., David M. Levitan, "The Foreign Relations Power: An Analysis of Mr. Justice Sutherland's Theory," 55 *Yale Law Journal* (1946), 467.

Yet the point of view remains and it cannot be dismissed cavalierly. The United States advanced it in arguing the tidelands oil cases. Since the idea of the marginal sea, together with whatever ownership there may be of the area, derives primarily from international law, the United States reasoned that the national government and not the states succeeded to whatever rights might have been held by the British Crown. Certainly the *Curtiss-Wright* case lends powerful support to this view.

One cannot, however, ignore historical fact. Further, in view of the numerous statements by the American courts concerning the influence of British law and the passing of Crown rights to the states, it appears to be more nearly correct to say that whatever the character of these rights, they vested in the original thirteen states as sovereign and independent entities.

Joseph Angell, an early commentator, went so far as to say that the Crown had already relinquished its rights in the submerged soils through the grants that had been made in the royal charters,[19] but it has already been seen in the previous chapter that such expressions do not give a complete picture.[20] A better view is expressed by Chief Justice Shaw of the Massachusetts Supreme Court in *Weston* v. *Sampson:*

. . . all the rights to the sea and sea-shores with the incidental rights of fishing, were granted to the colonies; . . . all the right, both to the soil under the sea, as far as by the law of nations one government is conceded to hold an exclusive right to the sea-coasts, and to the shores and arms of the sea, where the sea ebbs and flows, did vest in the grantees under those charters. Whatever right or jurisdiction, if any, remained in the crown after those grants, it is clear that it ceased on the establishment of independence, and has remained absolute in the States.[21]

At the time of the Revolution, therefore, each state succeeded to the rights or title of the Crown in the tidewaters within its territorial limits.[22] State and federal courts have followed this rule.[23]

[19] *Right of Property in Tidewaters*, 17–18.

[20] Pp. 17–19 above.

[21] 8 Cush. 347, 353 (Mass. 1851).

[22] John Melville Gould, *A Treatise on the Law of Waters* (2d ed., Chicago, Callaghan & Co., 1891), 74.

[23] *Appelby* v. *City of New York*, 271 U.S. 364, 381 (1926). Chief Justice Taft said: ". . . all the proprietary rights of the Crown and Parliament in, and all their dominion over, lands under tidewater vested in the several States."

Armour & Co. v. *Newport*, 110 Atl. 645, 646 (R.I. 1920): "During the time that Rhode Island was a colony of Great Britain the fee to the land within the Colony of New York became separated from the Crown of Great Britain, and a sovereignty resides in the people, and when the colony became independent the

Following the American Revolution, persons holding land under Crown grant generally continued in possession of the land where the grants were found to be valid. The remaining and unappropriated land was vested in the original state within whose border it was located. The jurisdiction of these new and independent states was coextensive with their boundaries at the time, whatever those boundaries might be.

The Supreme Court of the United States, in *United States* v. *Bevans,* described the extent and character of the jurisdiction which the state of Massachusetts possessed to prosecute for murder committed on a ship in the harbor of Boston when it said:

What then is the extent of jurisdiction which a state possesses? We answer, without hesitation, the jurisdiction of a state is coextensive with its territory; coextensive with its legislative power. The place described is unquestionably within the original territory of Massachusetts. It is, then, within the jurisdiction of Massachusetts, unless that jurisdiction has been ceded to the United States.[24]

In *Smith* v. *Maryland*[25] and *McCready* v. *Virginia*[26] are found statements holding that the states' power to exclude nonresidents from fishery benefits is based on the ownership of the soils below low-water mark as well as the legislative jurisdiction which the states hold over the

---

fee to lands passed to the state, which represents the sovereign power. . . ."

People v. *Trinity Church,* 22 N.Y. 46 (1860): "When, by the Revolution, the Colony of New York became separated from the Crown of Great Britain, and a republican government was formed, the people succeeded the king in the ownership of all lands within the State which had not already been granted away, and they became from thenceforth the source of all private titles."

People v. *N.Y. & Staten Island Ferry Co.,* 68 N.Y. 71, 77–78 (1876). The court showed that title to lands under tidewater in this country, which, before the Revolution, was vested in the King, became, upon the separation of the colonies, vested in the states within which they were situated; and the state legislatures exercised the same powers, which, previous to the Revolution, could have been exercised by the King alone, or by him in conjunction with Parliament.

[24] 3 Wheat. 336, 386–87 (1818). In this case the argument was advanced that the vesting of admiralty and maritime jurisdiction in the national government had carried with it an actual cession of the waters of the state which would give to the United States an exclusive jurisdiction to try the crime alleged. It was held that Massachusetts had the right to prosecute the crime. Chief Justice Marshall held that the cession of admiralty and maritime jurisdiction to the United States could not in any way be construed as a cession of the waters upon which admiralty or maritime cases might arise.

To similar effect see *United States* v. *Newark Meadows Improvement Co.,* 173 F. 426, 429 (1909).

[25] 18 How. 71, 74 (1855).

[26] 94 U.S. 391 (1877). These two cases did not, it is true, involve submerged lands in the open sea.

area. Similar statements to the net effect that territorial boundaries, jurisdiction, and ownership are coextensive are found in many decisions.[27]

These rights in the tidewaters, however, whatever their character may have been in the period between 1776 and 1789, are subject to any limitations which are present in the Constitution.[28] The case of *Martin* v. *Waddell* has stated the basic rule, a rule which has been much quoted in later cases: "When the Revolution took place, the people of each State became themselves sovereign; and in that character hold the absolute right to all their navigable waters and the soils under them for their own common use, subject only to the rights surrendered by the Constitution to the general Government."[29] The original states declared their intention of inheriting the rights held by the British Crown. Article XXV of the constitution of the state of North Carolina declares:

> Therefore all the territory, seas, waters, and harbours, with all their appurtenances, lying between the line above described, and the southern line of the State of Virginia, which begins on the sea shore, in thirty-six degrees thirty minutes, north latitude, and from thence runs west, agreeable to the said Charter of King Charles, are the right and property of the people of this State, to be held by them in sovereignty. . . .

Chapter 25 of the laws of New York of 1779 states that

> the absolute property of all lands, tenements, and hereditaments . . . and all rights and title to the same which next and immediately before the 9th day of July 1776, did vest in, or belong, or was due to the Crown of Great Britain be, and the same and each and every one of them are declared to be, and ever since the said 9th day of July 1776, to have been, and forever after shall be vested in the people of this State.[30]

[27] *Dunham* v. *Lamphere,* 3 Gray 268, 269, 272 (Mass. 1855); *Commonwealth* v. *Manchester,* 152 Mass. 230, 241 (1890); *Manchester* v. *Massachusetts,* 139 U.S. 240, 264 ff. (1891); *Martin* v. *Waddell,* 16 Pet. 367, 410 (1842); *Rhode Island* v. *Massachusetts,* 12 Pet. 657 (1838).

[28] 27 *Ruling Case Law* 1359.

[29] 16 Pet. 367, 410 (1842). To the same effect see *M'Ilvaine* v. *Coxe's Lessee,* 4 Cranch 209, 210 (1809); *Shively* v. *Bowlby,* 152 U.S. 1 (1894); *State* v. *Black River Phosphate Co.,* 32 Fla. 82, 93 (1893); *Broward* v. *Mabry,* 50 So. 826, 829 (Fla. 1909); *Broward* v. *Sledge,* 50 So. 831 (Fla. 1909).

[30] See *People* v. *Reilly,* 14 N.Y.S. 2d 589, 595 (1939), for a statement by a New York court tracing title to certain Brooklyn beaches and finding it to be in the borough of Brooklyn through grant by the state of New York.

Warren Gilman, assistant attorney general of the state of New York, traced the rights and title of New York in his "Brief for the State of New York against

Massachusetts declared a similar right of ownership.[31] The United States Supreme Court in *Smith* v. *Maryland* said:

> Whatever soil below low-water mark is the subject of exclusive propriety and ownership belongs to the State on whose maritime border, and within whose territory it lies, subject to any lawful grants of that soil by the State or the sovereign power which governed its territory before the Declaration of Independence.[32]

Although the land involved in this case was found in Chesapeake Bay,[33] it can still be seen that there was general agreement on one important point: each of the original thirteen states inherited from the Crown certain rights in the navigable waters within its territorial limits. The extent of those waters and the powers which the original states have exercised over them is a matter for further consideration.

As of the date of the Revolution, it appears that the thirteen original states held the title of the land beneath the navigable waters within their boundaries, at least to the line of low-water mark. The United States, on the other hand, at the time of the adoption of the Constitution held no land, either submerged or dry, within the boundaries of the original states, except that specifically granted to it by one of those states. While it might appear, at first glance, to be a waste of time to explore the possibilities along the frequently traveled trail of delegated and reserved powers, such an exercise is necessary.

The framers of the Constitution established a federal system of government, wherein certain powers were expressly granted to the central authority and the remaining powers either denied to the state or cen-

---

S.J. Resolutions 83 and 92," found in *Hearings* on S.J. Res. 83 and 92 (1939), 181–85.

[31] See *Commonwealth* v. *Boston Terminal Co.*, 185 Mass. 281, 282 (1904): "It must now be taken as settled that the territorial limits of the Commonwealth extend one marine league from its seashore at the line of extreme low water, and the title to the land within these boundaries, except as it may have been granted to others or acquired by them previously . . . by prescription is vested in the State."

[32] 18 How. 71, 74 (1855).

[33] In theory, the decisions in the *California, Texas,* and *Louisiana* cases pertain only to the open sea, for reasons which will be discussed later. Therefore the decision in *Smith* v. *Maryland* involving submerged lands in Chesapeake Bay is not, strictly speaking, in point. Chesapeake Bay is considered a closed or "historic" bay. John Bassett Moore, *A Digest of International Law* (Washington, Government Printing Office, 1906), I, 741–42. The difficulty of determining what areas are properly inland waters is dramatically highlighted by the series of hearings held before a special master following the decision in *United States* v. *California.* See pp. 236–38 and 260–65 below.

tral governments or both, or reserved to the states. Without arguing the "compact theory," it may safely be asserted that there was some agreement that certain powers were to be exercised by this new central authority. The lines of demarcation were not, however, clear; and the resulting conflict between state and national authorities has manifested itself down through the years on a myriad of issues.[34]

Prior to *United States* v. *California*, it was the contention, at least of the thirteen original states, that in establishing the Constitution there was no grant to the national government, either proprietary or jurisdictional, in the soils under navigable waters. The national government, the argument goes, is one of delegated powers only, and there is no delegation of jurisdiction or title in the soils under these waters.[35] The United States has, of course, acquired land through voluntary cession from the states or through its powers to exercise the right of eminent domain. The states have granted or leased lands beneath their navigable waters to private citizens. Except, however, for these grants or the portions of lands acquired by the United States through cession or eminent domain, "the original states today retain absolute title to and ownership of all such lands within their respective boundaries."[36] Whatever rights the original states may have possessed below high-water mark, there is no *direct* grant of these rights to the national government to be found in the Constitution.

Article IX of the Articles of Confederation had specifically provided that no "State shall be deprived of territory for the benefit of the United States." The national government under the Articles owned no land[37]

---

[34] Greaves (*op. cit.*, 32) believes that the Constitution was "in the nature of a compact between already existing powers." He points out (p. 28) that the idea of state governments distinct from a central authority established a check on the exercise of arbitrary power and appealed, therefore, to the framers with their belief in limited government.

[35] For typical statements in support of this position see "Memorandum in Opposition to S.J. Res. 208 of the American Association of Port Authorities," *Hearings* before the House Judiciary Committee on S.J. Res. 208, 75th Cong., 3d sess. (1938), 84–85; "Brief of the Attorneys General in Support of H.J. Resolutions 118 *et al.*," joint *Hearings* before the House Judiciary Committee and a Special Subcommittee of the Senate Judiciary Committee on H.J. Res. 118 *et al.*, 79th Cong., 1st sess. (1945), 13. These two hearings will hereinafter be cited as *Hearings* on S.J. Res. 208 (1938) and *Hearings* on H.J. Res. 118 *et al.* (1945) respectively.

To the same effect see Loret, "Louisiana's Twenty-Seven Mile Maritime Belt," 13 *Tulane Law Review* (1939), 256.

[36] "Brief of the Attorneys General in Support of H.J. Resolutions 118 *et al.*," *Hearings* on H.J. Res. 118 *et al.* (1945), 13.

[37] *Harcourt* v. *Gaillard*, 12 Wheat. 523 (1827).

until the various states, in an effort to settle their quarrels over certain western lands, executed a number of deeds to parts of the Northwest Territory. These deeds conveyed to the Congress of the Confederation the "title, jurisdiction and ownership" of the lands. In 1787, the Northwest Ordinance set the pattern for the creation of states out of the ceded territory, territory which passed from the Congress of the Confederation to the United States upon the ratification of the Constitution in 1789.[38] At the date of the adoption of the Constitution, therefore, the United States owned no public lands except those ceded by the respective states.

The Constitution itself recognizes that the national government may acquire land, specifically, (1) by cession by the states of an area not to exceed ten miles square for a seat of government, and (2) by purchase of land after gaining the consent of the state or states concerned.[39] To this must be added two other methods of acquiring land which have been recognized by the courts. The first is that of the exercise of the power of eminent domain, in which the consent of the state is not necessary.[40] The second, in the case of new states created out of territory of the United States, is reservation of specific land, not necessary for state sovereignty, through the inclusion of a specific description in the act admitting the state to the Union.[41] It is safe to make the assertion that the United States never acquired rights in the submerged soils below high-water mark in any of these four ways.

This argument that the original states never surrendered their rights in navigable waters was given added weight by the pronouncements of the courts, state and federal, down through the years. The statement that the "shores of navigable waters, and the soils under them, were not granted by the Constitution to the United States, but were reserved to the States respectively" is found frequently in leading cases.[42] In *Commonwealth* v. *Manchester,* Chief Justice Field of the Massachusetts Supreme Court declared that there "is no belt of land under the sea adjacent to the coast which is the property of the United States and

[38] Thomas Corwin Donaldson, *The Public Domain* (Washington, Government Printing Office, 1881), 64–81.

[39] Art. I, §8, cl. 17.

[40] *Kohl* v. *United States,* 91 U.S. 367 (1876); *United States* v. *Gettysburg R. Co.,* 160 U.S. 668 (1896).

[41] *Fort Leavenworth R. Co.* v. *Lowe,* 114 U.S. 525 (1885).

[42] *Pollard's Lessee* v. *Hagan,* 3 How. 212, 230 (1845); *County of St. Clair* v. *Lovingston,* 23 Wall. 46, 68 (1874); *United States* v. *Bevans,* 3 Wheat. 336, 338 (1818); *Corfield* v. *Coryell,* 6 Fed. Cases 546, 551 (1823), followed with approval in *Smith* v. *Maryland,* 18 How. 71, 74 (1855).

not the property of the states."[43] The original states continued to treat a belt of land for three miles below low-water mark as though it belonged to them. Regulations of fisheries were among the most common manifestations of their belief that it did. *Corfield* v. *Coryell* upheld the sale of a vessel seized as a prize under a New Jersey statute which prohibited the taking of oysters at certain times of the year, dredging for them at any time, or taking of oysters by residents of any state other than New Jersey.[44] *Commonwealth* v. *Manchester* applied Massachusetts fishery regulations to vessels enrolled and licensed under national law and operated by citizens of states other than Massachusetts, with a dictum to the effect that the "extent of the territorial jurisdiction of Massachusetts over the sea adjacent to its coast is that of an independent nation."[45] This application of Massachusetts law to vessels under United States registry was affirmed in *Manchester* v. *Massachusetts.*[46] *Smith* v. *Maryland*[47] and *McCready* v. *Virginia*[48] are other examples of Supreme Court cases wherein the court held that nonresidents could be excluded from the benefits of fishery in waters and soils below low-water mark and out to the three-mile limit, regardless of whether the fish were free swimming or attached to the soil.

But the Constitution had established an international entity. If, as may be admitted, there was no specific delegation of rights to the soils below low-water mark, could such be implied from other powers? Regardless of what, on the surface at least, appeared to be the obvious tenor of decisions and weight of authority, a few reasoned otherwise. For example, Leslie McNemar, then senior attorney in the Office of the Judge Advocate General of the Navy, argued that the three-mile belt

[43] 152 Mass. 230, 235 (1890). To the same effect see *Commonwealth* v. *Alger*, 7 Cush. 53 (Mass. 1851); *Commonwealth* v. *Roxbury*, 9 Gray 451 (Mass. 1857); *Arnold* v. *Mundy*, 1 Halst. 1 (N.J.L. 1821); *Gough* v. *Bell*, 1 Zab. 156 (N.J.L. 1847); *Shively* v. *Bowlby*, 152 U.S. 1 (1894); *Barker* v. *Bates*, 13 Pick. 255, 259 (Mass. 1832).

[44] 6 Fed. Cases 546 (1823).

[45] 152 Mass. 230, 247 (1890). In this case the Massachusetts Supreme Court was asked to overrule its previous decision in *Dunham* v. *Lamphere*, 3 Gray 268 (Mass. 1855), which had held that an action admittedly a violation of fishery regulations if committed by a Massachusetts citizen was equally a violation if committed by a citizen of Rhode Island acting under a coastal license of the United States. This case was not appealed to the federal courts. Chief Justice Shaw said (272–73): "The court are therefore of opinion that the right to the fisheries, and the power to regulate the use of fisheries on the coasts and in the tide waters of the State, are left, in the distribution of powers between the general and state governments, with the states. . . ." See also *Weston* v. *Sampson*, 8 Cush. 347 (Mass. 1851). [46] 139 U.S. 240 (1891).

[47] 18 How. 71 (1855). [48] 94 U.S. 391 (1876).

was given to the United States because it existed as a member of the family of nations; at the same time, in 1938, he believed in the territorial view which was then held by practically all persons concerned with the problem. He stated his position thus:

It must be remembered, however, that upon the ratification of the Federal Constitution the international entity of the several Thirteen Original Colonies ceased and became merged in the international entity of the United States of America and that the individual States of the United States were no longer sovereign within the meaning of international law. Thus when reference is made in international law to the territorial waters of a State extending at least a marine league or 3 geographic miles from the shore line it is the shore line of the United States that is intended and not the shore line of one of the municipal States thereof, such as New York, Texas, or California.[49]

It was claimed further that while the cases which have been cited appear to hold that the original states owned the submerged lands in the open sea below low-water mark to the three-mile belt, in actuality these cases dealt only with tidelands in the technical sense[50] or with lands under the inland waters of a state. It was contended that there are "pivotal distinctions" between the three-mile belt and the tidelands and inland waters. The three-mile limit, according to this line of reasoning, is a creature of international law, and therefore rights, powers, or duties arising from it belong to the national government and may be enforced as against other nations solely by the national government. The outstanding aspects of the zone are national rather than state. Therefore the jurisdiction and control of these submerged lands is more properly vested in the national government than in the states.[51]

Still, the basic argument advanced by those believing in the rights

[49] "Brief of Leslie C. McNemar in Support of S.J. Resolutions 83 and 92," *Hearings* on S.J. Res. 83 and 92 (1939), 76. Hereinafter cited as brief of Leslie C. McNemar. See also *Church* v. *Hubbart,* 2 Cranch 187 (1804).

[50] "Lands alternately covered and uncovered by the sea and between the dry upland and navigable waters are 'tidelands.' . . ."—*Baer* v. *Moran Brothers,* 153 U.S. 287 (1894). "Tidelands are made such by the water of the ocean flowing over them. Submerged lands are made such by the water standing over them." —*Carr* v. *Kingsbury,* 111 Cal. App. 165, 171 (1931). But cf. *San Pedro, etc., R. Co.* v. *Hamilton,* 161 Cal. 610, 614 (1911). In the period when the issue was first before the Congress, many of those testifying believed that there was no practical distinction to be made between "tidelands" and "submerged lands." See *Hearings* on S.J. Res. 83 and 92 (1939), 116–17, 121, 162, 178–79, 227, 246–47.

[51] United States brief, *California* case, 9–10.

of the states in the zone remains, namely, that there was in the Constitution no express delegation of jurisdiction over this area to the national government. To meet this objection, arguments utilizing the principle of implied powers were developed. Since the day of John Marshall, the principle of the supremacy of the national government acting within the scope of its area of power in the federal system has been settled. This fundamental principle of constitutional interpretation was the basis upon which the proponents of national jurisdiction within the three-mile zone built their arguments.

The delegated powers upon which principal reliance was placed were those of national defense and commerce. If the power of national defense had been ceded to the United States by the Constitution, then jurisdiction over the marginal seas, which must be protected from alien encroachment, must likewise have been ceded.[52] Further, had not the courts, including the Supreme Court of the United States, usually qualified statements allowing the state to exercise various types of control in the marginal seas with a remark that the exercise of these controls was always subject to such powers as the Congress might "justly exercise" in regulating commerce?[53]

The case of *Bailey and Fulgham* v. *United States* had held that the taking by the United States of oyster lands in the vicinity of Hampton Roads below low-water mark was within the rights of the national government to improve navigation and did not amount to a taking of private property for public use for which the lessees, renting the oyster beds from the state of Virginia, would be entitled to compensation.[54] Asserting that not every acquisition imposes an "obligation on the United States to pay," the Court of Claims said:

[52] Brief of Leslie C. McNemar, *Hearings* on S.J. Res. 83 and 92 (1939), 75. In *Hearings* before Subcommittee No. 4 of the House Judiciary Committee on H.J. Res. 176 and 181, 76th Cong., 1st sess. (1939), 42, McNemar testified as follows: "The rights to shore lands were expressly given in connection . . . with any definite power that was turned over by the States to the Federal Government, such as the power to regulate commerce, to provide and maintain a navy, and in connection with national defense, or one of the enumerated powers. . . . Insofar as those powers are concerned the sovereign states yielded up those powers to the Federal Government, and they do not now have them; . . . these States surrendered certain items of sovereignty to the United States of America as an international entity, which can be exercised only by the United States through its Congress and through its Government, and the States cannot now exercise these powers." These hearings will hereinafter be cited as *Hearings* on H.J. Res. 176 and 181 (1939).

[53] See, e.g., *Manchester* v. *Massachusetts,* 139 U.S. 240, 264 (1891). Numerous cases have contained such qualifying statements.

[54] 62 Ct. Cl. 77 (1926), certiorari denied, 273 U.S. 751 (1927).

But there is another principle upon which the defendant relies in justification of what was done and under which there is no liability to make
compensation, and that is the dominant right of the sovereign to do whatever may be necessary, in navigable waters, for the improvement of navigation. There can be no doubt the plaintiff's rights in these submerged
lands were subject to this dominant right of the sovereign without compensation.[55]

Destruction or taking of property without compensation by the United
States, even under the soils of inland navigable waters, as an incident
of the exercise of the commerce power has been upheld in a number of
cases where reasoning and issues were substantially those of the *Bailey
and Fulgham* case.[56] Those who proposed in 1938 and 1939 to declare
the jurisdiction and ownership of the United States in the marginal-sea
area, took the view that a state might exercise authority over the maritime belt until Congress asserted its superior authority. Under such a
declaration by the Congress, they argued, the three-mile zone would
come under the exclusive power of the United States by virtue of the
powers lodged in Congress to regulate interstate and foreign commerce.[57]

[55] 62 Ct. Cl. 77, 94–95 (1926). Although the naval officers at Hampton Roads
had been responsible for the taking of the oyster beds as incident to the
widening of a channel, the case was decided on the basis of the commerce power.
The court said that the "naval purposes" here involved included navigation;
indeed, the court was obviously chary of using the national-defense power as a
justification for the action in the case.

[56] *Lewis Blue Point Oyster Co.* v. *Briggs,* 229 U.S. 82 (1913); *Greenleaf
Lumber Co.* v. *Garrison,* 237 U.S. 251 (1915); *Scranton* v. *Wheeler,* 179 U.S.
141 (1900); *Hawkins Point Lighthouse Case,* 39 F. 77 (1889), reversed on other
grounds sub nom. *Chappell* v. *Waterworth,* 155 U.S. 102 (1894).

[57] A basis for this type of argument is found in *Ormerod* v. *New York, etc.,
R. Co.,* 13 F. 370, 371–72 (1882): "The shores of navigable waters and the lands
under the waters belong to the state within whose territorial limits they lie, or
to those who have derived title from the state. It is a familiar doctrine that the
right of eminent domain over the shores and the soil under the waters resides in
the state for all municipal purposes, and within the legitimate limitations of this
right the power of the state is absolute, and an appropriation of the shores and
lands is lawful. In the exercise of this right the state may directly, or indirectly
by delegation, authorize the construction of bridges, piers, wharves, or other
obstructions in navigable waters. Such obstructions are not nuisances, because
that cannot be a nuisance which is done by lawful authority. It is only when
the exercise of this power of eminent domain comes in collision with the paramount authority of the United States that it is inhibited and impotent. The power
of the state ends where that of the national sovereignty begins; but until Congress
has asserted its power to regulate commerce, and by legislation has assumed to
restrict the jurisdiction of the state over its navigable waters, no conflict can
arise, and the authority of the state is comprehensive."

Those who argued the case of the states made no attempt to deny the doctrine of the *Bailey and Fulgham, Blue Point Oyster, Hawkins Point Lighthouse,* and similar cases. They stated that these cases were merely illustrative of a right which the United States undoubtedly had. The crucial point in the development of their train of thought, however, was at the next step, where the believers in state ownership argued that under the commerce power the United States could not acquire *ownership* of any area. Congress could improve navigation, yes, but this did not mean that property not necessary to such an improvement could be expropriated.[58] They utilized the words of Justice Brandeis that the "right of the United States in the navigable waters within the several States is limited to the control thereof for purposes of navigation. . . . The character of the State's ownership in the land and in the waters is the full proprietary right."[59] They believed that the Supreme Court of the United States and the courts of the states had consistently construed the commerce clause as giving to the national government jurisdiction over the navigable waters of harbors for certain defined purposes, but not ownership as a proprietor.[60]

And while the representatives of the Navy tried to press, with little success, the argument that the power of national defense delegated to the national government carried with it the right to assume ownership and jurisdiction over the three-mile zone,[61] other groups sought to use other powers, primarily that over commerce, to accomplish the same objectives.

On a close evaluation of the evidence, one can but conclude that the states did derive from the Crown certain rights, including a right

[58] "Supplemental Memorandum of the Committee on Law and Legislation of the American Association of Port Authorities," *Hearings* on S.J. Res. 83 and 92 (1939), 248.

[59] *Port of Seattle* v. *Oregon & Washington R. Co.,* 255 U.S. 56, 63 (1921).

[60] See, e.g., brief of the Board of Harbor Commissioners of Los Angeles, found in *Hearings* on S.J. Res. 83 and 92 (1939), 250. To the same effect see the statement by Senator Tom Connally in *Hearings* on H.J. Res. 176 and 181 (1939), 25.

[61] Brief of Leslie C. McNemar, *Hearings* on S.J. Res. 83 and 92 (1939), 85–90. One cannot escape the impression in reading the vast mass of material pro and con that neither side was willing to press or argue at any length the basic issue of the extent of the national-defense power. Judicial expressions in this respect may be found in *United States* v. *New River Collieries Co.,* 262 U.S. 341, 343 (1923); *United States* v. *McIntosh,* 2 F. Supp. 244, 251 (1932); *United States* v. *Cohen Grocery Co.,* 255 U.S. 81, 88 (1920). These cases did not involve tidelands or submerged lands. The most important recent pronouncement of the court on the power of national defense is that of *Youngstown Sheet and Tube Co.* v. *Sawyer,* 343 U.S. 579 (1952).

of title, in soils beneath navigable waters down to low-water mark. The extent, however, of such rights of the states seaward of low-water mark is, at this point in the writing, indeterminable and requires a further consideration of problems and issues built upon the foundations just discussed. Of one point there can be no doubt: however erroneous the assumption, the original states did believe that they owned the bed of the sea out to the three-mile limit.

4 ·

Claims of Later States to Submerged Lands

Each new state, upon its admission to the Union, appears to have taken for granted that there was no reservation to the federal government of ownership of submerged soils under the navigable waters within the boundaries of the state as declared in its constitution. Each newly admitted state regulated its waterfronts and harbors and made grants of land in the soils under rivers, lakes, and harbors and in the open sea. By their actions, the later states evinced the same faith in the ownership of the soils that the thirteen originals had manifested. It is therefore necessary to determine upon what basis these later states acted in making such assumptions and taking such actions.

It has been seen that proponents of state ownership have traced a title from the Crown to the thirteen original states as independent, or at least quasi-independent, sovereigns. The nature and extent of these claims in the light of the adoption of the Constitution have been considered. The states which were admitted to the Union at a later date were admitted "on an equal footing with the said original States."[1] In

[1] The "equal footing" phrase antedates the Constitution and had its origins in the quarrels which arose over the various states' claims to western lands. These quarrels were threatening to wreck the government under the Articles of Confederation. Although the Articles were proposed in 1777, Maryland had not yet ratified in 1780. Finally, in 1780, Congress passed a resolution asking the various states to cede their western lands to the Congress, on condition that other states would be created from them with the "same rights of sovereignty, freedom, and independence, as the other states." New York ceded its lands in March 1781, after Virginia had made a similar cession in January of that year. Formal transfer of these two parcels was completed in 1784. Other cessions followed in 1784, 1785, and 1786. On 13 July 1787 the Northwest Ordinance, providing a system of governance for the Northwest Territory created out of these cessions, was passed. Section 13 of that act presumed the admission of

the main, territory acquired by the United States has been for the purpose of forming new states. This tracing of title from the Crown to original states and so to later states through the principle of "equality of states" is a constantly recurring theme in arguments which were presented in support of state claims to ownership of soils under navigable waters prior to *United States* v. *California.*[2] The argument is only as sound as the interpretation which may be given to the "equal footing" clause. In what respects must the states be "equal" upon their admission to the Union? What is the nature of the relationship so established? The general rule in this regard is that a state may not be placed in a position of political inferiority in the federal system. Restrictions of this character, placed on a state as a condition for admission, may be cast aside once the state has assumed full status.[3]

Insofar as the "equal footing" clause in relation to lands under navigable waters is concerned, the basic case is that of *Pollard's Lessee* v. *Hagan,*[4] which laid down the rule that ownership of soils under navigable waters is an attribute of state sovereignty. Therefore, such ownership cannot be denied to new states upon their admission to the Union. The facts in the case are relatively simple. Pollard and others brought an action of ejectment against Hagan and others in the Circuit

---

future states "to a share in the Federal councils on an equal footing with the original States." Article V of the articles of "compact" of the Ordinance is the basis of the clause later to be found in acts admitting states: ". . . such States shall be admitted, by its delegates, into the Congress of the United States, on an equal footing with the original States, in all respects whatever; and shall be at liberty to form a permanent constitution and State government. . . ." The first session of Congress under the Constitution continued the Northwest Ordinance by act of 7 August 1789. This résumé is drawn from Donaldson, *The Public Domain,* 64–81.

The acts admitting the various states to the Union are reproduced in Francis Newton Thorpe, *American Charters, Constitutions and Organic Laws* (Washington, Government Printing Office, 1909).

[2] See, e.g., "Brief of Joseph A. Loret for the State of Louisiana against S.J. Resolutions 83 and 92," *Hearings* on S.J. Res. 83 and 92 (1939), 192; testimony of Warren Gilman, assistant attorney general of the state of New York, *ibid.,* 176–78; "Memorandum in Support of H.J. Resolutions 118 *et al.* by the American Association of Port Authorities," *Hearings* on H.J. Res. 118 *et al.* (1945), 26.

[3] *Coyle* v. *Smith,* 221 U.S. 559 (1911). A state may not repudiate conditions imposed at the time of admission if the restrictions are such as could validly be imposed by federal legislation after its admission, e.g., those affecting control over federal lands within the boundaries of a state. *Stearns* v. *Minnesota,* 179 U.S. 223 (1900); *Economy Light and Power Co.* v. *United States,* 256 U.S. 113 (1921). A condition respecting the disposition of moneys derived from the sale of federal lands granted by the United States to the state of New Mexico was held valid in *Ervien* v. *United States,* 251 U.S. 41 (1919).

[4] 3 How. 212 (1845).

Court of Mobile County, Alabama. Pollard held patent to lands from the Congress of the United States. These patents had been issued in part to certain submerged lands in Mobile Bay, the submerged lands only being at issue in this case. The patents had been granted by Congress after Alabama had been admitted as a state; according to the act admitting Alabama to the Union, all the waste and unappropriated lands were reserved to the United States, and the state of Alabama was never to interfere with their disposal. Hagan claimed title to the same land based on an old Spanish grant. The lands in question had been litigated before, but the decisions had been concerned with points that need not be considered here.[5] This was the first case which presented squarely the question of the power of Congress to issue a patent to submerged lands under navigable waters within the boundaries of a state following its admission to the Union.

Alabama was created out of territory ceded by Georgia to the United States in April, 1802. The purpose of this, and the earlier cessions by other states, was to establish in the United States a trust, a binding obligation, to form new states. To that end, Justice McKinley said, the national government held only temporary powers over the territories, for

when Alabama was admitted into the Union, on an equal footing with the original States, she succeeded to all the rights of sovereignty, jurisdiction, and eminent domain which Georgia possessed at the date of cession, except so far as this right was diminished by the public lands remaining in the possession and under the control of the United States, for the temporary purposes provided for in the deed of cession and the legislative acts connected with it. Nothing remained to the United States, according to the terms of the agreement, but the public lands. And, if an express stipulation had been inserted in the agreement, granting the municipal right of sovereignty and eminent domain to the United States, such stipulation would have been void and inoperative; because the United States have no constitutional capacity to exercise municipal jurisdiction, sovereignty, or eminent domain, within the limits of a State or elsewhere, except in the cases in which it is expressly granted. . . . The right of Alabama and every other new State to exercise all the powers of government, which belong to and may be exercised by the original States of the Union, must be admitted, and remain unquestioned, except so far as they are, temporarily, deprived of control over the public lands.[6]

[5] *Pollard* v. *Kibbe*, 14 Pet. 353 (1840); *Mobile* v. *Eslava*, 16 Pet. 234 (1842); *Mobile* v. *Hallett*, 16 Pet. 261 (1842); *Mobile* v. *Emmanuel*, 1 How. 95 (1843); *Pollard* v. *Files*, 2 How. 591 (1844).

[6] 3 How. 212, 223–24. The words "eminent domain" are used here by Justice

It was insisted, however, by the plaintiffs that the disclaimer to public lands which Alabama accepted included within its purview the submerged lands in question. By the laws of Spain, which country had originally held the territory in question, the right to grant soils under navigable waters had resided in the King. Pollard argued that this right had passed to the United States. McKinley said, however, that territory acquired by the United States is held subject to the Constitution and laws of the United States and not those of the government ceding it. As a matter of fact, it appears from the record that Spain, in the Treaty of 1795, actually admitted to wrongful occupation, rather than ownership, of this area. Therefore Alabama was entitled to the "sovereignty and jurisdiction over all the territory within her limits" to the same extent that Georgia had possessed while holding it. McKinley's view of the matter was that to "maintain any other doctrine is to deny that Alabama has been admitted into the Union on an equal footing with the original States, the constitution, laws, and compact, to the contrary notwithstanding. But her rights of sovereignty and jurisdiction are not governed by the common law of England as it prevailed in the colonies before the Revolution, but as modified by our own institutions."[7] He then quoted with approval Taney's famous statement from *Martin* v. *Waddell* to the effect that after the Revolution the people of each state themselves became sovereign and in that character held the absolute right to their navigable waters and the soils under them.[8] The soils in question in *Pollard's Lessee* v. *Hagan,* therefore, belonged to the state of Alabama, and no compact might be made between her and the United States which might enlarge or diminish those rights.

There also had been, in the act admitting Alabama to the Union, a clause which guaranteed forever the "free navigability" to all American citizens of the rivers in the state. Since, under the commerce power, the Congress could apply this restriction to all states, new and original alike, the court held that this clause neither enlarged nor diminished the rights of Alabama under the "equal footing" clause. The "free navigability" phrase was, to McKinley, nothing more than a regulation of commerce with no applicability to the instant case. It did not constitute

---

McKinley as the right "which belongs to society, or to the sovereign, of disposing, in case of necessity, and for the public safety, of all the wealth contained in the State."

[7] *Ibid.,* 229.

[8] Taney was still chief justice at the time of *Pollard's Lessee* v. *Hagan* and was in accord with McKinley's opinion.

a source of power under which the Congress might issue a land patent to submerged soils, as Pollard had contended. In summary, the Justice then said:

> To give to the United States the right to transfer to a citizen the title to the shores and the soils under navigable waters, would be placing in their hands a weapon which might be wielded greatly to the injury of State sovereignty, and deprive the States of the power to exercise a numerous and important class of police powers. But in the hands of the States this power can never be used so as to affect the exercise of any national right of eminent domain or jurisdiction with which the United States have been invested by the Constitution. For, although the territorial limits of Alabama have extended all her sovereign power into the sea, it is there, as on the shore, but municipal power, subject to the Constitution of the United States, "and the laws which shall be made in pursuance thereof."[9]

Thus, in effect, the court said that one of the attributes of sovereignty protected by the "equal footing" clause is the right of a state to be secured, upon its admission to the Union, in the ownership of the soils beneath its navigable waters in the same fashion as the original states.

Justice Catron saw fit to dissent in this case. He made some significant statements presaging many of the developments which occurred almost a hundred years later. To him, the doctrine which assumed that "all lands temporarily flowed with tide water were part of the eminent domain and a sovereign right in the old States; and that the new ones when admitted into the Union, coming in with equal sovereign rights, took the lands thus flowed by implication as an incident of State sovereignty" was a doctrine which was "unheard of" in the courts of the land before 1840.[10] The doctrine had, he admitted, been put forward in political discussions, but always as an argument to bolster a theory

---

[9] 3 How. 212, 230. Note particularly in this quotation the last sentence, a clear intimation that the court had in mind the extension of territorial ownership below low-water mark by a state. The statement is, of course, dictum. *Pollard's Lessee* v. *Hagan* involved submerged lands under Mobile Bay, a closed bay which, even under *United States* v. *California,* remains in the possession of the state of Alabama or its grantees. The court was asked to overrule the *Pollard* case five years later but refused to do so. *Goodtitle* v. *Kibbe,* 9 How. 471 (1850).

In *Withers* v. *Buckley,* 20 How. 84, 93 (1857), the court reiterated its interpretation of the "equal footing" principle when it said that "Congress could exact of the new State the surrender of no attribute inherent in her character as a sovereign independent State, or indispensable to her equality with her sister States, necessarily implied or guaranteed by the very nature of the Federal compact." This case is followed with approval in many other cases, among them *Shively* v. *Bowlby,* 152 U.S. 1 (1894).

[10] 3 How. 212, 231.

that the new states obtained title to the *upland* because they held
title to the tidewaters. He could not but feel that the proper place for
the determination of the type of conflict presented in the *Pollard* case
was in the political departments of the state and federal government.[11]
Further, Catron contended, someone had to own these submerged
lands; Alabama could not, for she had "disclaimed" any right or title
to the waste or unappropriated lands. If, therefore, Alabama could not
own the lands in question, the United States must be the only governmental authority capable of ownership. Of course, Congress might have
granted away these very lands in question while Alabama was still a
territory. Catron denied the validity of the distinction between the uplands and the submerged lands made by McKinley as applied to waste
or unappropriated lands reserved to the United States. Catron maintained that equality was a political matter, and he did not want to see
this new idea of proprietary equality which, he felt, reversed previous
decisions.[12]

The arguments thus presented by the majority and the single dissent
have had their counterparts in the later controversy over the ownership
and jurisdiction of the submerged soils. Leslie McNemar, testifying before the Senate Committee on Public Lands, felt that the "equal footing" doctrine had only political significance in that it entitled each state
to two senators and at least one representative in the Congress and
guaranteed each state a republican form of government, protection
against invasion and domestic violence, and the other things that go
with statehood, so long as the state's laws do not conflict with the Constitution, laws, or treaties made by the United States.[13]

[11] The Justice thus foretold, with astonishing accuracy, the events which were
to occur in the Congress of the United States in the years following 1938.

[12] Comment, "Conflicting State and Federal Claims of Title in Submerged
Lands of the Continental Shelf," 56 *Yale Law Journal* (1947), 362. The previous
decisions referred to by Catron are those five which had involved the land claims
finally adjudicated in *Pollard's Lessee* v. *Hagan*. See footnote 5, this chapter.
These five cases were decided on points which are not pertinent to this discussion.

[13] *Hearings* on S.J. Res. 83 and 92 (1939), 58. In his brief filed in support of
these resolutions, McNemar noted particularly that the Constitution did not
guarantee to such new states as might be admitted into the Union that they
should be admitted on an equal footing with the original states in all respects
whatever. States have been admitted on unequal terms. Lands owned by the
United States in the original states were obtained by cession. On the other hand,
when foreign governments ceded land, or territory was otherwise acquired by
the United States, the vacant lands passed to the United States. The new states
formed from such lands had no right to these waste or unappropriated lands,
except as the United States saw fit to grant them. McNemar cited this discrepancy
as a typical example of the inequality on which states might be admitted to the
Union. *Ibid.*, 76–77, 81–82.

Thomas L. Blanton, a former member of Congress from Texas who was representing interests opposed to state control of tidelands oil in California, contended in the 1938 hearings before the House Committee on the Judiciary that the term "equal footing" meant only "identical political rights and privileges" and in no way involved title to property. The original states, when they declared their independence, derived an absolute right to their tidelands and submerged lands; they formed the Union retaining those rights. Texas, too, Blanton said, came into the United States retaining all its public lands.[14] "When States, however, like California and New Mexico came into the Union, they came in without public lands, as all public lands in such territories already belonged to the United States, and while they were admitted 'on an equal footing with the original States (concerning political rights) in all respects whatever,' they were not on an equal footing respecting ownership of public land, as they owned no public land whatever."[15] And, he continued, Congress had never granted to California or to any person any tide or submerged lands; these were a part of the "public lands" which the United States retained.[16] These statements are typical of the arguments which were advanced in reply to the veritable flood of decisions which have followed the rule laid down in *Pollard's Lessee* v. *Hagan.*[17]

[14] The situation of Texas is discussed in Chapter 6.

[15] *Hearings* on S.J. Res. 208 (1938), 11.

[16] *Ibid.*

[17] The case has been followed with approval in 52 Supreme Court decisions and 244 lower federal and state court decisions. Typical statements of such approval are found as follows:

UNITED STATES SUPREME COURT DECISIONS—

Mumford v. *Wardell,* 6 Wall. 423, 435–36 (1867): "California was admitted into the Union September 9, 1850, and the Act of Congress admitting her declares she is so admitted on an equal footing, in all respects, with the original States. . . . Settled rule of law in this court is that the shores of navigable waters and the soils under the same in the original States were not granted by the Constitution to the United States, but were reserved to the several States. . . ."

Weber v. *Board of Harbor Commissioners,* 18 Wall. 57, 65–66 (1873): "Upon the admission of California into the Union upon an equal footing with the original States, absolute property in and dominion and sovereignty over all soils under the tidewaters within her limits passed to the State, with the consequent right to dispose of the title to any part of said soils in such manner as she might deem proper."

Shively v. *Bowlby,* 152 U.S. 1, 57 (1894): "The new States admitted into the Union since the adoption of the Constitution have the same rights as the original States in the tide waters, and in the lands under them, within their respective jurisdictions."

For similar statements by the Supreme Court see *Barney* v. *Keokuk,* 94 U.S. 324, 338 (1876); *Escanaba & Lake Michigan Transportation Co.* v. *Chicago,*

Later cases have served to state in even more unequivocal terms the doctrine that when a state enters the Union with a reservation of public lands to the United States such a reservation does not apply seaward of high-water mark. The basic rule has been that the words "public lands" are habitually used to describe lands that are subject to sale or disposal under the general laws of Congress.[18] It was held in *Mann* v. *Tacoma Land Co.*[19] that holders of Valentine scrip[20] had no right to locate on tidelands, in this case certain lands covered by the ebb and flow of the tide at the head of Puget Sound, at the mouth of the Puyallup River. Congress, it was stated, could dispose of the title to tidelands before a state entered the Union, should it care to do so.[21] Congress had never, however, taken such a step, and it could be con-

---

107 U.S. 678, 688–90 (1882); *Cardwell* v. *American Bridge Co.*, 113 U.S. 205, 212 (1885); *Knight* v. *United Land Association*, 142 U.S. 161, 183 (1891); *Illinois Central R. Co.* v. *Illinois*, 146 U.S. 387, 435 (1892); *United States* v. *Mission Rock Co.*, 189 U.S. 391, 404 (1903); *Hardin* v. *Shedd*, 190 U.S. 508, 519 (1903); *Scott* v. *Lattig*, 227 U.S. 229, 242–43 (1913); *United States* v. *Coronado Beach Co.*, 255 U.S. 472, 487–88 (1921); *Port of Seattle* v. *Oregon & Washington R. Co.*, 255 U.S. 56 (1921); *Borax Consolidated* v. *Los Angeles*, 296 U.S. 10, 15 (1935); *Silas Mason Co.* v. *Tax Commission*, 302 U.S. 186, 239 (1937).

LOWER FEDERAL COURT DECISIONS—
United States v. *Ashton*, 170 F. 509, 517 (1909); *Dean* v. *San Diego*, 275 F. 228, 231 (1921).

STATE COURT DECISIONS—
Shively v. *Welch*, 10 Sawyer 136, 140–41 (Ore. 1884); *Wright* v. *Seymour*, 69 Cal. 122, 126 (1886); *Lux* v. *Haggin*, 69 Cal. 255, 335 (1886); *Bowlby* v. *Shively*, 22 Ore. 410, 417 (1892); *State* v. *Black River Phosphate Co.*, 32 Fla. 82, 93–94 (1893); *Broward* v. *Mabry*, 50 So. 826, 829–30 (Fla. 1909); *State* v. *Capdeville*, 146 La. 94 (1919); *Freed* v. *Miami Beach Pier Corp.*, 112 So. 841, 844 (Fla. 1927); *Lipscomb* v. *Gialourakis*, 133 So. 104, 106 (Fla. 1931); *People* v. *Kirk*, 162 Ill. 138 (1896); *Bodi* v. *Winous Point Shooting Club*, 57 Ohio St. 226 (1897); *Dwelle* v. *Wilson*, 14 Ohio Cir. Ct. R. 551 (1897); *People* v. *Silberwood*, 67 N.W. 1087 (Mich. 1896).

[18] *Newhall* v. *Sanger,* 92 U.S. 761, 763 (1875).

[19] 153 U.S. 273 (1894).

[20] The term was used to denote scrip issued by Congress to one Valentine in 1872, after he had proved that he had been unfairly dealt with in the confirmation of certain Spanish grants. The value of the scrip was presumed to equal the value of the lands he had lost and could be applied to the "unoccupied and unappropriated public lands of the United States, not mineral."

[21] In *Hinman* v. *Warren,* 6 Ore. 408, 411 (1876), the Supreme Court of Oregon said that the United States had no authority to so dispose of lands within a territory as to make it impossible to admit that territory into the Union on an equal footing with other states. The theory advanced by the court was that in all such matters the national government is simply a protector until such time as the territory becomes a state.

This view of the Oregon court is at variance with *Mann* v. *Tacoma Land Co.* The statement in the *Hinman* case is sheer dictum and constitutes one of the

sidered "settled that the general legislation of Congress in respect to public lands does not extend to tide lands."[22] Lindley says:

There is no principle involved in the consideration of the public land system better settled or more clearly enunciated than that lands under tidal waters, and below the line of ordinary high tide, are not "public lands." When a state bordering upon those waters is admitted into the Union it becomes, by virtue of its sovereignty, the owner of all lands extending seaward so far as its municipal dominion extends, . . . from the line of ordinary high tide on the shore of the open ocean seaward to the distance of three miles, or a marine league.[23]

---

few judicial declarations to the effect that Congress may not grant away tidelands before a state enters the Union.

Manley O. Hudson, formerly a member of the Permanent Court of International Justice, in answer to a question by Senator Wiley on this point stated: "I am disposed to say that the Federal Government cannot reserve the marginal sea to the exclusion of a new state." *Hearings* before the Senate Judiciary Committee on S.J. Res. 48 and H.J. Res. 225, 79th Cong., 2d sess. (1946), 260. These hearings will hereinafter be cited as *Hearings* on S.J. Res. 48 and H.J. Res. 225 (1946).

On the other hand, Leslie C. McNemar felt that the courts had incorrectly held that the term "public domain" did not include territory below high-water mark. Only Congress, he contended, could make such a distinction and Congress had never done so. *Hearings* on S.J. Res. 83 and 92 (1939), 80.

[22] *Mann* v. *Tacoma Land Co.*, 153 U.S. 273, 284 (1894). The rule in this case was followed in *Baer* v. *Moran Brothers*, 153 U.S. 287 (1894), decided the same day.

[23] Curtis H. Lindley, *A Treatise on the American Law Relating to Mines* (3d ed., San Francisco, Bancroft-Whitney, 1914), II, 1015–16. Insofar as the last phrase is concerned, *United States* v. *California, United States* v. *Texas,* and *United States* v. *Louisiana* unsettled Lindley's "clearly enunciated" principle.

45 *Corpus juris* 535, 537, states that lands under navigable waters are "public lands."

In *Brewer-Elliott Oil Co.* v. *United States*, 260 U.S. 77 (1922), lands under the Arkansas River were at issue. The court held that if the stream was navigable, the state would control; if the stream was not navigable, then the land would come under the definition of "public lands" which the United States might convey. On the facts of the case, the Arkansas River was held to be nonnavigable.

In *United States* v. *Utah*, 283 U.S. 64 (1931), a case involving the contested validity of a state oil lease as against a lease issued by the United States to lands under a navigable river, it was held that the state lease controlled. Only waste and unappropriated lands, those susceptible of continuous use and occupation, were reserved by the United States upon the admission of Utah to the Union. The term "public lands" did not include the lands under navigable waters within the boundaries of a state, for these were the property of the state upon its admission.

In *Barney* v. *Keokuk*, 94 U.S. 324, 338 (1876), the court said: "The United States has wisely abstained from extending (if it could extend) its surveys and grants beyond the limits of high waters."

Again in *Hardin* v. *Jordan*, 140 U.S. 371, 381 (1891), the court declared:

In furtherance of the doctrine frequently declared by the United States Supreme Court that the states hold title to the beds of all navigable waters within their boundaries, state courts have allowed the extension of state claims out to the three-mile limit. Thus the Alabama Court of Appeals upheld the conviction of persons who were shrimp fishing in the open sea three-fourths of a mile offshore in the Gulf of Mexico, on the grounds that the state of Alabama owned the sea bottom to a distance of one marine league.[24] Similar statements have been made by other courts.[25] *Corpus juris* declares that "within the three-mile limit, a state owns lands submerged by the sea."[26]

It is, of course, true that the United States Supreme Court, prior to *United States* v. *California*, had never passed directly on the issue of ownership or possible ownership in the submerged soils below low-water mark out to the three-mile limit. The Supreme Court had, however, used the "navigable waters" phrase to cover a state's ownership of navigable rivers,[27] tidelands in the technical sense,[28] lakes,[29] and

---

"With regard to grants of the government for lands bordering on tide-water, it has been distinctly settled that they only extend to high-water mark, and that the title to the shore and lands under water in front of lands so granted inures to the state within which they are situated, if a state has been organized and established there. Such title to the shore and lands under water is regarded as incidental to the sovereignty of the state . . . and cannot be retained or granted out to individuals by the United States." This particular language is quoted with approval in *Ross* v. *Burkhard Co.*, 90 Cal. App. 201, 207 (1928).

[24] *Borsage* v. *State*, 23 Ala. App. 18 (1928), certiorari denied, 219 Ala. 154, 208 U.S. 568. The request for certiorari to the United States Supreme Court was based on the theory that the area in question belonged to the United States rather than the state of Alabama and therefore the criminal jurisdiction of Alabama could not run in the three-mile zone.

[25] *State* v. *Pollock*, 239 Pac. 8, 10 (Wash. 1925): ". . . the jurisdiction and dominion of the state extends to the three-mile limit offshore."

People v. *Reilly*, 14 N.Y.S. 2d 589, 592 (1939): "The State owns and has jurisdiction over all lands under water within the three-mile limit."

To the same effect see declarations in these cases: *Lipscomb* v. *Gialourakis*, 133 So. 104, 106–107 (Fla. 1931); *Dunham* v. *Lamphere*, 3 Gray 268 (Mass. 1855); *Suttori* v. *Peckham*, 48 Cal. App. 88 (1920); *People ex rel. Mexican Telegraph Co.* v. *State Tax Commission*, 220 N.Y.S. 8, 18 (1927).

[26] 45 *Corpus juris* 540, n. 78 (b).

[27] *United States* v. *Utah*, 283 U.S. 64 (1931); *Barney* v. *Keokuk*, 94 U.S. 324 (1876). The latter case involved title to a portion of the bed of the Mississippi River.

[28] *Shively* v. *Bowlby*, 152 U.S. 1 (1894); *Borax Consolidated* v. *Los Angeles*, 296 U.S. 10 (1935).

[29] This holds true whether the lakes are contained entirely within the boundaries of a state or are international in character. In reference to the former situation, see *Louisiana* v. *Mississippi*, 202 U.S. 1 (1906), where the rule of the *thalweg* was applied in a boundary dispute involving Lake Borgne and Mississippi

bays.[30] The criterion, the opinions of the Supreme Court seem to hold, is based on the idea of the navigability of the waters rather than a distinction between waters above and below low-water mark. If waters within a state's boundary were navigable, then the soils under those waters belonged to the state; if the waters were not navigable, then the act admitting the state to the Union reserved such soils as a part of the "public lands" of the United States. In the first case, title to submerged soils accrued to the state as an incident of sovereignty. In the second·case, the submerged land belonged to the federal government, not as an incident of sovereignty, but merely because the federal government happened to be in the first instance the owner of the land.

Since Louisiana was one of the three states involved in the submerged lands cases before the United States Supreme Court, some special notice must be taken of the basis of claims made by that state to soils under the marginal sea. The stake of Louisiana in the submerged Gulf soils is a substantial one. The state has collected approximately forty-two million dollars in cash bonuses and rentals and over one million dollars in royalties[31] from lands brought into issue in *United States* v. *Louisiana*. Producing wells are located a considerable distance out in the Gulf. Senator Russell Long of Louisiana reported in 1949 that most of Louisiana's wells were fifteen to twenty miles offshore.[32] A well producing more than seven hundred barrels of crude oil per day was brought in twenty-five miles off the coast of St. Mary's Parish in 1950.[33]

Sound, which are inland waters. In reference to the latter situation, see *Massachusetts* v. *New York*, 271 U.S. 65 (1926), and *Illinois Central R. Co.* v. *Illinois*, 146 U.S. 387 (1892). In these cases Lake Ontario and Lake Michigan, lakes which constitute a part of an international boundary, were held subject to ownership by New York and Illinois out to the boundaries declared by those states. See also Cushing, Atty. Gen., 6 Op. Atty. Gen. 173 (1853), in reference to ownership of portions of the Great Lakes fronting on the same states.

In *United States* v. *Chandler-Dunbar Water Co.*, 209 U.S. 447 (1908), a bed of a river which formed an international boundary between the United States and Canada was held to be owned by a state rather than the United States. Justice Holmes wrote the opinion.

[30] *McCready* v. *Virginia*, 94 U.S. 391 (1876); *Smith* v. *Maryland*, 18 How. 71 (1855).

[31] Testimony of Lucille May Grace, register of the Louisiana State Land Office, *Hearings* before the Senate Committee on Interior and Insular Affairs on S.J. Res. 20, 82d Cong., 1st sess. (1951), 190. These hearings will hereinafter be cited as *Hearings* on S.J. Res. 20 (1951).

[32] *Times-Picayune* (New Orleans), 10 August 1949.

[33] *New York Times*, 12 April 1950. The well produced from a depth of 11,650 feet from an oil sand estimated at 250 feet in thickness.

The state of Louisiana reported in 1949 that "the records of operations in the

Although total production to date has not been great, and drilling and operating wells in the Gulf is more expensive than on uplands, no one can doubt the potentialities of production in the offshore areas of Louisiana.

The claim of the state of Louisiana to the submerged soils in the marginal sea off its coasts is substantially similar to that of all states which have been admitted to the Union since 1789, Texas only excepted.[34] In 1682, La Salle reached the mouth of the Mississippi River and took possession of the entire valley in the name of the King of France. In 1712, Antoine Crozat was granted a monopoly of trade in the territory extending from what is now Illinois to the Gulf of Mexico. Crozat surrendered this charter in 1717; a new one was granted in the same year to the Compagnie d'Occident. The coasts, harbors, lands, and title therein were granted to the Western Company as they had been to Crozat. Title and rights in the area reverted to the King of France in 1732, when the Western Company surrendered its charter and retroceded its rights. Operations in the area turned out to be highly unprofitable, a factor which weighed heavily in the thinking of Louis XIV when he agreed to cede the area to Spain following the Treaty of Paris in 1763.

The area was retroceded to France by the secret treaty of San Ildefonso, 1 October 1800. The treaty presented a serious threat to the United States. The order went to the Spanish intendant to suspend the right of deposit at New Orleans which had been granted by the Pinckney Treaty of 1795. On 30 April 1803, in violation of her agreement with Spain not to transfer Louisiana to any other power, France sold the Territory of Louisiana to the United States for eighty million francs. An area of magnificent size and untold wealth had been acquired.[35]

In the Treaty of San Ildefonso, it was agreed that "His Catholic

Gulf of Mexico off the coast of Louisiana reveal that 32 structures [or domes] have been drilled since 1945, but only 6 have produced oil. They show that on the 6 proven structures a total of 26 development wells have been drilled, but only 15 have been producers. Out of the other 26 structural prospects so drilled, 17 of the wells were dry and therefore failed to prove any productive character of the domes. The balance proved the existence only of gas. But in the total operations so conducted off Louisiana there has been a total investment of something like $190,000,000, although the gross value of the oil produced has amounted only to about $900,000, or less than one-half of one per cent of the investment made." "Brief of Defendant Opposing Plaintiff's Motion for Judgment and Supporting Defendant's Motion to Dismiss and Other Defenses," No. 12 Original, October Term 1949, pp. 109–10. This brief will hereinafter be cited as the Louisiana brief.

[34] The claim of Texas is discussed in Chapter 6.
[35] This short summary is based in major part on Samuel Eliot Morison and

Majesty promises and engages . . . to retrocede to the French Republic
. . . the colony or province of Louisiana, with the same extent that it
now has in the hands of Spain, and that it had when France possessed
it."[36]

The Treaty of Cession,[37] by which the United States gained Louisiana, declared that the "French Republic has an incontestable right to
the domain, and to the possession of the said territory," and "doth
hereby cede to the said United States, in the name of the French Republic, for ever and in full sovereignty, the said territory, with all its
rights and appurtenances, as fully and in the same manner as they have
been acquired by the French Republic."

Article II provided:

In the cession made by the preceding article are included the adjacent
islands belonging to Louisiana, all public lots and squares, vacant lands,
and all public buildings, fortifications, barracks, and other edifices which
are not private property.

Article III declared:

The inhabitants of the ceded territory shall be incorporated in the
Union of the United States, and admitted as soon as possible, according to
the principles of the Federal Constitution, to the enjoyment of all rights,
advantages and immunities of citizens of the United States; and in the
meantime they shall be maintained and protected in the free enjoyment of
their liberty, property, and the religion they profess.

Any right or title held by the United States must have come down
through the Treaty of Cession.

The claim of the state of Louisiana must rest upon the "equal footing" principle, which has been discussed above and which is taken up
in greater detail in the next chapter, in connection with the claims of
California. On 31 October 1803 the President was authorized to take
possession of the territory for the purpose of protecting it and the inhabitants.[38] The area was formally given territorial status by act of 26
March 1804.[39] On 20 February 1811 the persons resident in that part
of the territory ceded under the name of Louisiana by the Treaty of

---

Henry Steele Commager, *The Growth of the American Republic* (4th ed., New
York, Oxford University Press, 1950), I, 86–87, 389–93.
  [36] This portion of the Treaty of San Ildefonso which is quoted is found in the
Treaty of Cession, Article I.   [37] 8 U.S. Stat. 200 (1803).
  [38] 2 U.S. Stat. 245.   [39] 2 U.S. Stat. 283.

Cession were authorized "to form for themselves a Constitution and State Government."[40]

The act of 20 February 1811 set out certain limits:

Beginning at the mouth of the river Sabine; thence by a line to be drawn along the middle of said river, including all islands, to the thirty-second degree of north latitude; thence due north to the northernmost part of the thirty-third degree of north latitude; thence along the said parallel of latitude to the river Mississippi; thence down said river to the river Iberville; and from thence, along the middle of the said river and Lakes Maurepas and Pontchartrain, to the Gulf of Mexico; thence bounded by the said Gulf to the place of beginning, including all islands within three leagues of the coast. . . .

Under section 3 of the act, the people were required to disclaim right or title to "waste or unappropriated lands" lying in the boundaries set out. There was, however, no disclaimer of any rights of sovereignty. It has been seen, in *Pollard* v. *Hagan,* that the title to lands under navigable waters held by states other than the original thirteen is a part of state "sovereignty." Section 5 of the act provided that the "said State shall be admitted to the Union upon the same footing with the original states."

The state constitution, dated 22 January 1812, was prepared under the authority of this act and was approved by Congress in the act of 8 April 1812, which declared: "The said State shall be one, and is hereby declared to be one of the United States of America, and admitted to the Union on an equal footing with the original states, in all respects whatever, by the name and title of the State of Louisiana."[41] Under the rule of *Pollard* v. *Hagan* and the numerous cases which have followed the principle expressed in that decision, the state holds title to the beds of navigable waters as an incident of state sovereignty under the "equal footing" clause.

The state of Louisiana passed its first mineral leasing act in 1915,[42] a statute superseded by another act in 1936.[43] These statutes were based on the premise of title in the soils of the marginal sea, so far as their applicability to leases in the Gulf of Mexico were concerned. The state has set up a license system under which persons have been authorized

---

[40] 2 U.S. Stat. 641.

[41] 2 U.S. Stat. 701. By 2 U.S. Stat. 708, 14 April 1812, additional territory was added to the area set out in the 1811 act.

[42] Act 30 of 1915.   [43] Act 93 of 1936.

to remove gravel, shell, sand, and other materials of value from the beds of navigable waters.[44] The Department of Conservation of the state exercises general jurisdiction. Removal of oyster shells, for example, is authorized under license. Such shells may be removed "from any of the shell reefs within the boundaries of this State and located in or on the borders of the Gulf of Mexico or any of the bays, lakes, inlets, or waterways connected with or emptying into the said Gulf."[45]

In 1938, stimulated by actions in Congress which at that time appeared to presage an assertion of national authority over the offshore lands, the state legislature passed a boundary-extension act.[46] The statute was premised on the idea that the original limit of three marine miles set out in international law, based as it was on the range of cannon shot, was now outmoded. Since modern artillery had greater range, it was reasonable to extend the limit to twenty-seven marine miles. The act declared that the state's boundary prior to 1938 had been three marine leagues. Section 3 of the act minced no words: ". . . the State of Louisiana owns in full and complete ownership the waters of the Gulf of Mexico and of the arms of the said Gulf and the beds and shores of the Gulf of Mexico and the arms of the Gulf of Mexico, including all lands that are covered by the waters of the said Gulf and its arms either at low tide or high tide, within the boundaries of Louisiana, as herein fixed."

There can be no doubt that under the 1938 act, and under previous acts of a regulatory character, the state of Louisiana assumed that it held the ownership of the offshore lands. Nevertheless, the boundary-extension legislation, coming at a time when there was agitation to declare national control of the coastal lands, looked for all the world like an attempt on the part of the state to "grab" further land. There were those who disclaimed this motive and argued, in rather consistent fashion, that the extension measure was a perfectly sound and legal one.[47]

There can be little argument that the leasing of tide and submerged lands by Louisiana has been a profitable operation. As was previously noted, Lucille May Grace, register of the State Land Office, stated in 1951 that Louisiana had collected forty-two million dollars in cash bonuses and rentals and over one million in royalties from drilling in

---

[44] See *Gorham* v. *Alkali Works,* 27 So. 2d 299 (La. 1946).
[45] Act 42 of 1914.   [46] Act 55 of 1938.
[47] See Loret, "Louisiana's Twenty-Seven Mile Maritime Belt," 13 *Tulane Law Review* (1939), 252–57. The state of Texas enacted two boundary-extension acts. See p. 88, n. 44, below.

areas brought into question by the decisions of the United States Supreme Court.[48] Exploration and drilling operations are more extensive off the coast of Louisiana than in any other coastal area of the nation. The oil companies have poured hundreds of millions of dollars into the effort to develop producing fields. The Magnolia Petroleum Company spent twenty-six million dollars and drilled sixteen wells off Louisiana over a three-year period before bringing in a single producer. This Magnolia well is located twenty-five miles out in the Gulf off St. Mary's Parish.[49] The average cost of drilling for oil in shallow water is fourteen times greater than for a well of comparable depth on land;[50] yet even with this added cost, Louisiana has managed to do very well in bonus and royalty returns.

Since the legal basis of the Louisiana case is basically similar to that of California, attention will now be turned in detail to the claims to ownership of submerged soils made by the Golden State.

[48] *Hearings* on S.J. Res. 20 (1951), 190.
[49] Leigh S. McCaslin, Jr., "Along the Gulf," *Oil and Gas Journal,* 13 April 1950, p. 61.
[50] Letter from B. Orchard Lisle, joint publisher of *Oil Forum,* reprinted in *Hearings* before the Senate Committee on Interior and Insular Affairs on S.J. Res. 195, 81st Cong., 2d sess. (1950), 231. These hearings will hereinafter be cited as *Hearings* on S.J. Res. 195 (1950). See pp. 89–90 below, where the costs of offshore drilling are more fully discussed.

5.

California's Claims to Submerged Lands

Before the Mexican War in 1846, California was governed as a department within the Republic of Mexico. It included both Alta California and Baja California. The organic law was the Mexican constitution of 1837, a document which had confiscated the missions and substantially altered the previous government of the provinces. In northern California, however, actual governmental practice differed greatly from that contemplated by the Mexican constitution of 1837.

The United States declared war on Mexico on 13 May 1846. Commodore Sloat seized Monterrey on 7 July 1846 and proceeded to take other ports. By 17 August 1846 the occupation of California was complete. Hostilities ceased with the armistice effected through the Articles of Capitulation, signed at Cahuenga, on 16 January 1847, though the United States Supreme Court has held that the conquest of California itself was complete on 7 July 1846.[1] Peace was formally established by the Treaty of Guadalupe Hidalgo on 2 February 1848.[2]

From 7 July 1846 to 20 December 1849, the territory was governed by United States military commanders under authorization of the President. Local government was permitted to continue, and at no time did the Congress of the United States ever establish California's territorial status. Indeed, three times Congress adjourned without providing a civil government for California, though the question was before the Congress each time at the insistence of those who wished to establish a

[1] *Beard* v. *Federy*, 3 Wall. 478 (1866); *Merryman* v. *Bourne*, 9 Wall. 592 (1896).
[2] 9 U.S. Stat. 922. Ratifications were exchanged at Querétaro, Mexico, on 30 May 1848, and the treaty was proclaimed by the President of the United States on 4 July 1848.

state government, among them President Polk. After the third adjournment, General Riley, military governor of California, delayed no longer
but on 3 June 1849 called for a general election to be held 1 August
1849 to choose delegates to a state constitutional convention. On 1
September the group met at Monterey and by 11 October had approved certain "propositions" to be tendered to the Congress as conditions of admission. On 13 October the convention adopted the proposed constitution, which was ratified in the election of 13 November
1849. Congress passed, and the President approved on 9 September
1850, the "Act for the Admission of the State of California into the
Union," and the area became one of the United States.[3] This, in brief,
sketches the background against which the claims of California to the
soils of the submerged lands must be considered.[4]

The two key documents which must be examined in some detail are
the Treaty of Guadalupe Hidalgo and the statute admitting California
into the Union. By the treaty, the United States acquired complete
rights in the lands ceded by Mexico. These rights must have included
the rights under the soils of navigable waters, for there was no sovereign
power other than the United States in which such rights could vest
between 1848 and 1850. Mexico surrendered her proprietary rights and
title in, as well as her sovereignty over, California to the United States
and not to the state of California.[5]

The Treaty of Guadalupe Hidalgo stipulated that the valid grants of
the Mexican and Spanish governments were to be respected and their

---

[3] 9 U.S. Stat. 452.

[4] The material for this short history has been drawn from Paul Mason, "Consti-
tutional History of California," *Constitution of the State of California and of the
United States and Other Public Documents* (Sacramento, 1941), 1–39, and
Theodore H. Hittell, *History of California* (San Francisco, N.J. Stone & Co.),
II, 254, 713–14, 756–74. General Riley resigned his post as military governor of
California on 20 December 1849, and from that date until California was ad-
mitted into the Union no successor was appointed.

[5] Proponents of the Nye and Hobbs resolutions (1938) to declare the ownership of the United States in the marginal sea claimed that as a result of the
Treaty of Guadalupe Hidalgo the United States became the "owner, as the
paramount and supreme proprietor of all these lands ceded by Mexico, including
the tidelands and the submerged lands within the three mile limit." Brief of
Leslie C. McNemar, *Hearings* on S.J. Res. 83 and 92 (1939), 81. To the same
effect see testimony of Samuel A. King, attorney at law representing certain
citizens who had pending applications for prospecting permits under the Federal
Mineral Leasing Act of 1920 (*ibid.,* 405), and testimony of M. F. McCarthy,
representing certain California citizens who desired United States leases under
the Federal Mineral Leasing Act of 1920 (*Hearings* on S.J. Res. 208 [1938],
222–23).

holders secured in them. Congress provided by act of 3 March 1851[6] that a special tribunal would hear such claims in the first instance with the right of appeal to the federal courts, the action of this land commission constituting a declaration that the title asserted was valid under the laws of Mexico.[7] There were many so-called Spanish and Mexican grants in California which were confirmed pursuant to the Treaty of Guadalupe Hidalgo and the subsequent act of Congress. At least two of these grants involved soils under navigable waters.[8] Thus, by the treaty, while the United States assumed complete sovereignty of the ceded area, it assumed at the same time a trust insofar as the Spanish and Mexican grants were concerned, regardless of the character of those grants.

Under Spanish law, the precious minerals—gold, silver, and quicksilver—beneath the surface of the land belonged to the Crown. Each discoverer was required to pay a certain royalty to the Spanish Crown for the privilege of using the mine to extract its minerals. Rights to mines and minerals did not pass with a grant of the surface land. "Under the laws in force in Mexico at the date of the Treaty of Guadalupe Hidalgo, mines, whether in public or private property, belonged to the Supreme Government."[9] Within the public lands reserved to the United States upon the admission of a state to the Union, the Congress, since the middle of the nineteenth century, has retained the mineral rights unless they have been expressly granted away by the Congress;[10] Congress chose, however, until 1920, to allow an unlimited right of mining by any person who cared to enter upon the land and take the

---

[6] 9 U.S. Stat. 631.

[7] *Beard* v. *Federy,* 3 Wall. 478 (1866).

[8] The Carrillo Grant, litigated in *United States* v. *Coronado Beach Co.,* 255 U.S. 472 (1921), and the San Francisco Pueblo Grant, litigated in *Knight* v. *United Land Association,* 142 U.S. 161 (1891). Most of the Spanish and Mexican grants stopped at the line of high tide, but it is definitely known that one Spanish rancho asserted and was guaranteed by the commission a boundary out as far as "safe anchorage." See letter of E. W. Sawyer to Senator Gerald P. Nye in *Hearings* on S.J. Res. 83 and 92 (1939), 386. Sawyer was formerly assistant to Secretary of the Interior Ray Lyman Wilbur.

[9] Lindley, *A Treatise on the American Law Relating to Mines,* I, 199. See also statement of the United States Supreme Court in *Buford* v. *Houtz,* 133 U.S. 320 (1890). For a short, concise summary of Spanish mining law see *Moore* v. *Smaw,* 17 Cal. 199, 212–17 (1861).

[10] *United States* v. *Sweet,* 245 U.S. 563 (1918); *Morton* v. *Nebraska,* 21 Wall. 660 (1874). In *Work* v. *Louisiana,* 269 U.S. 250, 255–56 (1925), the court held that up to 1850 there was no settled policy of withholding minerals from disposal except under laws expressly including them.

risks of the business.[11] Unquestionably the interest in the minerals in the public lands in California passed to the United States as a result of the Treaty of Guadalupe Hidalgo.[12]

There remain further questions, however. To what extent did the United States grant, if indeed it needed to grant, rights to California in the soils of its navigable waters? And what of the mineral rights under the soils of such navigable waters? Did they pass to the state on admission, or were they retained by the national government?

The California Constitutional Convention did not discuss the general question of mineral rights. The state constitution which was sent to the Congress and which was used as the basis for admission of the state contained no request for land or for permission to take over mineral deposits. Under the "equal footing" doctrine, California automatically obtained fee simple title to the beds of all navigable waters down to a minimum low-water mark, for, as the Supreme Court said in *Weber* v. *Board of Harbor Commissioners:*

> Although the title to the soil under the tidewaters of the Bay was acquired by the United States by cession from Mexico, equally with the title to the upland, they held it only in trust for the future State. Upon the admission of California into the Union upon an equal footing with the original States, absolute property in, and dominion and sovereignty over, all soils under the tidewaters within her limits passed to the State, with the consequent right to dispose of the title to any part of said soils in such manner as she might deem proper. . . .[13]

It was argued, however, prior to the decision in *United States* v. *California,* that the "equal footing" doctrine, though applicable down to

[11] *Buford* v. *Houtz,* 133 U.S. 320 (1890).

[12] *United States* v. *San Pedro & Cañon del Agua Co.,* 17 Pac. 337 (N.M. 1888); *Moore* v. *Smaw,* 17 Cal. 199 (1861). The latter case overruled *Hicks* v. *Bell,* 3 Cal. 219 (1853), which had held that rights to mines of gold and silver were the property of the state of California by virtue of its sovereignty and not the property of the United States.

For an excellent brief arguing that the minerals vested in the United States included the petroleum in the submerged lands in the three-mile zone and therefore such lands could be leased by the United States under the Federal Mineral Leasing Act of 1920, see the "Brief of the Law Firm of Hudson, Creyke, and Hudson Supporting Appeals to the Secretary of the Interior on Behalf of Applicants for Leases in Submerged Lands under the Federal Leasing Act of 1920," in *Hearings* on S.J. Res. 83 and 92 (1939), 397–401.

[13] 18 Wall. 57, 65–66 (1873). See also *Wright* v. *Seymour,* 69 Cal. 122 (1886); *Los Angeles* v. *San Pedro, etc., R. Co.,* 182 Cal. 652 (1920); *San Francisco* v. *Le-Roy,* 138 U.S. 656 (1891); *Coburn* v. *San Mateo County,* 75 F. 520 (1896); *Dean* v. *San Diego,* 275 F. 228 (1921); *Hihn Co.* v. *City of Santa Cruz,* 170 Cal. 436 (1915); *Churchill Co.* v. *Kingsbury,* 178 Cal. 554 (1918).

low-water mark, should not extend into the open sea below that line of demarcation. The reasoning on this point was based on the terms of the act admitting California to the Union. In that act there was no express conveyance of these areas; neither can any express grant of submerged lands to the state be found in the subsequent statutes of Congress. Since California could obtain no rights not granted to it by the United States (as heir to the rights and privileges of Spain and Mexico), and since there had been no express conveyance, it should follow that California could not own the area below low-water mark in the open sea.[14] Similarly, it was possible to argue that the United States had not expressly granted away any mineral rights in the same marginal-sea area; and these mineral rights included oil and petroleum products which might be discovered below low-water mark.[15] The proponents of this line of reasoning were quite correct on one point: there were no statutes of this character.

More important, the act admitting California into the Union had contained a specific provision that "the said State of California is admitted into the Union upon the express condition that the people of said State, through their Legislature or otherwise, shall never interfere with the primary disposal of the public lands within its limits, and shall pass no law and do no act whereby the title of the United States to, and right to dispose of, the same shall be impaired or questioned."[16] At the same time California was "admitted into the Union on an equal footing with the Original States in all respects whatever."

There is evidence that Congress was aware of what it was doing in establishing the phrases which it used in admitting California. *Pollard's Lessee* v. *Hagan* was only five years old at that time, still fresh enough to have a certain novelty and provide a basis for argument. Further, that ruling had forced a reconsideration of the "equal footing" phrases which had been used almost automatically in previous acts of admission. In 1850, Senators Webster of Massachusetts and Soule of Louisiana argued the meaning of "equal footing" in terms of the *Pollard* case. There appears no doubt but that the Congress was aware of that decision and was in accord with it. The debate of Webster and

[14] United States brief, *California* case, 59.
Congress had authorized grants of land to the states in numerous instances, e.g., 9 U.S. Stat. 519–20, which gives swamplands to the states. Swamplands, being lands under nonnavigable waters, are reserved to the United States under the definition of "public lands."
[15] Brief of Leslie C. McNemar, *Hearings* on S.J. Res. 83 and 92 (1939), 74, 81; testimony of M. F. McCarthy in *Hearings* on S.J. Res. 208 (1938), 223–24.
[16] 9 U.S. Stat. 452.

Soule makes this point abundantly clear: lands beneath navigable waters were vested in the new states by virtue of their sovereignty, and the reservation of public lands, i.e., lands above high-water mark, to the United States was not an impairment of that state sovereignty.[17]

Congress, therefore, had the *Pollard* decision specifically brought to its attention. Yet it chose to admit the state of California to the Union on terms almost identical with those on which Alabama had been admitted, insofar as the reservation of "public lands" and the "equal footing" clause were concerned. If policy changes were to be made by the Congress in regard to reservation or possible reservation by the United States of submerged soils, 1850 was most certainly the time. Yet no changes were made; the Congress acceded to the interpretation of the Supreme Court which said, in effect, that "public lands" of the United States extended only to high-water mark and did not include lands beneath navigable waters. Congress knew what areas it was reserving for the United States when it allowed California to enter the Union with a reservation of these "public lands" to the United States.

Further than this, the proposed state constitution placed the boundaries of the state three "English miles" out in the Pacific. True, at the state constitutional convention, there was no awareness of any future implications of such a step, for the primary question of boundary delimitation was whether or not what is now Nevada and Utah should be included in the proposed state.[18] The boundaries of the California counties fronting on the Pacific Ocean have been so established as to coincide with the three-mile declaration.[19] The state constitution which the

[17] *Congressional Globe*, 31st Cong., 1st sess., Appendix, 960 ff., 1001.

[18] Mason, *op. cit.*, 21. Article XII, section 1, of the California constitution of 1849 defines the boundaries of the state as follows: "Commencing at the point of intersection of forty-second degree of north latitude with the one hundred twentieth degree of longitude west from Greenwich, and running south on the line of said one hundred twentieth degree of west longitude until it intersects the thirty-ninth degree of north latitude; thence running in a straight line in a southeasterly direction to the River Colorado, at a point where it intersects the thirty-fifth degree of north latitude; thence down the middle of the channel of said river to the boundary line between the United States and Mexico, as established by the treaty of May thirtieth, one thousand eight hundred and forty-eight; thence running west and along said boundary line, to the Pacific Ocean, and extending therein three English miles; thence running in a northwesterly direction and following the direction of the Pacific Coast, to the forty-second degree of north latitude, to the place of beginning. Also the islands, harbors, and bays along and adjacent to the coast."
The same boundaries are adhered to in the constitution of 1879, Article XXI, section 1, except that two words, not affecting context, are added in the last sentence. The constitution of 1879 is the one currently in force.

[19] Political Code of 1872. See, e.g., the boundaries of Del Norte County, §3916;

Congress accepted certainly did have in it a three-mile boundary declaration.

It is true that a close examination of the act of admission shows no express sanction of the boundary declaration. The latter clause of section 2 of the act of admission provided that "nothing herein contained shall be construed as recognizing or rejecting the propositions tendered by the people of California, as articles of compact in the ordinance adopted by the convention which formed the Constitution of the state."[20] Whether this clause refers to the state constitution itself or solely to the propositions[21] which accompanied it is problematical. The act of admission did accept the constitution, but no action was taken on the propositions. To that extent only may it be said that Congressional approval was given to the boundary lines. Futher, since California did hold proprietary rights to all soils beneath navigable waters down to low-water mark, it is possible to argue that she held similar rights out to the constitutionally defined three-mile limit. Indeed, the California courts have held that California,

... according to the decisions of the federal supreme court and the opinion of writers on international law, acquired, on her admission to the union, the sovereignty of an independent nation over a zone of waters three miles wide extending along the mainland, and also over similar zones or belts around the islands along and adjacent to her coast, unless, by her own definition of her boundary, the state has deliberately excluded such waters from her territory and jurisdiction. In defining its boundary in its organic law, the state has not ... expressed an intention to reject that sovereignty which, unless clearly renounced by her, she rightfully has over a belt of water, three miles wide. . . .[22]

This statement clearly shows in its first lines an argument by implication, for the Supreme Court had never, down to the decision in *United States* v. *California,* directly adjudicated the rights of a state in the three-mile zone in the open sea. The statement of the California

---

Humboldt County, §3920; Mendocino, §3931; Sonoma, §3975; Marin, §3929; San Mateo, §3949; Santa Cruz, §3952; Monterey, §3935; San Luis Obispo, §3948; and San Francisco, §3946. In the case of San Francisco County, its boundaries are so established as to include the Farallon Islands, which are some seventeen miles offshore in the open sea.

[20] 9 U.S. Stat. 452.

[21] These propositions related to grants of land for school purposes and to the defraying of the expenses of state government.

[22] *In re Marincovich,* 48 Cal. App. 474, 479 (1920). The case involved the right of California to regulate certain types of fishing within the three-mile belt around Santa Catalina Island in the open sea.

court is predicated on the carrying-over of federal decisions dealing with bays, rivers, inland lakes, and tidelands, the latter term being used in its technical sense.

The state of California has assumed that she held these submerged soils in the open sea below low-water mark in fee simple. She has exercised jurisdiction upon that basis, and it is proposed to examine in some detail at this point the manner and character of her actions, particularly in the regulation and encouragement of offshore oil production.

State regulation of oil production in the submerged fields has not always been successful, and a number of controversies have arisen over the subject in California. California has a coast line of roughly 1,200 miles, or an area of almost 3,600 square miles in the three-mile zone. Approximately 2,000 square miles of the area are probably not suited for oil production because of excessive water depth close inshore on the Pacific Coast. In a large portion of the remaining area, geological conditions are absolutely adverse for oil, thus eliminating about 1,430 additional square miles. About 170 square miles are left which show signs of possible commercial development. Inshore evidence appears to eliminate about 66 square miles of the 170, so that there are about 100 square miles that offer real possibilities for production.[23] Of this area, 10,688 acres were under state lease in 1949.[24] The first successful underwater oil development was in the Summerland field, discovered near Santa Barbara in 1897.

With the exception of the Summerland field, leases to operate in "state-owned" tide and submerged lands were granted after 1921. In 1949, there were twenty-two leases and fifty-four easement agreements in effect, covering 390 producing wells. Combined production from these wells was 42,640 barrels per day.[25] By 31 December 1950 the number of producing wells had increased to 483.[26] At the time of writing no determination had been made of what percentage of the pro-

[23] Testimony of Harry R. Johnson, consulting geologist and former member of the U.S. Geological Survey staff during the creation of Naval Oil Reserves 1 and 2, in *Hearings* on S.J. Res. 83 and 92 (1939), 331–32.

[24] Testimony of Ernie Pyles, assistant to the executive vice-president and general manager, Jergins Oil Co., *Hearings* before Subcommittee No. 1 of the House Judiciary Committee on H.R. 5991 and H.R. 5992, 81st Cong., 1st sess. (1949), 114. These hearings will hereinafter be cited as *Hearings* on H.R. 5991 and 5992 (1949).

[25] *Ibid.* The most important fields are Huntington Beach, Elwood, and Rincon, in that order. The easement agreements which are mentioned are discussed below (p. 71).

[26] Testimony of Rufus Putnam, executive officer, State Lands Commission of California, *Hearings* on S.J. Res. 20 (1951), 142.

ducing wells would come within the rule announced in *United States v. California*. Cumulative production to 1 March 1949 from state tide and submerged lands was 174,000,000 barrels, and reliable estimates of future reserves amounted to 178,000,000 barrels.[27]

Royalties paid to the state of California have been substantial. Down to the decision in *United States v. California* there was no coastal operation from which the state or its municipal subdivisions did not derive benefits. Rates of royalty paid on state leases were figured on a sliding scale of from 5 to 50 per cent, the average being approximately 27.5 per cent. These royalties were figured on gross production.[28] Some indication of the amount of royalties can be gained from the knowledge that in 1951 over twenty-seven million dollars was being held in escrow pending final settlement of the controversy. This sum represented royalties from June 1947, the date of *United States v. California*, to March 1951—roughly seven million dollars per year.[29] Thus the amount at stake by April 1953 was approximately forty-two million dollars. The state of California naturally did everything in its power to retain this revenue source.

Until 1921, there was no legislation in California to govern the extraction of oil and gas from submerged lands. In 1921 the California Legislature practically duplicated the Federal Mineral Leasing Act of 1920.[30] The California act reserved to the state all gas, oil, and other mineral deposits in the affected areas and authorized the issuance of prospecting permits to tide and submerged lands for a total period of four years. Provision was made for a lease of not more than 160 acres upon discovery. Royalty was set at 5 per cent. No permits could issue covering tide or submerged lands fronting on an incorporated city for one mile on either side thereof.[31] Between 1926 and 1929, over two

[27] Testimony of Ernie Pyles, *Hearings* on H.R. 5991 and 5992 (1949), 114–15. Estimates of probable recoverable oil must necessarily vary. Technological advances make possible the discovery of additional fields or a higher percentage of recovery in fields already in production. The figures given do not include production in waters owned by the cities of Los Angeles and Long Beach. Current production in these latter areas, according to Pyles, is approximately forty-four thousand barrels daily. Total capital investment by the state, cities, and persons acting under state or municipal lease is ninety million dollars. Approximately three billion dollars capital is invested in facilities and improvements on tide and submerged areas other than for petroleum production.

[28] Testimony of William W. Clary, formerly special assistant to the attorney general of California, *Hearings* on S.J. Res. 195 (1950), 122. For a schedule of oil royalty rates on each California state lease, see *ibid.*, 247.

[29] Testimony of Everett W. Mattoon, assistant attorney general of California, *Hearings* on S.J. Res. 20 (1951), 122.   [30] Calif. Stats. 1921, c. 303, p. 404.

[31] The act of 1921 was amended in 1923 to authorize leases in the Summerland

hundred persons filed applications for prospecting permits under the 1921 act covering tide and submerged lands in various parts of the Pacific Ocean, San Pedro Bay and Channel, Santa Barbara Channel, and Santa Monica Bay. A flood of applications came in after oil was discovered in the Elwood area in 1928.[32]

The surveyor general of California, whose duty it was to issue prospecting permits under the 1921 act, refused to issue certain permits in Santa Barbara Channel to test the constitutionality of the statute which allowed the issuance of such permits. Writs of mandamus were then asked to the California Supreme Court, which upheld the validity of the 1921 act and declared the *ownership* by California of the tide and submerged lands in the areas in which the petitioners were asking prospecting privileges.[33] The United States Supreme Court dismissed an appeal in this case[34] for want of a substantial federal question. It is quite proper to ask, in view of the categorical ruling of ownership made by the California court, whether the United States Supreme Court acted properly in refusing to review the case. If, as was contended in

---

field, which had not been previously covered, at a maximum 12.5 per cent royalty. Calif. Stats. 1923, p. 593. Seven leases were issued in this field under the amended act, but all have now been abandoned.

The Summerland operations were well known to the national government as early as 1907. The development of the Summerland field is described by Ralph Arnold in *Bulletin No. 321,* Department of the Interior, U.S. Geological Survey (Washington, Government Printing Office, 1907). Although the Summerland area involved tide and submerged lands, the United States made no claim.

[32] "Answer of the State of California," No. 12 Original, October Term 1945, p. 761. This work will hereinafter be cited as the California answer.

[33] *Boone* v. *Kingsbury,* 206 Cal. 148 (1928). The California court said at 170: "The minerals contained in the soil covered by tidal and submerged lands belong to the state in its sovereign right. . . . The proprietary rights of the owners bordering on tide water do not extend beyond the ordinary high-water mark." The reasoning of the California court in this case is based foursquare on *Pollard* v. *Hagan* and similar cases.

Another section of the 1921 act was considered in *Carr* v. *Kingsbury,* 111 Cal. App. 165 (1931). Carr was seeking a mandamus to force Kingsbury to issue a prospecting permit on certain "tide, overflowed or submerged lands" at Huntington Beach. This request was based upon the alleged unconstitutionality of the section of the act which provided that no permit should issue for lands fronting on incorporated cities or a distance of one mile on either side thereof. The court held, however, that the legislature had the power to set the terms upon which leases of tide and submerged lands it controlled might be issued. The court therefore refused to issue the mandamus. The *Carr* case was deemed controlling in *Cummings* v. *Kingsbury,* 111 Cal. App. 763 (1931); *Feisthamel* v. *Kingsbury,* 111 Cal. App. 762 (1931); *Maggart* v. *Kingsbury,* 111 Cal. App. 765 (1931); and *Joyner* v. *Kingsbury,* 97 Cal. App. 17 (1929), 111 Cal. App. 764 (1931). See also *Farry* v. *King,* 120 Cal. App. 118 (1932), and *Kelley* v. *Kingsbury,* 210 Cal. 37 (1930).   [34] *Workman* v. *Boone,* 280 U.S. 517 (1929).

1947, the presence of substantial national interests could override the prerogatives of the state, it would appear that these rights must also have been present in 1929. Without a doubt the action of the highest tribunal in the land lent support to those who advocated state ownership and control of the submerged lands.

The surveyor general of California was forced to grant the permits at issue in *Boone* v. *Kingsbury* at a 5 per cent royalty rate because proper legislation authorizing a higher rate was lacking in 1928. The lessees themselves for the most part did not drill, but sold their leases at a profit to others capable of drilling operations from wharves and piers.[35] About one hundred leases and permits were issued under the 1921 act in six or more separate offshore fields, some extending out as far as one-half mile. Roughly 350 wells were drilled under the act as amended.[36]

With the decision in *Boone* v. *Kingsbury* the prospecting fever hit a high pitch, and great numbers of persons, sure of their rights under the 1921 act, sought prospecting permits. The Legislature, meanwhile, passed an emergency act to gain time to consider the whole question of granting permits and leases in tide and submerged lands.[37] Soon thereafter, the Legislature passed an act amending the 1921 act so as to provide that no application for a prospecting permit should be received or granted by the state or any of its political subdivisions to cover tide and submerged lands.[38]

The difficulty with such a blanket prohibition of operations, however, was that it flatly ignored the "capture theory" and the geological realities of the submerged oil pools. *Brown* v. *Spillman* states the classic doctrine of the "capture theory."

Petroleum gas and oil are substances of a peculiar character, and decisions in ordinary cases of mining, for coal and other minerals which have a fixed *situs,* cannot be applied to contracts concerning them without some qualifications. They belong to the owner of the land, and are part of it, so long as they are on it or in it, or subject to his control, but when they

[35] Testimony of Thomas A. J. Dockweiler, *Hearings* on H.J. Res. 176 and 181 (1939), 122.

[36] "Brief for the State of California in Opposition to Motion for Judgment," No. 12 Original, October Term 1946, p. 146. A map set opposite p. 146 of the brief indicates the locations of these leases. This work will hereinafter be cited as the California brief.

[37] Calif. Stats. 1929, p. 11.

[38] Calif. Stats. 1929, p. 944. Persons having preferential rights prior to 17 January 1929 were not affected. The act prohibited the granting of leases in tide or submerged lands.

escape and go into other land, or come under another's control, the title
of the former owner is gone. If an adjoining owner drills his own land and
taps a deposit of oil or gas, extending under his neighbor's field, so that it
comes into his well, it becomes his property.[39]

The submerged pools could be drained in every case from the uplands. At Huntington Beach, especially, the situation was acute. A
number of wells had been drilled on the uplands which got production
at shallow levels. Standard Oil in the meantime had acquired rights to
a strip of shoreline known as the "P.E. Strip."[40] The company put
down some twenty to twenty-five wells and got a good production of
two to six thousand barrels per well at the outset. The discovery of what
was thought to be a fault line between the uplands and along the
shore led geologists to believe that the wells were being fed from the
ocean side. Experimentation showed that wells could be "whipstocked"
or slant-drilled out through the P.E. Strip into the submerged oil pools,
making the pools accessible to upland operators.[41]

Two courses of action had to be taken immediately. First of all, the
operators who had deliberately slant-drilled into "state" lands had to be
forced in some way to pay damages to the state for the oil already taken.
Many of the trespasses were innocent, for the art of directional drilling
had not been developed in the early 1930's to the state of perfection it
has today.[42] Secondly, the situation had to be remedied for the future

[39] 155 U.S. 665, 669–70 (1895).
[40] The strip is some 150 feet wide and lies between the right of way of the
electric trains of the Pacific Electric Company and the ocean. It is owned by
the Huntington Beach Company and the Pacific Electric Company, who trace
title from the Las Bolsas Spanish grant, confirmed under the act of Congress of
1851. "Report of the California Senate Committee to Investigate the Abstraction
of Oil and Gas from State Lands," reprinted in *Hearings* on S.J. Res. 83 and
92 (1939), 452.
[41] Testimony of Samuel A. King, *Hearings* on S.J. Res. 83 and 92 (1939),
411. There were eighty-six such wells whipstocked out from the uplands and
bottomed on "state-owned" land in 1938.
Once a well starts to produce in a field, there is a drainage of oil and gas
toward the well. As time goes on, the effects of this drainage extend farther and
farther into the outer reaches of the oil-bearing sands. If, after a lapse of time,
a second well be drilled within the sphere of drainage of the first, the second
well can never be expected to produce as much oil as the first, other things
being equal. This "adverse drainage" is the basis of all oil-well location and
offset programs between neighboring operators. The theory that drainage extends
only two hundred feet has long since been exploded. If wells are not properly
spaced, there will be a resulting loss in cumulative oil production. Oil which can
never be recovered will remain in the sand. "Technical Brief of Harry R.
Johnson," *ibid.*, 346–47.
[42] Wells today can be slanted out great distances off the perpendicular. Success-

by putting production from the submerged fields under the control of the state. This latter action was impossible under the 1929 act. In 1931 the Legislature amended section 675 of the Political Code to grant to the director of finance the power to make leases for the production of oil and gas on state-owned tide and submerged lands. This measure was defeated by referendum. Two initiative measures, one for tidelands drilling and one for slant-well operation, were also defeated.[43]

In an effort to control slant-drilling into state tidelands and to remedy the situation created by adverse drainage from the upland of the submerged pools, the Legislature in 1933 passed an amendment to the 1921 act, authorizing the negotiation of agreements to compensate for drainage of submerged pools "owned by California."[44] This 1933 act was never used. The state attorney general collaborated with the Department of Finance and other state departments in seeking injunctions to restrain the further taking of oil and gas and asking 100 per cent damages. Governor James Rolph, Jr., however, held a conference in 1934 with the trespassers; the result was a compromise calling for the issuance of easements and agreements to operators shoreward of the P.E. Strip with royalties at an average of 13.06 per cent by 1938.[45] The Olson Committee of the California Senate, created to investigate the situation, in its report in 1935 doubted the legality of these "agreements for easements," saying that they constituted a leasing of state land for which there was no authority.[46] The committee condemned this method of handling what was quite obviously a situation in which the public interest had been subordinated to the contest being waged. Yet many of the trespassers had been innocent; deliberate intent was difficult to prove.

At the date of the Olson report in 1935, no compromise had been

---

ful wells have been drilled and have produced with six hundred feet of deviation in seventeen hundred feet of vertical depth. George B. Parks, "Directional Drilling in Offshore Operations," *World Oil*, June 1949, p. 95.

[43] Testimony of Thomas A. J. Dockweiler, *Hearings* on H.J.Res. 176 and 181 (1939), 123.

[44] Calif. Stats. 1933, p. 1523.

[45] Testimony of Thomas A. J. Dockweiler, *Hearings* on H.J. Res. 176 and 181 (1939), 111.

[46] Reprinted in *Hearings* on S.J. Res. 83 and 92 (1939), 458–60. The independent upland oil operators who had drilled through the P.E. Strip to get to the state lands also were faced with the problem of getting separate settlements with the owners of the Strip.

The "easement" itself is rather interesting in that it constituted a right of way some thirty inches around the casings of the wells. Thus the "easement" is down in the ground a good many thousand feet. See testimony of Joseph Cunningham, private oil operator, *Hearings* on S.J. Res. 208 (1938), 230.

worked out with the Standard Oil Company and its affiliates. It was not until 1937 that a final agreement was reached between the state and Standard Oil, a compromise which settled the state's claims for approximately $500,000. The state's acceptance of this amount was bitterly assailed by Culbert L. Olson, who labeled the transaction "an outright gift by the State to the oil company of over $5,000,000 and a flagrant betrayal of the people." Charges of "incompetence or corruption" were leveled at State Finance Director Arlin R. Stockburger.[47]

Olson had not been successful in his attempt to secure passage of a law which would have allowed the state to get its own production from its own fields. In 1935, after his committee had submitted its report, the Governor vetoed a bill which would have allowed littoral owners to secure leases to drill into state-owned tide and submerged lands for a minimum one-sixth royalty. Charges have been made, and supported in some instances, that the oil operators financed the campaigns against those attempts in a deliberate effort to keep the whole question in a state of turmoil. To that end the Parent-Teacher Association and other civic groups were encouraged by the operators to go on record in opposition to such state leases, on the grounds that the beaches would be destroyed by unsightly oil derricks. Under the cover of confusion, the draining of the oil pools from the uplands proceeded as rapidly as possible.[48]

Earl Warren admitted in 1939 that down to 1938 the state of California had not been sufficiently diligent in conserving its oil.[49] It appears that this acknowledgment is a gross understatement of conditions, which, as has been shown, were chaotic. In 1938, however, the State Lands Act was passed.[50] This was a comprehensive statute relating to all California-owned lands. All state lands were placed under a State

[47] *Los Angeles Daily News,* 13 October 1937.

[48] Brief of Robert B. Keenan, attorney representing certain applicants for federal leases on tide and submerged lands under the Federal Mineral Leasing Act of 1920, *Hearings* on S.J. Res. 83 and 92 (1939), 445; *Hearings* on H.J. Res. 176 and 181 (1939), 266–67.

[49] Testimony, *Hearings* on H.J. Res. 176 and 181 (1939), 197. He expressed no opinion on whether or not the compromises effected in 1934 and 1937 were right or wrong. The important thing to him was that they were effected and that thereafter royalty payments of adequate amount were forthcoming to the state treasury.

[50] Calif. Stats., ex. sess., 1938, p. 23. Passage of this act was aided by the development of slant-drilling. Opposition to leasing state lands had been based in large part upon the claim that the beaches would be destroyed. This opposition was overcome when it was shown that the derricks could be placed on the uplands. As a matter of fact, the art of slant-drilling developed as a direct result of this controversy.

Lands Commission, which was empowered to issue leases or easements for the extraction of oil and gas in tide and submerged fields when lawful adverse drainage was taking place or about to take place.[51] The measure was thus a conservation as well as a leasing act. It called for the making of leases on the basis of competitive bidding[52] and eliminated the old prospecting permits of the act of 1921.[53]

In July 1938 the State Lands Commission invited bids for agreements to extract oil and gas from state tide and submerged lands in the Huntington Beach area to offset drainage of some fourteen upland wells. In September 1938 an easement of 835 acres was awarded to the Southwest Exploration Company. This agreement called for a maximum of eighty wells with provision for quitclaiming unproductive areas. Royalty was to be dependent on production, ranging from a 12 per cent minimum at eighty barrels or less up to a maximum of 66⅔ per cent. The average at two hundred barrels per day was 30.84 per cent.[54] Since this first agreement, ten other leases in seven fields containing tide and submerged lands have been issued under the Public Resources Code (§§6871 ff.).[55]

In the meantime, oil had been discovered in December of 1936 under permit of the Los Angeles Board of Harbor Commissioners on land belonging to the Los Angeles Harbor Department. Immediately a question was raised concerning the ownership and control of the oil.[56] An act of the California Legislature in 1911 had granted to the city of Los Angeles all the tide and submerged lands fronting on Los Angeles, out to the three-mile limit.[57] A similar grant was made to Long Beach in the same year.[58] The question, of course, was whether or not such a grant carried with it the right to minerals. In *Long Beach* v. *Marshall*,

---

[51] Art. 6, §85.   [52] Art. 6, §86.

[53] The State Lands Act was incorporated into the Public Resources Code by an act of the 1941 Legislature (Calif. Stats. 1941, c. 548, p. 1902). The sections relating to tide and submerged lands are now contained in Public Resources Code §§6871–78.

In 1939 the state of California promised that if any pools were discovered which were entirely below low-water mark, so that they could not be drained by upland operators, such pools would not be utilized until "public necessity calls them to use." "Brief of the State of California against H.J. Resolutions 176 and 181," *Hearings* on H.J. Res. 176 and 181 (1939), 203.

[54] Testimony of Thomas A. J. Dockweiler, *Hearings* on H.J. Res. 176 and 181 (1939), 112.

[55] For a record and map of each lease issued under this authority see California answer, 781–88.

[56] "Brief of the Board of Harbor Commissioners of Los Angeles," *Hearings* on H.J. Res. 176 and 181 (1939), 161.   [57] Calif. Stats. 1911, p. 1256.

[58] Calif. Stats. 1911, p. 1304.

in July 1938, it was held that the state's grant to a city did transfer the mineral rights and thus the city and not the state had the right to control the disposal thereof.[59] On 15 March 1939 the city of Long Beach entered into four drilling contracts with the Long Beach Oil and Development Company, which company by 1945 was operating 193 wells on filled, reclaimed, and submerged land in Long Beach Harbor, the revenues going into the Harbor Revenue Fund.[60]

Over all the internecine warfare being waged, there were the operations of a small but vocal group of individuals including Joseph Cunningham and Robert E. Lee Jordan. In 1934, Cunningham had been among the first to make application, under the Federal Mineral Leasing Act of 1920, for a federal prospecting permit in offshore areas in California. True, his application had been rejected by the Department of the Interior, the federal agency charged with the issuance of mineral prospecting permits under the Federal Mineral Leasing Act of 1920, on the ground that the department had no jurisdiction below the line of high-water mark. The department specifically ruled that California was the "owner" of such lands.[61] This, however, did not stop the group

[59] 11 Cal. 2d 609. See also *Miller* v. *Stockburger,* 12 Cal. 2d 440 (1938); but cf. *Stone* v. *Los Angeles,* 114 Cal. App. 192 (1931).

[60] California answer, 217–19. These drilling contracts were incorporated *in toto* into the *Hearings* on S.J. Res. 83 and 92 (1939), 296–330. The city took no chances in these agreements with the oil operators. In each contract, the city specifically inserted a clause which stated that the city made no covenant or warrant concerning its title or right of possession of these lands. This clause was inserted in spite of the fact that the California Supreme Court had specifically declared the city's ownership of these lands. The proposed drilling agreements were analyzed in an editorial in *Petroleum World,* January 1938, approximately a year before they were consummated.

According to testimony by George W. Trammell, then city attorney for Long Beach, the city retained entire control over the development program, with royalties to the Harbor Revenue Fund running from 30 to 85 per cent less operating costs. It was Trammell's contention that the life of the contracts would result in a 60 to 70 per cent royalty. *Hearings* on S.J. Res. 83 and 92 (1939), 285.

By 1952 it was reported that the city was realizing 85.5 per cent royalty on its 1939–42 contracts. In 1947 the Richfield Company made an agreement which gave the city 94.1 per cent royalty after drilling costs were paid. The arrangement has been called a "one-product kind of socialism" which amounted "very nearly to the ownership of the means of production." Oil companies like the arrangement because there is no risk involved. The shipping companies approve because all the money goes for harbor facilities. The wells in the upland areas help defray the cost of Long Beach city government. The entire picture would be rosy except for the fact that Terminal Island, key to harbor development, has sunk sixteen feet since 1937. Removal of the oil has been deemed a major factor in this sinking. Richard Dyer MacCann, "California Pays Big Price for Tideland Oil Income," *Christian Science Monitor,* 31 October 1952.

[61] *In re Joseph Cunningham,* 55 I.D. 1, 2 (1934).

from pressing its demands before the Congress in the various hearings which were held. Trade publications of the oil industry began to show a bit of reluctance to accept on faith and implication the argument that submerged soils below low-water mark belonged to the state of California. The *National Oil Derrick* indicated that there was "ample precedent" for national ownership;[62] another editorialized and warned California to go slow in legislating on submerged land development until "the question of proprietary ownership of such lands has been settled either by a decision of the United States Supreme Court or by an act of Congress ceding title to the State of California."[63] The airtight claim of the state, it appeared, was not quite so airtight, even at this relatively early date in the fight for control.

It was true that the state could bolster its petroleum claims with examples of its undoubted action in other commercial enterprises in the submerged lands. The state, as has been noted, had made grants of tide and submerged lands to municipalities;[64] state courts had upheld the validity of the grants;[65] and the cities had expended considerable sums of money in improving and reclaiming the lands so granted.[66] The

[62] 29 January 1938. The editorial pointed out that two attorneys, Arthur L. Ball and William G. Kenney, had advised a client to stop drilling operations in the Huntington Beach field, basing their advice on the federal claim then currently being made in Senate Joint Resolution 208.

[63] *California Oil World and Petroleum Industry*, 20 February 1938. The editorial warned that opening of new fields "while land titles are in doubt will prove unfortunate both for the State and its lessees."

[64] See, e.g., the act of the Legislature of 1 May 1911, Calif. Stats. 1911, p. 1357, granting such lands to San Diego; act of the Legislature of 12 April 1915, Calif. Stats. 1915, p. 62, granting such lands to Redondo Beach; and act of the Legislature of 10 April 1917, Calif. Stats. 1917, p. 90, granting such lands to Santa Monica. Grants to Los Angeles and Long Beach have been discussed above (pp. 73–74).

[65] *Oakland* v. *Oakland Water Front Co.*, 118 Cal. 160 (1897); *Bolsa Land Co.* v. *Burdick*, 151 Cal. 254 (1907); *Boone* v. *Kingsbury*, 206 Cal. 148 (1928); *Oakland* v. *Buteau*, 219 Cal. 745 (1934); *Long Beach* v. *Marshall*, 11 Cal. 2d 609 (1938). The United States Circuit Court of Appeals held in *Western Pacific R. Co.* v. *Southern Pacific R. Co.*, 151 F. 376 (1907), that a grant of tidelands to a city was expressly limited to the boundaries of the grant as of the time of the grant and that this boundary could not be extended by accretions to the granted lands.

[66] In the case of Long Beach, it is estimated that 95 per cent of the harbor facilities are constructed on reclaimed land. The city has invested $15,000,000 in harbor facilities and in 1945 contemplated a $52,000,000 postwar building program. Testimony of Irving Smith, city attorney of Long Beach, *Hearings* on H.J. Res. 118 *et al.* (1945), 114. Following the grants of tide and submerged lands to the city, Long Beach built a breakwater called Rainbow Pier and a Municipal Auditorium thereon extending into the Pacific Ocean and the Bay of San Pedro some 1,400 feet from shore. Total cost of the structure, completed

state had regulated the fisheries within the three-mile limit upon the assumption that it owned them. The state and federal courts had held that these fisheries were owned by the state and that the state could impose conditions for their use.[67] Since 1917 the state had leased kelp

------

in 1930, was in excess of $1,067,000. The filled and reclaimed land upon which the park and the auditorium are located comprises about eight acres. California answer, 755.

Los Angeles has no natural harbor. By 1938 total city investments in the harbor were $43,000,000 with $17,761,000 in bonds outstanding by the city for harbor improvements. Testimony of Clyde M. Leach, assistant city attorney of Los Angeles and attorney for the Board of Harbor Commissioners of Los Angeles, *Hearings* on H.J. Res. 176 and 181 (1939), 159; brief of the Board of Harbor Commissioners of Los Angeles, *Hearings* on S.J. Res. 83 and 92 (1939), 253. Arthur Eldridge, of the Harbor Commissioners, estimated that 6 per cent of the revenue of the harbor in 1945 was derived from oil. Testimony in *Hearings* on H.J. Res. 118 *et al.* (1945), 108.

Among the enterprises located on reclaimed land in San Diego are consolidated Aircraft Company, Solar Aircraft Company, Lindbergh Field, and the San Diego Civic Center. Testimony of Robert Kenny, attorney general of California, *ibid.*, 11.

Santa Barbara has a state university, for which certain tide and submerged lands were deeded in order to enable the school to move from its previous location. In addition, the oil fields of Summerland (before they gave out), Elwood, and Capitan have been taxed on the oil produced and the personal property and improvements. The city and county of Santa Barbara have derived $2,000,000 in revenues from this source. Testimony of Percy C. Heckendorf, district attorney of the city of Santa Barbara, *Hearings* on S.J. Res. 83 and 92 (1939), 276–77.

San Francisco is the only major harbor where title has remained in the state of California. Testimony of Senator Hiram Johnson, *ibid.*, 258. Much of San Francisco's business district is constructed on filled and reclaimed land. Testimony of Congressman Frank R. Havenner, *Hearings* on H.J. Res. 118 *et al.* (1945), 143.

The point will be discussed in detail later. It is the contention of the United States that these developments are not placed in jeopardy by *United States* v. *California.* The contention is based on the fact that these areas which have been listed are deemed to be in bays or inland waters and hence not covered by the scope of the Supreme Court's decision.

[67] *Darbee and Immel Oyster and Land Co.* v. *Pacific Oyster Co.*, 150 Cal. 392 (1907). This case declares state ownership of oyster beds.

People v. *Truckee Lumber Co.*, 116 Cal. 397 (1897); *In re Marincovich*, 48 Cal. App. 474 (1920); *Suttori* v. *Peckham*, 48 Cal. App. 88 (1920); *In re Phoedovius*, 177 Cal. 238 (1918). These cases deal with regulations in regard to size and method of use of nets in the three-mile zone and with general fishery regulation.

Paladini v. *Superior Court*, 178 Cal. 369 (1918); *People* v. *Stafford Packing Co.*, 193 Cal. 719 (1924); *People* v. *Monterey Fish Products Co.*, 195 Cal. 548 (1925); *Bayside Fish Flour Co.* v. *Zellerbach*, 124 Cal. App. 564 (1932); *Bayside Fish Flour Co.* v. *Gentry*, 297 U.S. 422 (1936); *Van Camp Sea Food Co.* v. *Department of Natural Resources*, 30 F. 2d 111 (1929). These are cases dealing with the power of the state to regulate the percentage of fish which may be

beds, the greater number of which lie approximately one mile below low-water mark in the open sea.[68]

The state of California and its municipal subdivisions have made frequent grants of tide and submerged lands to the national government and its agencies under the impression that the state, or its subdivisions through grant from the state, owned the areas which they gave

---

rendered into fish flour and meal, regardless of the fact that such fish may have been taken from outside as well as within the three-mile limit.

Santa Cruz Oil Corporation v. Milnor, 55 Cal. App. 2d 56 (1942); *Mirkovich v. Milnor,* 34 F. Supp. 409 (1940); *Ocean Industries, Inc. v. Greene,* 15 F. 2d 862 (1926). These cases held that California might, in effect, regulate floating canneries which plied their trade beyond the three-mile limit, on the grounds that indirect regulation was necessary to effect the "preservation of its fisheries." California had no jurisdiction over the floating canneries while they were processing fish beyond the three-mile limit, but could take jurisdiction over them the moment they entered the three-mile zone.

Fishing is big business in California. It greatly exceeds in value petroleum and and other minerals taken from the sea. The table below shows the value of fish (exclusive of clams, lobsters, abalone, and crabs) and fish products marketed by California between 1942 and 1945.

	Fish Sold by Fishermen	Canned Fish	Fish Meal and Fish Oil
1942	$26,100,000	$67,432,689	$13,998,542
1943	31,900,000	70,496,100	15,386,369
1944	36,100,000	79,074,776	19,694,321
1945	38,830,400	79,755,151	13,557,169

In the years 1942–45, 310,311 tons of fish from California waters were delivered to the armed forces. The total income from California fisheries and related enterprises for the year 1945 was $147,000,054.

These figures are taken from the California brief, No. 12 Original, October Term 1946, pp. 8–9, and *Fisheries Resources of the United States,* S. Doc. 51, 79th Cong.

[68] There are forty-five kelp beds off the coast of California with a total area of 108.84 square miles. The act regulating these operations was passed in 1917 (Cal. Stats. 1917, c. 513, p. 646). Beginning in that year, 17,024 tons of kelp were harvested at three cents per ton rental. In 1918, 438,956 tons were harvested. In 1919, 13,403 tons were taken and operations ceased.

Operations were recommenced in 1932. The three-cent per-ton rental remained for the leased beds. Operators were also granted licenses to take kelp from open beds at one and one-half cents per ton until 1941, at which time the charge was raised to five cents. Between 1932 and 1945, 366,963 tons were taken from the leased beds and 243,667 tons from the open beds, a total of 610,630 tons.

On the basis of these figures the net return to California has been roughly twenty-five thousand dollars over the seventeen-year period, or an average of about two thousand dollars per year. This certainly does not make kelp a major industry. It is indicative, however, of an industry which operates below low-water mark and which has been subject to royalty payments in a fashion similar to oil operations.

These figures are a part of the official records of the Fish and Game Commission of the state of California and are reproduced in Appendices A to I to the California brief, No. 12 Original, October Term 1946, pp. 137–40.

title to. In the briefs filed by California in both 1945 and 1946, great space is given to a discussion of the circumstances surrounding each of some ninety-two outright grants, leases, and easements issuing from California or its municipal subdivisions to the federal government.[69]

Although the United States met this argument with the claim that but five of the ninety-two instances actually involved California land below low-water mark,[70] it is important to note that such instances have occurred. Further, there have been instances in which other littoral states have made grants or leases or have given easements to the federal government.[71]

The controls and regulations which have been exercised and the assertions of title upon which the states and their grantees have relied are admitted. The state of California believed with some justification that it held title to the three-mile zone off its coast. The state constitution, accepted by Congress, had set the state boundary three English miles out in the Pacific. By statutory declaration, the state had been proclaimed the owner of all land below ordinary high-water mark "within the state."[72] Prior to 1937, no federal officer appeared to contest the title.

[69] California answer, 89–440; California brief, 158–65; Appendix to California brief, 169–253.

These actions trace back to 1897, when all right and title of the state in lands extending out three hundred yards from low-water mark around United States military reservations was granted to the United States. (Calif. Stats. 1897, p. 74.) Some seventeen different pieces of submerged lands, part of which were admittedly in the open sea, were conveyed at this time to the United States. It is entirely proper to ask where the state got the right to transfer such lands and why the United States felt it necessary to ask such grant if the United States already had rights in these areas. This question will be considered in some detail in later discussions.

[70] United States brief, *California* case, 167–68, 227–42. The remaining eighty-seven cases, claimed the United States, involved grants of land under bays, rivers, inland waters, or tidelands, and not submerged lands under the open sea.

[71] The United States admits that there have been nine such grants which definitely involved areas of land in the open sea beyond low-water mark. In the case of the five California grants and the four from other states, however, it was the contention of the United States that the federal officials concerned merely acted out of "an abundance of caution." *Ibid.*, 167–68, 244–58.

[72] Cal. Civ. Code, §670. The act was passed in 1872.

6·

Texas' Claims to Submerged Lands

The capacity of Texans for extolling the virtues of the largest member of the federal union is too well known to necessitate any elaboration in a work of this type. Texans are wont to suggest at considerable length that the state is unique in a variety of respects, ranging from the beauty of their women to the material resources of their lands. While most such claims have been received in a spirit of amused toleration by residents of other states, there is at least one respect in which the Texans' boast is correct: Texas alone among the thirty-five states which have been added to the Union was a truly independent nation before its annexation. The fact of Texas' independence places the state in an extraordinary position so far as its possible claims to submerged soils in the Gulf of Mexico are concerned. In some respects, its claims are stronger than those of the thirteen original states. Most certainly the Texas position is better than that which the state of California sought to establish.

As will be shown in detail later in this chapter, the financial stake in oil in the submerged lands off the coast of Texas is considerable, some estimates placing the possible revenue to be realized from oil production in these lands in the neighborhood of $1,000,000,000.[1] Petroleum production below low-water mark in the submerged lands of the marginal sea has reached the quantity stage. Texas has already derived income running into the millions of dollars from these operations. Letting leases under competitive bidding, the state had realized by 1949 some

[1] Testimony of Beauford H. Jester, then governor of Texas, joint *Hearings* before the House Judiciary Committee and the Senate Judiciary Committee on S. 1988, 80th Cong., 2d sess. (1948), 120. These hearings will hereinafter be cited as joint *Hearings* on S. 1988 (1948).

79

$7,212,000 in lease bonuses alone—an average of approximately $20 per acre for unproved wildcat submerged land.[2] All bonuses went into the permanent school fund of the state, and future royalties are similarly pledged.

The 380-mile coast line of the state contains proved submerged fields and other possible oil resources as yet undiscovered. In the thirty-mile-wide strip off the coast of Texas there are an estimated 245 structures which show promise of oil.[3] Exploration, mainly through geophysical operations, has been much more extensive off Texas than off the coast of California, though California production is much greater.

The claims of the United States to the territory a portion of which is now Texas were renounced by the United States in the Transcontinental Treaty with Spain in 1819.[4] The United States relinquished "forever" all "rights, claims, and pretensions" to all the territory west and south of a line which began "on the Gulph of Mexico, at the mouth of the river Sabine, in the sea" and continuing north.[5] The line marked what is today, substantially, the eastern boundary of Texas. Two interpretations of the words of the treaty are possible. One theory places the boundary's point of commencement at rather than out in the Gulf of Mexico, thus implying that there was no concept of territorial ownership in the marginal sea at the time of the treaty; the other, and to the writer the more logical, interpretation places emphasis on the phrase "in the sea," thus inferring the existence of a territorial concept. In other respects the terms of the 1819 treaty are clear; whatever rights the United States may have had in this portion of the North American continent were renounced.

In 1821, Mexico seceded from the Spanish Empire and became an independent nation, succeeding to the Spanish claims and title. These claims included those resulting from Spain's position as a member of

[2] Testimony of Bascom Giles, commissioner of the General Land Office of Texas, *Hearings* before the Senate Committee on Interior and Insular Affairs on S. 155 *et al.*, 81st Cong., 1st sess. (1949), 165. These hearings will hereinafter be cited as *Hearings* on S. 155 *et al.* (1949). At 168–77 in these hearings appears a list of all Gulf of Mexico leases made by Texas. Each lease is described, together with a statement of the date of the lease, cash bonus, rental, and royalty obligations.

[3] Robert Moora, feature article, *Oakland Tribune*, 13 June 1948.

[4] 8 U.S. Stat. 252. The treaty was signed 22 February 1819 and was ratified by the Senate two days later. There was suspected fraud, however, and it was necessary to resubmit the treaty. Final ratification was not secured until 19 February 1821. For a history of the negotiations surrounding the treaty see Samuel Flagg Bemis, *Diplomatic History of the United States* (New York, Henry Holt & Co., 1936), 188–95.

[5] 8 U.S. Stat. 252, 256.

the family of nations, as well as those rights renounced by the United States in the treaty of 1819. Commencing in 1821, Mexico sought to encourage the colonization of the Texas territory by Americans. Stephen F. Austin and others procured substantial grants of land upon their promise to settle certain numbers of families there. Although the total number of persons emigrating to Texas under these conditions was not great, trouble with the Mexican authorities began soon after the first settlers arrived, and by 1830 open outbreaks of violence had occurred.

In 1836 the Texans revolted against Mexican rule and on 2 March 1836 established the independent Republic of Texas,[6] followed soon thereafter by the adoption of a constitution.[7] This nation succeeded to all rights and title formerly held by Mexico. The Republic of Texas, up to the date of its annexation to the United States in 1845, held unquestioned sway over the areas freed by the revolution from Mexican dominion and power.

The independence of Texas was recognized by many of the major powers of the day. On 1 March 1837 the Senate of the United States resolved that Texas' independence was established and ought to be recognized.[8] Two days later, Congress voted the money to pay a diplomatic representative to Texas.[9] On this same day, Andrew Jackson appointed a minister to the new nation, and the appointment was confirmed by the Senate on 7 March 1837.[10] France concluded a treaty of "amity, commerce, and navigation" with Texas 25 September 1839, accomplishing "the formal recognition . . . of the independence of the Republic of Texas."[11] A year later the Netherlands[12] and Great Britain[13] acknowledged Texas as a member of the family of nations by the signing of treaties. Full diplomatic relations between these nations and Texas were maintained. Even Mexico was willing to recognize the independence of Texas on condition that Texas would not allow herself to be annexed to any other nation.[14] There can be little doubt that Texas was a full-fledged member of the family of nations, with such rights and jurisdiction over the waters of her marginal seas as other nations of that period maintained.

Immediately after Texas gained her freedom, the Congress of the

---

[6] 1 Laws Repub. Tex. 3–7.   [7] 1 Laws Repub. Tex. 9–25.
[8] *Congressional Globe*, 24th Cong., 2d sess., 45.   [9] 5 U.S. Stat. 170.
[10] This entire story is well told in Bemis, *op. cit.*, 215–31.
[11] 2 Gammel's *Laws of Texas* 655.   [12] 2 Gammel's *Laws of Texas* 905.
[13] 2 Gammel's *Laws of Texas* 880, 886, 889.
[14] John Bassett Moore, *A Digest of International Law,* I, 456.

Republic of Texas passed an act extending the civil and political jurisdiction of the nation to the territory "beginning at the mouth of the
Sabine River, and running west along the Gulf of Mexico three leagues
from the land to the mouth of the Rio Grande."[15] This three-league
boundary, approximately ten and one-half rather than the customary
three miles, has been doggedly maintained by representatives of the state
of Texas as the legal boundary,[16] even after the decision of the United
States Supreme Court in *United States* v. *Texas* in 1950.[17] Yet it is
significant that Buchanan, while Secretary of State, in a note to the
British minister rejected any notion that this three-league limit had substantial effect in international law. According to Buchanan, the United
States allowed the limit as a matter of "mutual convenience." At the
same time he conceded that a one-league (three-mile) "territorial jurisdiction" was "acknowledged by international law."[18] And in simple
justice to the claim of Texas, it must be acknowledged that Buchanan
did admit that the United States, the nation which was to annex the
Republic of Texas in 1845, did recognize the three-league demarcation.

The discussion between Crampton and Secretary of State Buchanan
arose from the wording of the Treaty of Guadalupe Hidalgo, which
ended the war between the United States and Mexico in 1848.[19] Article
V of this treaty stipulated that "the boundary line between the two Republics shall commence in the Gulf of Mexico, three leagues from land,
opposite the mouth of the Rio Grande otherwise called Rio Bravo del

[15] 1 Gammel's *Laws of Texas* 1193; 1 Sayles' *Early Laws of Texas*, Art. 257.

[16] See, e.g., testimony of Price Daniel, attorney general of Texas, *Hearings* on
S. 155 *et al.* (1949), 123, 132–33; testimony of Bascom Giles, *ibid.*, 151, 155,
156–57, 159–60.

[17] See, e.g., testimony of J. M. Combs, member of Congress, Second Texas
District, *Hearings* on S.J. Res. 20 (1951), 169, 180; joint statement of Allan
Shivers, governor of Texas, Price Daniel, and Bascom Giles, *ibid.*, 100–101.

[18] John Bassett Moore, *A Digest of International Law,* I, 730. The note to
Crampton, dated 19 August 1848, says in part: "I have had the honor to receive
your note of the 30th April last objecting on behalf of the British Government,
to that clause in the fifth article of the late treaty between Mexico and the
United States by which it is declared that 'the boundary line between the two
Republics shall commence in the Gulf of Mexico 3 leagues from land,' instead
of 1 league from land, which you observe 'is acknowledged by international law
as the extent of territorial jurisdiction over the sea that washes the coasts of
states.'

"In answer I have to state that the stipulation in the treaty can only affect the
rights of Mexico and the United States. If for their mutual convenience it has
been deemed proper to enter into such an arrangement, third parties can have
no just cause for complaint. The Government of the United States never intended
by this stipulation to question the rights which Great Britain or any other power
may possess under the law of Nations."

[19] 9 U.S. Stat. 922.

norte." Throughout the period of negotiations on the treaty, Nicholas P. Trist, who spoke for the United States, insisted on the establishment of the same boundary line which had been previously claimed by the Republic of Texas.[20] On 30 December 1853 the Gadsden Treaty was concluded between the United States and Mexico,[21] once again specifying that the boundaries of the United States begin "in the Gulf of Mexico, three leagues from land,"[22] and thus again following the old Texas declaration. The indication, it would appear, is clear.

In 1845, nine years after becoming an independent nation, the Republic of Texas was annexed by the United States, the only state to be so joined to the Union. These proceedings for annexation were conducted between two independent members of the family of nations. The story is an important one in understanding the claim which Texas has made to the ownership of the submerged lands in the Gulf of Mexico.

The first overtures by the Texans, in 1837, looking to annexation were summarily rejected by the United States. The issue could not, however, go long unresolved, and on 12 April 1844 a treaty of annexation engineered by Calhoun was concluded in Washington.[23] This treaty called for the Republic of Texas to cede to the United States "all of the territories of Texas," including "all public lots and squares, vacant lands, mines, minerals, salt lakes and springs, public edifices, fortifications, barracks, ports and harbors, navy and navy-yards, docks, magazines, arms, armaments, and accoutrements, archives and public documents, public funds, debts, taxes and dues unpaid at the time of the exchange of the ratifications of this treaty."[24] By Article V of the treaty the United States agreed to assume and "pay the public debts and liabilities of Texas, however created, for which the faith or credit of her government may be bound at the time of the exchange of the ratifications of this treaty; which debts and liabilities are estimated not to exceed, in the whole, ten millions of dollars."

On 8 June 1844 this instrument failed, by a vote of 35–16, to gain the approval of the United States Senate. The reasons for the defeat of the treaty are many and varied. The slavery controversy undoubtedly loomed large in the minds of many so-called "free state" senators. A

[20] For thorough documentation of treaty negotiation on this point see "Brief for the State of Texas in Opposition to Motion for Judgment," No. 13 Original, October Term 1949, pp. 84–85. This brief is hereinafter cited as Texas brief.
[21] 10 U.S. Stat. 1031.
[22] Art. I.
[23] A copy of this unratified treaty is found in the Appendix of the Texas brief, 50–57.
[24] Art. I.

further factor was objection to assumption by the United States of the Texas public debt, contracted in the War of Independence and variously estimated at from ten to thirteen million dollars.[25] Calhoun and Polk favored the annexation, but Henry Clay and his party opposed it, among other reasons, on the debt issue. President Tyler felt that the United States could not, "with honor," take over the public lands of Texas without assuming the payment of the debt.[26] Some members of Congress argued that the Texas lands were worthless in comparison to the total debt. J. R. Ingersoll, for example, argued that "so much of the country was covered with swamps and overflowed by marshes, with rivers too shallow to drain them, that the production of the great southern staple to any large extent was a matter of doubt."[27] Others with greater vision argued that the United States would receive the best of the bargain. Ezra Dean stated, after pointing out that the Texas debt might be greater than ten million dollars: "Well, admitting it is so, we shall, I think, still be the gainer by the bargain. For we shall receive of her rising of one hundred and thirty-six millions of acres of land, and some of it of the best quality."[28]

In 1844, James Knox Polk won the presidency on a platform calling for the addition of Texas to the Union. Congressional lame ducks now acted more expeditiously, finding the solution to the problem in annexation through a joint resolution of Congress.[29] Approximately fifty bills and resolutions were introduced for the purpose, but the one finally adopted was introduced by Congressman Brown of Tennessee. His original resolution provided that Texas should cede to the United States all "mines, minerals, salt lakes, springs, and also all edifices, fortifications, barracks," and so forth, after which the new state should keep the remainder of her lands and her public debt.[30] This resolution, introduced 13 January 1845, and others containing similar provisions were much debated. On 28 January 1845, Brown introduced a substitute resolution with the words "mines, minerals, salt lakes, and springs" omitted on the justifiable grounds that if Texas were to utilize the public lands to pay the debt she had contracted she should not be deprived of the major portion of what were then considered to be the

[25] *Congressional Globe,* 28 Cong., 1st sess., Appendix, 686; 28 Cong., 2d sess., 141, and Appendix, 275.

[26] *Ibid.,* 28 Cong., 2d sess., 141.

[27] *Ibid.,* Appendix, 58.

[28] *Ibid.,* Appendix, 105.

[29] 5 U.S. Stat. 797.

[30] *Congressional Globe,* 28th Cong., 2d sess., 129.

valuable lands.[31] This substitute resolution was adopted. It specifically stated:

Said State, when admitted into the Union . . . shall retain all the public funds, debts, taxes, and dues of every kind which may belong to or be due and owing said Republic; and shall also retain all the vacant and unappropriated lands lying within its limits, to be applied to the payment of the debts and liabilities of said Republic of Texas, and the residue of said lands, after discharging said debts and liabilities, to be disposed of as said State may direct; but in no event are said debts and liabilities to become a charge upon the Government of the United States. . . .[32]

Thus Texas came into the Union retaining her "worthless" lands and her debt. It was upon the basis of this contract that Texas was unsuccessfully to argue her claims before the Supreme Court of the United States in the case of *United States* v. *Texas*.

The final form of the "Joint Resolution for Annexing Texas"[33] provided for two separate and distinct possible bases for annexation. Sections 1 and 2 read:

Resolved by the Senate and House of Representatives of the United States of America in Congress assembled, That Congress doth consent that the territory properly included within, and rightfully belonging to the Republic of Texas, may be erected into a new state, to be called the state of Texas, with a republican form of government, to be adopted by the people of said republic, by deputies in Convention assembled, with the consent of the existing government, in order that the same may be admitted as one of the States of this Union.

2. *And be it further resolved,* That the foregoing consent of Congress is given upon the following conditions, and with the following guarantees, to-wit: *First*—said state to be formed, subject to the adjustment by this government of all questions of boundary that may arise with other governments; and the constitution thereof, with the proper evidence of its adoption by the people of said republic of Texas shall be transmitted to the President of the United States, to be laid before Congress for its final action, on or before the first day of January, one thousand eight hundred and forty six. *Second.* . . . [Here followed the provision leaving to Texas the "unappropriated lands" as well as the debt. Other technical matters, not here at issue, were also incorporated into section 2.]

By section 3 of the joint resolution a totally different plan of annexation, a plan which was never used, was set out in these words:

[31] *Ibid.,* 193.   [32] 5 U.S. Stat. 797–98.   [33] 5 U.S. Stat. 797.

3. *And be it further resolved,* That if the President of the United States shall in his judgment and discretion deem it most advisable, instead of proceeding to submit the foregoing resolution to the Republic of Texas, as an overture on the part of the United States for admission, to negotiate with that Republic; then, *Be it resolved,* That a state, to be formed out of the present Republic of Texas, with suitable extent and boundaries, and with two representatives in Congress, until the next apportionment of representation, shall be admitted into the Union, by virtue of this act, on an equal footing with the existing states, as soon as the terms and conditions of such admission, and the cession of the remaining Texian territory to the United States shall be agreed upon by the Governments of Texas and the United States: And that the sum of one hundred thousand dollars be, and the same is hereby, appropriated to defray the expenses of missions and negotiations, to agree upon the terms of said admission and cession, either by treaty to be submitted to the Senate, or by articles to be submitted to the two Houses of Congress, as the President may direct.

President Tyler's term of office was about to expire, and he determined to act at once under sections 1 and 2 of the joint resolution; he rejected specifically undertaking the negotiations contemplated in section 3. Accordingly he sent instructions to the American chargé d'affaires in Texas to present annexation proposals based on sections 1 and 2. President Polk did not disturb the decision of his predecessor upon his assumption of office.[34] The American chargé d'affaires presented the proposal of the United States, exclusive of section 3. By joint resolution the Congress of Texas accepted the annexation proposal, the resolution of acceptance omitting section 3 of the United States joint resolution.[35]

The Texas Convention on 4 July 1845 gave its assent in the following words:

. . . WHEREAS the President of United States has submitted to Texas the first and second sections of the said resolution of the United States, as the basis upon which Texas may be admitted as one of the States of the said Union; and

WHEREAS the existing government of the Republic of Texas has assented to the proposals thus made, the terms and conditions of which are as follows. . . . [Here the Texas action incorporates sections 1 and 2 of the joint resolution of the United States Congress of 1 March 1845; section 3 was not incorporated.]

Now, in order to manifest the assent of the people of this Republic as

[34] Miller, *Treaties of the United States,* IV, 706–708.
[35] 2 Gammel's *Laws of Texas* 1225. The date was 23 June 1845.

required in the above recited portions of the said resolutions; We the deputies of the people of Texas in convention assembled, in their name and by their authority, do ordain and declare, that we assent to, and accept the proposals, conditions and guarantees contained in the first and second sections of the resolution of the Congress of the United States aforesaid.[36]

This convention then drafted a constitution for the new state of Texas which provided that rights of property which had been acquired under the Republic should remain precisely as before.[37] The constitution was accepted by the Congress of the United States on 29 December 1845.[38] The process of annexation was complete.

Rather lengthy reference has been made here to the fact that this annexation was not accomplished under section 3 of the joint resolution of annexation. Section 3 is the only portion of the resolution which contained reference to the "equal footing with the existing states." There is nothing in sections 1 and 2 of the resolution of Congress, in the actions of President Tyler or Polk, or in the actions of the duly designated representatives of Texas which in any way indicates that the "equal footing" principle was at issue. It is for this reason that the argument of the United States more than one hundred years later in *United States* v. *Texas,* premised as it was to some extent upon the "equal footing" clause, proceeded partially upon a historically erroneous precedent.[39] Even the majority opinion of the Supreme Court cited the unused section 3 as support in ruling that the "equal footing clause of the Joint Resolution Annexing Texas" meant that the Republic of Texas had given up to the United States its control over the submerged lands in the marginal sea.[40]

Yet it is incontestable that the final act of Congress on 29 December 1845 did contain the reference to Texas' having been admitted on an equal footing with the other states.[41] This action was a unilateral declaration, true. There was never any such consent given by the Republic

[36] 2 Gammel's *Laws of Texas* 1228.
[37] Constitution of Texas, Art. VIII, §20.
[38] 9 U.S. Stat. 108.
[39] United States brief, *Texas* case, 52–63.
[40] 339 U.S. 707, 715. See pp. 204–205, where this argument is developed at greater length.
[41] 9 U.S. Stat. 108. The pertinent language is as follows: "*Resolved by the Senate and House of Representatives of the United States in Congress assembled,* That the State of Texas shall be one, and is hereby declared to be one, of the United States of America, and admitted into the Union on an equal footing with the original States in all respects whatever."

of Texas, which understood, precisely and finally, that the annexation was being accomplished under sections 1 and 2 of the annexation resolution. But the final operative document which contained the disputed clause was the means of admission. From this point of view, it is possible to argue that whether the state agreed to the "equal footing" clause or not, it could only have joined the Union upon the same basis as other states. The matter is not clean-cut on either side.

On 29 April 1846 the Texas Legislature reaffirmed the declarations which had been made while the state was a republic. By joint resolution the Legislature declared the exclusive right of the state to jurisdiction over the soil included within the boundaries of the state[42]—and the Congress of the Republic had declared those boundaries to extend three leagues out into the Gulf of Mexico. Further, as previously noted, the United States in 1848 was to give implied sanction to this declaration by the Treaty of Guadalupe Hidalgo. Since the United States Supreme Court in *New Mexico* v. *Colorado* later declared that the right of a state, upon its admission to the Union, to rely upon its established boundaries could not be impaired by subsequent action on the part of the United States,[43] Texas felt her jurisdiction over submerged lands to be secure.

Formal provision for leasing and development of "that portion of the Gulf of Mexico within the jurisdiction of Texas" was not accomplished until 1919.[44] Previous acts of the Legislature in 1913[45] and

[42] 2 Gammel's *Laws of Texas* 1461; Hartley's *Digest,* Arts. 1631, 1634.

[43] 267 U.S. 30, 41 (1925).

[44] Gen. Laws Tex. 36th Legis. 2d called sess., 51. Since in 1919 the boundaries were legally established at three leagues out in the Gulf of Mexico, the 1919 act covered 2,608,774 acres of submerged lands. Testimony of Bascom Giles, *Hearings* on S. 155 *et al.* (1949), 158. In 1941 the Texas Legislature unilaterally extended its boundaries out to a limit of twenty-seven miles from the old three-league boundary. Gen. Laws Tex., 47th Legis., 454. The Legislature based its action on the increased range of cannon fire. In May 1947, just before the decision of the United States Supreme Court in *United States* v. *California,* the Texas Legislature took the unprecedented and again unilateral action of declaring that state boundaries extended to the edge of the continental shelf. Gen. Laws Tex., 50th Legis., 451. The action was taken on the theory that submerged lands are appurtenant to the upland.

In 1949, Attorney General Price Daniel admitted that Texas had consummated leases out beyond the original three-league limit. Testimony, *Hearings* on S. 155 *et al.* (1949), 138. The writer has grave doubts of the validity of all actions taken by the state of Texas in respect to submerged lands beyond the three-league limit. He is of the frank opinion that by its actions the Texas Legislature may have laid itself open to charges of "land-grabbing."

[45] Gen. Laws Tex., 33d Legis., 409. The first lease for purposes of oil production to lands under water (not in the open sea) was negotiated in 1913. "Brief

1917[46] had provided for mineral development on state lands generally, fresh-water lakes, islands, bays, and the beds of navigable rivers. The 1919 act extended the provisions for mineral leases of state lands found in the earlier acts to the submerged lands of the Gulf of Mexico. By act of 1949[47] the commissioner of the General Land Office of Texas was authorized to issue permits for "geological, geophysical, and other surveys" of areas not already under lease and within tidewater limits.

The procedure requires that leases to submerged lands be made on the basis of sealed bids, with the highest bidder for a particular parcel securing the lease. Texas averaged approximately $20 per acre bonus on 350,000 acres of tidelands and submerged lands leased prior to *United States* v. *Texas;* the return to the state's school fund from this source alone, without including returns from rentals or royalties, was $7,212,000. It is interesting to note that the United States, under the Federal Mineral Leasing Act of 1920, would have realized only a miserly twenty-five cents per acre, or a total of $87,500 bonus for these same lands.[48] The submerged lands, including some under the beds of rivers and lakes not directly affected by the decision in *United States* v. *Texas,* had returned down to 1948 over $25,000,000 for the school fund of Texas.[49]

Oil companies seeking to operate off the coasts of Texas and Louisiana encounter extremely adverse weather and geophysical conditions, which increase the costs of exploration and drilling. While some of the undersea pools can be tapped by whipstocking, as in California, many others require the building of expensive drilling platforms in the Gulf. The experience of the Ohio Oil Company has been typical. This corporation holds a lease from the state of Texas to some 120,000 acres of

---

of the Land Commissioner of Texas Supporting Resolutions to Quiet Title," *Hearings* on H.J. Res. 118 *et al.* (1945).

[46] Gen. Laws Tex., 35th Legis., 158.

[47] Gen. Laws Tex., 51st Legis., 603.

[48] Testimony of Price Daniel, *Hearings* on S.J. Res. 195 (1950), 41. Daniel noted that Louisiana had averaged ten dollars per acre for its lease bonuses.

[49] Statement of Congressman Olin E. Teague, joint *Hearings* on S. 1988 (1948), 1687. Six of the twelve coastal counties of Texas have proved salt domes. Testimony of Robert A. Stuart, *Hearings* on H.J. Res. 176 and 181 (1939), 78. Where a lease was made in the submerged lands of the Gulf of Mexico, that lease was entered on the tax rolls of the littoral county. Testimony of Price Daniel, joint *Hearings* on S. 1988 (1948), 1098. By 1939 evidence was offered that the submerged lands, inland as well as coastal, had been leased or granted to some six hundred individuals and corporations, subject to royalties and bonus payments in favor of the public school fund. "Brief of the Texas State Teachers Association against S.J. Resolutions 83 and 92," *Hearings* on S.J. Res. 83 and 92 (1939), 153.

submerged lands. The Ohio Company paid $1,400,000 for the leases and expended a similar amount on geophysical operations. The company spent $5,500,000 drilling three dry holes and a gas well and has yet to produce any oil.[50] To 15 July 1951 a total of $234,000,000 had been spent by oil producers in exploring, drilling, and operating in the Gulf of Mexico area, including lands off the coasts of both Texas and Louisiana. Total revenues to the oil companies to 1 June 1950 amounted to $6,300,000, with monthly costs running $3,500,000 and revenues averaging $870,000 per month. The Humble Oil Company spent $1,200,000 in the construction of a single large platform and an average of $280,000 on each of sixteen smaller ones.[51] And for the most part, operations in the Gulf of Mexico are still in the wildcat stage.

The passage of legislation providing for mineral exploration and development of the lands beneath the marginal sea is not the only evidence that the governmental agencies of Texas had operated for many years on the principle that ownership of such submerged soils was vested in the state. State statutes termed the fish in these areas as "property"[52] and provided stringent regulations for the control of the taking of them commercially or for sport. The production and taking of oysters had been governed by statute.[53] Extensive regulations had been developed providing for the taking of sand and gravel below low-water mark in the Gulf of Mexico—regulations based on the assumption that the state held title to these areas.[54] The Legislature in 1941 granted to cities of more than sixty thousand persons the right of use and occupancy of the tidelands proper and for a distance of two thousand feet out into the Gulf where such land was to be utilized for park purposes. The state of Texas expressly retained, by the statute, full rights to any oil,

[50] Testimony of Clayton L. Orn, attorney for the Ohio Oil Company, *Hearings on S.J. Res. 195* (1950), 58–59.

[51] Statement of Rex G. Baker, director and general counsel, Humble Oil Company, *ibid.*, 83.

[52] Vernon's Tex. Civ. Stat., Art. 4026; *Stephenson* v. *Wood*, 119 Tex. 564 (1931).

[53] Vernon's Tex. Civ. Stat., Arts. 4027, 4035–43.

[54] *Ibid.*, Arts. 4051–55. Article 4051 reads as follows: "Property of the State. All the islands, reefs, bars, lakes, and bays within the tidewater limits from the most interior point seaward co-extensive with the jurisdiction of this State, and such of the fresh water islands, lakes, rivers, creeks and bayous within the interior of this State as may not be embraced in any survey of private land, together with all the marl and sand of commercial value, and all the shells, mudshell or gravel of whatsoever kind, . . . are included within the provisions of this chapter, and are hereby placed under the management, control and protection of the Commissioner."

gas, and other minerals which might be found under land so granted.[55] Without title, the state would have had no right to make any such grant and retain the mineral rights thereunder.

Texas courts recognized the right of the Texas Legislature to issue patents to land below low-water mark in the open sea. A grant of land in Galveston Bay below low-water mark, made while Texas was still a republic, was held valid by the Texas Supreme Court in *Galveston* v. *Menard*.[56] The Joint Resolution for Annexing Texas was interpreted in a number of cases. In *Galveston* v. *Mann*[57] the Texas court held that the terms of the annexation resolution unquestionably recognized Texas' "ownership of the waters and submerged lands" in the Gulf of Mexico.[58]

The issue was clear in *State* v. *Jadwin*.[59] In a contest involving title to certain lands at the east end of Galveston Island, defendants pleaded that they were the agents of the United States and held possession by virtue of the national government's alleged title. The Texas Court of Civil Appeals answered in the negative the question of whether or not the United States had received any land at the east end of Galveston Island by virtue of the resolution annexing Texas to the United States. After pointing out that any title which the United States held to such lands must have derived from the annexation resolution, the court said:

The state showed that the land sued for was within its borders. . . . It may also be mentioned . . . that the United States has, since the admission of Texas into the Union, purchased a tract of land on the east end of the island, and one in the shallow waters adjacent, and in neither instance was any assertion of title made to the lands in question. . . . The land upon the island belonged to the state. Equally the waters of the bay and the gulf for three leagues from the shore. As between Texas, as the grantor, and the United States, as grantee, the grant could not be enlarged by accretion. What Texas granted to the United States was the specific lands devoted to purposes of public defense.[60]

[55] Gen. Laws Tex., 47th Legis., 10; Vernon's Tex. Civ. Stat., Art. 6081g. Agreements have been worked out between state officials and the officials of the city of Galveston so that no oil derricks have been placed on city beaches. This arrangement is typical of the co-operation between state and city in this matter. Testimony of Price Daniel, *Hearings* on S.J. Res. 195 (1950), 40.
[56] 23 Tex. 349 (1859). See also *State* v. *Delesdenier*, 7 Tex. 76 (1851); *State* v. *Bradford*, 121 Tex. 515 (1932).
[57] 135 Tex. 319, 143 S.W. 2d 1028 (1940).
[58] 143 S.W. 2d 1028, 1032–33, 1034.
[59] 85 S.W. 490 (1904).
[60] *Ibid.*, 492.

The case was carried to the United States Supreme Court, but the action was dismissed on motion of the solicitor general of the United States.[61] This officer asked for voluntary dismissal, for, as he put it, there was "no ground upon which this case can now be reversed." The United States had recognized that its only claim to the disputed lands, which at one time had been under water either in the Galveston Bay or in the Gulf, was derived from the section of the annexation resolution which called for the Republic of Texas to cede "fortifications, barracks, ports and harbors, navy and navy-yards, docks, magazines, arms, armaments, and all other property and means pertaining to the public defense."[62]

In *Amaya* v. *Stanolind Oil and Gas Co.*[63] the United States District Court for the Southern District of Texas was faced with questions of title to land between the Rio Grande and the Nueces River. Judge Hannay set out in detail the Texas boundary act of 1836 and then stated:

> This act of Texas has never been repealed, and at the time that Texas was finally admitted to the United States . . . a new constitution was adopted which expressly provided for the continuation of such prior enactment in full force. . . .
> The United States recognized that in view of the annexation agreement, Texas was the superior sovereign, so far as land and land titles in Texas were concerned. . . .
> Prior to annexation, Texas as a republic had complete control of all land within its borders. . . .
> In view of the repeated statements of the Supreme Court of the United States, both before and after annexation and the Treaty of Guadalupe Hidalgo, it is most unreasonable to argue that the Treaty of Guadalupe Hidalgo in any way takes away any of the sovereign rights of Texas respecting land.[64]

The Fifth Circuit Court of Appeals affirmed the decision,[65] and the United States Supreme Court denied certiorari.[66] The federal district judge's statements in the *Amaya* case are dicta insofar as the issue of submerged lands is concerned. Yet there can be little doubt that Judge Hannay was considering the total effect of the boundary act of 1836.

[61] 209 U.S. 553 (1908).
[62] 5 U.S. Stat. 797, 798.
[63] 62 F. Supp. 181 (1945).
[64] *Ibid.*, 185, 197, 198, 200.
[65] 158 F. 2d 554 (1946).
[66] 331 U.S. 808 (1947), rehearing denied, 331 U.S. 867 (1947).

The decision is significant in its interpretation of the resolution of annexation.

Upon the request of national officials, the state conveyed parcels of submerged lands in the Gulf of Mexico to the United States. Over 650 acres of land on Galveston Island, together with submerged lands upon which Galveston Jetty was built, were granted to the United States in 1912.[67] In 1880, land covered by water in the Bolivar Point Lighthouse area of Galveston Harbor was conveyed to the United States.[68] Other similar examples could be cited.[69] As a matter of fact, it would appear that the Department of State recognized the three-league boundary as the international boundary, for this was the line surveyed in 1911.[70]

It was not until 1938, with the actions of political officials in the executive and congressional branches of the national government, that any national representative sought to question a title of Texas, by that time almost one hundred years old. Texas' pride was wounded and Texas' ire aroused. The people of the state were genuinely concerned. In 1949 they considered the controversy over the submerged lands as the biggest problem facing Texas, ranking it above the cost of living, employment, health, education, housing, and even the problem of racial equality. In 1948, the submerged lands controversy had ranked sixth among the ten most important Texas problems.[71] Typical Texas enthusiasm was now centered on an issue in which the national government was attempting to breach what was, to many Texans, a sacred agreement.[72]

[67] Patent No. 47 of the General Land Office of Texas, Vol. XXXIX, file 103.

[68] Patent No. 633 of the General Land Office of Texas, Vol. XXXII, p. 633.

[69] See Texas brief, 187–88. The two examples just cited are drawn originally by the writer from the Texas brief (p. 186).

[70] Map sheets 29 and 30, Department of State, *Proceedings* of the International Boundary Commission, United States and Mexico, joint *Report* of the Consulting Engineers on Field Operations of 1910–1911, American Section (Washington, Government Printing Office, 1913).

[71] Joe Belden, director of the Texas Poll, in *Austin* (Texas) *American,* 27 November 1949.

[72] In a letter to the writer, the late Secretary of the Interior Harold L. Ickes raised a novel legal point respecting the Texas title to the submerged lands. He had made the public statement, after the decision of the United States Supreme Court in *United States* v. *California,* that, "parenthetically, Texas may have a legal right to its tidelands because it came into the Union voluntarily and as an independent country." Address over the ABC Network, 14 October 1948. In making this statement, he was relying upon the chain of reasoning which has been sketched in this chapter.

But in 1950, a friend of his who was a member of the California Bar raised a point to which few persons, including Ickes, had given thought. As Ickes expressed it in a letter to the writer dated 18 August 1950: "It is true that Texas came in as an independent sovereignty and with a reservation as to certain titles and rights. But subsequently, Texas rebelled against the United States. Texas was defeated, along with the other rebellious states, and surrendered rights that were not definitely restored to it. And title to its tidelands, if they belonged originally to Texas, has never been restored." Quoted with the permission of former Secretary Ickes.

Certainly this approach is most unusual and at first blush appears to have some substance. Yet the ruling of the United States Supreme Court in *Texas* v. *White*, 7 Wall. 700 (1869), would appear to answer the propositions advanced by Ickes. Legally, the rebellious states never left the Union; the majority of the court refused to go along with the argument advanced by Justice Grier in his dissent to *Texas* v. *White* that the Southern states were, in fact, no longer members of the Union during that period of time they were waging hostilities against the United States. 7 Wall. 700, 737–41. President Lincoln, as a matter of history, waged the war throughout on the principle that the seceding states never really left the Union. When General Philip Sheridan took over as military governor following the Civil War, one of his first official acts was to declare the Texas Act of Secession null and void. It is true that Texas tried to leave the Union, but she did not legally or actually succeed in doing so. Therefore, she could not have lost by the Act of Secession her rights to the submerged lands off her coast.

7.

Congressional Policy on Submerged Lands
Prior to World War II

Having traced in some detail the basis of the legal claims of the individual states to submerged lands, it is now necessary to examine the actions of the political branches of the national government in the matter. If claims to the submerged soils were made prior to the decisions in *United States* v. *California, United States* v. *Louisiana,* and *United States* v. *Texas*, those claims must have been asserted by either the Congress or the executive branch. Equally, if claims are to be made as a result of these decisions, the claims must be initiated by political branches.

It can be established that prior to 1937 the Congress did not regard the areas below low-water mark as constituting a part of the public lands belonging to the United States. No evidence can be found in Congressional hearings or debates prior to that date which would offer any support to a view that the marginal sea was held in property by the United States rather than the individual states. Under the Constitution, Congress alone has the power "to dispose of and make all needful Rules and Regulations respecting the Territory or other Property belonging to the United States."[1] The United States has obtained new territory by treaty, war, and discovery, but such acquisitions have not enlarged the boundaries of the Union.[2] Congressional action alone has

[1] Art. IV, §3.
[2] *Fleming* v. *Page,* 9 How. 602, 615 (1850). The United States acquired the Louisiana Territory by cession, the Northwest Territory by discovery and occupation, and California by conquest.

made the territory so acquired an integral part of the United States.[3] Congress has never taken affirmative action to annex the marginal sea in the name of, and as territory of, the United States. That much is certain.

The nation does have the power to acquire and govern territory.[4] Any question of the disposal of such lands is within the power of Congress alone. This right of Congress over the public lands has been recognized by the Supreme Court from the inception of the government.[5] The power of Congress in this regard is plenary, for "Congress has the sole power to dispose of the public domain, and to declare the dignity and effect of titles emanating from the United States, and as it is not restrained by the Constitution from passing such a law, its propriety and constitutionality can not be questioned."[6] Laws for the disposition of the public lands must come from Congress.[7] In *United States v. Holt Bank* the Supreme Court declared that the "United States early adopted and constantly has adhered to the policy of regarding lands under navigable waters in acquired territory, while under its sole dominion, as held for the ultimate benefit of future states, and so has refrained from making any disposal thereof, save in exceptional circumstances."[8] This policy, if policy it may be called, of noninterference with the soils under navigable waters was consistently followed by the Congress down to 1937. The claim of California in 1947[9] that the Congress had never made any provision for the general "sale, homesteading, donation or other conveyance whatever, of any tide or submerged lands" was completely correct.

In *Pollard's Lessee v. Hagan,* Mr. Justice McKinley had gone so far as to imply, in dicta, that Congress might not grant the tide or submerged lands of an area in territorial status.[10] Justice Gray set this dis-

---

[3] *Foster* v. *Neilson,* 2 Pet. 253, 309 (1829); *United States* v. *Arredondo,* 6 Pet. 691 (1832); *Dorr* v. *United States,* 195 U.S. 138 (1904); *Balzac* v. *Porto Rico,* 258 U.S. 298, 308 (1922).

[4] *American Insurance Co.* v. *Canter,* 1 Pet. 511, 546 (1828).

[5] *Johnson* v. *McIntosh,* 8 Wheat. 543 (1823); *United States* v. *Cook,* 19 Wall. 591 (1873); *Beecher* v. *Wetherby,* 95 U.S. 517 (1877).

[6] *Parkinson* v. *Bracken,* 39 Am. Dec. 296, 297 (Wis. 1842). To the same effect, *Bagnell* v. *Broderick,* 13 Pet. 436, 450 (1839).

[7] *United States* v. *Castillero,* 2 Black 17 (1862); *Heydenfeldt* v. *Daney Gold Mining Co.,* 93 U.S. 634 (1876).

[8] 270 U.S. 49, 55 (1926).

[9] California answer, 447.

[10] The reporter's headnote on the point reads as follows: "It results from these principles that the right of the United States to the public lands, and the power of Congress to make all needful rules and regulations for the sale and disposition thereof, conferred no power to grant land in Alabama which was

crepancy aright when he said of the *Pollard* case in *Shively* v. *Bowlby:* "So much of the reasoning of the learned justice [McKinley] as implied that the title in the land below high-water mark could not have been granted away by the United States after the deed of cession of the territory, and before the admission of the State into the Union, was not necessary to the decision. . . ."[11] This was the same general rule which Chief Justice Taney had followed a number of years before in holding that Congress might have granted tidelands or confirmed a Spanish grant of them before Alabama became a state.[12] This in turn has been elaborated until the rule has become well established that the United States, while holding an area as a territory, may grant, for appropriate purposes, title or rights in the soil below high-water mark; the national government, that is, the Congress, has never chosen to do so, however, by any general laws.[13]

In this respect . . . the United States . . . merely holds the tidelands or foreshore as trustee for the benefit of the future State or States afterwards to be carved out of the territory. Congress has, however, the power to make grants of tidelands whenever it becomes necessary to do so in order to perform international obligations or to effect the improvement of such lands for the promotion and convenience of commerce or to carry out other public purposes appropriate to the objects for which the United States holds such territory, but Congress has never undertaken to dispose of tidelands by general laws. . . . Congress may . . . dispose of the foreshores or tidelands if it considers it expedient to do so.[14]

In at least one case, in Alaska, a specific grant of tidelands was made by the Congress,[15] but the statement that Congress has never chosen to make any general grant or to enact general laws in relation to the submerged lands is corroborated by a search of cases and statutes.

In this lack of action, Congress was aware of the course it was following. It has been shown how the members of Congress knew and de-

---

below usual high water-mark at the time Alabama was admitted into the Union." 3 How. 212.

[11] 152 U.S. 1, 28 (1894). Justice Catron, dissenting in *Pollard* v. *Hagan,* points out this same error in the opinion of Justice McKinley. 3 How. 212, 234.

[12] *Goodtitle* v. *Kibbe,* 9 How. 471, 478 (1850).

[13] *Shively* v. *Bowlby,* 152 U.S. 1 (1894). A grant of public lands by the United States carries with it no force or title below high-water mark to waters and submerged lands bordering such grants. *Ibid.*

[14] Instructions by Commissioner Tallman to the Commissioner of Education on a question of the reservation of tidelands in Alaska for the use of the natives. 44 L.D. 441, 443–44 (1915).

[15] The tidelands so granted were in Cordova Bay. 35 U.S. Stat. 598 (1909).

bated the holdings of the Supreme Court to the effect that the term "public lands" of the United States did not include lands below high-water mark in navigable waters.[16] As Justice Brewer has pointed out, there is no doubt that Congress was aware of its policy in this regard.[17] The general legislation of Congress, as presently constituted, does not apply to submerged lands.[18]

It has been argued, however, that since the Congress never specifically granted away title or rights in the area below low-water mark and out to the three-mile limit, in this area right or title must inhere in the United States.[19] This contention is based upon the premise that the failure of Congress to act does not mean that it did not consider such lands to be owned or controlled by the United States. Further, this lack of action on the part of Congress, it is contended, does not constitute a positive recognition of title in the state.[20]

Such contentions, however, are based upon the assumption that the Congress was not aware of what it was doing, a theory clearly not provable. One finds, for example, that the homestead law for the Territory of Alaska provides that

. . . nothing in this Act contained shall be construed as impairing in any degree the title of any State that may hereafter be erected out of said District or any part thereof, to tide lands and beds of any of its navigable waters, or the right of such State to regulate the use thereof, nor the right of the United States to resume possession of such lands, it being declared that all such rights shall continue to be held by the United States in trust for the people of any State or States which may hereafter be erected out of said District. The term "navigable waters," as herein used, shall be held to include all tidal waters up to the line of ordinary high tide and all nontidal waters navigable in fact up to the line of ordinary high-water mark.[21]

Without attempting to prove, at this point, anything in respect to the extent of the lands under the "navigable waters" mentioned, it can be

---

[16] Pp. 63–64 above.

[17] *Mann* v. *Tacoma Land Co.*, 153 U.S. 273, 283–84 (1894).

[18] *Ibid.*, 284. See p. 189 below.

[19] United States brief, *California* case, 8.

[20] *Ibid.*, 185–86. Arguments utilizing this line of reasoning are found in Congressional hearings in 1938–39. See testimony of Samuel A. King, *Hearings* on S.J. Res. 83 and 92 (1939), 410–11; and M. F. McCarthy, *Hearings* on S.J. Res. 208 (1938), 222–24.

[21] 30 U.S. Stat. 409; 48 U.S.C.A., §411. For a discussion of the general background of this statute and specific references to the section above quoted see *Heine* v. *Roth*, 2 Alaska 416 (1905).

seen that the Congress did have some sort of policy in regard to such lands. That policy, by Congressional declaration, was to hold these areas in trust for future states.[22] In conformity with that policy, the application of one seeking to placer mine on the tidelands in the Bering Sea was rejected on the grounds that "such lands are not public lands belonging to the United States, within the meaning of the mining laws."[23]

Congress was aware of the riches to be found in the marginal sea, yet no action was ever taken to declare such areas under national jurisdiction. In 1911, a report was submitted by the Department of Agriculture to the Congress on the possibilities to be found in the marginal sea in the production and taking of kelp.[24] This report calculated that there were possibilities that thirty-five million dollars' worth of potash could be produced annually from kelp available off the West Coast, with the by-products, such as iodine, sufficient to pay for the total cost of production. This report, moreover, asked the Congress to give special attention to the policing and regulation of the area, though the solicitor general of the Department of Agriculture stated that, in his opinion, the right to so regulate lay with the states rather than the national government.[25] Congress, however, did not attempt to lease or regulate the taking of kelp in any way, though it was perfectly aware that Oregon and California had passed leasing and regulatory laws.[26] Congress has never asserted any rights with respect to kelp.

In 1912 the Supreme Court held that a portion of a federal statute relating to the taking of sponges in the marginal sea off the coast of Florida was applicable only to ocean waters outside the state's boundaries. The court declared that if the act were construed to apply to the area from low-water mark out to the three-mile limit, the measure would be unconstitutional.[27] The national act had prohibited the landing or sale of sponges taken by means of diving apparatus in the "Gulf of Mexico or the Straits of Florida."[28] Since the court held, however, that the act could be applied only to areas outside the three-mile limit, libel by the United States of a vessel operating within the three-mile

[22] For interpretations of the act extending the homestead laws to Alaska, see *Alaska Pacific Fisheries* v. *United States,* 248 U.S. 78 (1918); *Alaska Gold Recovery Co.* v. *Northern M. & T. Co.,* 7 Alaska 386 (1926); *McCloskey* v. *Pacific Coast Co.,* 160 F. 794 (1908).
[23] *In re James W. Logan,* 29 L.D. 395 (1900). To the same effect see *In re Jesse C. Martin,* 32 L.D. 1 (1903); *In re Red Star Olga Fishing Station,* 26 L.D. 533 (1898).   [24] S. Doc. 190, 62d Cong. 2d sess.
[25] *Ibid.,* Appendix I, 129.   [26] See p. 77, n. 68, above.
[27] *The Abby Dodge,* 223 U.S. 166 (1912).   [28] 34 U.S. Stat. 313.

zone was not possible. Of greater importance than the decision was the fact that the Congress, two years later, adopted the decision of the court by making the act effective only in waters outside the state's territorial limits. Some years later, Chief Justice Hughes remarked in an aside, in passing on the validity of a Florida statute regulating the taking of sponges within the three-mile limit, that the previous statute of Congress might now be held valid.[29] The statement was sheer dictum, however, and does not detract from the force of Congressional action taken in acceding to the earlier decision of the court.

In making grants of public lands, the Congress did reserve the mineral rights to the United States.[30] Such rights, by the settled policy of Congress, were disposed of only in specific terms.[31] Thus California asked the United States to grant to the state certain public lands following California's admission to the Union. Sections 16 and 36 were granted to the state for various purposes, and other grants gave additional lands for educational and other uses. California, in turn, gave Standard Oil a lease to section 36 in one portion of the state, and Standard extracted oil. The United States sued to recover damages, alleging that the lands were known to be mineral lands at the time of the grant and hence were reserved to the United States. The defense argued that the lands were not known to contain oil when the grant was made. The district court granted damages, on the ground that grants of public lands did not include mineral rights, where known, unless such a grant specifically included that right.[32] Here the Congress, in its control over public lands, clearly established a policy. Although the whole system of public land control under the Congress has been remarkably liberal[33]—some might argue entirely too liberal—the fact of its liberality does not deny the existence of a policy, however ill conceived or unco-ordinated. Since, as has been seen, submerged lands are not "public lands," this policy of reserving the mineral rights in known mineral lands cannot be held to apply to the submerged lands.

It is true that a state cannot confer on an individual rights in the public lands of the United States,[34] but the state does have the power to exercise a certain jurisdiction over such lands. Thus an Idaho statute

---

[29] *Skiriotes* v. *Florida,* 313 U.S. 69, 74–75 (1941).

[30] *United States* v. *Sweet,* 245 U.S. 563 (1918); *Morton* v. *Nebraska,* 21 Wall. 660 (1874).

[31] *United States* v. *Sweet,* 245 U.S. 563, 572 (1918).

[32] *United States* v. *Standard Oil Co.,* 21 F. Supp. 645 (1937).

[33] *Buford* v. *Houtz,* 133 U.S. 320, 326–27 (1890).

[34] *Doran* v. *Central Pacific R. Co.,* 24 Cal. 246 (1864). Only Congress has this power.

providing that sheep could not be grazed within two miles of any residence, except when a person was grazing his own sheep next to his own domicile, was held valid as applied to one grazing sheep on United States public lands within two miles of another's house. This was a valid exercise of the state's police power, even though the area affected was owned by the United States.[35]

It can be seen, therefore, that the Congress of the United States, by its very inactivity, has had a policy toward the three-mile belt. The attitude of that body had been consistently, down to 1937, that the areas below low-water mark in the navigable waters of the territories were held in trust for the future state, and though the Congress might grant rights in these areas while the land was still in territorial status, it has refrained from doing so. The Congress, down to 1937 at least, contributed its bit toward building a belief that the states held jurisdiction and property rights in the marginal-sea areas.

On 15 April 1937, Senator Gerald P. Nye of North Dakota introduced Senate Bill 2164, which, in effect, declared that lands under the marginal seas of all the coastal states were a part of the public domain of the United States. This bill marks the starting point of the controversy in the Congress over the ownership and control of the three-mile zone. No hearings were ever held on the bill, for the Senate Public Lands Committee, according to Senator Nye, discovered a fundamental inconsistency in the measure. If the properties under the marginal sea were already a part of the public domain, then it was felt that the purpose could better be served by the introduction of a joint resolution directing that the rights of the federal government in the area be asserted.[36]

The original stimulus for the bill, it appears, was furnished by the then Secretary of the Interior Harold L. Ickes, for in a letter to the writer he stated that he "personally" asked Senator Nye to take such action. Nye was chosen because, as Ickes put it, there was no oil in North Dakota and Senator Nye would not be subjected to local pressures. Ickes assumed a great deal of responsibility for guiding the course of legislation designed to declare the rights of the United States in coastal waters.[37]

[35] *Bacon* v. *Walker,* 204 U.S. 311 (1907).
[36] Testimony of Senator Nye, *Hearings* on S.J. Res. 208 (1938), 5.
[37] This letter is dated 29 November 1947. All references to and quotations from correspondence which the writer had with Secretary Ickes are used with the former official's generous permission.

Senate Bill 2164 being deemed inadequate, the North Dakota Senator withdrew the measure and substituted for it, in the third session of the Seventy-fifth Congress, Senate Joint Resolution 208. This resolution asserted that all submerged lands below low-water mark and within the three-mile limit were the property of the United States; and, since certain persons were entering upon them and removing oil, it directed the Attorney General of the United States to "assert, maintain, and establish the title and possession of the United States to the submerged lands aforesaid." This resolution was passed by the Senate in the closing days of the session with no hearings held; the date was 19 August 1937.[38]

On 23, 24, and 25 February 1938 the House Committee on the Judiciary under Chairman Hatton W. Sumners of Texas, held hearings on Senate Joint Resolution 208, the first hearings in a lengthy and notable series. The substance of these and subsequent hearings is discussed later in the chapter. The House committee, by a vote of 10–8, reported the resolution favorably to the House—after striking out everything after the enacting clause and substituting a declaration that the conservation of petroleum deposits in the submerged lands "adjacent to and along the coast of the State of California" was essential for national defense, maintenance of the Navy, and protection and regulation of interstate commerce. In this amended resolution there was no declaration of "title." The right of the United States in this area was declared to be an "attribute of its sovereignty, paramount and exclusive." The Attorney General was directed to maintain this right against trespassers through appropriate judicial proceedings.[39] This measure, even with the favorable, albeit divided, committee report, failed to come to a vote in the House and died on the calendar of the Seventy-fifth Congress.

In the Seventy-sixth Congress, Senator Nye resumed the fight, introducing a resolution which substantially duplicated his earlier Senate Joint Resolution 208 declaring title.[40] He soon changed this measure, however, until it resembled closely the House-amended version of his

[38] A search of the *Congressional Record* of this date discloses no debate on the floor of the Senate. Senator Walsh made a few remarks in which he called Senate Joint Resolution 208 "desirable legislation." There is no other evidence of discussion on the floor. 81 *Congressional Record* 9326. There was no record vote on the resolution.

[39] H.R. Rept. No. 2378, 75th Cong., 3d sess., submitted 19 May 1938. Representative Sam Hobbs submitted the majority report with Representative Tolan of California speaking for the minority.

[40] S.J. Res. 24, 76th Cong., 1st sess.

resolution of the previous session.[41] Senator Walsh introduced a similar measure.[42] In the House, Representative O'Connor of Montana introduced a resolution which was directed to an assertion of title in the submerged lands by the United States,[43] while Representative Hobbs introduced legislation which was substantially that for which he had submitted a majority report at the previous Congress.[44] With the exception of Senate Joint Resolution 24 and House Joint Resolution 181 the measures related only to the submerged lands off the coast of California and were based upon an assertion of superior and paramount national rights in the area. House Joint Resolution 181 clung to a blanket assertion of the United States' title to all the submerged lands of the marginal seas. Under House Joint Resolution 176, the control of the area would have gone to the Navy Department, but under House Joint Resolution 181, the Interior Department was to administer the entire expanse of coastal lands.[45] While hearings were held in both the House and the Senate on these measures,[46] neither House nor Senate took any action.

The hearings present a strange mixture of contradictions. While it is, of course, true that there was a basic division of opinion between those persons of a states' rights persuasion and those who favored national control, there were numerous shades of argument advanced by both factions. A careful study of the hearings during the period 1937–39 provides a foundation for the clearer understanding of the decisions in *United States* v. *California, United States* v. *Louisiana,* and *United States* v. *Texas.*

The National Resources Committee, in its report to the President on 28 January 1939, stated:

> Another problem affecting petroleum reserves which merits attention here is that of national policy toward ownership of petroleum and natural gas lying beneath the submerged areas off the coast of the United States between low-water mark and the 3-mile limit. Unsettled questions of law are involved, but the very existence of doubt offers an opportunity for the bold assertion of the national interest in any petroleum or natural-gas re-

[41] S.J. Res. 92, 76th Cong., 1st sess.
[42] S.J. Res. 83, 76th Cong., 1st sess.
[43] H.J. Res. 181, 76th Cong., 1st sess.
[44] H.J. Res. 176, 76th Cong., 1st sess.
[45] It should not be necessary to add that the Navy was not in favor of House Joint Resolution 181. See testimony of Leslie C. McNemar, *Hearings* on H.J. Res. 176 and 181 (1939), 49.
[46] *Hearings* on S.J. Res. 83 and 92 (1939); *Hearings* on H.J. Res. 176 and 181 (1939).

serves that may be found beneath those areas. It is one of the unfortunate errors of our national development that early in our history the public ownership of all subsurface mineral wealth was not declared; such a step would have been so simple at an early stage and would have meant so much in terms of conservation, and it would be so complex and costly at this stage—not to speak of the wastes of irreplaceable resources that have already taken place. But here and now in 1939 we have one last opportunity to take steps which will reserve to the nation petroleum deposits that may be of considerable extent. In the third session of the Seventy-fifth Congress a joint resolution, asserting the Government's rights to these deposits and setting them aside as a naval petroleum reserve, was introduced, passed by the Senate, reported with amendments by the House Committee of the Judiciary and committed to the Committee of the Whole House. No final action was taken, owing doubtless to the pressure of other matters and to the early adjournment of Congress. It is recommended that the substance of this resolution again be presented to the Congress. At this stage in our history it is sheer folly to overlook any opportunity for safeguarding the national interest in petroleum reserves.[47]

The inference here is clear: a desperate need, the committee said, existed for oil reserves. What did the Congress propose to do about it?

The emphasis of the advocates of national control at the 1938–39 hearings was centered on this very problem of the conservation of petroleum reserves. Just six days after Senator Nye introduced his original Senate Bill 2164 at the behest of Secretary of the Interior Ickes, the Navy Department transmitted a letter to the chairman of the Senate Public Lands Committee in which the Congress was urged to enact a law declaring that the submerged lands were a part of the "public domain" of the United States so that federal mineral laws might be applied for the "conservation" of mineral resources.[48] Again after Senator Nye introduced his Senate Joint Resolution 208, which asserted national "title" to the marginal-sea areas, the Navy Department, the Department of Justice, and the Department of the Interior drafted proposed changes to the resolution, changes based not on an assertion of "title" but upon a declaration that "large petroleum deposits" were to be found in submerged lands below low-water mark. The departments suggested that the resolution state the conservation of petroleum resources to be essential to the national defense and maintenance of the

---

[47] Quoted in *Hearings* on S.J. Res. 83 and 92 (1939), 21; *Hearings* on H.J. Res. 176 and 181 (1939), 19. Harold L. Ickes was chairman of the National Resources Committee.

[48] The letter is reprinted in *Hearings* on S.J. Res. 208 (1938), 31.

Navy, thus providing a basis for the executive branch of the national government to assert the paramount rights in this area arising out of such necessity for conservation.[49]

In supporting the 1939 resolutions, Assistant Secretary of the Navy Charles Edison wrote, prophetically, to the speaker of the House of Representatives that the depletion of oil reserves was a serious matter to a Navy likely to need them badly in the future. Depletion was especially serious, he said, in the submerged fields off the coast of California. The production of California petroleum, he claimed, was excessive, contributing only to an already overglutted market. Of California reserves, he stated: "During the past 9 years the State's reserves have been depleted by nearly 20 percent, due primarily to withdrawals in excess of actual normal needs, whereas the reserves of the Nation outside of California have shown a very pronounced increase. . . ."[50] He felt justified, therefore, in asking the passage of resolutions to declare the paramount rights of the United States in the submerged oil fields off the shore of California.

Leslie C. McNemar, who carried the burden of the Navy's legal testimony in the 1939 hearings, emphasized that the Navy was interested only in a petroleum reserve, not in setting up a "straw man to get somebody to declare something or other so that some decision will be rendered by the court."[51] A few moments later he gave emphasis to this point when he stated: "Let us get our position clear on this. We want only the petroleum deposits under the Territorial waters of the United States beyond the low-water marks. We want them as a naval reserve, because as Captain Stuart, who has preceded me, tells you in his opinion and the Navy's opinion, it is necessary."[52]

In 1938, Captain H. A. Stuart, director of the Naval Petroleum Reserves, had argued that the Navy had to prepare itself against the day when oil might no longer be easily obtainable. According to him, the United States owned no further public lands which offered oil possibilities. The submerged lands presented a sort of last "opportunity" for the government "to fortify itself with a prospective additional supply of petroleum products."[53] In 1939 he pointed out that the government was dependent on two kinds of reserves: industrial reserves and governmental reserves. Eighty-seven per cent of the known industrial reserves were located east of the Rocky Mountains. A Pacific war would draw

[49] *Ibid.*, 3.
[50] The letter is reprinted in *Hearings* on S.J. Res. 83 and 92 (1939), 21–22. It was dated 20 February 1939.   [51] *Ibid.*, 67.   [52] *Ibid.*
[53] Testimony, *Hearings* on S.J. Res. 208 (1938), 37.

heavily on the 13 per cent of industrial reserves in California. With no pipelines to the Pacific, the running of tankers through the Panama Canal would be at best a gamble. Condemning the oil industry in California, he said: "The Government cannot depend on the industry in California to conserve any significant amount of oil for the national defense. The commercial interests of that industry are concerned primarily with profits, immediate and sustained."[54]

The emphasis on conservation in California was, however, unfortunate, for geologically the California submerged fields could not be constituted a naval petroleum reserve. Control or ownership by the national government of the submerged lands could not solve the problem of adverse drainage created by upland owners drilling on their own lands.[55] Geologically, the Navy was asking for something it couldn't have. Harry R. Johnson, a consulting geologist, in his technical brief, put the situation this way: "The creation of a sealed oil reserve for the United States Navy or for anyone else in the offshore area of the Wilmington field is therefore an impossibility unless the large number of private wells creating the adverse drainage therein are condemned and shut in until future production in the offshore area indicates that a balanced drainage condition has come into existence."[56]

In addition, the Navy's hands were not clean in the matter of managing the reserves which it had held for many years. Teapot Dome was still fresh in the minds of the nation's citizens. The opponents of the resolutions were able to mount attacks on the conservation arguments by merely airing the already proved facts of the Navy's maladministration in Elk Hills and elsewhere.[57] Even Harold Ickes said in 1947 that "the Navy's administration of its reserve in Elk Hills was so careless and inadequate that the Standard Oil Company of California was

[54] *Hearings* on S.J. Res. 83 and 92 (1939), 48–49. Captain Stuart spent a great deal of time quoting statistics on oil reserves in an effort to prove that the submerged lands off California were absolutely necessary to the Navy's defense scheme. He described in detail the known areas and proved reserves in the Navy's Oil Reserve Areas: Elk Hills, Buena Vista, Teapot Dome, and Alaska. The Navy had in addition, in 1939, three oil shale reserves, two in Colorado and one in Utah, as future sources of synthetic production. *Ibid.*, 49–51; *Hearings* on S.J. Res. 208 (1938), 34–36; *Hearings* on H.J. Res. 176 and 181 (1939), 29, 270.

[55] Brief of the American Association of Port Authorities, *Hearings* on S.J. Res. 83 and 92 (1939), 230; testimony of Earl Warren, *ibid.*, 373; testimony of George W. Trammell, *Hearings* on H.J. Res. 176 and 181 (1939), 173.

[56] *Hearings* on S.J. Res. 83 and 92 (1939), 347.

[57] Testimony of Thomas Dockweiler, *ibid.*, 262–63; testimony of Earl Warren, *ibid.*, 375; minority report of John W. Tolan on S.J. Res. 208 in H.R. Rept. No. 2378, p. 5.

able to extract large quantities of oil from wells sunk on the edge of the reserve. The Navy did not have sense enough to put down off-set wells, with the result that an estimated 150,000,000 barrels of oil were lost to the Navy."[58] Representative Michener of Michigan, a member of the House Judiciary Committee, twitted Captain Stuart on the "sudden" interest taken by the Navy in oil reserves. Oil, Congressman Michener pointed out, had been discovered off the shores of California many years before, and he wrung an admission from the Captain that the Navy was just now, for the first time, suddenly interested in the area as a possible reserve.[59]

Regardless of the protestations of the Navy Department that oil and its conservation were the sole objective, opponents of the legislation continued to look on it with suspicion. Advocates of the legislation did nothing to allay these fears, for they were not decided among themselves what tactics and policies to pursue. They abandoned almost at once the declaration of general policy applicable to all the marginal seas in favor of a declaration aimed solely at the California offshore areas. Representative Sam Hobbs of Alabama, who pushed the resolutions, stated frankly that he favored a resolution of general application. Having tried and failed on that point, he was now trying for California alone to see if he could get that much—the old divide-and-rule principle.[60]

The arguments in the hearings were centered mainly on questions of title. In contrast, Representative Hobbs advanced his "nonownership" theory, which was to be followed to a considerable degree by the Supreme Court eight years later in *United States* v. *California*.

I maintain that title is not a question nor an element in our consideration. Title means, as I understand it, that which comes from some muniment of ownership. We claim no fee-simple title, or I claim no fee-simple title in the Government to any part of the ocean—surface, body, or bed. I maintain that under international law, which is just as well recognized as ABC, that fee-simple title, subject to the littoral nations' absolute control even to appropriation, rests in the family of nations. . . . There is no fee-simple title of any State to any part of the submerged lands, or in the tide lands for that matter.[61]

[58] Letter to the writer dated 29 November 1947. Ickes noted that during his stay in the Interior Department he had "never found that the Navy fought hard for the public interest with respect to oil."

[59] *Hearings* on S.J. Res. 208 (1938), 40. It should be remembered that oil was first discovered off the California coast in 1897. See p. 66 above.

[60] *Hearings* on H.J. Res. 176 and 181 (1939), 4–5.

[61] *Hearings* on S.J. Res. 83 and 92 (1939), 19. On the next page of his testi-

In other words, it was contended that neither the states nor the federal government had any title to the oil.[62] The lands containing oil-bearing sands are actually nothing but the bed of the ocean, which in turn belongs to the family of nations, subject only to the right of the United States to assert "ownership" within the three-mile limit—which assertion Representative Hobbs claimed had never been made by the United States and which he sought to effect by means of these resolutions.[63] The Navy adopted the main outlines of this position.[64] To add to the general confusion, the Justice Department said it wasn't sure whether title to the lands lay with the states or the United States or whether, as Hobbs claimed, there was no title at all.[65]

The opponents of the resolutions classed Hobbs' doctrine of nonownership as a "dangerously novel theory" and called it "completely and demonstrably fallacious."[66] Under the doctrine, they contended, the lands of the marginal sea, being ownerless, could be appropriated

---

mony Hobbs did modify the last phrase of his statement and conceded to the states a "99.9 percent fee-simple title" in the tidelands, using that word in its technical sense as the area lying between high- and low-water marks.

[62] *Ibid.,* 28.

[63] *Hearings* on H.J. Res. 176 and 181 (1939), 9–10. For similar statements of Hobbs' position see *Hearings* on S.J. Res. 83 and 92 (1939), 25–26, 28–30, 44–45; *Hearings* on S.J. Res. 208 (1938), 17–18, 42–43, 72, 131–32.

[64] Testimony of Philip Buettner, principal attorney, Judge Advocate General's Office, Navy Department, *Hearings* on S.J. Res. 208 (1938), 258. Buettner did an extremely inept job of testifying, allowing himself to become confused and to be caught in numerous contradictions. Had it not been for Representative Hobbs, who was present at this hearing and who asked him a number of leading questions requiring only yes and no answers, the entire position of the Navy Department would have been so confused as to be incomprehensible. *Ibid.,* 44–50.

Leslie C. McNemar adopted Hobbs' interpretation, though it must be admitted that he leaned more heavily upon the "necessity" for the resolutions than upon the Hobbsian theory of "nonownership." *Hearings* on S.J. Res. 83 and 92 (1939), 73, 76; *Hearings* on H.J. Res. 176 and 181 (1939), 36, 42–43. The following dialogue from the latter hearings (p. 40) is indicative of McNemar's testimony:

"MR. MICHENER. Now, what we have here involves a question of title.

"MR. McNEMAR. A question of title? Not title.

"MR. MICHENER. If it were not a question of title, you would start your proceedings at once.

"MR. McNEMAR. It is not a question of title. Title has a definite relation to public or private lands; or, if you are talking about personal property, it may have a definite relationship there.

"MR. MICHENER. Or to real property.

"MR. McNEMAR. Or to real property; real or personal. We are not talking about either of those things here, and the term 'title' has no application below the high-water mark, so far as I can find out."

[65] Testimony of Frank Chambers, special assistant to the Attorney General, Department of Justice, *Hearings* on S.J. Res. 208 (1938), 59–60, 111–12.

[66] Brief of Texas, *Hearings* on S.J. Res. 83 and 92 (1939), 95.

by the first nation, even an enemy one, making a claim to such lands. And even if the littoral nation alone had the right to make such a declaration, each original state after the Revolution was free and independent and came into the right, if it existed at all. The original states did not divest themselves of it when establishing the Constitution. They must, therefore, have retained the right. Even under Hobbs' theory, moreover, California had set her boundaries in her constitution and had assumed this very right.[67] And, argued the opponents, what real difference did it make anyhow? Call it fee simple title, paramount rights, or what have you, the end result was the same—the taking of the oil in a manner exactly as though the United States did, in fact, have ownership.[68]

The small but vociferous group that had been interested for years in getting the Department of the Interior to issue to them federal leases to the submerged and tidelands areas off the coast of California tossed a third idea into the title–no-title argument by contending that the United States had obtained title to the areas from Mexico through the Treaty of Guadalupe Hidalgo. The United States, they claimed further, had never severed that title. Therefore these applicants were appearing before the Congressional committees to demand that some action be taken to force the Department of the Interior to issue federal leases to them.[69]

Senate Joint Resolutions 83 and 92 and House Joint Resolution 176 had not been based on an open assertion of title by the United States. These resolutions stated that

. . . the conservation of petroleum deposits underlying submerged lands adjacent to and along the coast of the State of California, below low-water mark and under the territorial waters of the United States of America, is hereby declared to be essential for national defense, maintenance of the Navy, and regulation and protection of interstate and foreign commerce, and that in the exercise of the paramount and exclusive powers of

[67] "Supplemental Memorandum of the Committee on Law and Legislation of the American Association of Port Authorities," *ibid.*, 240–41.

[68] Testimony of R. W. Fairchild, *ibid.*, 106; testimony of Robert A. Stuart, *Hearings* on H.J. Res. 176 and 181 (1939), 78.

[69] Testimony of Samuel A. King, *Hearings* on S.J. Res. 83 and 92 (1939), 404–405, 408–10; "Brief of the Law Firm of Hudson, Creyke, and Hudson Supporting Appeals to the Secretary of the Interior on Behalf of Applicants for Leases in Submerged Lands under the Federal Leasing Act of 1920," reprinted *ibid.*, 397–401; testimony of Thomas L. Blanton, *Hearings* on S.J. Res. 208 (1938), 9–10.

the United States for those purposes, there are hereby reserved and set aside as a naval petroleum reserve any and all such deposits. . . .[70]

As Representative Hobbs expressed it: "We claim absolutely that neither the State nor the Federal Government has title to this oil, but we think that the Federal Government has the absolute right to take and use it in the performance of its constitutional powers."[71] The Navy, the Coast Guard, and the Revenue Service needed oil to run their ships. Within the marginal seas, he contended, the federal government had absolute control for the purposes specified in the Constitution: (1) regulation of navigation and control of foreign and interstate commerce, (2) national defense, (3) provision and maintenance of a navy, and (4) "national sovereignty." The federal government thus held rights superior to any other right within the area below low-water mark and out to the three-mile limit.[72]

The Navy Department argued that in this zone the United States could exercise any authority necessary for national defense.[73] The exercise of the power of eminent domain was not necessary below low-water mark. McNemar stated the position:

The primary jurisdiction over upland territory is in the individual, under the system of American jurisprudence as we received it from England. We superimposed upon that State jurisdiction and the right of eminent domain to take for compensation, and we superimposed upon that United States jurisdiction, and we can take from either one or both, as the case may be; and in the case of uplands compensation has to be paid because the fifth amendment to the Constitution provides it, but below high-water mark it does not apply.[74]

In answer to a question by Senator Holman as to whether or not the federal government could take possession, without compensation to a state or anyone to whom a state might have deeded or leased these areas, McNemar answered an unequivocal yes.[75] Assuming always that

[70] The three resolutions are identical in this respect.

[71] *Hearings* on S.J. Res. 83 and 92 (1939), 28.

[72] *Hearings* on S.J. Res. 208 (1938), 50.

[73] Leslie C. McNemar, *Hearings* on H.J. Res. 176 and 181 (1939), 42. He stated his belief that the Navy could take, without compensation, oysters in this marginal-sea area, were it proved that oysters were absolutely necessary to the maintenance of the Navy.

[74] *Hearings* on S.J. Res. 83 and 92 (1939), 430–31.

[75] *Ibid.*, 431. Senate Joint Resolutions 83, 92, and 208 and House Joint Resolution 176 were specifically drawn to exclude any possibility of claims of compensation. See section 3 of each of these resolutions.

the necessity has been shown, under this argument the United States has the right to take the oil in the submerged pools in the marginal sea without compensation; to obtain oil in upland pools, however, the national government is subject to the revisions of the Fifth Amendment.[76]

Cases were cited in which the United States did destroy, without compensation, certain lands and valuable assets below low-water mark as an incidental exercise of federal power.[77] Among these cases were the *Hawkins Point Lighthouse Case*, the *Bailey and Fulgham* case, the *Blue Point Oyster* case, and the *Greenleaf Lumber* case previously discussed.[78] Unfortunately, argued McNemar, these cases seem to indicate by "incorrect language" that the United States has such a power only in connection with the exercise of the commerce power. Actually, so he said, "nothing was ever further from the truth. The United States Government has those powers [to take land without compensation as an incidental exercise of delegated powers] in connection with every power conferred upon it by the Constitution. All it has to show, under the decision in *McCulloch* v. *Maryland*, is that it reasonably applies and it is one of the powers that it has and that it is a reasonable exercise of

[76] *Hearings* on H.J. Res. 176 and 181 (1939), 280. Although Hobbs and McNemar were in essential agreement on most points, it is typical of the lack of co-ordination among the advocates of these measures that McNemar measured the superior rights from high-water mark, whereas Hobbs conceded to the states an almost clear title to the area between high- and low-water marks, or the "tidelands" in the technical sense. See n. 61 this chapter.

[77] *Hearings* on S.J. Res. 83 and 92 (1939), 84.

[78] Pp. 39–42. The writer has found a case which was not discussed by McNemar. Yet the case ties in perfectly with his statement that eminent domain does not apply below high-water mark. It might have supplied an additional stone for an otherwise weak structure. Curiously enough, this case seems to have been ignored by both sides all the way through the controversy. While it is true that this is only a district court case (as were some of the cases upon which McNemar relied), the court held that the shore and lands under waters of the navigable streams and waters of New Jersey, which prior to the Revolution had belonged to the Crown as a part of the *jura regalia* of the Crown, passed to the state at the close of the war. But the state succeeded to them as trustee for the people at large, the right of the state not constituting property such as is susceptible of pecuniary compensation; the lands were not private property within the meaning of the Fifth Amendment to the Constitution, providing that private property shall not be taken for public use without just compensation. *Stockton* v. *Baltimore & N.Y. R. Co.,* 32 F. 9 (1887).

All of these cases say, in effect, that investments made in navigable waters are always subject to destruction without compensation upon the exercise by the central government of its admitted powers over interstate commerce. Persons making such investments are presumed to have knowledge of this risk. The cases do not say that agents of the national government may seize property simply because it lies below low-water mark.

that power."[79] Commander Harold Biesemeier of the Navy Judge Advocate General's Office stated that he did not want to rest the Navy's case solely upon the commerce power but that he wanted to see the power of "national defense stand on its own feet."[80]

The Navy attempted to bolster its case by giving the impression that the executive branch of the government could stop drilling by powers already delegated, but that the executive vastly preferred to have the sanction of Congress as expressed in the resolutions. An act of Congress of 8 August 1917[81] was cited, which empowered the President to establish defensive sea areas in the navigable waters of the United States and to issue such regulations governing the conduct of persons within those areas as might be necessary for national defense. What was to prevent the President from establishing a defensive sea area in the submerged oil fields and then issuing regulations to stop the drilling operations?[82] Of course, it was admitted, this would not get the oil for the Navy or prevent upland operators from continuing to pump,[83] but it would "force the private interests to desist from wantonly destroying these petroleum deposits . . . and prevent this oil from being . . . supplied to a certain Asiatic nation under circumstances inimical to our national defense."[84]

Or, it was insinuated, what was to prevent the Secretary of War from re-establishing the harbor lines at Long Beach, for example, so as to recapture all of the harbor below mean high-water mark filled in since 1850—all this without compensation? This would force the surrender of the oil wells in operation in the area, though it would not give the Navy the thing it supposedly wanted, a naval petroleum reserve.[85] Or perhaps the President could simply close the port of Long Beach, with the remedy against the abuse of this power coming from the Congress and not the courts.[86] In other words, the Navy was gently waving a large stick over the opponents of the resolutions and saying, in effect,

[79] *Hearings* on S.J. Res. 83 and 92 (1939), 431.
[80] *Hearings* on S.J. Res. 208 (1938), 124.
[81] 40 U.S. Stat. 250, §8.
[82] Testimony of Commander Harold Biesemeier, *Hearings* on S.J. Res. 208 (1938), 119.
[83] *Ibid.*, 122.
[84] Brief of Leslie C. McNemar, *Hearings* on S.J. Res. 83 and 92 (1939), 88.
[85] *Ibid.*, 87.
[86] The Navy, all the way through its arguments, almost completely ignored the geologically proved fact that this area could not be created a reserve. It is amazing that, in the face of overwhelming evidence to the contrary, the Navy could continue to talk in terms of a "reserve," for such an accomplishment was impossible.

"If we can't get our naval petroleum reserve, we will at least see to it that you don't get to operate your wells."

The opponents of the resolutions met these arguments with a single basic attack. W. Page Keeton summed it up quite well when he said, in a law review commentary, that the cases, such as the *Blue Point Oyster* case and the *Bailey and Fulgham* case, holding that the federal government may appropriate, as an incident of the commerce power, lands below the surface of the water, were not authority for the idea that oil "can be utilized by the Government as an aid to the defense of the country and the operation of a navy." If oil is needed for such a purpose, it can be condemned or purchased just as it can elsewhere in the United States and subject to the same limitations.[87] The United States, it was argued, holds only an easement or servitude over these areas for the improvement and regulation of commerce.[88] If these oil deposits can be taken without payment simply because the Navy "needs" them, why would it not be possible to "appropriate the Capitol Building of the State of Texas . . . to provide a barracks for housing the Army . . . without compensation to the State?"[89] Why not take shoes, by Congressional declaration, because the Army needs them, saying of course that the Army isn't taking title but merely wearing the shoes out because of the "necessities" of national defense?[90]

The commerce power carries with it no right, so the opponents of the resolutions argued, to take the soil itself for any but a purpose incident to the improvement of navigation. And even under such circumstances the title does not pass; the federal government has only an easement. The right of the United States in this regard is strictly limited to the purposes of facilitating and regulating navigation.[91]

The executive departments were in accord on one phase of their various presentations to Congress in support of these resolutions. They were uniformly agreed that, in order to accomplish their purpose, it was necessary for the Congress to assert some right, to assert a policy in regard to the marginal sea, and then to direct the Attorney General

[87] W. Page Keeton, "Federal and State Claims to Submerged Lands under Coastal Waters," 25 *Texas Law Review* (1947), 262, 268.

[88] Testimony of R. W. Fairchild, *Hearings* on H.J. Res. 176 and 181 (1939), 95.

[89] Testimony of R. W. Fairchild, *Hearings* on S.J. Res. 83 and 92 (1939), 136.

[90] Testimony of William McCraw, then attorney general of Texas, *Hearings* on S.J. Res. 208 (1938), 253.

[91] "Brief of the State of California against Resolutions 176 and 181," *Hearings* on S.J. Res. 83 and 92 (1939), 367; brief of Texas, *ibid.*, 99, 101; testimony of R. W. Fairchild, *ibid.*, 134–35.

of the United States to push that declaration. Leslie McNemar felt that it would be impossible to get a judicial determination of a case involving submerged lands in the absence of such a declaration. A mere directive to the Attorney General to bring a suit to determine the rights of the national government as against the states would not be sufficient.[92] The Department of Justice representatives stated officially that the department wanted a resolution, such as those proposed by Nye and Hobbs, which would cover all eventualities. The possibility that the area might not be owned by anyone was covered by a declaration asserting the right of occupancy. True, if the question was simply one of title, there was no need for a declaration before action could be taken, but the Nye and Hobbs resolutions covered all the possibilities.[93]

The O'Connor resolution, House Joint Resolution 181, did not meet the Navy's test, for it did not make the bringing of the suit mandatory on the part of the Attorney General, but merely directed him to conduct an investigation and then to proceed at his discretion. In addition, the O'Connor resolution was unsatisfactory to the Navy in that it would have placed the submerged lands under the control of the Interior Department.[94]

Congressman Hobbs considered the resolutions necessary to call into play the dormant powers of Congress, for "there are three coordinate branches of the Federal Government. The executive branch has no policy-making function. All it can do is execute the laws enacted by Congress. The courts can say what the law is, can interpret it, but the Congress and the Congress alone has the power to legislate, which is to make laws, and to make declarations of public policy, such as this."[95] Further, if the United States already had title to the area, or if a resolution were enacted taking occupancy under the nonownership theory,

---

[92] *Ibid.*, 55–56. He thus guessed incorrectly on the manner in which *United States* v. *California, United States* v. *Texas,* and *United States* v. *Louisiana* were finally brought.

[93] Testimony of Frank Chambers, *Hearings* on S.J. Res. 208 (1938), 59–60; testimony of William B. Jones, attorney for the Department of Justice, *ibid.*, 206.

The Navy had wanted the Justice Department to proceed to take action, declaration or no declaration; but since the Justice Department had to handle the action, and since it felt that there was some doubt as to title, the Navy acceded to the argument of the Justice Department. Testimony of Commander Harold Biesemeier, *ibid.*, 129–30.

[94] Testimony of Representative James F. O'Connor, *Hearings* on H.J. Res. 176 and 181 (1939), 190–91.

[95] *Hearings* on S.J. Res. 83 and 92 (1939), 27. To the same effect see brief of Leslie C. McNemar, *ibid.*, 74; testimony of same, *ibid.*, 65; letter from Charles Edison, Assistant Secretary of the Navy, dated 20 February 1939, reprinted *ibid.*, 21–22.

the petroleum deposits would then become property subject to the disposition of Congress under the Constitution. Thus the resolutions, with their declaration that the areas were established as a naval petroleum reserve were, in effect, a disposition of property by Congress.[96]

One section of the outside group of Californians who hoped to secure federal leases to already proved and producing submerged lands went on record as favoring the necessity for the resolutions. Saying that the average citizen wished to see these resources developed by "legitimate capital" rather than "pirates," one attorney for these interests said that the Attorney General would welcome and need the backing of Congress to bring the suits.[97] Representative Murdock thought the resolutions should be passed to force the Attorney General to action, and contended that Congress should advise and even command when it saw the executive branch of government not taking an action which it was its duty to take.[98]

Opponents of the resolutions countered that if the United States already owned these lands, then no resolution was necessary for the Attorney General to take the requisite action. If the United States did not have title, the passage of resolutions would not create it.[99] At the most, urged the opponents, if a declaration is deemed necessary by the Congress, make it only a simple direction to the Attorney General to bring suit.[100] Thus, if the states were forced to meet such a suit, the two parties would come into court equal, without the possible prejudice to the states' case which might result from a declaration of national paramount rights or ownership.[101]

Such arguments ignored the nonownership theory of Congressman Hobbs. How could the Attorney General act if these lands were, in fact, not capable of ownership? The representatives of the states never

[96] Testimony of Leslie C. McNemar, *ibid.,* 423, and in *Hearings* on H.J. Res. 176 and 181 (1939), 273.

[97] Brief of Robert B. Keenan, *Hearings* on S.J. Res. 83 and 92 (1939), 448. The inference was that those seeking federal leases constituted "legitimate interests," whereas those operating under the authority of California leases were "pirates."

[98] *Hearings* on S.J. Res. 208 (1938), 179. The representative drew no line between valid and invalid Congressional interference with the administrative branch of the government.

[99] Testimony of Robert A. Stuart, *Hearings* on S.J. Res. 83 and 92 (1939), 159; brief of same, *ibid.,* 148; testimony of same, *Hearings* on H.J. Res. 176 and 181 (1939), 77; testimony of Joseph A. Loret, *Hearings* on S.J. Res. 83 and 92 (1939), 203.

[100] Statement of Senator Tom Connally, *Hearings* on H.J. Res. 176 and 181 (1939), 20.

[101] Testimony of Joseph A. Loret, *Hearings* on S.J. Res. 83 and 92 (1939), 203.

really answered this basic question. They chose instead to argue that
one authority or the other must own the area and therefore the ideas
expressed by Hobbs were so much theoretical nonsense. In the light of
events which transpired in 1947 and 1950, they should not have dismissed the argument so lightly.

The representatives of the states feared that the executive branch of
the national government was attempting to get something for nothing
without allowing the issue to be met justiciably at all.[102] This fear was
engendered by a portion of a letter written by the Secretary of the
Navy, Claude Swanson, to the chairman of the Senate Committee on
Public Lands in answer to a query by the committee on the stand of
the Navy Department on Nye's earlier resolutions:

> Such an act [passage of the resolution] would be of a political nature,
> and therefore it would be sustained by the courts. It is not the province of
> the courts to participate in the discussion of questions arising out of juris-
> diction or dominion, for they are of a political nature, and not judicial.
> National dominion and sovereignty may be extended over the sea as well
> as over the land, and in our Government, when Congress and the Presi-
> dent assert dominion and sovereignty over any portion of the seas, or over
> any body of water, the courts are bound by it.[103]

It was contended, therefore, that the Navy was afraid to go into court
without a Congressional declaration asserting title or paramount interest—a declaration which would then be used to prevent the court from
taking jurisdiction on the grounds that the issue was a political one.[104]
The assertions of the Navy that this controversy was generated by the
"unfortunate wording" of the letter and that the Navy was not seeking
to pull a "double cross" and close the issue as against possible judicial
determination were unavailing.[105] The advocates of the states had
found a weak point that could be exploited, and exploit it they did.
Whether the statement in the letter was meant as it sounded or not is
a matter which cannot be determined. Nevertheless, its effects were felt,

---

[102] Testimony of Earl Warren, *ibid.*, 372.

[103] The letter is dated 21 July 1937 and is reprinted in *Hearings* on S.J. Res.
208 (1938), 31. The Secretary cited in support of his statement these cases:
In re Cooper, 143 U.S. 472 (1892); *Wilson* v. *Shaw,* 204 U.S. 24 (1906); *The
James G. Swan,* 50 F. 108 (1892); and *The Kodiak,* 53 F. 126 (1892).

[104] Testimony of Robert A. Stuart, *Hearings* on S.J. Res. 83 and 92 (1939),
159; testimony of Laurence A. Truett, assistant attorney general of Florida, *ibid.*,
189; testimony of Daniel J. Doherty, assistant attorney general of Massachusetts,
ibid., 174; testimony of R. W. Fairchild, *ibid.*, 124–25.

[105] Testimony of Leslie C. McNemar, *ibid.*, 71–72, 430.

and attempts to explain it away merely caused the opponents of the resolutions to stress the point the more.[106]

The advocates of state control concentrated their fire on each of the points of the government as noted; at the same time they endeavored to establish positively that the state of California and not the United States already owned the specific land under discussion. It is not necessary here to go into the legal arguments advanced, as they are substantially those covered in detail in Chapters 2 through 6. Instead of splitting the opposition by choosing to aim at the coastal lands of California alone, the representatives of the federal government merely solidified the states, inland and coastal alike, in a firm stand against the resolutions. No state official appeared in support of the resolutions or in any way indicated anything but opposition to them. Representative Hobbs stated frankly, as has been noted, that he felt the substance of his resolution should be asserted everywhere; but since he had been unable to get such a resolution reported favorably, he had decided to concentrate on California.[107] The Navy thought that a resolution covering all the coastal states would be "fine," but it was interested solely in the establishment of a naval reserve.[108] The Navy couldn't understand why the resolutions had seemed to "stir up" conditions,[109] or why the states

---

[106] A careful reading of the cases which the Secretary cited discloses that none were within the three-mile zone off the shore of any state. Most of them involved Alaskan waters beyond the three-mile limit. The quotation from the "unfortunately worded" letter is almost verbatim from *The Kodiak*, 53 F. 126, 130 (1892). The word "political," therefore, seems advisedly chosen. One has only the statements of the two contending parties as to the motives involved, and no accurate way of determining what the Navy Department really had in mind at the time the letter was written. The writer's opinion is that the Navy would have followed the course predicted by the opponents of the resolutions, had such resolutions passed.

[107] *Hearings* on S.J. Res. 208 (1938), 19; *Hearings* on S.J. Res. 83 and 92 (1939), 18; *Hearings* on H.J. Res. 176 and 181 (1939), 5.

The late Senator Hiram Johnson of California gave Senator Nye a bit of a lecture about the singling out of California when he said: "I cannot, for the life of me, see, first, what the interest of Senator Nye is, unless it be a patriotic duty. Secondly, I cannot understand why, having asked the Congress for this authority as to all the States, he did not persist in having all the States agree; in having all the States included in the one [resolution] that is now before us." *Hearings* on S.J. Res. 83 and 92 (1939), 69.

Senator Nye answered Johnson by saying that his interest was, indeed, "purely patriotic." Conceding that it was "rather futile to hope for the accomplishment" of his original resolution, he argued that a slice is better than no bread at all. *Ibid.*, 69–70.

[108] Testimony of Leslie C. McNemar, *Hearings* on S.J. Res. 83 and 92 (1939), 68.

[109] *Ibid.*, 432.

found it impossible to believe Navy protestations that only an oil reserve was wanted.

Representatives of the states were quite certain that the principle which Hobbs and Nye sought to enunciate for California's petroleum-rich submerged lands would apply equally to the submerged lands off the coasts of all the states. Californians and others alike agreed on this point.[110] By 1945, when hearings were held on resolutions which would have "quitclaimed" any possible national rights in the marginal-sea areas, this opposition had crystallized; forty-six of the forty-eight state attorneys general supported a brief in opposition to the claims of the United States.[111] The attempt to split the inland states away from their coastal sisters had been singularly unsuccessful, once the entire problem had been blasted out in the open at Congressional hearings. Senator Connally had it figured thus: the advocates of national supremacy in the marginal-sea areas calculated that the thirteen original states and Texas had the strongest case and therefore picked California as being the most vulnerable to attack. If the proposition "worked" with California, advocates of national control would then be ready to push their claims elsewhere.[112]

Generally the states endeavored to argue that the issue was one solely of title. On that basis, the various representatives urged that the history of the submerged lands and the actions of the courts and the political branches of the federal government had all tended to establish title in the states. More important, the states had acted as though they held the title.[113] They did not now wish to see that title, which

---

[110] Testimony of Joseph A. Loret, *Hearings* on S.J. Res. 83 and 92 (1939), 203; brief of same, *ibid.*, 192; brief of California, *ibid.*, 354; Representative Tolan's minority report in H.R. Rept. 2378, p. 4; statement of Senator Tom Connally, *Hearings* on S.J. Res. 83 and 92 (1939), 10–11; statement by same, *Hearings* on H.J. Res. 176 and 181 (1939), 23; testimony of James V. Allred, governor of Texas, *Hearings* on S.J. Res. 208 (1938), 81; testimony of Earl Warren, *Hearings* on S.J. Res. 83 and 92 (1939), 372; testimony of Laurence A. Truett, *ibid.*, 189–90; statement of Senator Morris Sheppard, *ibid.*, 6–7.

[111] Reprinted in *Hearings* on H.J. Res. 118 *et al.* (1945), 12 ff. This group was most active throughout the entire quarrel. Walter R. Johnson, attorney general of Nebraska, as president of the group, conducted a lively battle on behalf of California; he became their Washington lobbyist, pressing for quitclaim legislation. The activities of this organization will receive consideration later.

[112] *Hearings* on S.J. Res. 83 and 92 (1939), 10–11.

[113] Typical of such arguments are those developed by the "Supplemental Memorandum of the Committee on Law and Legislation of the American Association of Port Authorities," *ibid.*, 247; brief of the Land Commissioner of Texas, *ibid.*, 144; brief of Robert A. Stuart for the Texas State Teachers Association, *ibid.*, 149–51; brief of the American Association of Port Authorities, *ibid.*, 230; testimony of R. W. Fairchild, *ibid.*, 103–104; "Memorandum in Opposition

they contended they held, clouded by a Congressional assertion of title or paramount right. The net result would be a heavy burden of litigation on the states, port facilities, and others holding rights to submerged lands granted by the states. Water-front financing would be gravely hampered during the interim period between the passage of the resolution and a court declaration; and although the state advocates expressed their complete confidence that the court decision would be in their favor, they were much discouraged by what they felt was an unfair attempt by the federal government to commence a running fight on all facilities and wealth in the marginal sea.[114]

Some attention must be paid to the interests involved in terms of economic and political considerations. Mention has already been made of the fact that no state representatives supported in any way the resolutions which were proposed between 1937 and 1939. Indeed, aside from the national governmental agencies involved, only one organization was formally on record in the hearings as favoring the resolutions: that organization was the National Association of Audubon Societies.[115] Individuals went on record as favoring the resolutions, but without exception each of these had interests in federal applications for prospecting permits in the producing submerged areas offshore from California, the areas covered by the resolutions.[116] If in some way these federal

to S.J. Resolution 208 of the American Association of Port Authorities, Committee on Law and Legislation," *Hearings* on S.J. Res. 208 (1938), 84; "Memorandum in Opposition to S.J. Resolution 208 of the Port of New York Authority," *ibid.,* 89–96; testimony of Gaston Porterie, *ibid.,* 175, 182.

[114] Testimony of Earl Warren, *Hearings* on H.J. Res. 176 and 181 (1939), 198; "Memorandum in Opposition to S.J. Resolution 208 of the American Association of Port Authorities, Committee on Law and Legislation," *Hearings* on S.J. Res. 208 (1938), 86–87; testimony of Wilbur LaRoe, Jr., associate counsel of the Port of New York Authority, *ibid.,* 96; testimony of James V. Allred, *ibid.,* 82–83; brief of California, *Hearings* on S.J. Res. 83 and 92 (1939), 354–55; testimony of George W. Trammell, city attorney of Long Beach, *ibid.,* 287; testimony of George F. Nicholson, representing the American Association of Port Authorities, *ibid.,* 225–26; testimony of Robert A. Stuart, *ibid.,* 166.

[115] A letter from this group to Senator Nye said that they supported his resolution because they felt it would cut down the oil pollution of navigable waters and areas where the birds breed. Letter reprinted in *Hearings* on S.J. Res. 208 (1938), 8.

[116] Thus a letter from one E. W. Sawyer, formerly assistant to Ray Lyman Wilbur while the latter was Secretary of the Interior, intimated that Mark Megladdery, Joe Rosenthal, Carl B. Sturzenacher, Donald Richberg, and Congressman Tolan comprised an Oakland "gang." This group in turn was tied in, according to Sawyer's accusations, with the Santa Fe Railroad and the Standard Oil Company. The port authorities for the city of Oakland (California) were being forced to oppose the Nye and Hobbs resolutions because the Santa Fe Railroad held property in the city. The Standard Oil Company controlled Signal

leases could be granted, these individuals stood to make fortunes, even though they had never hazarded a dime in exploration or other costs which would have to be met before a "probable" area becomes a producing one. From the hearings, at least, one can only presume that there were few organized groups or persons without direct pecuniary interests willing to come to the support of these national officers seeking the enactment of federal control legislation.[117]

The advocates for the states were extremely successful in organizing a campaign of resistance to the resolutions, whatever may have been the motives involved. The hearings are filled with resolutions and memorials of various groups throughout the nation asking the Congress for the defeat of the measures. Some of the groups had an obvious tie-in either with oil companies or with port authorities. No representative of any oil company testified on these resolutions, and no briefs or statements were filed by any oil company. Only one private business corporation, the Santa Fe Railroad, ever appeared to protest the resolutions.[118] The overwhelming bulk of memorials against the resolutions came from public corporations, service groups, and legislative bodies.[119]

Oil Company, which in turn dominated the Long Beach and Southwest Exploration Companies, the major producer in the California submerged lands at the time Sawyer made his charges. William Randolph Hearst, too, according to Sawyer, had interests; since no congressman could be elected from California against Hearst's opposition, each member of the California Congressional delegation had to appear in opposition to the resolutions or face trouble with Hearst. Sawyer characterized the lobby against the Nye and Hobbs measures as "more insidious and vicious than either the bonus or the Townsend lobbies." Reprinted at Senator Nye's request in *Hearings* on S.J. Res. 83 and 92 (1939), 386–87. At the time Sawyer wrote the letter, he was the applicant for federal lease No. 053181 in the heart of the proved and producing Wilmington field.

[117] In the *Hearings* on H.J. Res. 176 and 181 (1939), 124, there is mention of a United Landowners Association, which appears to have been a group spearheaded by Robert E. Lee Jordan and associates of his who had applications for federal leasing permits in the California offshore lands and, therefore, a direct interest in the outcome of the legislation. This organization never appeared formally, however, and the only mention of it is made by one opposed to the resolutions. Jordan's name crops up occasionally in the controversy.

[118] Testimony of F. W. Clements, attorney for the Atchison, Topeka & Santa Fe Railroad Co., *Hearings* on S.J. Res. 208 (1938), 220 ff.

[119] Groups in opposition to the resolutions with statements in *Hearings* on S.J. Res. 83 and 92 (1939), 205–24, 368–69, 383–85, 392–93: National Rivers and Harbors Congress; Texas Ports Association; Legislature of Alabama; Legislature of New Jersey; City Council of Milwaukee; State Council of Parks of the State of New York; Greater Harbor Association of Los Angeles (a group representing two hundred merchants, shippers, and transportation firms); Civil and Structural Engineers Association of Long Beach; Board of Port Commissioners of the City of Oakland; Council of the Borough of Stone Harbor, New Jersey; Board of Supervisors of Santa Barbara County; State Port Authority of Virginia; Board

There was, on the side of the states, a considerable amount of money expended to get these various groups to act in concert in order to give the appearance of spontaneity. But charges that advocates of state ownership were in the "pay" of large oil interests are not true. The oil companies could hardly have purchased the support of so diversified a list.

In summary, those favoring the enactment of the Nye and Hobbs resolutions believed (1) that the United States either had title or had superior rights in the marginal-sea area off the coast of California, such superior rights accruing to the United States by implication from the powers delegated to the national government; and (2) that the Congress of the United States, in order to bring these paramount rights into play, must declare the existence of such rights by appropriate legislation.

Opponents of the resolutions, while giving casual recognition to the superior-rights argument, chose rather to center their attack around the single issue of which authority had title to the area. They thus presented a united front in pushing the single idea that title to the area below low-water mark belonged to the littoral states. They committed a tactical error in so discounting the nonownership theory of their opponents; the advocates for the states could not shake loose from the well-beaten paths of legal thought into which they had strait-jacketed themselves. Their total arguments against the measures were far superior to those advanced in attempting to establish positively their own position. Perhaps this is due in no small measure to the fact that they were on the defensive, fighting against the passage of a legislative measure; their tactics could, therefore, be devoted to the destruction of the arguments of their adversaries rather than to an attempt to build a solid foundation for their own ideas. The argument of the states was a legal one; the argument of the agencies of the national government was only incidentally legal and was built upon the foundation of need for national security.

---

of Harbor Commissioners of the City of Los Angeles; Legislature of California; Philadelphia Chamber of Commerce; City Council of Ashtabula, Ohio; San Francisco Chamber of Commerce; Albany Port District Commission; and Railway Commission of the State of Texas. Other groups in opposition: Board of Commerce and Navigation of New Jersey, South Jersey Port Commission, and Texas Bankers Association, with statements in *Hearings* on S.J. Res. 208 (1938), 34, 135–36, 207; delegation of the state of Louisiana in Congress, with statement in *Hearings* on H.J. Res. 176 and 181 (1939), 178.

8 ·

Executive Policy on Submerged Lands
Prior to United States *v.* California

It has been shown that the Congress prior to 1937 had assumed that the submerged lands belonged to the littoral states. It was only after the actions of Senator Nye and, later, Congressman Hobbs that the issue of national ownership or control was pressed. The Navy Department, the Department of Justice, and the Department of the Interior very definitely favored the adoption of the Nye and Hobbs resolutions in 1938 and 1939; there can be no doubt that these departments supported the principle of national control, if not ownership, at that time. What had been the policy of the executive branch of the government toward ownership and control of the submerged lands prior to the introduction of the Nye and Hobbs resolutions? Were the executive departments prior to 1938 quiescent as the Congress had been?

The United States, acting through its executive departments in furtherance of Congressional declarations of policy, requested and received from the states bordering the oceans some 195 grants of land, leases, or easements involving areas under navigable waters. In at least 15 of these instances, the land concerned was located below low-water mark in the open sea; in the other instances the lands were under rivers, lakes, harbors, or bays.[1]

In the case of land grants, the executive officers of the United States asked for and obtained from the states certificates of title passing title in fee simple to the United States. The national officers did not assert

[1] Admission of these facts and discussion of the 195 grants is contained in United States brief, *California* case, 227 ff.

122

a claim to the submerged lands which were requested, either on the basis of title or on the basis of superior rights in the United States. Indeed, prior to the bringing of action against the Pacific Western Oil Company in 1945,[2] it appears that no executive officer of the government of the United States ever asserted formally on behalf of the United States a claim to any portion of the coastal waters of any state. At least no mention of such an instance was made in the United States brief in the case of *United States* v. *California*. It would be supposed that such an assertion would have been mentioned had one ever been made, for the *California* answer was full of examples of rulings by national officers that title to submerged lands lay with the states. As James V. Allred of Texas said, the Attorney General of the United States and the Secretary of the Interior were very "zealous" men with competent staffs, yet down to the time of the hearings on the Nye and Hobbs resolutions they had never attempted to assert a title or superior national right in these areas.[3]

Under an 1899 act of Congress,[4] the War Department was charged with the responsibility for determining whether the construction of jetties, oil rigs, and other structures in navigable waters interfered with navigation or commerce. In California (except for the oil rigs erected in the Summerland field prior to 1899), Louisiana, and Texas, every lessee under state authority received the permission of the War Department to erect each derrick. In every case the lessee advised the War Department that he held a permit or lease from the state.[5]

[2] *United States* v. *Pacific Western Oil Corp.,* filed 29 May 1945 in the Federal District Court for the Southern District of California. The suit was dismissed upon the filing of *United States* v. *California.*

[3] *Hearings* on S.J. Res. 208 (1938), 79.

[4] 30 U.S. Stat. 1151.

[5] See California answer, 788. At 789–95 is sketched a typical example of such a War Department permit, in this case for a lease which was at issue in the *Pacific Western* suit and described in paragraph 6 of the complaint in *United States* v. *California*. On 18 April 1929, S. M. Spaulding made written request to the War Department for permission to construct a pier. He told the War Department that he held California permit or lease No. 92 and wanted to build a two-thousand-foot pier. He accompanied his request with a drawing (reproduced in the answer at 790). On 4 May 1929 the War Department granted Spaulding his permit to construct the pier according to the drawing submitted; on 26 September 1929 the Pacific Western Corporation advised that it now held permit No. 92 and asked permission of the War Department to extend the pier. On 9 October 1929 the War Department authorized the extension and other work. On 17 November 1932, Pacific Western asked for a time extension to complete the work. Permission for time extension was granted by the district

A permit was secured from the War Department for the construction of the Rainbow Pier and Municipal Auditorium at Long Beach, California, a structure extending out into the open sea some 1,400 feet. The pier is of semicircular design and encloses some forty-seven acres of tide and submerged lands.[6] On 27 November 1925 the Miami Beach Pier Corporation, Miami Beach, Florida, applied for and later received from the War Department a waiver of objections to construct the Miami Beach Pier.[7] Robert A. Stuart cited an instance in which the consent of the War Department was secured to the drilling of an oil well in Galveston Bay. Some years later, the state of Texas received the permission of the Army to make further seismograph soundings. The citizens of Galveston protested the drilling of further wells, and a public hearing was held with the Army sitting in on the proceedings. The official report of the Army to Washington stated that so long as navigation was not being interferred with, the Army had no right to stop the drilling of wells on the Texas coast.[8] The state of New York had made "thousands" of grants in underwater areas around the state. When an application for such a grant was received, New York cleared it with the War Department. If the War Department stated that the projected application would interfere with navigation or commerce, the state denied the application.[9]

In 1938, Harry W. Edelstein, of the Department of Justice, affirmed that these actions had been in line with the traditional policy of the War Department.[10] The War Department made no effort to protect whatever interest the United States may have had in the areas below low-water mark. Indeed, it is possible to cite numbers of instances in

---

engineer on 28 November 1932. On 12 July 1933, Pacific Western wrote the United States district engineer, advising him of the portion yet to be finished. Permission was asked to construct an additional lateral pier. On 31 July 1933 the War Department granted permission to construct the lateral pier. On 18 August 1933, Pacific Western submitted a request for a change in design and location of the lateral pier. On 29 August 1933 the change was approved by the War Department. On 18 March 1934 the War Department granted a further time extension and permission to construct two additional piers. On 29 March 1935 a permit was granted for an extension to an existing pier on submerged lands. On 6 May 1935, Pacific Western was given War Department permission to widen and lengthen an existing pier.

No question of rights of the United States was ever broached or in any way suggested during the course of these negotiations.

[6] *Ibid.,* 755.

[7] *Freed* v. *Miami Beach Pier Corp.,* 112 So. 841 (Fla. 1927).

[8] *Hearings* on S.J. Res. 208 (1938), 136–37.

[9] Testimony of Warren H. Gilman, *ibid.,* 183.

[10] *Ibid.,* 65–66.

which representatives of the War Department, customarily the district engineer, went so far as to say that the state held title to tide and submerged lands.[11]

The Attorney General of the United States is required by statute to render his opinion on title to any and all lands acquired or received by the United States before the erection of any improvements.[12] In *United States* v. *California* the state argued that the Attorney General of the United States down through the years had followed a consistent policy of ruling that lands under navigable waters were the property of the state. Most of the rulings, however, do not involve lands in the open sea. In the case of two opinions by Attorney General John G. Sargent involving certain areas off the shore of the Fort Canby Military Reservation, the inference can be drawn that the state of Washington as grantor could have granted more land, less land, or nothing at all—in which case the United States would have had to condemn the submerged areas in order to obtain them. The area involved, however, seems to have been along the Columbia River rather than the Pacific Ocean, though the rulings do not make the point clear.[13]

In 1915 the city of Los Angeles, California, exchanged nine and three-quarters acres of submerged lands in front of Fort McArthur for lands adjacent to Deadman's Island owned by the United States. The

[11] See, e.g., H.D. No. 349, 68th Cong., 1st sess., 46–47, where the district engineer pointed out that the construction of a breakwater would allow the reclamation of "large areas" of valuable land to which the city of Long Beach would "have title." The plan for the development of Long Beach Harbor recommended by the chief of engineers was adopted by Congress. 43 U.S. Stat. 1189.

See also California answer, 91–117, 504–27; California brief, 158–60, 170–71; Appendix to California brief, 174–94. It should be noted that the Navy Department made requests for grants. There are circumstances where Naval officials declared title to a particular portion of submerged lands to be in the state. The details of these transactions, which need not be covered here, are fully documented in the California briefs.

[12] 5 U.S. Stat. 468, now embodied in Rev. Stat., §355, and in 34 U.S.C.A., §520, as amended by act of 28 June 1930 and by act of October 1940; and also embodied in 40 U.S.C.A., §255, and 50 U.S.C.A., §175. The section reads: "No public money shall be expended upon any site or land purchased by the United States for the purpose of erecting thereon . . . [a] public building, of any kind whatever, until the written opinion of the Attorney General shall be had in favor of the validity of the title. . . ."

[13] 34 Op. Atty. Gen. 428 (1925); 34 Op. Atty. Gen. 531 (1925). The United States, in meeting the California argument that the Sargent rulings did apply in the open sea, was still in doubt as to the extent of the area. Thus the United States said that the area "appears" to have been in the Columbia River rather than the open sea. United States brief, *California* case, 244.

United States attorney for the Southern District of California, speaking for the United States Department of Justice, addressed the Los Angeles city attorney as follows:

I have to advise that the Attorney General has passed the title of the City of Los Angeles to the 9.75 acres of land in the outer harbor at Los Angeles, California, which the City of Los Angeles had been heretofore authorized to transfer to the United States government in exchange for a like amount of land lying on the westerly side of the entrance channel to the inner harbor at Los Angeles, and has found the title good.

Pursuant to his instructions, a deed from the City of Los Angeles to the United States has been placed on record and I understand that the actual exchange of the property took place some time ago.[14]

This Deadman's Island transfer was classified by the United States in 1947 as being in the "doubtful" class; that is, representatives of the national government believed that there was uncertainty as to whether or not the affected areas were in the open sea.[15] Again, in 1927, William D. Mitchell, then Attorney General of the United States, found title to certain lands in San Pedro Bay to be in the city of Los Angeles.[16] Much earlier Attorney General Caleb Cushing had ruled, in respect to certain overflowed lands at Mare Island, California, that he was

. . . satisfied that the State of California may set up, and probably maintain, title, as against the United States, to so much of Mare Island as is subject to overflow by water whether periodically or otherwise, that is, at least, to all below high water mark. . . .

It is immaterial, under these decisions, whether the general sovereignty of the United States, and their right of domain, came by treaty with a foreign power or otherwise. In all cases, on the admission of any State into the Union, the land of the shores below high water mark passes to and vests in that State, by virtue of the Constitution.[17]

One does not find, down to 1937, any assertion by the Attorney General or his subordinates in the Justice Department that the United States ever held title to any area beneath navigable waters within a state's boundaries Indeed, in *United States* v. *Brewer-Elliott Oil and*

---

[14] Quoted in California answer, 266. Italics used by the author of the California brief have been omitted.

[15] United States brief, *California* case, 233–34.

[16] California answer, 453–54.

[17] 8 Op. Atty. Gen. 422, 425 (1853). Obviously Mare Island is not in the open-sea category, for it is located in the northern part of San Francisco Bay.

Gas Co., it was agreed that if the Arkansas River was navigable the soils under it belonged to the state of Oklahoma; if nonnavigable, the area belonged to the United States.[18] The question of title turned on navigability.

There is an opinion by Edmund Randolph as Attorney General which might be taken to indicate a claim of the United States to the submerged soils under navigable waters. In a ruling issued concerning the validity of the seizure of a British ship by a French vessel in Delaware Bay, he said:

From a question originating under the foregoing circumstances, is obviously and properly excluded every consideration of a dominion over the *sea.* The solidity of our neutral right does not depend, in this case, on any of the various distances claimed on that element by the different nations possessing the neighboring shore. But if it did, the field would probably be found more extensive and more favorable to our demand than is supposed by the document above referred to; for the *necessary* or *natural* law of nations, (unchanged as it is, in the United States), will, perhaps, when combined with the treaty of Paris in 1783, justify us in attaching to our coasts an extent into the sea beyond the reach of cannon shot. The cornerstone of our claim is, that the United States are proprietors of the lands on both sides of the Delaware, from its head to its entrance into the sea.

The high ocean, in *general,* it is true, is insusceptible of becoming property. It is a gift of nature, manifestly destined for the use of all mankind—inexhaustible in its benefits—not admitting metes and bounds. But the rivers may be appropriated, because the reverse is their situation: were they open to all the world, they would prove the inlets of perpetual disturbance and discord; would soon be rendered barren by the number of those who would share in their products; and, moreover, they may be defined.[19]

The opinion is not quite clear on some points and is contradictory on others, in that it appears to accept the idea of the territorial character of the marginal sea and then in turn rejects it. This difference is manifested in the references made to "cannon shot." At the same time, the criterion to be used as basis for appropriation is definitely set out, a criterion which may be as easily applied to a three-mile zone. Randolph does speak of "attaching" territory to the coasts of the United States. Some confusion arises from the phrase "the United States are proprietors." This last statement, on its face, is patently incorrect, for the

[18] 249 F. 609 (1918), affirmed, 260 U.S. 77 (1922).
[19] 1 Op. Atty. Gen. 32, 34 (1793).

United States did not then own and could not own the land above high-water mark. The assumption must be made that the Attorney General was using the word "proprietor" in a general sense. He was speaking in terms of international law and saying that Delaware Bay was bounded on both sides by the "territory" of the United States. There is little in this letter to support the claim that the United States was a proprietor as the term is normally used.

The Department of Justice and the Attorney General, down through the years, did follow a consistent policy in regard to submerged lands, a policy based upon the idea that the states held title to the soils beneath their navigable waters. If the rulings of these individuals did not always concern lands in the marginal seas, the inferences down to 1937 appear clear. The United States, in its briefs, did not offer any opinion of the Attorney General which was contrary to those indicated; yet, as stated before, one would have expected the Department of Justice to produce such opinions to bolster its arguments if there had been any.

The most hotly contested point is the attitude of the Department of the Interior in regard to the whole controversy. The focal point is the late Harold L. Ickes, who held the position of Secretary of the Interior during President Franklin Roosevelt's entire administration and who resigned the post under President Truman amid circumstances attributable in part to this very tidelands oil controversy. In a letter to Olin S. Proctor, of Long Beach, in 1933, Ickes refused an application for a federal mineral prospecting permit in the submerged lands off the coast of California. The letter reads as follows:

DEPARTMENT OF THE INTERIOR
WASHINGTON, December 22, 1933

Mr. Olin S. Proctor
Long Beach, Calif.

MY DEAR MR. PROCTOR:

I have received, by reference from the Department of State, copies of your letters of October 15 and November 22.

As to the jurisdiction of the Federal Government over lands bordering on tidewater, the Supreme Court of the United States has held in the case of *Hardin v. Jordan* (140 U.S. 371), as follows:

"With regard to grants of the Government for lands bordering on tidewater, it has been distinctly settled that they only extend to high-water mark, and that the title to the shore and lands under water in front of lands so granted inures to the State within which they are situated, if a

State has been organized and established there. Such title to the shore and lands under water is regarded as incidental to the sovereignty of the State —a portion of the royalties belonging thereto and held in trust for the public purposes of navigation and fishery and cannot be retained or granted out to individuals by the United States."

The foregoing is a statement of the settled law, and therefore no rights can be granted you either under the Leasing Act of February 25, 1920 (41 Stat. 437), or under any other public-land law to the bed of the Pacific Ocean either within or without the 3-mile limit. Title to the soil under the ocean within the 3-mile limit is in the State of California, and the land may not be appropriated except by authority of the State. A permit would be necessary to be obtained from the War Department as a prerequisite to the maintenance of structures in the navigable waters of the United States, but such a permit would not confer any rights in the ocean bed.

I find no authority of law under which any right can be granted to you to establish your proposed structures in the ocean outside the 3-mile limit of the jurisdiction of the State of California, nor am I advised that any other branch of the Federal Government has such authority.

Sincerely yours,

HAROLD L. ICKES

Secretary of the Interior[20]

Ickes, no stranger to a hot fight, could not have foreseen the trouble which this routine letter was to bring him. He said plainly that "title to soil under the ocean within the 3-mile limit is in the State of California, and the land may not be appropriated except by authority of the State." What clearer declaration of policy could be made by one in high authority, especially one charged with administration of the public lands of the United States and presumably knowing the law and settled policies in regard to what were, and what were not, considered lands of the United States? Ickes' letter of 1933 stands as clear and unmistakable evidence that he, at that date, held none of the thoughts which he was to nourish and support in the later thirties.

His letter was perfectly consistent with all previous interpretations of the General Land Office and the Department of the Interior. In 1882, Commissioner H. C. McFarland had rejected an application for the filing of a placer claim on California tidelands with the following letter:

---

[20] This famous letter was reprinted in *Hearings* on S.J. Res. 83 and 92 (1939), 23–24; *Hearings* on H.J. Res. 176 and 181 (1939), 172–73; and *Hearings* on H.J. Res. 118 *et al.* (1945), 18. Constant reference is made to it in all Congressional hearings and debates which are concerned with the tidelands question.

Wm. E. Morris, Esq.
678 24th Street, Oakland, California.

SIR:

I am in receipt of your letter of the 15th ulto., asking "whether or not placer claims on the Pacific coast, lying on the beach, between high and low tide, are open to location and patent under United States mining laws."

In reply, I have to state that the mineral lands, to which the laws of the United States are applicable are, as stated in the original mining act of July 4, 1866, "mineral lands of the public domain."

"The shores of navigable waters and the soils under them . . . were reserved to the States respectively. The new States have the same rights, sovereignty, and jurisdiction over this subject as the original States." This is the language of the court in Pollard v. Hagan, 3 Howard 212; 15 Curtis 391; and in the case of Ward v. Mulford, 32 Cal. 365, it was specifically stated by the court "that land covered and uncovered by the ebb and flow of the neap or ordinary tides, the State owns by virtue of its sovereignty."

Hence this Department has no jurisdiction over such lands.

H. C. McFARLAND, *Commissioner.*[21]

F. W. Clements, for thirty-five years a law officer of the Department of the Interior, testified that all requests for entry or claim in the submerged lands during his experience in the department "were uniformly turned down."[22] Under the Swamp Land Grants Act of Congress in 1850, there were similar decisions by the Land Office or the Depart-

---

[21] 9 Copp's *Landowner* 5.

For decisions to the same effect see *In re James Kasson,* 13 L.D. 299 (1891), rejection of tidelands claims; *In re Red Star Olga Fishing Station,* 26 L.D. 533 (1898), declaration that a survey of Alaskan land that embraces tidelands within its limits will not be approved; *Gillespie* v. *Nebraska,* 28 L.D. 124 (1899), holding that the Missouri River is a navigable stream with control and rights to lands under it therefore vested in the state of Nebraska; *In re James W. Logan,* 29 L.D. 395 (1900), rejecting application to placer mine on tidelands in the Bering Sea; 44 L.D. 441 (1915), instructions by Commissioner Tallman to the commissioner of education on the reservation of tidelands in Alaska for the use of the natives, no controversy involved.

In Alaska, the Department of the Interior did have some limited control below the line of low-water mark. Under a statute of Congress creating an Indian reservation, an order allowing only Indians to erect fish traps in certain navigable waters off the coast of Annette Island was upheld. *Alaska Pacific Fisheries* v. *United States,* 248 U.S. 78 (1918).

[22] *Hearings* on S.J. Res. 208 (1939), 220. Clements was a very old man when he testified or else the dates are incorrect, for this thirty-five-year period of service was put in prior to 1913. Thus, if he were only twenty years old at the time he entered the Department of the Interior, he was eighty at the time of his testimony. In these hearings, he was representing the Santa Fe Railroad.

ment of the Interior which further bear witness to the fact that the policy stated by Ickes in 1933 was exactly the one which had been followed by his predecessors.[23]

The basic Interior Department decision on this issue came in 1934 and arose over the application filed by Joseph Cunningham for a prospecting permit to cover some 1,600 acres lying west of Huntington Beach, California.[24] The commissioner of the General Land Office rejected the application, saying that if the area was below the line of ordinary high tide, jurisdiction was in the state of California, since it became the "owner" of all lands "extending seaward so far as its municipal domain extends." Cunningham appealed, listing eleven grounds on which he based his action.

The Secretary of the Interior, on the appeal, declined even to hold an oral hearing, saying:

It is clear that this Department has no jurisdiction. The State of California asserts title to tide and submerged lands under the common law as it has repeatedly been laid down by the Supreme Court of the United States. If any question of title to such lands as between the State of California and the United States is to be tried, it is for the Federal courts.[25]

[23] For five such illustrations from Florida, see the testimony of Fred C. Elliot, state engineer of Florida, in *Hearings* on S.J. Res. 83 and 92 (1939), 186–87. Two of these are definitely in the open sea, while one is doubtful and two are clearly inland-waters cases.

For two such illustrations from Louisiana see brief of Louisiana, *Hearings* on H.J. Res. 118 *et al.* (1945), 80.

[24] *In re Joseph Cunningham,* 55 I.D. 1 (1934).

[25] *Ibid.,* 3. On motion for rehearing, the decision was again affirmed. Then Cunningham moved that the Secretary exercise his supervisory authority and grant oral argument. The Secretary denied this motion on the ground the state had title, according to the interpretations of the Supreme Court; therefore Interior had no jurisdiction, since it was not free to disregard these decisions.

The rule of the Proctor and Cunningham decisions was followed by Secretary Ickes and his subordinates in the following decisions of the commissioner of General Land Office: decision rejecting applications of W. G. Clark and five others, 18 September 1934, affirmed on appeal by Secretary Ickes, 7 February 1935; decision rejecting application of J. H. Dolan and A. M. Weirick and three others, 23 October 1934, and affirmed on appeal by Secretary Ickes, 21 February 1935; decision rejecting application of F. Dewart, C. P. Ritter, and K. Weyant, 4 April 1935, affirmed on appeal by Secretary Ickes, 24 October 1935; decision rejecting application of O. L. Dillman, 27 September 1935, affirmed on appeal by Secretary Ickes, 12 March 1936; decision rejecting application of J. B. Primm, 2 October 1935, affirmed on appeal by Secretary Ickes, 12 March 1936; decision rejecting application of E. L. Stanton, filed 12 March 1935; decision rejecting application of W. H. Taylor, 4 November 1935, affirmed on appeal by Secretary Ickes, 9 February 1936; decision rejecting application of S. K. Strickler and others, 12 January 1937; decision rejecting application of Chester Mann, 28

The statement is not so blunt and forthright as Ickes' letter and some of the earlier decisions, but the same basic assumption is present: California asserts title under the decisions of the Supreme Court. A further note is injected, however, in that the Secretary says, and properly, that any question of title between the United States and California is for the federal courts to settle. If this statement is merely a rehash of the idea of the court as an umpire of the federal system, it contains absolutely nothing that was not implicit in every other decision made by the Interior Department. There was, however, the possibility that the Secretary was beginning to have doubts about the categorical statements of state title he had made previously, and was now hedging a bit by intimating that, after all, perhaps the best thing to do, as was argued by the proponents of the Nye and Hobbs resolutions, was to get a test case in a federal court to settle the ticklish question once and for all.

It is difficult to determine just when Ickes began to change his mind or for precisely what reasons. In 1946 he stated that the earlier policy of the department, which held that the submerged lands belonged to the state and could not therefore be leased by the Interior Department, was begun in 1926 "without much investigation of the problem."[26] He admitted the authorship of the 1933 letter just discussed and stated that he followed its policy till 1937. However, the applicants for federal leases and their lawyers were most persistent and continued to insist that the United States owned these lands and that the Interior Depart-

---

September 1935, subsequently affirmed by Secretary Ickes; decision rejecting application of R. J. Clark, 22 September 1935, affirmed on appeal by Secretary Ickes, 13 October 1936; decision rejecting application of C. A. Weigel and two others, 18 November 1936; decision rejecting application of H. F. Jones and three others, 26 October 1936, affirmed on appeal by Secretary Ickes, 9 April 1937; decision rejecting application of J. L. Griffith, 23 March 1937; decision rejecting application of T. A. Johnson, 25 September 1937; decision rejecting applications of G. G. Fisher and three others, 8 September 1937; decision rejecting applications of F. E. Pendell and one other, 25 June 1936, affirmed on appeal by Secretary Ickes, 25 September 1936, affirmed on rehearing by decision of Secretary Ickes, 4 February 1937; decision rejecting applications of C. B. Reynolds, Jr., Myrtle A. McCurry, and two others, 27 October 1936, affirmed on appeal by Secretary Ickes, 13 January 1937; decision rejecting application of Myrtle A. McCurry and two others, 26 October 1936, affirmed on appeal by Secretary Ickes, 56 I.D. 60; and decision rejecting applications of Robert E. Lee Jordan and five others, 8 June 1937.

In most of the above mentioned decisions, written opinions were given both by the land commissioner and Secretary Ickes, holding that submerged lands below high-water mark were owned by the state and that no public land of the United States was involved. This list was prepared by William W. Clary. It was inserted into *Hearings* on S.J. Res. 20 (1951), 562.

[26] It has already been demonstrated that the policy antedates the year 1926.

ment had the power to grant the leases. "So," said Secretary Ickes, "we began to have doubts."[27]

Ickes at one time considered the issuance of a single lease to precipitate a test suit to settle the issue;[28] this was rendered unnecessary by the action of the United States Attorney General in the *Pacific Western* and *United States* v. *California* actions.[29] In a letter written 3 April 1939, Ickes attempted to rationalize his 1933 refusal of Proctor's application and his support of the Hobbs resolution by saying that the resolution would pave the way for a judicial determination of the question, exactly his attitude all along.[30] By 1946, he had become aware of the fact that he could not, consistently with his 1933 action, suddenly espouse the cause of the federal government. Although he had attempted to rationalize the two actions in 1939, in 1946 he said frankly of his advocacy of a court decision on the subject:

This, I most readily concede, was a change from the earlier action of myself and of the Department.

I did not, when I assumed office a good many years ago, take an oath that I would always be right, nor even that I would never change my mind. I did take an oath to do my duty, and I viewed my duty in this matter as plain, once I realized that the ownership of submerged coastal lands had not in fact been settled by the courts. Show me a man who takes stubborn pride in the fact that his mind, once made up, is unchangeable, and I will show you a man who is not fit to be a public servant.[31]

Until 1937 the Interior Department had consistently followed the policy that has been outlined. It appears that Ickes' friendship with an applicant for a federal leasing permit marks a possible turning point in

[27] *Hearings* on S.J. Res. 48 and H.J. Res. 225 (1946), 4.
[28] See, e.g., *Los Angeles Times*, 5 March 1945, where Ickes is quoted as saying he would issue a lease in the Long Beach–Seal Beach area to precipitate a settlement.
According to Clyde Doyle, member of the House from California's Eighteenth Congressional District, Ickes told him in an interview, on 21 February 1945, that he intended to approve certain applications for leases held in the Long Beach–Seal Beach area as soon as the legal descriptions thereof were corrected by the applicants. A few days later, Ickes "firmly restated" his position to Doyle, who was accompanied this time by Long Beach City Manager Vickers. *Hearings* on S.J. Res. 48 and H.J. Res. 225 (1946), 204–206.
[29] See letter by Ickes reprinted in *Hearings* on H.J. Res. 118 *et al.* (1945), 159–60. The letter is dated 20 June 1945.
[30] *Hearings* on H.J. Res. 176 and 181 (1939), 133.
[31] *Hearings* on S.J. Res. 48 and H.J. Res. 225 (1946), 5. For a complete listing of all applications filed for federal leases to tide and submerged lands down to February 1948, see list submitted by C. Girard Davidson, Assistant Secretary of

that attitude. In a personal letter to the writer, Ickes made the following statement:

It developed that the Department of the Interior had accepted the view that the tidelands belonged to the State of California. The result was that subsequent applications for leases were turned down either by the Registrar of the Land Office or the Department of the Interior in Washington. No new Secretary taking over can review all of the decisions of policy that have been made prior to his accession. If he should undertake such a task, he could not possibly have time or energy for administration. This matter was not brought to my attention until a citizen of San Francisco, who was interested in an application for a lease that had been filed under the Federal Leasing Act, and who happened to know me personally, called on me in Washington. His lawyer had advised him that title to these lands belonged in the United States instead of in California. . . . I asked for a full report on the case. . . . I further instructed that office [General Land Office] not to determine any question of title without first bringing this matter to me.

When the files reached my desk, it seemed to me to be obvious that the United States at least had enough color of title so that the matter should be presented to the courts for final determination. . . . I regarded it as a question of law, that only the courts should pass on.[32]

Whatever the reasons that Secretary Ickes may have had for changing his mind, the fact is that holding in abeyance all applications for federal leases after 1937 raised some very serious problems. Such action established clouds on title of many activities and individuals not associated with the production of oil. Leander Shelley, general counsel of the Port of New York Authority, correctly pointed out in 1946 that Ickes' refusal to act on the applications resulted in an unwillingness on the part of the Authority to undertake improvements, on the justifiable ground that the national government might take them over in event of

---

the Interior, joint *Hearings* on S. 1988 (1948), 1285–94. At 1285, the following summary is made:

State	No. Applications before 23 June 1947	No. Applications after 23 June 1947	Total
California	278	82	360
Washington	0	3	3
Texas and Louisiana	29	629	658
Total	307	714	1,021

[32] The letter is dated 29 November 1947.

a court decision allowing (or requiring) the issuance of a federal leasing permit in California.[33]

Some of the applicants for federal leasing permits were offering for sale at varying amounts fractional rights in these undenied lease applications. The purchaser of such fractional rights got nothing but an indefinite promise on a highly unlikely future eventuality. Robert Kenny, then attorney general of California, classed these activities as a "racket," pointing out that many of the applications were being filed in order to sell the fractional rights to "suckers."[34]

The decision to suspend action on applications was condemned not only by those who believed that title to the submerged lands was in the respective states but also by those seeking federal leases. Ickes was forced to defend two suits brought against him by those who desired federal leases and who sought to compel the Secretary to issue them.[35] Though unsuccessful, the actions illustrate that Ickes was not, by this time, in the good graces of at least two of the three parties to the controversy.

Once Secretary Ickes had made up his mind where the equities lay in the controversy, his actions were as vigorous as his language was salty. His accusation that forty of the forty-six attorneys general who supported the brief filed by the National Association of Attorneys General in support of California's position were actually "representing clients other than those States and Commonwealths where they held office"[36] is typical of his blunt comments. He even went so far as to intimate that the attorneys general had not studied the briefs and the issues involved but had merely appended their names in response to a "telegraphic solicitation."[37] While there may have been an element of truth in this latter statement in 1946, it is not true of the years after 1946, when the issues were well known, and when the National Association of Attorneys General continued its support of the position taken by California, Texas, and Louisiana.[38] Secretary Ickes characterized the inland states' support of California's position as that of "an innocent

[33] *Hearings* on S.J. Res. 48 and H.J. Res. 225 (1946), 217–18.

[34] Kenny cited names, dates, and places in his testimony. *Ibid.*, 68–70. For a more complete discussion of the activities of these persons, see pp. 242–46 below.

[35] *Dunn* v. *Ickes,* 115 F. 2d 36 (1940), certiorari denied, 311 U.S. 698 (1940); *United States ex rel. Jordan* v. *Ickes,* 55 F. Supp. 875, 143 F. 2d 152 (1944), certiorari denied, 320 U.S. 801, 323 U.S. 759 (1944).

[36] Letter by Ickes, dated 20 June 1945, reprinted in *Hearings* on H.J. Res. 118 *et al.* (1945), 161.

[37] *Hearings* on S.J. Res. 48 and H.J. Res. 225 (1946), 7.

[38] See, e.g., resolutions of the organization, adopted 12 December 1950, reprinted in *Hearings* on S.J. Res. 20 (1951), 92–93.

bystander who is somehow persuaded to grab a rock and throw it instead of going peaceably home."[39]

There is no doubt in the writer's mind that Ickes was altruistically interested in one thing: the conservation of oil. He sincerely believed that conservation could best be accomplished under national administration. To the time he resigned his post as Secretary of the Interior, he viewed the contest as one solely involving oil, and he continued to hold that view as a private citizen. His every letter, newspaper and magazine article, and piece of testimony from 1938 to the day of his death breathes this spirit. In 1946 he could say, "I persist in viewing this contest as one over oil."[40] The arguments of those who opposed him

[39] *Hearings* on S.J. Res. 48 and H.J. Res. 225 (1946), 8.

[40] *Ibid.*, 7. He did not confine the reach of his remarks to California alone but spoke of oil possibilities in the Gulf of Mexico.

There is only one point in the entire controversy where questions have been raised as to his motives. The incident involved a series of correspondence over the application of the Consolidated Petroleum Company, a Nevada corporation organized by C. P. Ritter and W. W. Chapin for the apparent purpose of filing for a federal lease to submerged lands off the shore of California in the Seal Beach area. The oil and gas lease application of this company was filed with the Department of the Interior on 10 June 1944 as No. 056460.

On 17 May 1944 the commissioner of the General Land Office sent a letter to the registrar of the Land Office in Los Angeles ordering any application by Ritter or Chapin forwarded immediately to Washington. On 24 June 1944 a follow-up telegram was sent by the commissioner asking where the papers were. The registrar sent a reply enclosing the application of Consolidated Petroleum. He stated in his letter of transmittal that "Mr. Ritter presented a letter from the Secretary of the Interior suggesting that he file an application and stating that he would get to the bottom of this matter pertaining to tideland."

The above facts, standing alone, constitute nothing irregular. However, two previous applications had been filed for this same area: S. B. Osborne, No. 053281, filed 14 April 1938; and John Tweed Dale, filed 18 December 1943. Ickes stated publicly on several occasions that he was going to grant the Ritter and Chapin application. Why, if he was only interested in a test case, did he not grant one of the previous applications already on file? Had the Chapin and Ritter application been upheld in a court test, it was charged, Ickes would have been guilty of playing "fast and loose" with the rights of the previous applicants.

Source of this summary: *ibid.*, 67–68; statement by Robert W. Kenny and William W. Clary, *The Truth about the Legislation Quieting Titles to Lands beneath Tidal and Navigable Waters* (Washington, Judd and Detweiler, 1946). This was an official California publication; it advocated a point of view and should be so judged.

This is the only instance where even a faint shadow of suspicion may be cast on Ickes' motives. The difficult, almost impossible, part of the tale to understand is why Ickes did not fly to his own defense in his usual inimitable fashion. The writer is somewhat inclined to believe that Ickes considered the insinuations so patently absurd that he would not dignify them with an answer. The fact that the leases were never issued still does not provide a completely satisfactory explanation of the incident.

and screamed that his actions were violative of states' rights merely caused him to shake off his tormentors and return again to his basic point. He called himself "an advocate of legitimate States' rights."[41] He sarcastically noted that it was not his understanding that "one of the inalienable rights of a State is to escape litigation when it claims land to which the National Government also asserts title."[42]

The complete story of the controversy in which Secretary Ickes and Edwin W. Pauley were the principal actors will perhaps never be known. There is, however, enough information on the incident to point up the single fact that political pressures in the tidelands controversy tended to increase as the whole issue builded to a conclusion, ultimately transcending the doctrinaire arguments of the so-called advocates for the parties and culminating in the behind-the-scenes activities of those striving for political power and prestige.

Secretary Ickes discussed the tidelands controversy with President Roosevelt. Ickes himself notes that for a long time the President gave him no decision on possible courses of action, but finally, shortly before Roosevelt's death, authorized Attorney General Francis Biddle to file a suit.[43] Biddle took action, but, to Secretary Ickes' dismay, the suit was brought against the Pacific Western Oil Company in the District Court for the Southern District of California,[44] rather than against California in the original jurisdiction of the United States Supreme Court. Secretary Ickes argued at length that the whole question of the ownership and control of submerged lands could be settled only by an original action against California, but Attorney General Biddle would not change his mind.

With President Truman's accession to office, there was more pro-

---

[41] *Hearings* on S.J. Res. 48 and H.J. Res. 225 (1946), 7.

[42] *Ibid.*

[43] Letter of Ickes to the writer, dated 29 November 1947. Ickes may have been in error as to President Roosevelt's authorization of the suit. In testimony in 1948, Ickes referred to a discussion that he had on the topic in 1937 with the President and Harry Hopkins. He based his testimony on his diary. Subsequently, some of the diary entries, particularly one showing Congressman Hatton Sumners as favoring a suit against the states, were shown to be incorrect. Further, persons like Price Daniel stated publicly that President Roosevelt did not authorize the suit. No challenge was made of this statement. Ickes' own testimony at the 1948 hearings would appear to contradict the assertion made in his letter to the writer. He testified, in effect, that the suit was authorized after President Roosevelt's death. Joint *Hearings* on S. 1988 (1948), 1119, 1124–31, 1188–89. See pp. 159–61 below, where the *Pacific Western* suit is discussed, and especially Attorney General Biddle's remark in 1945 that the decision to bring suit in that year was a "recent one."

[44] See n. 2, this chapter, and p. 161 below.

crastination and delay. After the resignation of Attorney General Biddle, the whole process had to be repeated. Ickes was becoming increasingly irritated at the delaying tactics being employed by the California oil interests, acting, he contended, through the agency of Edwin Pauley, whose position in the Democratic party machinery in California gave him a powerful lever which could be exerted on the policies of the national administration. The enmity between these two public servants —Ickes and Pauley—if not born of the tidelands issue, was nurtured into flaming hatred by the events which were to transpire.

Secretary Ickes tried to persuade Tom Clark, after the latter became Attorney General, to dismiss the *Pacific Western* action and substitute for it an original action in the United States Supreme Court against the state of California. This the Attorney General refused to do, on the ground that he did not want to disturb an action of his precursor. Ickes expresses the belief that Clark's refusal was generated by the pressure of Texas oil interests; but, pressure or not, President Truman was persuaded by Secretary Ickes' arguments and ordered Clark to drop the *Pacific Western* suit and adopt Ickes' plan. Attorney General Clark delayed, until Ickes, at lunch with the President one day, again applied the pressure; Truman, in turn, told Clark he wanted no more delay. The suit was finally filed. Ickes was convinced that Attorney General Clark wanted to see the United States lose the case.[45] There is some indication, too, that President Truman, even though he allowed himself to be pushed, was not altogether happy about taking action.[46]

The *Pacific Western* suit had been filed on 29 May 1945. Little outward opposition had appeared to it among the advisers immediately surrounding President Roosevelt. This exterior atmosphere of calm carried over to Truman's administration and to the end of 1945. Secretary Ickes was unable to restrain himself longer, however, when President Truman nominated Edwin Pauley to the post of Undersecretary of the Navy early in 1946. Opposition to Pauley's nomination developed immediately among the members of the Senate Naval Af-

[45] This résumé is taken from letters, dated 29 November 1947 and 18 August 1950, from Secretary Ickes to the writer.

[46] The *Los Angeles Times,* 29 May 1945, said in a news dispatch (datelined Washington) in regard to the *Pacific Western* action: "If Biddle decides to act, political observers believe it will be against the wishes of the Truman administration. It is understood that President Truman did not favor attempts made earlier this year by Secretary of the Interior Ickes to stir up a court fight on the issue."

Ickes states, on the other hand, that he had "no reason to doubt his [Truman's] sincerity." Letter to the writer, 18 August 1950.

fairs Committee, who based their objection on the fact that Pauley had
been an oil operator of some wealth and influence in California, where
he had headed the Petrol Corporation.[47]

So far, the Ickes-Pauley feud had no outward bearing on the question at issue. Ickes saw fit, however, to appear twice before the Senate
Naval Affairs Committee in February, 1946, and there gave testimony
to the effect that Pauley was unfit to be confirmed to the post to which
he had been nominated by President Truman. It was the contention of
Ickes that on 6 September 1944 he had had a conversation with
Pauley concerning the difficulty of raising campaign funds for the
1944 presidential campaign. At this meeting, Ickes alleged, Pauley
promised to raise three hundred thousand dollars for the Democratic
war chest if in turn Ickes would see that the federal government no
longer pushed its claims to the submerged lands. Ickes now fought
Pauley's nomination with every means at his disposal. He traced the
background of Pauley's operations in California oil. He aired the dirty
linen of the Navy in regard to methods used in the naval reserves at
Elk Hills, showing the incompetence of the Navy and insinuating that
the Navy was unable to take care of those reserves over which it already
had control.[48]

Pauley replied in kind. The controversy was sharply fought; and
even while Pauley's major share in the hearings was yet to take place,
Ickes resigned on 13 February 1946 in protest against President Truman's continued support of Pauley.[49] Ickes' allegations concerning the
campaign fund deal were never really proved or disproved in the

[47] *New York Times,* 20 January 1946, p. 11; *ibid.,* 27 January 1946, §4, p. 10,
by-lined Cabell Phillips.

[48] The whole affair was most bitter. Ickes called Pauley's offer the "rawest"
ever put to him. He claimed Pauley even tried to lobby for the tidelands interests
in a railroad car following the burial of Franklin Roosevelt at Hyde Park. Pauley
insisted that Ickes must be mistaken; Ickes retorted that maybe he didn't understand the English language. *New York Times,* 6 February 1946, by-lined Anthony
Leviero. President Truman likewise felt Ickes "must be mistaken." *Ibid.,* 8
February 1946.

[49] Arthur Krock predicted Ickes' resignation. *New York Times,* 8 February
1946.

Ickes' farewell dripped with acid. He stated that he would not stay in an
administration where he had to commit perjury for the party. He suggested that
his resignation take effect 31 March, but Truman made it effective 15 February.
Ickes sounded a general warning for the Democratic party, recalling the events
leading up to the Teapot Dome scandal. The texts of his letter of resignation,
interview, and radio speech are given in the *New York Times,* 14 February 1946.
Editorially, the *Times* stated that the resignation indicated that Truman preferred
Pauley to Ickes, and the *Times* indicated that it considered this a most unfortunate state of affairs. It lauded Ickes as a great public servant. *Ibid.*

Pauley hearings. As nearly as can be determined, Ickes never mentioned the affair to either Roosevelt or Truman. Even Abe Fortas,
Undersecretary of the Department of the Interior and Ickes' right-
hand man and confidant, could not recall on the witness stand that
Ickes ever told him of such an occurrence.[50] Pauley admitted that he
had had a talk with Ickes and that campaign funds had been discussed,
even a three-hundred-thousand-dollar figure. Pauley contended, however, that this sum represented a hoped-for contribution from the District of Columbia and not from Pauley interests. Pauley stated that he
never made any promise to Ickes to raise funds in return for a guarantee on the part of the executive officers of the federal government to
take no further action on the tidelands issue.[51] Regardless of the truth
or falsity of Ickes' contention, Pauley had been a California oil operator for many years, and his previous connections would have placed his
nomination in jeopardy even without Ickes' sensational charges.

The remainder of the story is well known. After a series of claims
and counterclaims, recessed hearings, vindictive name-calling, and
general spite work on both sides, Pauley agreed to a withdrawal of his
nomination on the condition that the committee would affirm confidence in his integrity. Truman issued a statement declaring his faith in
Pauley, and the episode which had caused the resignation of one of
the most famous and able of the secretaries of the interior was to all
appearances closed.[52]

Yet the tidelands issue, once relatively unimportant, had exploded
into page-one prominence. It had assumed an importance sufficient to
force the resignation of an able and, who can gainsay, forthright Secretary of the Interior. It was important enough to force a man nominated for high office to defend his activities in regard to that issue and
sufficient in the end to be a contributing factor to the withdrawal of
his nomination. And this was in early 1946, before the arguments in
United States v. *California*. More noteworthy, the event which had provided the basis for the sensational allegation concerning Pauley's activities had occurred in 1944, before any official action whatsoever
had been taken by the Attorney General. The apparent calm which
existed during the war belied the powerful undercurrents.

Whether Pauley had made such an offer in 1944 is relatively im-

[50] *Ibid.*, 8 March 1946. Ickes took the stand again in opposition to Pauley's
confirmation, but though his remarks were a bit more vitriolic, no new facts
came to light.
[51] *Ibid.*
[52] *Ibid.*, 6, 8, 9, and 14 March 1946.

material to this study.[53] The fact that Ickes thought that Pauley had, and said so, is indicative of the tremendous shift of opinion toward control of the submerged lands in the Department of the Interior between 1933 and 1939. In 1933, Ickes had said the ownership of the tidelands lay with the states, but in the later thirties and early forties he encouraged the filing of suits to test the validity of the states' claims.

There had been a corresponding shift in attitude on the part of the representatives of the Navy and Justice departments, for in 1938–39 they had indicated they could take no action without a Congressional resolution declaring ownership and directing the Department of Justice to bring suit to enforce the declaration. In 1945 the Department of Justice did bring a suit, couched in terms similar to the Nye and Hobbs resolutions of 1938–39, without the blessing of having such a resolution passed. And a year later the United States filed its complaint in the case of *United States* v. *California,* without benefit of that Congressional action deemed to be indispensable a few short years before.

As though to emphasize more strongly this change in basic attitude on the part of the executive departments, President Truman in 1945 issued a proclamation announcing to the world that the United States regarded the "natural resources of the subsoil and sea bed of the continental shelf" as territory appertaining to the nation. The proclamation stated:

Having concern for the urgency of conserving and prudently utilizing its natural resources, the Government of the United States regards the natural resources of the subsoil and sea bed of the continental shelf beneath the high seas but contiguous to the coasts of the United States as appertaining to the United States, subject to its jurisdiction and control. In cases where the continental shelf extends to the shores of another State, or is shared with an adjacent State, the boundary shall be determined by the United States and the State concerned in accordance with equitable principles. The character as high seas of the waters above the continental shelf and the right to their free and unimpeded navigation are in no way thus affected.[54]

[53] Senator Wiley's attitude on the Pauley affair was caustic but to the point. He stated: "I do not know who is telling the truth. It might probably be well to have a lie detector put on both of them." *Hearings* on S.J. Res. 48 and H.J. Res. 225 (1946), 125.
[54] Pres. Proc. No. 2667, 28 September 1945, 10 Fed. Reg. 12303.

It is significant that in the same year, with the tidelands issue plainly before him, the President could proceed to declare the right and jurisdiction of the United States in the continental shelf off the coasts of the United States—and California, Texas, and Louisiana particularly. It is significant, too, that he made no effort to vest any proprietary interests in the United States as against the states in the three-mile zone; the *Pacific Western* suit had been filed, and the entire issue was yet to be adjudicated. The President was not trying to foreclose a settlement of the issue of the ownership of the submerged lands "in accordance with equitable principles."[55]

The proclamation was, of course, a political one. Because of the extent of the claim, its validity in international law would seem doubtful. So far as domestic law is concerned, however, the President's action would be binding on American courts under the rule of *In re Cooper*,[56] *Wilson* v. *Shaw*,[57] *United States* v. *The James G. Swan*,[58] and *United States* v. *The Kodiak*.[59] While the President had made no effort to apply his proclamation to the three-mile zone, he had by his action effectively foreclosed any future assertions by the states beyond the boundaries established in 1945.[60]

By executive order[61] issued on the same day as the proclamation, President Truman ordered that these natural resources covered in the proclamation be placed under the "jurisdiction and control" of the Secretary of the Interior "pending the enactment of legislation in regard thereto." Again the President emphasized that nothing in these

[55] A press release issued from the White House contemporaneously with the Presidential proclamation contained the following statement: "The policy proclaimed by the President in regard to the jurisdiction over the continental shelf does not touch upon the question of Federal versus State control. It is concerned solely with establishing the jurisdiction of the United States from an international standpoint." 13 Dept. State Bull. 484.

[56] 143 U.S. 472 (1892).

[57] 204 U.S. 24 (1907).

[58] 50 F. 108 (1892).

[59] 53 F. 126 (1892).

[60] Thus the action of the Texas Legislature taken in 1947 extending the boundaries of Texas in the Gulf of Mexico to the edge of the continental shelf could not have the effect of creating any rights in the state of Texas.

[61] Exec. Order No. 9633, 10 Fed. Reg. 12305. Presidential Proclamation No. 2668, of the same date, declared the policy of the United States with respect to coastal fisheries in these areas of the high seas. The proclamation was based on the need for "conservation and protection of fisheries resources."

The executive order was rescinded by Executive Order 10426, 18 Fed. Reg. 405, issued 16 January 1953. Truman's action in issuing the rescinding order, which provided for the transfer of administrative control of the continental shelf from the Interior to the Navy Department, was hotly criticized. See pp. 257–58.

actions should be taken as prejudicing the question of ownership of the submerged lands: "Neither this Order nor the aforesaid proclamation shall be deemed to affect the determination by legislation or judicial decree of any issues between the United States and the several states, relating to the ownership or control of the subsoil and sea bed of the continental shelf within or outside of the 3-mile limit."[62]

Here, then, was no action by the Congress; the proclamation and order constituted an unqualified declaration of right by the executive branch of the government. The proclamation was a dramatic manifestation that the attitude of the executive departments had shifted. The federal government might, through its lack of diligence over one hundred years of practice, have lost its right to exploit the submerged soils in the marginal sea out to the declared boundaries of the coastal states. From those boundaries outward, however, the presidential proclamation served as a notice of future national intent.

[62] 10 Fed. Reg. 12305.

9.

The Quitclaim Attempt in 1945

The actions of Secretary of the Interior Harold L. Ickes and other executive officers of the federal government, together with the introduction of the Nye and Hobbs resolutions, forced those who believed in state ownership of the submerged soils in the maritime belt to devote thought to the development of counter strategy. Negative strategy had sufficed for the defeat of the Nye and Hobbs measures, but the mere introduction of the bills and the actions of Secretary Ickes in withholding decisions for federal leasing permits in the submerged soils were sufficient to cloud titles in the area. If these clouds were to be permanently removed, positive action was absolutely necessary.

Although World War II brought a temporary halt to the type of actions which had been attempted in 1938 and 1939 by those espousing federal control, the possibility of a renewal of the fight at the first opportunity was always present. Even before the filing of the *Pacific Western* action, therefore, proponents of state ownership of submerged soils in the maritime belt had introduced into the Congress a number of bills and resolutions under which the United States would have released, remised, and quitclaimed all "right, title, interest, claim, or demand," in the submerged soils.[1]

[1] H.J. Res. 118, 79th Cong., 1st sess., introduced by Hebert. The following resolutions of similar or identical form were also introduced at this same session of Congress: S.J. Res. 48, by McCarran of Nevada; II.J. Res. 119, by Brooks of Louisiana; H.J. Res. 122, by Doyle of California; H.J. Res. 123, by Boykin of Alabama; H.J. Res. 125, by Tolan of California; H.J. Res. 128, by Bender of Ohio; H.J. Res. 129, by Reed of Illinois; H.J. Res. 130, by Havenner of California; H.J. Res. 134, by All of Louisiana; H.J. Res. 137, by Colmer of Mississippi; H.J. Res. 138, by Hale of Maine; H.J. Res. 146, by Patterson of California; H.J. Res. 148, by Welch of California; H.J. Res. 153, by Phillips of California;

At the time these resolutions were introduced, no official action had yet been taken by an executive officer of the federal government, except that, since 9 June 1937, Secretary Ickes had refused to deny applications for prospecting permits to submerged soils which were sought under the Federal Mineral Leasing Act of 1920; he had been holding such applications in abeyance. The filing of the *Pacific Western* suit was merely a final spur to action, if further stimulus were needed. Representative Hatton Sumners, chairman of the House Judiciary Committee, announced on 30 May 1945, the *Pacific Western* suit having been filed the day previous, that hearings on House Joint Resolution 118 and the other resolutions which "would definitely establish title to all submerged lands in the maritime belt in the states" would be scheduled to begin 18 June 1945.[2]

Two series of hearings were held on what will be referred to from this point on as the "quitclaim" legislation. The hearings before the House Judiciary Committee and a subcommittee of the Senate Judiciary Committee were held 18, 19, and 20 June 1945; and hearings before the Senate Judiciary Committee, 5, 6, and 7 February 1946. House Joint Resolution 225, quitclaiming "right, title, interest, or claim" in submerged lands in the three-mile limit, passed the House 21 September 1945 and the Senate 24 April 1946, in slightly different versions. The resolution was sent to conference, approved in final form 23 July, and sent to the President. Truman vetoed it 2 August 1946 for reasons to be stated shortly. Such is the legislative history of the attempts at quitclaim measures prior to *United States* v. *California*.

There is no particular reason to state in detail the arguments advanced in these hearings. For the most part the contentions were mere repetitions of the previous hearings on the Nye and Hobbs resolutions, which have already received much attention. It might be of interest to recall that in 1939 Thomas Dockweiler, a former member of Congress from California, had suggested exactly the course which was pursued in 1945 and 1946. He was perfectly in favor of a Congressional declaration, but he wanted the declaration to quitclaim forever all pretense of title in the submerged lands on the part of the United States, rather than proposing that the United States assert title or paramount rights.[3]

H.J. Res. 172, by Johnson of California; H.J. Res. 193, by Mealy of California; and H.J. Res. 217, by McDonough of California.

[2] *Los Angeles Times,* 30 May 1945. While Biddle's action was in the "hot rumor" stage, Senator Pat McCarran of the Subcommittee of the Senate Judiciary Committee indicated that his group was proceeding to a consideration of the quitclaim measures. *Ibid.,* 29 May 1945.

[3] *Hearings* on S.J. Res. 83 and 92 (1939), 264.

It is almost impossible to assess the arguments of those who opposed or who might have opposed a quitclaim measure if only the 1945 hearings are considered. Only one person, and that person a private party, appeared before the committees to oppose actively the quitclaim action in 1945.[4] Attorney General Biddle did not testify in person, but stated his views by letter in reply to a request by Senator McCarran. The concluding paragraph of Biddle's communication was as follows:

The question whether the resolution should be adopted is one of legislative policy to be considered by the Congress. If the Congress should decide to adopt a resolution of the kind proposed without awaiting judicial determination of the questions involved, the controversy would largely become moot, although, of course, a number of questions of construction and application of the resolution would be likely to arise. In view of the history and complexity of the issue, and the value of the rights in question, the Congress may well desire to have the controversy determined by judicial proceedings in order that there may be a more adequate basis for the consideration of proposals to alienate the right, title, and interest of the United States.[5]

Biddle's opposition is stated in the mildest of terms. Secretary Ickes, too, sent only a noncommittal letter to Senator McCarran in which he stated the view that the question of a quitclaim was a policy issue to be left to the determination of Congress.[6] Although he stated in 1946 that this communication recorded his "emphatic opposition" to the quitclaim proposals,[7] that opposition is not apparent. In 1946, Ickes excused his failure to oppose quitclaim more actively in 1945 by saying that it was his rule never to appear before Congressional committees unless invited, and he had not been in 1945.[8] According to Chairman Sumners, however, the Departments of Justice, Navy, and Interior were all asked in 1945 if they had anything to contribute.[9] The two letters noted constitute the returns from these groups. The State Department,

---

[4] Raymond M. Hudson, of the law firm of Hudson, Creyke, and Hudson, was the sole individual to appear at the 1945 hearings in opposition to quitclaiming the rights of the United States. His firm represented some ten or twelve applicants for federal prospecting permits in the submerged areas offshore from California. *Hearings* on H.J. Res. 118 *et al.* (1945), 129–34.

[5] The letter, dated 6 June 1945, is reprinted *ibid.*, 19. The *Pacific Western* suit, it should be remembered, was filed 29 May.

[6] Reprinted *ibid.*, 159–61. He sent a similar letter to Congressman Sumners. *Ibid.*, 19.

[7] *Hearings* on S.J. Res. 48 and H.J. Res. 225 (1946), 3.

[8] *Ibid.*

[9] *Hearings* on H.J. Res. 118 *et al.* (1945), 121.

in a communication signed by Acting Secretary Grew, refused to touch the political "hot potato" and said that the issue was a purely domestic one, not within the purview of the department.[10] Representative Michener called this general attitude of the executive departments "unusual,"[11] but it does not appear from the record that anything was done to get a fuller representation of views by those who might be opposed to the resolutions. The only congressman to suggest even vaguely at the hearings that there might be something quite wrong in the procedure was Hugh DeLacy, who wanted to let the courts settle the matter because such a decision "wouldn't affect the interests of the State of Washington."[12] Every other individual present and testifying at the 1945 hearings favored the quitclaim.

The 1946 hearings were similarly weighted in favor of the proponents of quitclaim legislation. Harold Ickes was the only executive officer of the federal government to appear in opposition—and he was to resign his post less than a week after testifying. His view of the event is stated thus:

. . . the oil and other sympathetic interests began to press for legislation, that, in effect, would quitclaim all of the land to the State of California. The bill went through the House practically by acclamation. When I was in London negotiating the oil treaty with Great Britain in the fall of 1945, my office cabled me that Senator McCarran was apparently determined to rush this legislation through the Senate. Thereupon, I cabled Senator Mc-Carran, pointing out my interest in the bill and asking for a chance to be heard. So Senator McCarran held the bill over until I returned to Washington in October, and subsequently, he held a hearing of a sub-committee that he had appointed, with himself as Chairman. I could see that everything had been cut and dried. McCarran gave me time to make a formal statement, but it was significant to me that neither he nor any member of the committee had any questions to ask. . . . At this hearing the then Attorney General Kenny of California and his supporters, not only from California, but from other states, were present in force. I believe that I was the only one to support the case of the Government. The Bill was rushed through and sent to the President.[13]

---

[10] *Los Angeles Times,* 29 May 1945.
[11] *Hearings* on H.J. Res. 118 *et al.* (1945), 138.
[12] *Ibid.,* 139–40. DeLacy did not appear personally but sent a statement.
[13] Letter to the writer, 29 November 1947.
As a matter of fact, according to the record, Ickes' statement concerning the lack of questions is not quite correct. The late Senator Kenneth Wherry of Nebraska asked a number of questions of Ickes, though it is true he was the only one to do so. *Hearings* on S.J. Res. 48 and H.J. Res. 225 (1946), 13.

Robert E. Lee Jordan, aged erstwhile oil operator who had made frequent applications for federal permits in the California submerged lands, appeared in opposition, along with his attorney, Orin DeMotte Walker, who did most of the talking for him. Indeed most of the opposition, in terms of argument, was presented by Walker. One other applicant for a federal lease appeared personally in opposition, one E. J. Preston, who described himself as an independent oil operator. One individual, applicant for a federal lease, and one law firm, representing other applicants, sent letters recording opposition to the proposed quitclaim. That constituted the total extent of opposition in the 1946 hearings. No state governmental agency or municipal corporation filed any protest, though numerous states and cities, inland and coastal, had personal representatives who testified in support of the measures or filed letters and statements in support of the quitclaim. Of 476 pages of testimony taken at the two hearings, a total of only 53 pages is devoted to the arguments and statements of the opposition; and of these 53 pages, 47 were recorded at the 1946 hearings. This is a commentary on the disorganization of those favoring federal control or ownership as well as a demonstration of the excellently planned and executed maneuvers of those favoring the quitclaim.

The united front presented by the states in these two hearings is little short of phenomenal. Seldom has such unanimity of opinion been demonstrated. Forty-six of forty-eight state attorneys general supported the brief filed in support of the quitclaim. Attorney General Robert Kenny, in the 1945 hearings, called this brief a landmark in legislation, saying that never before had there been evidenced such co-operation.[14] Undeniably, there was a surprising concord. Washington and Arizona were the only states whose top legal officers did not join in the brief. The attorney general of Washington was still in Germany, and communication was somewhat hampered; in the 1946 hearings, Harold A. Pebbles, his assistant, stated that his chief was in agreement with the principles laid down in the brief.[15] This statement by Pebbles was in answer to a specific suggestion made by Ickes that the attorney general of Washington could not support the brief because of a basic disagreement with the thesis which it stated.[16]

The agreement among the state attorneys general may have resulted from the fact that many, as was intimated by Ickes, simply did not study the problem.[17] On the other hand, this support continued

---

[14] *Hearings* on H.J. Res. 118 *et al.* (1945), 5.
[15] *Hearings* on S.J. Res. 48 and H.J. Res. 225 (1946), 116.
[16] Ickes' statement to this effect appears *ibid.*, 8.   [17] *Ibid.*, 7–8.

throughout the pleadings and arguments in the cases of *United States* v. *California, United States* v. *Texas,* and *United States* v. *Louisiana.* After the decision in *United States* v. *California* the attorneys general filed a brief as *amicus curiae* supporting a California petition for rehearing.[18] In the space of time between 1945 and decision in 1947, it would have been impossible for any attorney general to remain incognizant of the issues involved. It would appear that this unanimity of opinion stemmed from something much deeper. The fact that this group chose to support the quitclaim legislation indicates a fairly basic agreement among them rather than a surprising hold by the oil interests on this particular officer of the state governments. Secretary Ickes' protestations to the contrary, the issues involved much more than mere oil beneath a relatively small area of land off the California, Texas, and Louisiana coasts.

The representatives of the states and cities were afraid. They were concerned, not so much that California, Texas, and Louisiana might lose certain rights to petroleum products, but rather that if the national government should have such power over petroleum, it must have a similar power over all other products and, more importantly, present and future installations below low-water mark. Orrin Judd, solicitor general of the state of New York, said bluntly that New York would not allow the Department of the Interior to follow the policy of divide-and-conquer; New York would support California to the limit.[19] The representatives of other states present at the hearings backed this sentiment to the fullest extent. Inland and coastal state alike presented a united front in supporting the demands of the proponents of state ownership of submerged lands in the maritime belt.

The attempt of the Interior Department to concentrate the attack on California oil was characterized as an attempt to divide the states

---

[18] "Brief of the National Association of Attorneys General, Amicus Curiae, in Support of Defendant's Petition for a Rehearing and Objections to the Plaintiff's Proposed Decree," No. 12 Original, October Term 1946. This brief will hereinafter be cited as brief of the National Association of Attorneys General, *amicus curiae, California* case.

[19] *Hearings* on H.J. Res. 118 *et al.* (1945), 94.

Richard B. Keech, corporation counsel of the District of Columbia, who appeared favoring quitclaim legislation on behalf of the National Institute of Municipal Law Officers, called Ickes' concentration on the question of oil a sham raised to confuse the issue. He said: "We want this committee to clearly understand that this is not an 'oil' case, but it is rather a case in which the Federal Government is raising a broad principle in a specific case which does involve oil-producing lands. The Federal officials apparently do not or will not follow their claims to the ultimate conclusion and see the Nation-wide consequences which flow from them." *Ibid.,* 54.

among themselves and to "prevent unified and coordinated action by the States."[20] If the federal government could destroy ownership in one state, it was argued, it would follow "automatically" that the principle would apply in any state.[21] "There is and can be no middle ground. If Mr. Ickes can seize 1 square foot of tide or submerged lands in any State and maintain his seizure, it will be the official duty of Federal officers everywhere to complete the conquest of all like areas in all the States."[22]

This same group argued that a rule of property had been established down through the years in the submerged lands. In the belief of the existence of that rule, large sums had been expended in various types of developments: harbors had been built, land reclaimed, and royalties taken from petroleum operations. The actions of Secretary Ickes, in holding in abeyance and refusing to dismiss applications for federal leases in the submerged areas, combined with the Nye and Hobbs resolutions of 1938–39, had created an "unwarranted cloud" on such properties, a cloud which should be removed by a quitclaim or release passed by the Congress.[23]

An "unfounded and unwarranted assertion of title" had been made.[24] Hirsh Freed, assistant corporation counsel of Boston, expressed the need for a quitclaim in these words: "The principal value, it seems to me, of this joint resolution is not in having the Federal Government actually convey to the States that which they do not now have. I regard this joint resolution as declaratory of an existing state of affairs, namely, to quiet, or, rather, to remove from the area of doubt any question as to where title to these submerged lands is."[25] Others favored the resolutions on the mere ground of utility, couching their arguments in terms of the unsettled state of affairs which would result if the United States, through some turn of events, actually did get title to the submerged lands in the marginal sea.[26] Some even justified a quitclaim on the ground that the judiciary would act too slowly in the matter and therefore was an inappropriate agency for the prompt determination of the controversy.[27]

Most of those who testified in favor of quitclaim believed that the long series of Supreme Court cases, combined with lower federal and

---

[20] Brief of the Attorneys General, *ibid.*, 12.
[21] *Ibid.*   [22] *Ibid.*   [23] *Ibid.*, 13–16.
[24] Testimony of Robert Kenny, *ibid.*, 9.   [25] *Ibid.*, 58.
[26] Statement of Overton Brooks, member of Congress from Louisiana's Fourth District, *ibid.*, 142.
[27] Testimony of Grover Sellers, then attorney general of Texas, *ibid.*, 44.

state court decisions,[28] was sufficient to justify an assertion that the issue had already been settled by the courts. The "Memorandum of the American Association of Port Authorities" said, regarding the *Pacific Western* suit:

If those desiring to expropriate submerged lands are unwilling to abide by the past decisions of the Supreme Court there is no reason to believe that they will abide by its decision in this newly initiated case. Only Congressional action can put an end to the matter. The initiation of the present suit, accompanied as it has been by an announcement casting doubt upon the title to submerged and reclaimed lands throughout the country, is a strong argument for the adoption of the pending bills.[29]

The forces favoring a quitclaim were certain of one thing: they saw no reason to fight the issue out in the courts. They felt deeply that a Congressional resolution should be the instrument for halting the controversy once and for all.[30] Court decisions had been, and could be in the future, overruled.[31] The Congress had the power to settle this vexing question and should do so immediately,[32] for only Congress could settle it finally now that the issue had been raised.

Paradoxically enough, the very people who had opposed with might and main the proposed Nye and Hobbs resolutions in 1938 and 1939 now labored just as diligently for a resolution of their own. The 1938–39 hearings, as has been pointed out, were replete with arguments on the part of the advocates of the states to the effect that no resolution such as those proposed by Nye and Hobbs was needed. "If you must pass a resolution," they said in effect, "pass one which will merely direct the Attorney General of the United States to bring suit against us. We can meet a court fight, but don't prejudice our case with a Congressional declaration of national rights in these submerged areas." In

[28] These cases have been discussed in detail in Chapters 3–6.

[29] *Hearings* on H.J. Res. 118 *et al.* (1945), 28. This group suggested that the proposed quitclaim measures be amended to make clear that the resolutions meant low-water mark as it once was, thus assuring that no claim could be levied against filled and reclaimed lands.

[30] See, e.g., testimony of Leander Shelley, *ibid.*, 21; testimony of Robert Kenny, *ibid.*, 5–11; testimony of Gessner McCorvey, special assistant attorney general of Alabama, *ibid.*, 69–70; statement by Frank F. Truscott, city solicitor of Philadelphia, *ibid.*, 57; testimony of Richmond B. Keech, *ibid.*, 54.

[31] The testimony of Abram Staples, attorney general of Virginia, in *Hearings* on S.J. Res. 48 and H.J. Res. 225 (1946), 93, emphasized this very obvious point.

[32] Testimony of Walter J. Mattison, president of the National Institute of Municipal Law Officers, *ibid.*, 106. His statement is typical of numerous ones which may be found merely by leafing through these 1946 *Hearings*.

1945–46 these same individuals protested just as loudly that Congress should pass a resolution to exclude the very possibility they themselves had suggested, albeit unwillingly, in 1938–39. Yet they detected no inconsistency in their later requests, nor did they admit any. The opponents of the quitclaim, weak numerically though they were, made no effort to seize on this inconsistency and exploit it. No opponent of the quitclaim legislation ever pointed out this reasonably obvious shift in states' rights tactics.

Further, what might have been developed into the strongest argument of all against the quitclaim measures was never broached at all. It may be argued that under a quitclaim the United States would be surrendering its valid claims in the area, if it had any. No agent of the national government, Congress included, may surrender power granted to the national government by the Constitution. In the case of a quitclaim, Congress might be surrendering the legitimate authority of the national government over the marginal-sea area, granting for the moment that it had such authority. Thus, it appears to the writer, an excellent argument against the quitclaim could have been developed on the basic issue of constitutionality.[33]

Had those who opposed the quitclaim made use of the possibilities offered in this line of reasoning, the argument might possibly have received a hearing, if not consideration, from the members of the Congressional committees, who were predominantly lawyers. On the contrary, however, the brief of Raymond Hudson in opposition to quitclaim measures commences with an admission that Congress could give up these areas to the states but that he did not see why the Congress should be so generous.[34] He preferred to couch his arguments in terms of national acquisition from Mexico of the submerged areas, which had never been granted specifically to the states, and which were therefore still under the control of the national government. The Department of the Interior, he reasoned, had the power to issue, and should issue to his clients, federal prospecting permits in the maritime belt.[35] At a later

[33] In 1938–39, Leslie McNemar and Congressman Hobbs made statements on which this line of reasoning is based. *Hearings* on S.J. Res. 176 and 181 (1939), 19. McNemar briefly mentioned the possible constitutionality of a quitclaim measure when one was suggested by Thomas A. J. Dockweiler. He did not develop the argument, however. In 1951, Solicitor General Philip B. Perlman expressed doubt that Congress could "quitclaim," thus bolstering the idea expressed by the writer. *Hearings* on S.J. Res. 20 (1951), 37–40. See pp. 230–33 below, where this argument is discussed in detail and where the writer states his reasons for believing that the line of argument, though interesting, is not basically sound.   [34] *Hearings* on H.J. Res. 118 *et al.* (1945), 132.
[35] *Ibid.*, 132–34.

stage in his argument, however, he reasoned that the dispute was a purely legal one over which the Congress had no constitutional authority of determination.[36] With this last statement he threw himself into the inconsistent position of saying in the first place that Congress could take action and then, at the end, that it could not.

Secretary Ickes, perhaps because of his position, expressed no opinion on the legal questions presented by the quitclaim measures; instead, he said of House Joint Resolution 225:

As to the resolution in its present form, I place my case on a few simple and, I believe, unassailable propositions: The United States and California are now litigating in the Supreme Court their opposing claims to ownership. The question has never before been decided, and no one knows the outcome. It would be an almost unprecedented abuse of legislative power if Congress were to take the issue away from the Supreme Court by presenting to the defendant State the Government's claims. The result would be bad government, not only because it would be an invasion by the legislative branch of the judicial function, but because it would constitute the waste of a national asset which some day might be crucial to our survival.

For these reasons, House Joint Resolution 225 should be rejected.[37]

---

[36] *Ibid.*, 130–32.

[37] *Hearings* on S.J. Res. 48 and H.J. Res. 225 (1946), 12. Sarcastically, Secretary Ickes prefaced his remarks by noting: "This resolution contains also a good deal of argument about an unsettled question of law, and seems to express the view that the United States not only should give away any claim that it may have to the submerged lands but should also apologize for having mentioned it." *Ibid.*, 3. He then outlined the events which brought him to doubt his 1933 attitude.

He flatly stated, and correctly so if viewed in a narrow and highly technical sense, that the issue had never before been adjudicated and denied that he was trying to "seize" these lands. He condemned bitterly the combined actions of the state attorneys general and accused this and similar groups of clouding the main issue, which he contended was oil.

Although the quitclaim legislation had been introduced before any suit had been filed by the national government, he compared the resolution to quitclaim with the situation in *Ex parte McCardle*, 7 Wall. 506 (1869). He called the reconstruction case the "only example" in history in which the Supreme Court was deprived of its jurisdiction in a pending case. Orrin Judd and Robert Kenny, however, cited a number of illustrations in which Congressional action in a pending suit modified substantially the jurisdiction of the court. The most notable and recent example is that in *United States* v. *Southeastern Underwriters*, 322 U.S. 533 (1944), where the fact that an indictment was pending and awaiting trial did not deter Congress from passing a statute to limit the application of the antitrust laws, with the remaining steps in the action being conducted in conformance with the changed law. *Hearings* on S.J. Res. 48 and H.J. Res. 225 (1946), 43–44, 46.

Ickes accused California of having "always" used its petroleum resources

Orin DeMotte Walker, as attorney for Robert E. Lee Jordan, and E. J. Preston, who, with Secretary Ickes, constituted the opposition to the quitclaim, made absolutely no use of any argument based on constitutionality. Instead, they believed that the thirteen original states and Texas held a fee simple title to the submerged lands in the marginal sea. Walker, Jordan, and Preston contended that a quitclaim could not be applied to the thirteen original states and Texas because it would be giving them something they already had.[38] They were interested, financially, in California submerged lands; California's status was different. The territory of California was obtained through treaty with Mexico, and the Congress had never granted the submerged areas to the state. Although the Congress had the power to give the quitclaim, under the power to dispose of the public lands of the United States, they contended, it would be poor public policy.[39]

What was being ignored was the possibility that there might be present here a concept greater than title. Representative Hobbs had come close to it in 1939 with his nonownership theory as applied to the marginal sea, but Hobbs at that time had not carried the idea through to its logical conclusion. Throughout all the hearings there is the constantly recurring theme, a belief that the issue could be decided on the basis of title conceptions. If the question was one merely of title to land, then admittedly the Congress could, through its powers over the public domain, quitclaim the area to the states. But suppose the concept was broader than mere title? Suppose, as the Supreme Court was to presume later in *United States* v. *California, United States* v. *Texas,* and *United States* v. *Louisiana,* the issue in the marginal-sea lands transcended title? Suppose that it was a question of power, of superior authority to exercise a certain right under the federal system with its division of powers between state and nation? Could the Congress, under such circumstances, constitutionally grant to the states those

---

"wastefully and recklessly"; he then sketched for the committee a proposed federal policy for the conservation of the oil in the submerged lands, should the Supreme Court decide they were "federally owned." This policy included recommendations to establish the area as a reserve, to explore its potentialities to the fullest possible extent, to lodge administrative authority in the Department of the Interior, to establish co-ordinated working agreements with the state or upland operators where the submerged lands might be drained from the upland area, and to protect the valid interest of navigation by co-ordinating the total program with the War Department. A special act would have to be passed to give leasing authority, according to Ickes, for he felt that the 1920 Mineral Leasing Act was not applicable to submerged lands.

[38] *Hearings* on S.J. Res. 48 and H.J. Res. 225 (1946), 16–17, 267.
[39] *Ibid.,* 21.

powers which belonged to the federal government? Obviously the possibilities of such an argument were not explored, when to do so might have been to the advantage of those believing in the right and/or title of the United States.

It would serve little purpose to list all of the various groups—municipal, state, and professional—that favored the quitclaim legislation. Reference to the index of the 1945 and 1946 hearings will provide that information in abundant measure. They were a diverse lot, representing inland and coastal states and communities: state officials acting singly and in concert, inland and coastal chambers of commerce, port authorities, educational groups, real estate operators, state legislatures, and plain citizens. The list is indeed most impressive.

House Joint Resolution 225 was reported with a unanimous recommendation for passage.[40] There was little opposition to the measure in the House. Hobbs argued at some length that the United States was quitclaiming a title it never had, for there was no such thing as title to lands in the marginal sea.[41] He filed a brief in opposition in which he said:

> Be it not thought, because there is no specific grant conveying fee-simple title into the people of the United States, that their right to conserve, take and use the petroleum in question is less clear or strong. This right is inherent in the sovereignty of the Federal Government created by the Constitution. . . . The right of all the people of the United States, acting through their Government, to use this oil is like their right to breathe air—necessary to the maintenance of constitutional vigor.[42]

He then told the members of the House to vote as they pleased. They had the votes to pass the measure, he admitted, but they had no right to shut their eyes to the duty which the Congress ought to perform.[43]

No member of the House came actively to the support of Representative Hobbs. Representative Voorhis of California supported an amendment introduced by Hobbs which would have retained control of the oil for the United States. Said Voorhis: "I am frank to say that one reason I am going to support the Hobbs amendment is that I do not believe that by and large the States have successfully or effectively protected the public interests of the American people in those oil resources which lie in these submerged lands."[44] The Hobbs amendment, Voorhis claimed, would quitclaim title of the marginal-sea areas to the states,

---

[40] 91 *Congressional Record* 8840. [41] *Ibid.*, 8842.
[42] *Ibid.*, 8849. [43] *Ibid.*, 8864. [44] *Ibid.*, 8865.

but the United States would retain the mineral rights, which was exactly what he wanted.[45] Representative Gallagher remarked that House Joint Resolution 225 was being passed to allow the oil companies to exploit the country.[46] Representative LaFollette stated: "I find a rather unique coincidence in the rise of Ed Pauley in the Democratic Party and the removal of Mr. Biddle and the naming of Mr. Clark. I am wondering if the Republican Members have made appropriate arrangements for their share of any campaign funds that may arise out of the passage of this legislation."[47] Thus, aside from a few slighting and sarcastic remarks directed at the opposition, Hobbs got no support in carrying on his singlehanded battle. His amendment was voted down; House Joint Resolution 225 passed the House by a vote of 108 to 11.[48]

Opposition to the quitclaim in the Senate centered in Senators Barkley, Tobey, Fulbright, and Donnell, with the last-named doing most of the talking and developing a highly legalistic argument that ran on for pages.[49] The gist of Donnell's remarks was that no case before decided was exactly in point and therefore the Supreme Court should be allowed to reach a decision. Tobey called the resolution "a final act of prodigality in disposing of public lands and interests in public lands which are vested in the United States."[50] There was, however, no numerical opposition from a debate standpoint, and the measure passed the Senate by a vote of 44 to 34 with 18 senators abstaining.[51] Party lines meant nothing in the vote, Republicans and Democrats being about equally split on both sides. The measure was then sent to the President.[52]

President Truman vetoed the resolution. Ickes intimated that, in view of the fact that Franklin Roosevelt had resisted the terrific political pressures which had been brought to kill tidelands action, President Truman could not have done otherwise.[53] The grounds of the President's veto were simple and apparently reasonable; he stated that the issue was currently before the Supreme Court for decision and should not be disturbed. Although *United States* v. *California* had not been argued at the date of the veto, 2 August 1946, the briefs had long since been filed. The President wanted determination on the legal issues involved.[54] His veto was sustained.[55] We have only the word of Secretary

---

[45] *Ibid.*   [46] *Ibid.*   [47] *Ibid.*, 8860.   [48] *Ibid.*, 8869.
[49] 92 *Congressional Record* 9524 ff.   [50] *Ibid.*, 9642.   [51] *Ibid.*
[52] *Ibid.*, 10496.   [53] Letter to the writer, 29 November 1947.
[54] 92 *Congressional Record* 10660.
[55] *Ibid.*, 10745. The vote took place in the House. The results were 193 yeas, 95 nays, and 196 not voting.

Ickes that President Roosevelt would have acted similarly; said Ickes, "I think that, at heart, he was with me on this issue all the time."[56]

Out of the welter of claims and counterclaims which mark the actions of the national government down to 1947 and *United States* v. *California,* it is possible to draw certain general conclusions:

1. No evidence can be found that the Congress of the United States prior to 1937 considered the area below low-water mark as a part of the public lands of the United States or considered the area to be under such control of the national government that oil in the submerged lands in the marginal sea might be taken by federal authority. Indeed the action, or inaction, of Congress appears to indicate that before 1937 the contrary view was held; for although the Congress had the power to grant lands below low-water mark while an area was in territorial status, it never did so by any general legislation.

2. The introduction of the Nye and Hobbs resolutions marks the first attempt on the part of Congress to assert a right in the submerged areas; the attempt was not successful. The singling out of California merely resulted in the establishment of a cohesive bloc among the states as a whole, a bloc which has continued and grown in strength down to the present day.

3. The executive departments, prior to 1937, when Secretary Ickes began to hold in abeyance applications for federal leasing permits in the submerged areas, appear uniformly to have acquiesced, without argument, in the activities of the states in the marginal sea, except where those activities infringed on the admitted powers of the national government to control commerce and navigation.

4. After 1937 the Navy and Interior departments spearheaded the attack to get the Nye and Hobbs resolutions passed, primarily on grounds of necessity, but stating their arguments as much as possible in terms of the application of the implied-powers doctrine. The position of the executive departments to January 1953 was one of attempting to confine the argument, with a conspicuous lack of success, to the single question of oil.

5. The arguments of both sides were stated primarily in terms of a concept of title, ignoring to a considerable extent the very basis upon which the Supreme Court was to decide in favor of the United States in *United States* v. *California, United States* v. *Texas,* and *United States* v. *Louisiana.*

---

[56] Letter to the writer, 29 November 1947.

6. Regardless of the fact that the executive departments couched the problem in terms of oil, the principle on which they advocated national control of the oil in submerged lands would be applicable equally to all commodities, including the soil itself, below the line of low water in the open sea. To condemn, therefore, as did Secretary Ickes, the almost unanimous opposition of the states to the extension of federal control is to ignore the basic fact that the issue could not be confined to the single one of oil. The states were quite within their province, in a federal system, in fighting as they did to secure that which they felt to be their right.

7. The real stimulus to national control, as evidenced by the lack of opposition to the quitclaim measures, had been furnished by a few persons of the caliber of Secretary Ickes. Whether time will prove him correct and wise or incorrect and foolish remains to be seen. Although some may have called him scoundrel and charlatan, it is virtually impossible to question the Secretary's sincerity in his advocacy of federal control.

10 ·

United States *v.* California

In the triumvirate of cases declaring the paramount authority of the United States in the submerged lands of the marginal sea, the most important is, of course, the case of *United States* v. *California*. The later cases of *United States* v. *Texas* and *United States* v. *Louisiana* are built upon the foundation of the earlier case; indeed, it is possible to say that *United States* v. *California* was decided in the fashion that it was because of the certainty that the issue of control of submerged lands in the Gulf of Mexico would inevitably arise. It is for this reason that the 1947 case must now be considered in detail.

At 12:30 P.M., 29 May 1945, the Department of Justice issued a press release which stated that a suit to enjoin the Pacific Western Oil Company from "extracting additional oil in the rich submerged Elwood Field near Santa Barbara" had been filed in the Federal District Court for the Southern District of California.[1] As has been previously noted, the Pacific Western Company had been operating in this area under lease from the state of California. The action transferred the battle for the control of California offshore oil from the political branches to the judicial department of the national government.

This so-called "death bed act"[2] of Attorney General Biddle resulted in an immediate acceptance by California of the challenge to battle, with Attorney General Robert Kenny promising a fight. For though the action was directed against a private company, Kenny believed with

---

[1] *Los Angeles Times,* 30 May 1945. The suit was filed by Special Assistants Francis B. Critchlow and Eugene D. Williams and United States Attorney Charles H. Carr.

[2] *Ibid.* The phrase is Robert Kenny's and is based on the fact that Attorney General Biddle had just announced his retirement effective as of 1 July 1945.

Secretary Ickes that the action was in effect one against the state of California. Declaring the suit brought by the United States to be an attack on state sovereignty and contrary to President Truman's announced policy of federal-state co-operation, Attorney General Kenny stated that the only way the United States could enjoin the state was in the Supreme Court of the United States.[3]

The lease of the Pacific Western Oil Company which was thus attacked covered 144.07 acres in the Goleta area, but Biddle pointed out that suit was being brought to determine the legal rights of the United States and the state of California, a clear indication that the views of Secretary Ickes and Robert Kenny were on sound ground by the admission of the Attorney General himself. The suit, Biddle claimed, would also determine legal rights as between the United States and "other coastal States where there are oil deposits." Thus covered, according to the statement of the Justice Department, would be 2,100 acres with 73,500,000 barrels of recoverable oil. Furthermore, oil possibilities were supposed to be present in an additional 5,000 acres with an estimated 200,000,000 barrels recoverable. All of these areas would be immediately affected, it was stated, together with oil fields in the submerged areas off Texas, Florida, and Mississippi.[4]

Attorney General Biddle admitted that the decision to take action was a recent one, for the idea of filing such a suit had been dropped by the Department of Justice some years before. Impetus had been supplied, however, by the fact that "several licensees" had been attempting to get permission of the Department of the Interior to drill on these lands.[5] Norman Littell, when he testified at the Pauley hearings, took a somewhat different view of Biddle's reasons for taking action after the project had been abandoned. Littell had been one of the "bright young lawyers" who found their way to Washington with the New Deal. He had held the post of assistant in the Attorney General's Office, from which position he had been removed by President Roosevelt.[6] Littell

[3] *Ibid.* Grover Sellers correctly pointed out that the settled method of determining boundary disputes between states or between the United States and a state has been by an original proceeding in the Supreme Court. *Hearings* on H.J. Res. 118 *et al.* (1945), 43.

[4] *Los Angeles Times,* 30 May 1945. These figures on recoverable oil, believed to be correct in 1945, are now out of date as the result of the discovery of new fields. The press release omitted Louisiana.

[5] *Ibid.*

[6] The grounds of Littell's removal are open to dispute. See letters from Littell and William W. Clary in *Hearings* before a subcommittee of the Senate Judiciary Committee on S. 1988, 80th Cong., 2d sess. (1948), 334–35. These hearings will hereinafter be cited as *Hearings* on S. 1988 (1948). They should be distinguished

contended that in 1942 Biddle had publicly announced the suit was dead. The reason it was resurrected, Littell alleged, was that "Tommy the Cork" Corcoran had a great deal of influence with Attorney General Biddle. It was Corcoran who had persuaded Biddle to change his mind, and Corcoran, it was charged, was a direct representative of persons who would benefit from federal control of the submerged fields.[7] The truth or falsity of this statement was never proved, but *something* happened to change Biddle's mind. No official denial of the Littell testimony was ever entered, insofar as this writer has been able to discover.

The *Pacific Western* action did not involve tidelands in the technical sense or lands under inland waters, though, said Biddle, "the status of these will no doubt be clarified to some extent by the decision."[8] This statement caused Attorney General Kenny to say later in rejoinder that "a man could be clarified right out of title."[9] The cryptic remark of Biddle was never further explained. In the light of the many decisions which have definitely held that the states have title to lands beneath navigable waters to low-water mark, Biddle must have been thinking of some possible judicial reappraisal of the whole question, not just a determination of the status of submerged lands in the marginal sea.

At any rate, the *Pacific Western* action was dropped 19 October 1945, at which time Attorney General Tom Clark filed an original action against the state of California in the Supreme Court of the United States. Mention has been made of the fact that Secretary Ickes took the credit for this development. He had been extremely unhappy when the *Pacific Western* action was filed. When Clark took over, the Secretary of the Interior tried to get the suit dismissed and an original action against California substituted. When the Attorney General demurred, Ickes went directly to President Truman and explained the situation to him, whereupon the President ordered Clark to follow Ickes' suggestion. After much pushing, Clark finally took the necessary steps to kill the *Pacific Western* suit and filed a complaint in the original jurisdiction of the Supreme Court of the United States.[10] Paragraph 2 of the complaint against California alleged as follows:

---

from the joint *Hearings* on S. 1988 (1948), which were held earlier the same year.

[7] Littell's testimony is summarized in the *New York Times,* 2 February 1946.
[8] *Los Angeles Times,* 30 May 1935.
[9] *Hearings* on H.J. Res. 118 *et al.* (1945), 5.
[10] Letter of Ickes to the writer, 29 November 1947.

At all times herein mentioned, plaintiff was and now is the owner in fee simple of, or possessed of paramount rights in and powers over, the lands, minerals and other things of value underlying the Pacific Ocean, lying seaward of the ordinary low water mark on the coast of California and outside of the inland waters of the State, extending seaward three nautical miles and bounded on the north and south, respectively, by the northern and southern boundaries of the State of California.[11]

The prayer was for a decree declaring the rights of the United States as against the state of California and for an injunction against the state of California and persons claiming under the state from trespassing on the area.

Attorney General Tom Clark, in a speech before the National Association of Attorneys General at Jacksonville, Florida, 27 November 1945, explained the reason for acting solely against the state of California:

In filing the action in the Supreme Court against the State of California alone, there was, of course, no intention to discriminate against that state. There are many other coastal States of the Union as well as thousands of individuals and corporations who assert claims in the marginal sea area under authority of the states. The decision of the Supreme Court, we hope, will settle the question as to all coastal states of the Union.[12]

Here, at long last, an executive officer of the national government admitted that the issue was not one of oil alone. Clark did not attempt to confine the argument to oil. He stated frankly and clearly that "thousands" of persons would be affected, and that all of the coastal states, rather than one, might find the status of the lands off their coasts in question. The amazing thing about this whole controversy is the attempt which was made to center the argument on oil alone, probably in an effort to get the inland states to withdraw their active opposition. Yet a few short months before the case was to be argued, the Attorney General of the United States flatly stated that the adoption by the Supreme Court of the rule he was proposing would be equally applicable to the marginal sea of all the coastal states. From this point on, the protestations of Ickes and others that the issue was solely one of oil fell on deaf ears indeed.

In answer to the complaint, California filed what Ickes called the

[11] Supreme Court of the United States, No. 12 Original, 1945 Term.
[12] Press release of the Department of Justice of that date.

"most elaborate and complicated pleading on record in the Supreme Court—an answer in three volumes, running to 822 printed pages and weighing 3 pounds 9 ounces."[13] This is the work which Manley O. Hudson, after the decision in *United States* v. *California,* said he doubted if the members of the Supreme Court had even read, for the court was "ignorant" of many of the state's "brilliant arguments."[14] Of course it should be noted that Judge Hudson had been retained by the state of California and had helped the state prepare materials on the international-law aspects of the case.

The Department of Justice was not at all satisfied with this three-volume work. After California had filed its answer, the United States filed a motion to strike answer on the ground that the answer was so "prolix and so replete with arguments, evidentiary matter and conclusions, both of law and of fact, that it is virtually impossible to segregate and identify the well-pleaded facts for the purpose of determining the issues to be tendered." On 22 April 1946 the Supreme Court ordered the attorney general of California to file a "succinct statement, without argument or statement of evidence, of the several propositions of law and fact, separately stated and enumerated, which he deems to have been placed in issue by the answer." California filed the statement, and the United States submitted a memorandum in regard to it. A pretrial conference was held in the chambers of Justice Black, the result of which saw the state of California filing a new and condensed answer on 21 May 1946, with the understanding that the three-volume original was to remain on file with the court for such use as the court or the parties to the action might make of it, and with the further provision that the original answer was not to be treated as a part of the pleadings. The United States then withdrew its motion to strike answer.[15] The issue was joined; the case was argued 13 and 14 March 1947.

---

[13] *Hearings* on S.J. Res. 48 and H.J. Res. 225 (1946), 9.

[14] Report of Charles B. Degges, Washington correspondent, on the February 1948 quitclaim hearings on S. 1988, *Oakland Tribune,* 26 February 1948. It appears that Judge Hudson and other witnesses locked horns with Senator Donnell, opponent of the quitclaim. According to Degges, Judge Hudson "practically laughed Donnell out of committee when the Missourian tried his usual browbeating tactics on him."

[15] This account of what happened to the original California answer is taken from the United States brief, *California* case, 5–6 n. In March 1947, California filed a two-volume document consisting of a "Brief in Opposition to Motion for Judgment" and Appendices A to I. This material was prepared in answer to the "Brief of the United States in Support of Motion for Judgment." The March California effort totaled 508 pages; the weight was not reported.

The United States made four major contentions. The first of these, after definition of basic terms, argued that the development of a territorial concept in the three-mile zone was a modern idea, not accepted in international law until sometime after the adoption of the national Constitution.

The second argued that while the state of California was admitted to the Union on an "equal footing," such admission endowed the state with governmental powers only. The state had no rights in public lands except as such lands were granted to the state by the United States. The United States, admittedly, had never made an express cession of lands; the government argued that there had never been any implied grant. This conclusion was based on the view that the "equal footing" clause should not be so construed as to imply any grant of land in the marginal sea.

The third point characterized the decisions cited by the state as not controlling because (1) these decisions had dealt with inland waters and tidelands (in the technical sense) only; (2) ownership of the marginal sea, if such there be, was more closely an attribute of national than of state sovereignty; (3) the original states never claimed or owned the marginal-sea areas off their coasts, and the crystallization of the territorial concept of the marginal sea, coming after the adoption of the Constitution, could only result in the vesting of such property rights in the national government; and (4) even if the original states had owned the area off their coasts to the three-mile limit, California could not hold similar ownership because the ownership of such submerged lands is not an indicium of sovereignty at all.[16]

The fourth major contention of the national government dealt with the arguments advanced by the state of California that estoppel, laches, adverse possession, and *res judicata* precluded an assertion of national right in the area. The United States argued that (1) there was not present a "long-continued and uniform acquiescence" on the part of the federal government as alleged by the state, for the vast bulk of the instances cited by the state did not occur in the open sea but in inland or tideland areas; (2) while there may have been expenditures

---

[16] The United States brief, *California* case, 11, makes the following comment on this point: ". . . we submit that ownership of submerged lands is not related to sovereignty at all, and that the decisions of this Court dealing with the tidelands and lands under inland waters have proceeded upon a false premise. The Government does not ask that these cases be overruled; indeed, it suggests that in the interest of clarity and certainty they be reaffirmed herein; but the Government does ask that the unsound rule of those cases be not extended to the marginal sea."

by private persons in the marginal sea which Congress might well recognize, the total value so far expended was infinitesimal in comparison with the total worth of the area yet to be explored and therefore should not preclude an assertion of federal right; (3) estoppel could not run against the United States anyhow because of any mistaken or unauthorized actions performed by the agents of the national government; (4) the issue was of recent origin, for oil had been but recently discovered and the United States had not delayed action unduly; and (5) insofar as the argument of *res judicata* was concerned, this particular issue had never been adjudicated, for all the cited cases dealt with inland or tideland areas and were not, therefore, applicable.

Thus did the advocates of the United States declare the substance of their arguments.[17]

The complexity of the California pleadings makes it difficult to state the arguments in the same concise form as those of the United States. A great deal of factual and historical material had to receive consideration, for such material formed a major part of the California case.

Two arguments of a somewhat technical character were presented at the outset. In the first place, the jurisdiction of the Supreme Court was questioned on the basis that there was no "case or controversy" present which would bring the case properly before the court under Article III of the Constitution. There was only a difference of opinion between federal and state officials over a subject matter so vaguely defined as to be impossible to identify. Secondly, California argued that even if the court did have jurisdiction, the fact that Congress for over one hundred years had, allegedly, recognized the ownership of the states presented a serious question as to whether or not the Attorney General had the authority to maintain the action.

Of the 192 pages of the California brief, 108 were devoted to affirmative defenses attempting to prove California's right and title in the submerged lands below low-water mark out to the three-mile limit. To this end, the rights of the British Crown were traced through the thirteen original states which succeeded to the rights of the Crown. These states, it was alleged, never surrendered the lands in the marginal seas off their coasts, one of the attributes of sovereignty which they took over from the Crown. The new states admitted to the Union held the same rights of ownership in the beds of navigable waters as the original states under the "equal footing" rule. Decisions of the Supreme Court, down through the years, were held to have established a rule

---

[17] This summary is taken from *ibid.,* 7–15.

of property in the marginal-sea area; and, even if the original decisions were incorrect (which the state of California would not grant), the rule of property so established should not now be disturbed.

To this basic argument, which constituted California's primary defense in the case, were added arguments involving the doctrines of estoppel, prescription, acquiescence, laches, and *res judicata*. These arguments were buttressed in detail by discussions of numerous instances in which, presumedly, the federal government through the acts of its agents had in effect recognized and established a title to the submerged soils in the state.

Property rights and questions of title were held to be matters of municipal law; the United States, in the exercise of its constitutional functions, could not thereby acquire title to property. The United States, through its position as a member of the family of nations, did not come into possession of property. Since it was established, according to the contentions of California, that the territorial concept of the marginal sea was a part of international law prior to 1776, it must therefore follow that the states and not the national government must hold title to submerged lands of the maritime belt.

These are the California arguments summarized.[18]

The arguments of both parties proceeded on the fundamental premise that rights to property were involved. The action was conducted on the part of the disputants as though the issue were purely one of title. It is true that the United States, in its complaint, spoke of the national government as having "paramount rights" in the area, if, indeed, it did not have title. The tenor of the pleadings of the United States departed almost immediately from this idea, however, and a few pages later the assertion was made by the United States that "the Government contends only that the area in question became the property of the United States and that it has never conveyed that area to the state."[19] While the United States made a number of asides, throughout its arguments, which touch on the doctrine of "paramount rights," the basis of which must have been the arguments of Congressman Sam Hobbs in 1938 and 1939, the argument was basically one of title. The California pleadings were stated almost entirely in terms of property

---

[18] The summary was prepared by the writer on the basis of the 192-page California brief.

[19] United States brief, *California* case, 5. Attorney General Tom Clark opened his oral argument before the court by stating: "The question is a simple one. It merely involves the proprietary right, the ownership to land underlying this three mile belt. . . ." *Proceedings,* Oral Transcript, *United States* v. *California,* 1.

concepts. Since the case of the United States was premised on that line of reasoning, there was no reason for California to do otherwise.

These were lawyers arguing, on the legal bases with which they were familiar, a concept of title and all that title implies. It appears that they saw no reason to argue the larger but ephemeral concept of "paramount rights," a doctrine of far greater importance to the general theory of federalism than to the more prosaic and legalistic concept of title. Whether the outcome could or would have been different if the state of California had chosen to devote the bulk of its pleadings to this more inclusive theory is a matter for pure conjecture. In a letter to the writer dated 13 August 1952, William W. Clary stated frankly that the failure of California to argue the paramount-powers theory was a basic error. In view of the nature of the pleadings, however, he and his associates need feel no remorse for failure to give consideration to the theory. The fact remains that the case was argued entirely on one basis and decided on another, as will presently be shown.

The arguments in regard to title need not be further developed than the statement which has been made of them at this point. For the most part they were legal restatements of the years of argument and counter argument of 1938–39 and 1945–46. The extensive discussion previously entered on these points[20] is sufficient for the purpose here. Each advocate brought out much the same ideas, using the same cases, as had the disputants before Congressional committees. The phraseology was smoother and the organization vastly superior, but the essence of the arguments remained generally the same.

In a divided opinion the Supreme Court held for the United States. Mr. Justice Jackson took no part in the consideration or discussion of the case, and Justices Frankfurter and Reed registered strong dissents. The writing of the majority opinion fell to the lot of Mr. Justice Black, who blazed a new judicial trail of great moment to the nature of the American federal system as it will or must operate in the future. As has been true of many decisions of the highest tribunal of the land, the ramifications of *United States* v. *California* extend beyond the mere question of power over and rights to oil out of one minute portion of the marginal sea off one state's coast.

Noting that the legal issues had been exhaustively and thoroughly covered by the briefs and oral arguments, Justice Black said that the

---

[20] Chapters 2–9.

time was "now ripe for determination" of these issues. Before this case
could be considered on its merits, however, it was necessary to dispose
of the two somewhat more technical issues involving the right of the
court to adjudicate the claim of the national government in this type
of proceeding. These two issues had been raised by the state of California, though they were not argued orally. Counsel for the state felt
that the limited time available for oral presentation could be used more
advantageously in establishing California's affirmative defenses.

The first of the two technical issues involved the contention of the
state that there was not present a "case or controversy" within the scope
of Article III, section 2, of the Constitution. This argument was based
on a belief (1) that there was no dispute in a legal sense, but only a
disagreement between federal and state officials, and (2) that there
was no way to identify the subject matter of the suit so as to be able
to render a proper decree. Justice Black made short work of this contention. More was involved here, he said, than a mere difference of
opinion between officials of the state and federal governments; it was
a "concrete conflict" involving the question of who owned or who
might exercise paramount rights in the marginal sea off the coast of
California. This type of conflict was a controversy in the "classic legal
sense." "The justiciability of this controversy rests therefore on conflicting claims of alleged invasions of interests in property and on conflicting claims of governmental powers to authorize its use."[21]

Further than that, though California might argue that the national
government had not sufficiently demarcated the subject matter of the
suit, determination of the boundary was "not impossible." True, said
Justice Black, it might be difficult to determine whether or not a given
land indentation was or was not a true bay, but it could be done. There
was nothing to prevent later and more detailed hearings to determine
disputed boundary areas in specific sections. The Supreme Court had
frequently fulfilled the function of boundary arbiter in numerous equitable proceedings between the states. The contention of California
presented no "insuperable obstacle" to the exercise of jurisdiction by
the high court.[22]

---

[21] 332 U.S. 19, 25.

[22] *Ibid.,* 26. What Justice Black said, in effect, was that further proceedings
would be necessary if the holding was favorable to the national government.
Justice Black tacitly invited future litigation, without saying so openly. In criticism of the Justice's treatment of this point, it may be stated that litigation over
land rights ordinarily does not come to trial until the issue is settled as to exactly
what areas are in dispute. Five and one-half years after the *California* decision,
proceedings over the drawing of the boundary line of inland waters and the open

The second of the technical issues involved a contention by California that the Attorney General of the United States did not have the authorization requisite to the filing and maintenance of the suit. This is a technical argument, the state claiming that the powers of the Attorney General in regard to the instant case were limited by implication in that the Congress had twice failed to grant authority to the Attorney General to maintain exactly the kind of action he was now bringing. Justice Black had no difficulty disposing of this argument. All he had to say was that the Congress had never amended the statutes imposing on the Attorney General of the United States the duty of protecting the interests of the federal government through the instrument of the courts.[23]

The arguments of the parties on this point present some strange contradictions. In 1938 and 1939, California had argued that neither the Nye nor the Hobbs resolutions were necessary because the Attorney General of the United States already had the requisite authority to bring an action should he care to exercise it. The implication at that time was that he was afraid to bring the suit because he knew his case was too weak. On the other hand, the United States had also abandoned its 1938 position. At that time, it will be recalled, the Justice and Navy departments did not feel they had authority to bring suit without a resolution requiring them to do so.

Having disposed of the two relatively minor jurisdictional points, Black now came to grips with the problem of deciding the case on its merits. Significantly, he prefaced his remarks on the heart of the case in this fashion:

The crucial question on the merits is not merely who owns the bare legal title to the lands under the marginal sea. The United States here asserts rights in two capacities transcending those of a mere property owner. In one capacity it asserts the right and responsibility to exercise whatever power and dominion are necessary to protect this country against dangers to the security and tranquillity of its people incident to the fact that the United States is located immediately adjacent to the ocean. The Government also appears in its capacity as a member of the family of nations. In that capacity it is responsible for conducting United States relations with other nations. It asserts that proper exercise of these constitutional re-

---

sea off the coast of the Golden State continued. Did Justice Black's pronouncement on this point violate the established principle requiring determination of the areas in controversy before allowing the cause to come to trial?

[23] The authority given to the Attorney General in this regard is found in 5 U.S.C., §§291, 309.

sponsibilities requires that it have power, unencumbered by state commitments, always to determine what agreements will be made concerning
the control and use of the marginal sea and the land under it. . . . In the
light of the foregoing, our question is whether the state or the Federal
Government has the paramount right and power to determine in the first
instance when, how, and by what agencies, foreign or domestic, the oil
and other resources of the soils of the marginal sea, known or hereafter
discovered, may be exploited.[24]

The conclusion is inescapable that arguments of title are of little
moment to Justice Black. He is saying that the majority opinion will
ignore the vast bulk of arguments presented by both sides and choose a
new path irrespective of these arguments. A careful study of the briefs
of both sides will not substantiate the emphasis which Black places upon
the disregard of title. If one reads only the majority opinion, the inference can be made that the United States argued the case on the basis
of the statements which have just been quoted. Such an inference
would be incorrect. The United States argued its case primarily from
the standpoint of title and made only the most incidental mention of the
points which Justice Black chose to emphasize. Although the Justice
had the incontestable right to ignore the references on title and to strike
out on his own, it should be made clear that he did not rely upon the
brief of the national government as a support for his opinion.

According to Justice Black, California based its claims to ownership
upon these points: (1) that the Constitution adopted by the state of
California in 1849, prior to the admission of the state to the Union,
placed the state's boundaries three English miles out in the marginal
sea; (2) that the enabling act admitting California to the Union admitted the state on "an equal footing with the original States in all
respects whatever"; and (3) that therefore ownership by California
of the marginal sea must follow the rule announced by the Supreme
Court in the case of *Pollard's Lessee* v. *Hagan,* with its declaration that
since the thirteen original states owned the navigable waters within
their boundaries, it must follow that later states admitted on an equal
footing must hold similar rights as an inseparable part of state sovereignty.

The United States did not and could not deny the existence of the
rule in the *Pollard* case, but it did argue that the rationale of the
Pollard decision should not be extended to the area of the marginal

[24] 332 U.S. 19, 29.

sea.[25] As Justice Black analyzed the brief of the United States, he noted that the claim was that the thirteen original states did not own the marginal sea area off their shores; that the federal government did not assert its "increasingly greater rights"[26] in the marginal sea until "after the formation of the Union"; and that the United States had not granted any of these rights to the states, but had retained them as "appurtenances of national sovereignty."

Justice Black waived aside with two short paragraphs the contention that the thirteen original states owned the three-mile belt off their coasts. Without meeting in any way the arguments advanced by California, he stated: "From all the wealth of material supplied, however, we cannot say that the thirteen original colonies separately acquired ownership to the three-mile belt or the soil under it, even if they did acquire elements of the sovereignty of the English Crown by their revolution against it."[27] The thirteen original states did not own the marginal sea, Black said, because the territorial concept of the marginal sea was only a "nebulous suggestion" at the time of the Declaration of Inde-

---

[25] The fact that the United States could not deny the existence of the *Pollard* rule did not prevent criticism of it. Thus in the United States brief, *California* case, 143, it is stated in regard to the line of decisions of which the *Pollard* case is the keystone: "Finally, in the alternative, we contend that the equal footing rule is inapplicable because the concept of ownership as an attribute of sovereignty within the meaning of the equal footing clause is unsound and should not be extended to the marginal sea. In making this contention we do not urge that the decisions applying the rule to tidelands and inland waters be overruled. Indeed we suggest that the Court reaffirm those decisions lest any doubts be permitted to arise as to the rights established by them. But we submit that the unsound rule of those decisions should not be extended to the marginal sea."

Again, at 153: "It thus appears that the concept of ownership as an attribute of State sovereignty is a legal fiction which was adopted rather fortuitously for the purposes of the so-called tideland rule only and which being an unsound exception to the usual notion of property ownership, ought not to be extended now to apply to the marginal sea."

[26] 332 U.S. 19, 31. The phrase is Justice Black's; it does not occur in the pleadings of the United States. Its use is open to serious question, for the phrase poses the question of what may be the source of "increasingly greater rights." Either the Constitution gives certain powers to the federal government or it does not, albeit the dividing line is sometimes not clear and is subject to interpretation. Through the exercise of the doctrine of implied powers and the situation of the times, the national government may exercise powers at one time which it may not have before exercised. To use the bare words, however, and to speak of "increasingly greater rights" is a mere redundancy. How may a right be "increasingly greater"?

[27] *Ibid.* Justice Black, in a footnote, cites a number of authors who supposedly bore out his contentions. As has already been seen in Chapter 2, however, there are notable statements to the effect that such a territorial concept did exist. As is his prerogative, Justice Black listed only those that supported his statement.

pendence. He asserted that "there is no substantial support in history for the idea" that the early settlers in this country "wanted or claimed a right to block off the ocean's bottom for private ownership and use in the extraction of its wealth."[28] This statement was, as has been shown, incorrect. The early settlers did block off sea areas for a number of purposes, such as oyster cultivation. To say that early charters granted by the Crown did not specifically give the three-mile zone to the new colonies would be correct; but Justice Black was saying something quite different—that no document to which the Supreme Court had been referred showed any intent or purpose to grant the use of the marginal-sea areas. Some of the charters, as has been shown in Chapter 2,[29] very probably did contemplate the exclusive utilization of these areas by the early settlers.

Further, as has also been shown in Chapter 2, the territorial concept of the marginal sea was decidedly more than a "nebulous suggestion" in 1789. It is true that the exact extent of the area may have been in doubt, but it is not true that there was no territorial concept of the marginal sea at this time. To say that there is "no substantial support in history" for this view is to ignore the vast amount of documentary material which was submitted to the court showing the very reverse to be within the realm of possibility, though admittedly subject to argument. Justice Black relied on *Queen* v. *Keyn* in support of his views that the concept of territoriality was in doubt as late as 1876. It has already been demonstrated, however, that this case is but one opinion, and badly divided at that, while the entire weight of British practice falls on the opposite, the territorial, side.[30]

Justice Black then proceeded to cite instances in which the political branches, i.e., the executive, of the national government had asserted "broad dominion and control" over the three-mile marginal belt. These assertions—though in no case which he cited was there ever a question of title or opposition of state and national interests—he now held to be "binding" on the court. Not only was there never any declaration of title in the instances which he cited, but the Continental Shelf Proclamation of President Truman on which he relied, specifically exempted the claims of the states in the marginal-sea area, a fact he did not mention.

The amazing thing about this statement that the declarations were binding on the court was that after using it, Black proceeded to decide

[28] *Ibid.,* 32–33.   [29] Pp. 17–18.
[30] See pp. 15–17 above, where *Queen* v. *Keyn* is discussed.

the case on its merits. The cases on which the Justice relied[31] in proving the assertions of the political branch binding on the court state unequivocally that such declarations are political questions which the court may not review. If, therefore, declarations of the political branches of the government in these areas are binding on the courts, why was it necessary to spend more time in argument? Why not say that the entire controversy was a political one and therefore allow the assertions of the federal government to stand, for whatever they might be worth? Although it is true that such an answer would constitute no practical solution, it seems quite useless to assert that these expressions of "national dominion" are "binding upon this Court" and then to proceed to argue the whole question at great length.

At any rate, said Justice Black:

Not only has the acquisition, as it were, of the three-mile belt been accomplished by the National Government, but protection and control of it has been and is a function of national external sovereignty. . . . The belief that local interests are so predominant as constitutionally to require state dominion over lands under its land-locked navigable waters finds some argument for its support. But such can hardly be said in favor of state control over any part of the ocean or the ocean's bottom. . . . The three-mile rule is but a recognition of the necessity that a government next to the sea must be able to protect itself from dangers incident to its location; . . . insofar as the nation asserts its rights under international law, whatever of value may be discovered in the sea next to its shores and within its protective belt, will most naturally be appropriated for its use. . . . What this Government does, or even what the states do, anywhere in the ocean, is a subject upon which the nation may enter into and assume treaty or similar international obligations. . . . The very oil about which the state and nation here contend might well become the subject of international dispute and settlement.[32]

The decision in *United States* v. *California* is to the effect that California does not own the contested area and that the United States has paramount rights therein; the United States is nowhere declared to have title. Here, however, Justice Black gave some slight indication that he regarded the area as having been "acquired, as it were" by the United States. As to what his criteria are for "acquisition," he gives no hint. Acquisition implies in most minds a physical possession. This is one of

[31] *Jones* v. *United States*, 137 U.S. 202, 212–14 (1890); *In re Cooper*, 143 U.S. 472, 502–503 (1892).
[32] 332 U.S. 19, 34–35.

the very few times when Black allowed himself the luxury of slipping
into phraseology which might be used by those arguing title. Though
not important in the instant case, these words might require reinterpre-
tation at some future date, for the word "acquisition," standing in
splendid isolation, may have many an effect not presently foreseen.

The net effect of the paragraph just quoted, however, is to pose the
proposition that the United States holds this area of the marginal sea
as an attribute of national sovereignty. Because it is a member of the
family of nations, its power in this zone must not be encumbered,
but must be free to allow for dealing with other members of the international family without the restraints that state ownership of the area
might entail. What these restraints might be, the Justice did not say.
The fact that the oil—and Black limited his remarks rather strictly
to that subject—might be a subject of a treaty assumes a position of
importance in the statement of his position.

This argument, however, in the light of *Missouri* v. *Holland*,[33] can
be held to apply to almost any phase of national economic, political, or
social existence. What subjects are there that may not become the subject of a treaty and thereby removed from the control of the states?
Without arguing the question, a case can be made that there are very
few indeed. The important fact to note, it appears to this writer, is that
these items would become subjects of national control only after such
a treaty were concluded. The argument that a given area of power
might be the subject of an international treaty, it is submitted, affords
no answer to the question of ownership of submerged soils. To say that
oil in the marginal sea may be subjected to the control of the national
government because it might be the subject of a treaty contributes
nothing and proves nothing. If such oil actually were the subject of
such a treaty, the statement would stand in an undeniably different
relationship to the constitutional power of the national government
than it apparently does as used by Justice Black.

On the other hand, the Justice's argument that this area bears a
fuller relationship to national than to state sovereignty is an eminently
practical realization of the circumstances. As indicated by him in a following paragraph,[34] the states are not equipped to defend this area;
its protection is a function solely of the national government. The responsibility to the family of nations for the area is a charge on the
national government and not on the individual states. If one were to
consider the relations of the area in cold logic, the conclusion that would

[33] 252 U.S. 416 (1920).   [34] 332 U.S. 19, 35–36.

1

be reached pragmatically in every case would be that the area must bear a closer tie to the national than to the individual state governments.

The flaw in the argument is that a federal system is not always or necessarily a logical system. There are many areas of power which are reserved to the states which might, conceivably, be better placed in the hands of the national government. The muddled state of divorce law in this country argues nothing so much as the necessity for uniformity in divorce procedures and law.[35] The argument for uniformity, however, does not thereby impart to the national government the power to procure it. Justice Black's statement, therefore, tells only the cold logic of the situation, which admittedly may be the law in this case, but which must be examined in the light of the American federal system.

Justice Black would concede police power in the three-mile zone, but would argue that a state's right to exercise such power cannot detract from the paramount rights of the federal government in the area. The state of California could, and did, counter with the argument that the national government has undeniable rights to regulate commerce and navigation in the marginal sea and to make the oil therein contained the subject of a treaty, but that the title to the area remains with the state. Justice Black answered this argument, however, with a discussion of the *Pollard* case, in which he stated his belief that if the rationale of the case is valid as a basis for concluding that a state has paramount rights in its inland waters, then by the same token the national government must have paramount rights in the three-mile zone.

He was not, however, insensible of the fact that the *Pollard* decision might very well be read as California had interpreted it.

As previously stated, this Court has followed and reasserted the basic doctrine of the Pollard case many times. And in doing so it has used language strong enough to indicate that the Court then believed that states not only owned tidelands and soil under navigable inland waters, but also owned soils under all navigable waters within their territorial jurisdiction, whether inland or not. All of these statements were, however, merely paraphrases or offshoots of the Pollard inland water rule, and were used, not as an enunciation of a new ocean rule, but in explanation of the old inland water principle. Notwithstanding the fact that none of these cases either involved or decided the state-federal conflict presented here, we are urged to say that the language used and repeated in those cases forecloses

[35] Since the decision in the case of *Williams v. North Carolina,* 325 U.S. 226 (1944), even though somewhat qualified by *Sherrer v. Sherrer,* 334 U.S. 343 (1948), and *Cook v. Cook,* 342 U.S. 126 (1951).

the Government from the right to have this Court decide that question
now that it is squarely presented for the first time.[36]

The *Pollard* case could not, Black said, foreclose a ruling in the instant
case, for this was the first time the issue had been before the court; the
Pollard decision dealt only with inland waters.

There were three cases, Black thought, which lent weight to California's contentions. These were *Manchester* v. *Massachusetts*,[37] *Louisiana* v. *Mississippi*,[38] and *The Abby Dodge*.[39] The first he dismissed
with the remark that no question of title or paramount rights in the
open sea was or could be raised because the case involved a fishery
regulation in Buzzard's Bay, inland waters of Massachusetts; and
even then the court had "specifically laid to one side any question as
to the rights of the Federal Government to regulate fishing there."[40]
In the second case, a boundary dispute between Louisiana and Mississippi, while acknowledging that the court had used language susceptible
of interpretation that the states might hold sway over their maritime
belts, Black correctly stated that there was not present any dispute between the state and federal governments; therefore this case, too, was
inapplicable.

The case of *The Abby Dodge* was more difficult to rationalize. The
facts and general reasoning of this case have already been considered.[41]
Of the court's decision in this case Black said:

This Court construed the statute's prohibition as applying only to
sponges outside the state's "territorial limits" in the Gulf. It thus narrowed
the scope of the statute because of a belief that the United States was
without power to regulate the Florida traffic in sponges obtained from
within Florida's territorial limits, presumably the three-mile belt. But the
opinion in that case was concerned with the state's power to regulate and
conserve within its territorial waters, not with its exercise of the right to
use and deplete resources which might be of national and international

---

[36] 332 U.S. 19, 36–37. The writer would emphasize that the rationale of the
series of cases, of which *Pollard* v. *Hagan* is one, is based squarely on the principle
of the navigability of the waters and not on the question of whether or not the
waters are inland waters.

[37] 139 U.S. 240 (1891).

[38] 202 U.S. 1 (1906).

[39] 223 U.S. 166 (1912).

[40] His statement ignored the obvious fact that the freedom or gaolibility of the
person involved depended upon the application of a state fishing regulation as
opposed to a national license which, when issued, gave to the individual the very
right which was prohibited by state law.

[41] Pp. 99–100 above.

importance. And there was no argument there, nor did this Court decide, whether the Federal Government owned or had paramount rights in the soil under the Gulf waters. That this question remained undecided is evidenced by *Skiriotes* v. *State of Florida,* 313 U.S. 69, 75, 61 S. Ct. 924, 928, 85 L. Ed. 1193, where we had occasion to speak of Florida's power over sponge fishing in its territorial waters. Through Mr. Chief Justice Hughes we said: "It is also clear that Florida has an interest in the proper maintenance of the sponge fishery and that the [state] statute *so far as applied to conduct within the territorial waters of Florida, in the absence of conflicting federal legislation, is within the police power of the State.*"[42]

One may draw a number of conclusions from this statement. The first and inescapable one is that the national government could regulate, if it chose, the sponge industry being carried on within the three-mile zone off the coast of Florida in the Gulf of Mexico; such regulation would find adequate foundation, at this date, in an expression of the power of Congress over interstate and foreign commerce. Such an expression would not, however, touch the title to the sponges, granted that the state held such a title. A second, and less charitable, inference which may be drawn is that Justice Black is measuring the case of *The Abby Dodge* against that of *United States* v. *California* in terms of the intrinsic value of the products involved. Sponges, being of less value to national defense, are therefore less likely to come under the paramount-powers doctrine than oil, the lifeblood of modern warfare. Yet sponges are attached to the soil and are, in effect, products of the soil; oil is a product of the soil. In *The Abby Dodge,* the state of Florida had an "interest" in the maintenance of the sponge fishery. Is the "interest" of California in the submerged oil reserves less? Further, Florida retained control over its sponge fishery in the absence of "conflicting federal legislation"; there had been no federal action by Congress asserting any control over the submerged soil areas for oil production purposes. Once again, Black's bit of rationalization may be justified pragmatically, but it is difficult to see from his statements just how he drew this line which separates two products of the soil—the one necessary to national defense and the other not. One cannot, however, quarrel very much with his assertion that there is no case exactly in point on which to base a decision in *United States* v. *California.*[43]

---

[42] 332 U.S. 19, 37–38. The emphasis is Justice Black's.

[43] Judge Manley O. Hudson had taken what is, in the thinking of this writer, the correct view. In *Hearings* on S.J. Res. 48 and H.J. Res. 225 (1946), 260–61, he says: "What I think I can say is that there has been a consistent current of judicial opinion with respect to the question before the committee, to the effect

On the merits, therefore, Justice Black said (1) that the thirteen original states did not own the three-mile belt of marginal sea off their coasts because the territorial concept of the marginal sea had not yet crystallized in 1776; (2) that assertions of dominion by the political branches of the national government over the marginal sea are binding on the court; (3) that the protection and control of the marginal sea is a function of national sovereignty which gives to the federal government, in its capacity as a member of the family of nations, paramount rights to remove therefrom such objects of value as it may choose; and (4) that although the state may exercise certain police powers in the area, the rationale of the *Pollard* case and similar decisions cannot be extended to the waters of the open sea so as to prevent the national government from exercising paramount powers in the area. Therefore, "we decide for the reasons we have stated that California is not the owner of the three-mile marginal belt along its coast, and that the Federal Government rather than the state has paramount rights in and power over that belt, an incident to which is full dominion over the resources of the soil under that water area, including oil."[44]

Justice Black then proceeded to answer the California arguments based on the doctrines of estoppel, laches, and adverse possession. Admitting that many acts of the political branches of the national govern-

---

that the States are on equal basis in regard to the ownership of the bed of the marginal sea. . . . I cannot say that there is an exact precedent for the determination of title to the land of the marginal sea. . . . Yet I should find it very difficult to explain the results reached in many of the cases if one did not accept the general principle which would fix the same rule to the bed of the sea under the marginal sea, namely, that that bed is the property of the States. . . . I think the cases which have been cited by the attorneys general show the application of a general principle of law. Perhaps one may say that the principle is stated in this or that case a little too broadly for the purposes of the decision to be made, but the general principle has run consistently through 1842 down to our time, over 100 years, and that general principle refuses to distinguish between brown dogs, for example, and red dogs among our States."

Keeton, 25 *Texas Law Review* (1947), 269–70, says: "Nevertheless, with respect to navigable waters within the states, the law is well settled. As regards submerged lands under coastal waters, it has been urged that the cases in which state ownership has been asserted do not involve land below the low-water mark and outside of harbors and bays. But the fact that the courts have used as a principle one that was broader than necessary to decide the case does not, of course, make the use of the principle dictum. . . . If there is anything to the principle of *stare decisis* as regards property rights, and there is more justification for it in this field than perhaps any other, then it would seem that the law is well settled to the effect that the states formed out of territory are in no different position from the thirteen original states as regards ownership of submerged lands. . . ."

[44] 332 U.S. 19, 38–39.

ment would tend to give substance to the view that the national government had recognized the title of the states to the marginal sea, Black stated that the issue did not appear until after the discovery of oil. Therefore, he felt that the officers of the national government acted with reasonable diligence in prosecuting the federal interest. Over and above that, however, he felt that even though the agents had been negligent, the rights of the national government could not be forfeited as a result. The federal government holds these paramount rights in trust for the people and cannot be deprived of them "by the ordinary court rules designed particularly for private disputes over individually owned pieces of property."[45] Government officers, who have no authority to dispose of government property, cannot lose these paramount rights of the national government through laches or similar action or inaction.

As for the money which had been expended by the states and their lessees in the marginal-sea area, the Justice offered the following condolences:

> . . . we are faced with the issue as to whether state or nation has paramount rights in and power over this ocean belt, and that great national question is not dependent upon what expenses may have been incurred upon mistaken assumptions. Furthermore, we cannot know how many of these improvements are within and how many without the boundary of the marginal sea which can later be accurately defined. But beyond all this we cannot and do not assume that Congress, which has constitutional control over Government property, will execute its powers in such way as to bring about injustices to states, their subdivisions, or persons acting pursuant to their permission.[46]

Mr. Justice Black held, therefore, that the national government was entitled to the relief prayed for and suggested that the parties get together before September 1947 on a decree to be presented to the Supreme Court to carry the decision of the court into effect. This, in itself a relatively unusual procedure, is suggestive of the fact that Black was perfectly aware of the ramifications of the ruling and desired to get the two parties to work out a solution between themselves; thus com- ·

---

[45] *Ibid.*, 40.

[46] *Ibid.* In the last sentence, Black once again allowed the "property concept" to break out. Improvements have been made in these areas; he had said the states did not own them; he refused now, and refused later (see pp. 192–94 below), to say that the national government owned them. Why then talk of Congress' power over government "property"?

plete acquiescence to a final decree would be assured. As will be seen, the attempt was not successful.

Justices Frankfurter and Reed could not go along with the majority in the case. Both based their dissent on ideas of property rights; neither was able to accept the doctrine of paramount rights on which Black based his decision. Frankfurter pointed out that an injunction "normally presupposes" property rights; the majority granted the prayer in the case, but in so doing did not find and declare that the United States had title. Declaring that California did not own the area, he said, did not mean that the United States did. He found it "significant that the Court does not adopt the Government's elaborate argument, based on the dubious and tenuous writings of publicists, that this part of the open sea belongs, in a proprietary sense, to the United States. . . . Instead, the Court finds trespass against the United States on the basis of what it calls the 'national dominion' by the United States over this area."[47] To speak of "dominion," he said, carried with it ideas of property. There was no doubt whatsoever, in Frankfurter's mind, that the United States had paramount rights in these waters—rights to regulate commerce, to condemn land, to make treaties, and to make war. But these are rights under those constitutional powers delegated to the national government. This case, he believed, did not involve these rights at all, but rather there was presented a simple question of ownership. This ownership he thought the United States had not proved and certainly never acquired. The presence or absence of oil deposits had nothing to do with the question so far as he was concerned.

Frankfurter was not sure that California could claim ownership either. He inclined to the view that the area was "unclaimed land" to which the political branches of the national government might lay claim, though, he emphasized, they have never done so. Such a decision, he properly pointed out, would be outside the realm of judicial scrutiny. Then he read the majority a lecture by saying: "Today this Court has decided that a new application even in the old field of torts should not be made by adjudication, where Congress has refrained from acting. . . . Considerations of judicial self-restraint would seem to me far more compelling where there are obviously at stake claims that involve so many far-reaching, complicated, historic interests, the proper

[47] *Ibid.,* 43.

adjustments of which are not readily resolved by the materials and methods to which this Court is confined."[48]

Justice Reed affirmed his belief that ownership of the marginal-sea area was sufficiently proved to be in the state of California. This ownership carried with it the right to the minerals contained in the lands. Ownership of the area turned, for him, upon whether or not the original states owned their marginal-sea belts. Utilizing the same cases which the majority opinion had used, he concluded that the thirteen original states did own the lands of the marginal sea. Since California was admitted on an equal footing with the original states, she therefore, according to Reed's views of the problem, must hold similar rights in the three-mile zone off her coasts as did the original states. Again using the same cases as Black had used, he concluded:

This ownership in California would not interfere in any way with the needs or rights of the United States in war or peace. The power of the United States is plenary over these undersea lands precisely as it is over every river, farm, mine, and factory of the nation. While no square ruling of the Court has determined the ownership of those marginal lands, to me the tone of the decisions dealing with similar problems indicates that, without discussion, state ownership has been assumed.[49]

Thus the dissenting opinions placed emphasis upon concepts of property as determinative of a ruling in the case. The dissenting judges were not able to see the paramount-rights doctrine toward which Black had been driving. Like the lawyers who argued the case, the minority justices thought that the concept of an area surrounding the United States, a veritable no man's land insofar as title was concerned, was unthinkable. The dissenting judges failed, as had the lawyers, to grasp the true significance of the point which Black was attempting to make; they failed to see the background and importance of what he was attempting to do, of the new concepts he was establishing for the conduct of federal-state relations.

[48] *Ibid.*, 46. The case to which he was referring is that of *United States* v. *Standard Oil of California*, 332 U.S. 301 (1947).
[49] 332 U.S. 19, 42–43.

11 ·

The Immediate Aftermath
of United States *v.* California

Representatives of the state of California did not consider the battle finished. Less than a month after the decision, 18 July 1947 to be exact, California's attorney general, Fred N. Howser, filed a formal petition for rehearing.[1] This forty-page petition, stripped of the verbiage of its predecessors filed by the state, is a short, concise statement of what the state had been contending all along. Apparently misconstruing Justice Black's paramount-rights doctrine, California based its petition upon the premise that no proprietary interest in the lands in the marginal sea could accrue to the national government in the exercise of national dominion in the area. Objections were entered that an extensive shift of powers had been made in the federal system without a detailed or exhaustive discussion of the problem.[2]

The state contended that the Supreme Court had overlooked "at least" six basic propositions of law. The first of these dealt with the proposition that the various powers granted to the national government, including the power over external affairs, did not carry with them any cession of territory or necessitate the general national ownership of property within a state. The second was based on an opinion by Justice Holmes which purportedly rejected the very basis upon which Justice Black had based his opinion. Justice Black had stated that

[1] "Motion for Leave to File Petition and Petition for Rehearing and Reconsideration of Majority Opinion," No. 12 Original, October Term 1946. This petition will hereinafter be cited as California petition for rehearing.
[2] *Ibid.,* 2–3.

182

paramount authority over these marginal-sea areas was a necessary corollary of the power of the federal government over external affairs. In *United States* v. *Chandler-Dunbar Co.*[3] Justice Holmes had rejected a contention of the United States solicitor general that the power of the United States over external affairs carried with it ownership of beds of navigable waters connecting the Great Lakes; Justice Holmes held, as between a grantee of the state of Michigan and a grantee of the United States, that even though the waters in question constituted an international boundary, the beds of such waters were held in title by the state. Thus, argued California, if waters which are an international boundary do not come under the rule announced in 1947 by Justice Black, why should marginal-sea areas which are not even boundaries come under the dominion of the national government because of its power over external affairs?

Third, California contended that the court had ignored the established rule that territory may not be annexed or acquired by the United States except by Congressional action; this action, the state claimed, had never been taken by Congress. Indeed, it was contended, Congress had acted to opposite effect, if at all. Fourth, the state sought to show that the court had not taken into consideration the "rule established by prior decisions . . . holding that the original thirteen states, and not the National Government, own the marginal belt along their coasts." Fifth, California stated that even though the decision might be correct, the court was ignoring a settled principle of law which declares that where property rights have been established on the faith of previous decisions, or even dicta, the rights will not be overturned, no matter what the present views of the court may be.

Lastly, the state argued that the opinion of the majority had shorn the state of its sovereignty and "relegated" it to the position of a private individual. Prescription and acquiescence, it was claimed, could run as between sovereigns, and in the federal system such is the case. The court had made an error in treating California as it would treat any private person in similar circumstances.

The state argued at some length that there could not be in law a distinction between inland waters and the waters of the marginal sea. The sole criterion, it was contended, was whether or not the waters were in fact navigable. That, the state said, was the basis for all previous decisions by the court; that, it was argued, must be the decision

[3] 209 U.S. 447 (1908).

of the court upon rehearing. An artificial distinction was being created for the "first time in history" by the high tribunal.[4]

The petition concluded with a series of statements which should be quoted, for they illustrate the states' rights philosophy which permeated the thinking of those believing in the essential justice of the state position:

The majority opinion, if it is allowed to stand, will deprive every coastal State of enormous areas of property and of valuable property rights which have long been held and occupied by them under their respective State laws as actual and legal owners. We desire respectfully to call attention to the fact that in support of the majority opinion not one previous decision of this Court is or can be cited, although, as the Court says, there are many of its own decisions which flatly declare the States to be the owners of these properties. There is not one decision of any State court which supports the majority opinion although a multitude of decisions of able State courts uphold State ownership. There is not one constitutional provision cited in support of the majority opinion except those general grants of power which this Court has held carry with them no proprietary rights. There is not one Federal statute cited in support of the majority opinion, although there are many statutes, particularly those dealing with kelp and sponges, which clearly support State ownership and there are a great many State statutes which declare and assert State ownership. There is not one decision or opinion of any department of the Federal Government prior to 1937 which supports the majority opinion, although there are many decisions of the Interior Department, the Attorney General, the War and Navy Departments, the Department of Agriculture and other departments which specifically uphold State ownership. Not one Federal officer has ever attempted to assume rights of ownership or possession of the three-mile belt, although State officials and State grantees and lessees in every coastal State under State laws have actually occupied large portions of the three-mile belt as owners or lessees. In a word, there is absolutely nothing upon which the Federal claim in this case is or can be predicated except the unsupported declaration of the majority of this Court that national power gives the Federal Government the right to appropriate these properties to its own use, a proposition which as we have shown is contrary to all past decisions on the subject. If this decision should stand, no one today could foretell the extent to which future Federal administrations may go in asserting the right to expropriate private property and property rights on the basis of the vague concept of "national power" which is relied upon therein.

It is respectfully urged that this petition for rehearing and reconsidera-

---

[4] This material is summarized from California petition for rehearing, 4–6.

tion of the majority opinion should be granted and that the majority
opinion should be reversed on the grounds set forth herein; or, in the alternative, that the petition should be granted and the case set for further
argument.[5]

The California petition for rehearing struck a particularly telling
blow when it emphasized the opinion of Mr. Justice Holmes in the
Chandler-Dunbar case. California had discussed the case previously,[6]
but the concern with the case had been primarily one of title. The state
had not then stressed it as a counterargument to the paramount-rights
theory, since the obvious tenor of the arguments of both sides was concerned almost solely with title. On petition for rehearing, however, even
though California still emphasized aspects of title, the *Chandler-
Dunbar* case was utilized as a powerful argument which the court has
not yet to this day successfully countered.

The case involved the bed of the St. Marys River, an international
boundary between the United States and Canada, with grantees of
Michigan and the United States contesting ownership. Mr. Justice
Holmes held for the Michigan grantee, on the ground that the stream
was navigable and therefore the state held title to it under the innumerable previous decisions announced by the court. No question was raised
as to whether or not the waters were inland waters; the criterion was
navigability.

Now how is it possible to rationalize this decision with the decision
in *United States* v. *California?* How is it possible for a river which is an
international boundary (and which *has been* the subject of a treaty)
to bear a different relationship to a state from waters in the marginal
sea which border only on the littoral state? If *United States* v. *California* is to be considered as ruling, which it of course is, was not the
Chandler-Dunbar case overruled *sub silentio?* It is true that the waters
in the latter case may be classed as inland waters, but is such a classification pertinent or even necessary in the light of Black's interpretation
of the power of the national government in external affairs? It appears
that the possible conclusion can be drawn that where waters constitute
a part of an international boundary, they thereby come under the new
rule announced in *United States* v. *California.*[7]

[5] *Ibid.*, 38–40.
[6] California brief, 70–71.
[7] The rule enunciated in the *Chandler-Dunbar* case was followed in *Massachusetts* v. *New York*, 271 U.S. 65 (1926), holding that the state of New York
was the owner of the bed of that portion of Lake Ontario within the state's
borders. The boundary between the United States and Canada runs through

Shoulder to shoulder with the representatives of California were the attorneys general of the other states, forty-three of them at this time, to be exact. This group filed a supporting brief as *amicus curiae* asking for rehearing and reversal of the majority opinion.[8] Although this brief was filed after certain stipulations, to be discussed presently, had been agreed to and therefore contains specific objections which do not appear in the California brief, it is substantially the same. The supporting brief did not emphasize the *Chandler-Dunbar* case though mention was made of it.[9] As might be expected, the attorneys general placed greater emphasis upon the possible consequences of the decision in *United States* v. *California* to titles under the beds of inland waters— rivers, lakes, and the like. They were particularly concerned with the fact that the majority opinion placed no apparent restrictions on the doctrine of paramount rights; the court had said that title of the states even to lands underlying inland navigable waters was "qualified." As a result, said the attorneys general, "the principles of this decision are not limited to mere property rights. Its doctrine of 'full dominion' as an incident to certain Federal regulatory powers which apply to all public and private property in the Nation could be used as an opening wedge for nationalization or Federal control of all land use and natural resources. This, in spite of the fact that such exclusive control goes far beyond the extent necessary for proper exercise of the delegated paramount Federal powers."[10]

In the meantime, while California's representatives were filing petitions for rehearing, they were also conferring with representatives of the United States to perfect interim arrangements to be effective until a final decree disposing of the area might be drawn. This was a form of insurance in case the Supreme Court acted adversely on the petition for rehearing. Such interim arrangements were absolutely necessary. Oil was badly needed, and production had to be kept up. There was danger of damage to equipment and to the fields themselves if abrupt shutdowns occurred.

In the days immediately following the announcement of the decision, shares of Signal Oil stock dropped fifteen points on the Los Angeles

---

Lake Ontario. See also *Illinois Central R. Co.* v. *Illinois*, 146 U.S. 387 (1892).

The arguments developed in this paragraph are those of the writer. California did not carry the *Chandler-Dunbar* case to these precise conclusions.

[8] Brief of the National Association of Attorneys General, *amicus curiae, California* case. Walter R. Johnson, then attorney general of Nebraska, was chairman of the Committee on the Brief, with representatives from Massachusetts, Texas, Ohio, Louisiana, and Kansas. The representation was carefully chosen to assure inland support.   [9] *Ibid.,* 17, 33.   [10] *Ibid.,* 3–4.

Stock Exchange, and Hancock of California dropped eight. These two companies, together with smaller operators, had some fifty million dollars invested in tidelands fields; the court decision left them with little idea of the status of that investment.[11] There was even doubt about whether or not they might be liable for damages for the oil they had already taken.

California State Finance Director James S. Dean announced 14 July 1947 that temporary agreement had been reached whereby inland waters would remain under the control of the state, whereas royalties from companies operating in affected areas, though they would continue to be paid to the state of California, would be held in a reserve fund pending final disposition. This temporary arrangement was the result of almost two weeks of conferences between representatives of California and Interior Department officials. Business was to continue as usual for the time being.[12]

The Governors' Conference, meeting in Salt Lake City on 15 July, was, meanwhile, one of the first groups to go on record as memorializing the Congress of the United States to pass legislation which would recognize state ownership of submerged lands and resources, thus, in effect, overruling the decision of the Supreme Court.[13]

On 26 July the Departments of Justice and Interior issued a joint press release which stated that two stipulations had been entered into by representatives of the United States and California. This five-page release was the first really authoritative statement to be issued by the national government following *United States* v. *California.* The agreement received about a quarter of a column in the *Oakland Tribune;*[14] its content merits greater consideration here.

The release made an attempt to point out the great problems raised by the decision. The major difficulty was that of trying to draw accurately the line which would define those areas within the purview of the decision and those outside its operation. This final demarcation, it was stated, would "probably" involve further court proceedings.

[11] *Time Magazine,* 7 July 1947, p. 84. Signal Oil sold at 120 just before the decision. The stock dropped to 105 on 24 June 1947. The price rose rapidly, however, and sales were at 120 by 26 July 1947.

[12] *Oakland Tribune,* 14 July 1947.

[13] *Ibid.,* 15, 16, and 22 July 1947. Governor Beauford Jester of Texas introduced the resolution in the Governors' Conference. The latter date of the *Tribune* contains an editorial wherein the paper praises the action of the conference and notes that the memorial "serves notice on the still-doubting few that the question is not one confined to California or to oil lands. . . . Involved are the rights of all 48 states and this the governors recognized and proclaimed."

[14] 27 July 1947.

In order to reassure harbor investors and keep oil production up, therefore, the interim arrangements were completed. Three areas were listed as specifically outside any possible operation of the decision of the court:

1. That part of San Francisco Bay landward of a line drawn from Point Diablo, Marin County, California, to Fort Point, City and County of San Francisco, California.

2. That part of San Diego Bay landward of a line drawn from Point Loma to Zuninga Point, on the southwestern end of North Island, San Diego County, California.

3. That part of San Pedro Bay landward of a line drawn from Point Fermin in a northeasterly direction through a point 300 feet due south of the southeasterly extension of the Navy mole and breakwater to the line of ordinary low tide in the City of Long Beach, Los Angeles County, California.[15]

The fact that other waters were omitted was stipulated to be without prejudice to the rights of either party to make further claims.

The second stipulation provided, in the main, for "business as usual" operation in the affected oil fields. New wells could be drilled where necessary to prevent adverse drainage, and operations in general were to continue as before. The royalties were to be collected by California and placed in a special fund, pending final determination of the exact line of demarcation. It was realized, of course, that many wells were operating in borderline areas, being drilled in or on tidelands (in the technical sense) and therefore not immediately affected by the decision. Many of the wells would have to be electrically gauged to determine whether or not they were slanted out into the area of United States dominion. Affirmations of good will were made by the executive officers of the United States, who promised to see that the fair thing was done for those who had developed the areas now under United States jurisdiction. A provision was inserted that no claim for entry was to be made for any operations carried on prior to 23 June 1947. The stipulations were stated to be purely interim arrangements, subject to revocation by the Congress, and in no case to run beyond September 1948.[16] Congress, incidentally, was informed of the stipulations before they were announced.[17]

[15] Press release by the Departments of Justice and Interior, 26 July 1947, p. 3.

[16] The submerged fields are still, at this writing, being operated under state-national stipulations, though some changes in the original agreements have been made. See pp. 234–36 and 257–58 below.

[17] Press release by the Departments of Justice and Interior, 26 July 1947, p. 3.

On 29 August 1947, Attorney General Tom Clark sent the following letter to Secretary of the Interior J. A. Krug:

My dear Mr. Secretary:

You have asked by opinion on the question whether the Mineral Leasing Act of February 25, 1920, as amended (41 Stat. 437, 30 U.S.C. 181, *et seq.*), authorizes the issuance of oil and gas leases with respect to the submerged lands below low tide off the coasts of the United States and outside the inland waters within the States.

In considering the steps which should be taken to protect the interests of the United States in the submerged lands off the Coast of California, following the decision of the United States Supreme Court rendered on June 23, 1947, in *United States* v. *California,* No. 12 Original, October Term 1946, one of the questions which your Department and this Department had to examine was whether the provisions of the Mineral Leasing Act required that the procedures set forth in that act be followed with regard to the property which the Supreme Court held in that case to be that of the United States. The Acting Solicitor General and the Solicitor of your Department concluded that the act imposed no such requirement. After consideration, I reached the same conclusion, and I now adhere to it. The stipulations were signed on that basis.

Sincerely yours,

Tom C. Clark

Attorney General[18]

This letter meant that the Congress would have to take affirmative action and pass a new statute before federal leases could be granted in the areas affected by the decision.

The peculiar feature of the letter, however, occurs in the middle of the second paragraph, where the Attorney General noted that the Supreme Court had held this area to be the "property" of the United States. The Supreme Court did not declare that the three-mile zone was the property of the United States. Justice Frankfurter made this point incontrovertibly clear. Yet the Attorney General of the United States made this basic error in an official communication; this action

---

[18] The letter is reprinted in *Hearings* on S.J. Res. 20 (1951), 501. A previous opinion to the same effect had been given by Mastin G. White, solicitor of the Department of the Interior, on 8 August 1947. White's opinion, reprinted *ibid.*, 498–500, is an excellent piece of work and stands as an adequate rebuttal to those who contended that the Mineral Leasing Act did apply to the submerged soils in the marginal sea. Testifying in 1946, Secretary Ickes had said that the "Mineral Leasing Act of 1920 is not applicable to submerged lands." *Hearings* on S.J. Res. 48 and H.J. Res. 225 (1946), 11. But Ickes later changed his mind. See p. 235 n. below.

constitutes further proof that Justice Black's opinion was not understood by persons accustomed to dealing only in legalistic conceptions of title. As will be presently demonstrated, the Supreme Court was to declare again in a few short weeks, in clear and unmistakable terms, that the United States did not "own" the area in controversy.

On 13 September 1947 the United States filed with the Supreme Court a proposed decree and brief supporting it.[19] The United States asked the court to order, adjudge, and decree as follows:

1. The United States of America is now, and has been at all times pertinent thereto, possessed of paramount rights of proprietorship in, and full dominion and power over, the lands, minerals and other things underlying the Pacific Ocean lying seaward of the ordinary low-water mark on the coast of California, and outside of the inland waters, extending seaward three nautical miles and bounded on the north and south, respectively, by the northern and southern boundaries of the State of California. The State of California has no title thereto or property interest therein.

2. The United States is entitled to the injunctive relief prayed for in the complaint.

3. Jurisdiction is reserved by this Court to enter such further orders and to issue such writs as may from time to time be deemed advisable or necessary to give full force and effect to this decree.[20]

The decree was drawn in general terms because it was impossible at that date to establish a demarcation line with any degree of exactness. Thus the United States asked the court, in effect, to approve the interim operating stipulations[21] which have already been covered in detail.

The state of California interposed objections to the granting of the decree.[22] The first was based upon the fact that California's petition for rehearing was pending. Specifically, the state objected to the words "of proprietorship" and "full dominion and power over" in paragraph 1 of the decree. The state objected to paragraph 2 *in toto*. California was quite correct in objecting to the reference to proprietary rights, when the court had not held proprietary rights to be lodged in the

[19] "Decree Proposed by the United States and Memorandum in Support of Proposed Decree," No. 12 Original, October Term 1947. This work also includes a formal copy of the stipulations entered into by the state of California and the United States, which have just been discussed. This material will be cited hereinafter as United States proposed decree, *California* case.

[20] *Ibid.*, 1–2.   [21] *Ibid.*, 3–6.

[22] "Objections to Decree Proposed by Plaintiff and Memorandum in Support of Objections to Proposed Decree," No. 12 Original, October Term 1947. This work will be cited hereinafter as California objections to proposed decree.

United States. Over and above this obvious objection, however, California contended that the national government was asking the Supreme Court to declare the existence of abstract powers which might or might not be exercised at some future time as the Congress of the United States might see fit. Congress would have to act, though it had not yet done so, before the court could enter a valid decree to carry the opinion into effect. The remaining arguments were rephrasings of the same contentions which had been made throughout the entire controversy.[23]

On 13 October 1947 the Supreme Court dealt California's hopes another, though not unexpected, blow. The court on that date refused to reconsider its previous decision and denied the California petition for rehearing.[24] The court did not, however, enter a final decree.

In the meantime, other persons were endeavoring to protect their own interests. Robert E. Lee Jordan filed a petition in the Supreme Court[25] praying that he be permitted to file a motion *amicus curiae* or as an intervenor to have the stipulations which had been entered into 26 July 1947 set aside and declared null and void. He contended that the Attorney General of the United States and the Secretary of the Interior were without power to enter into agreements which would effectively surrender the paramount rights of the United States in the submerged areas. Primarily, of course, Jordan was interested in obtaining a lease from the federal government to start drilling operations of his own in these already proved fields; this possibility was effectively estopped by the operating stipulations which had been concluded. The court denied his petition.[26]

On 21 October 1947, Norman M. Littell, former Assistant Attorney General of the United States under Biddle, asked leave to file a brief *amicus curiae*[27] directed against the operating stipulations. Littell's motion fired indiscriminately at both sides of the controversy as he endeavored, so he said, to set forth "material information and considerations" not brought to the court's attention by either the United States or California. The gist of his allegations was that the operating stipulations entered into by the representatives of the United States

[23] *Ibid.*, 4–24.　　　[24] 332 U.S. 787.

[25] The summary of Jordan's allegations is taken from the order and decree entered by the Supreme Court on 27 October 1947, in the case of *United States v. California*, No. 12 Original, October Term 1947. 332 U.S. 804–805.

[26] 332 U.S. 804, 805; 332 U.S. 828.

[27] "Motion for Leave to File Brief *Amicus Curiae*," Supreme Court of the United States, No. 12 Original, October Term 1947. Leave to file was granted. 332 U.S. 806.

and California were invalid. Littell's wrath was directed primarily to the contention that the stipulations ignored the question of whether or not the original operations were conducted by the oil companies in good faith.[28] The treatment of the situation, he contended, was greatly to the detriment of the United States, as was a provision allowing the drilling of new wells, an item which he claimed usurped the function of Congress.[29]

On 27 October 1947 the Supreme Court handed down its order and decree.[30] In a few short pages, it proceeded to read the Attorney General of the United States a lecture. Describing the two stipulations entered into, the court stated that

. . . the Attorney General and the Secretary of the Interior purport to renounce and disclaim for the United States Government paramount governmental power over certain particularly described submerged fields in the California coastal area.[31] In such stipulations the United States Attorney General and Secretary of the Interior furthermore purport to bind the United States to agreements which purport to authorize state leases of California coastal submerged lands to continue to occupy and exploit those lands, and which agreements also purport to authorize California under conditions set out to execute leases for other submerged coastal lands.[32]

The court ordered the stipulations stricken as "irrelevant to any issues" before it and entered an order and decree in which paragraphs 2 and 3 followed the language requested by the United States. Paragraph 1 was changed in one important respect, however: the words "of proprietorship" were stricken. The Supreme Court thus reiterated its earlier stand, which the Attorney General appears to have completely misinterpreted, that the United States had "paramount rights and national dominion" in the submerged area. The court refused to say

[28] Prior to the decision in *United States* v. *California*, Keeton (25 *Texas Law Review*, 273) believed that if the states did not own the submerged lands and if the doctrine of estoppel did not apply (both of these conditions were held effective by the Supreme Court), then persons acting in the submerged lands were trespassers and liable in damages for products removed therefrom.

[29] "Motion for Leave to File Brief *Amicus Curiae*," 1–3. See also newspaper summary and comment in the *Oakland Tribune*, 21 October 1947.

[30] *United States* v. *California*, Supreme Court of the United States, No. 12 Original, October Term 1947. 332 U.S. 804.

[31] It will be recalled that these areas were found in San Francisco, San Diego, and San Pedro bays. It should also be recalled that the area described in San Francisco Bay has been held specifically to be under the ownership of the state of California. *United States* v. *Mission Rock Co.*, 189 U.S. 391 (1903).

[32] Order and decree, 332 U.S. 804.

that the United States held title or had rights of property in the submerged zone.

One should notice carefully the wording in which the stipulations were discussed and then stricken as irrelevant. These stipulations, the Supreme Court said, "purport" to bind the United States. The court would not admit, even in the case of a bay where specific previous rulings held that title was in the state, that the Attorney General could make a binding agreement. And after a short discussion of the stipulations, the court struck them as irrelevant. If they were irrelevant, why discuss them at all, especially in terms which carried overtones of disapproval of the procedure which the Attorney General of the United States and the Secretary of the Interior had followed? The stipulations, incidentally, were not thereby invalidated, but were merely disregarded by the court. Solicitor General Philip B. Perlman, after the court's order and decree, said that the private drilling stipulations "remain in full force and effect."[33]

Once again, in the face of the fact that the Supreme Court had stricken the words "of proprietorship" from the decree which the United States had proposed, Attorney General Tom Clark, at a later meeting of the National Association of Attorneys General in Boston, stated: "The position of the Government continues as it has—that the Government owns the lands. We now will get up recommendations to Congress as to how this property shall be managed and operated."[34] From California Attorney General Fred Howser, in Boston for the meeting at which Clark had made his incorrect analysis of the Supreme Court's order and decree, came the statement that only legislation by Congress could now give the "ownership" of the controverted areas to California.

In the face of the Supreme Court's refusal to declare ownership, lawyers still explained that someone had to have title and, since the court had declared that California did not, then the United States must.

[33] *San Francisco Chronicle,* 28 October 1947; *Oakland Tribune,* 30 October 1947.

[34] *San Francisco Chronicle,* 28 October 1947. Some months later, Clark was asked to explain this apparently contradictory stand. In reply to questions posed by Senator McCarran, he said that he had consulted *Bouvier's Law Dictionary* for definitions of "dominion." Clark reasoned that the court dropped the words "of proprietorship" because they were superfluous. "Proprietorship" is included within "dominion" in Clark's interpretation—as based on his reading of Bouvier. Joint *Hearings* on S. 1988 (1948), 673.

If Clark's interpretation be the correct one, which this writer strongly doubts, it can only be said that the Supreme Court has not always been so chary of excess verbiage.

This, presumably, was the basis for Attorney General Clark's supposition. The legal profession had simply not grasped the full import of Justice Black's ruling. When the court specifically refuses, on a number of occasions, to include a declaration of title in the United States, there is more to its action than mere perverseness.

The curtain was temporarily rung down on the court battle. The fight shifted to other fields, primarily the political. The time had come for appraisal and evaluation. Events had moved so rapidly, and had been so beclouded by arguments based on emotion, that there had been little time to analyze and weigh the meaning of the ruling. From this point on, it would be necessary to move in the light of the decision in *United States* v. *California*—that the United States has paramount rights in the zone below low-water mark out to the three-mile limit in the open sea.

12 ·

United States *v.* Louisiana
and United States *v.* Texas

The representatives of the states of Texas and Louisiana were under no illusions about what would transpire in the next act of the drama. In typical and picturesque Texas fashion, Bascom Giles, land commissioner of the state, called the decision of the Supreme Court in *United States* v. *California* "claim-jumping" and said he "would favor seceding before giving up these valuable [Texas] lands!" Texas Attorney General Price Daniel called the decision the greatest "blow against property rights of the states since the Civil War."[1] The President of the United States might say in a 1948 campaign speech that "Texas is in a class by itself; it entered the Union by treaty,"[2] but there was no doubt that both Texas and Louisiana would soon be faced with the situation of defending in the Supreme Court of the United States their claims to submerged soils.

The loss of a battle on the judicial front did not necessarily mean the loss of the war. Following the decision in *United States* v. *California,* advocates of state ownership and control introduced in the Eightieth Congress a number of quitclaim bills[3] patterned after the measure which had been vetoed by the President in 1945. It was at the hearings

[1] *Oakland Tribune,* 24 August 1947.

[2] Speech at Austin, Texas, 27 September 1948. Some indication of the importance of the controversy over submerged lands is found in the fact that President Truman, in seeking re-election, found it necessary to comment on the point and to "reassure" the Texans.

[3] E.g., S. 1988; H.J. Res. 51, 52, 67, 157, 263, 286, and 299; H.R. 5010, 5099, 5105, 5121, 5128, 5132, 5136, 5162, 5167, 5238, 5273, 5281, 5288, 5297, 5308, 5320, 5349, 5372, 5380, 5443, and 5461.

in early March 1948 on Senate Bill 1988, one of these proposed quit-claim measures, that the rumors of impending suits against Texas and Louisiana were confirmed. Under questioning by Congressman Ed Gossett of Texas, Attorney General Tom Clark, who was appearing in opposition to the adoption of the quitclaim measure, admitted that a case against Texas had not yet been filed, but was "now in preparation along with the case of Louisiana, and possibly the case against two or three of the other states in the Gulf."[4]

The die was cast on 21 December 1948, when the United States filed motions for leave to file complaints against Texas and against Louisiana. In both cases the complaints alleged that the United States "was and now is the owner in fee simple of, or possessed of paramount rights in, and full dominion and power over, the lands, minerals and other things underlying the Gulf of Mexico" off the coasts of Texas and Louisiana out to the edge of the continental shelf. Although the Supreme Court had refused to adopt the contention of ownership in *United States* v. *California,* the United States was still doing business at the same old stand.[5]

Both Texas[6] and Louisiana[7] opposed the national government's motions on jurisdictional grounds, leave to file to oppose the motions being granted 3 January 1949. Oral argument was had in early May 1949; and on 16 May 1949 the Supreme Court overruled the objections of the two states and granted to the national government leave to file a complaint against each state.[8] Process was ordered to issue, returnable 1 September 1949. Neither state filed an answer to the complaint against it on the return date. Texas filed, instead, a motion to dismiss on jurisdictional grounds and a motion for a more definite bill of particulars; Louisiana filed a somewhat similar motion. The United States thereupon moved for judgments as prayed in the complaints.

On 10 October 1949, at the opening of the new term of court, both sets of motions to dismiss were denied,[9] and each state was allowed thirty days within which to file an answer to the complaint against it. On 29 November 1949 the United States moved for judgment in both

---

[4] Joint *Hearings* on S. 1988 (1948), 616. Clark said further: "It is my present intention to file a suit against every State that I think is affected by the decision [in *United States* v. *California*]."

[5] Attorney General Clark very explicitly made the point (*ibid.*, 609) that the United States had a "property ownership, complete, and perfect" in the submerged soils off the coast of California. While the interpretation is patently incorrect, the Attorney General should be credited with persistency.

[6] 335 U.S. 901.   [7] *Ibid.*   [8] 337 U.S. 902.
[9] 338 U.S. 806.

cases, and on 5 December 1949 the court ordered the cases set 1
February 1950 for argument on the motion.[10] Texas then asked leave to
file an amended answer, which was allowed on 16 January 1950, with
the cases being reset for argument 13 March 1950.[11] On 13 March
1950 the cases were reassigned for argument on 27 March 1950, after
motions to pass made by Texas and Louisiana were denied.[12] The case
of *United States* v. *Louisiana* was argued on its merits on 27 March
1950 and that of *United States* v. *Texas* one day later.

With one major exception, the arguments advanced by the United
States were fundamentally the same in both the Texas and the Louisiana actions. The national government based its arguments squarely on
United States v. *California,* contending that the principles enunciated
therein governed control or ownership by the United States of submerged lands off the coasts of Texas and Louisiana. So far as the
boundary-extension legislation which had been passed by the legislatures of both states was concerned, the United States made it clear that
the rule of *United States* v. *California* was applicable in the area outside the three-mile zone and that state acts could not take precedence.[13]

Attacking the Texas defense, the United States contended that the
defense must stand or fall on the merits of the claim to "exceptional
status." The "alleged special reasons" of Texas for claiming exceptional
status and exemption from the rule laid down by the court in *United
States* v. *California,* said the United States, did not differentiate the
Texas case. It was true that the state of Texas claimed all "vacant and
unappropriated lands" lying within its borders at the time of the annexation agreements; but, said the United States, lands under the
marginal-sea belt are not to be considered as being in this classification.
Grants and reservations must be read in the light of the intent of the
parties making them; and, claimed the United States, the purpose of
the retention clause had been to let the state pay its debts by selling

[10] 338 U.S. 895.   [11] 338 U.S. 945.

[12] 339 U.S. 908. In the oral argument of *United States* v. *Texas,* United States
Solicitor General Philip B. Perlman criticized the maneuverings of the states in
these cases. He said: "Look at all these documents filed by both Louisiana and
Texas, every kind of dilatory motion that it is possible to make to prevent this
thing from coming to issue, and to have that issue determined." *Proceedings,*
Oral Transcript, 152.

[13] United States brief, *Texas* case, 11, 17–18; "Brief for the United States in
Support of Motion for Judgment," No. 12 Original, October Term 1949, 8–9.
This latter brief will hereinafter be cited as United States brief, *Louisiana* case.

land. At that time the submerged soils had had no sales value and could not have been considered as "vacant and unappropriated lands." Rather the phrase "vacant and unappropriated lands" was to be considered as synonymous with the phrase "public lands," a phrase which has been held traditionally as not including tide and submerged lands.[14]

Further, as a part of the annexation agreement, the United States was to take over all "public edifices, fortifications, barracks, ports and harbors, navy and navy-yards, docks, magazines, arms, armaments, and all other property and means pertaining to said Republic of Texas." The terms of the agreement admitting Texas to the Union were, therefore, carefully drawn to preserve the paramount rights of the United States in respect to these essential functions of national sovereignty, to which paramount rights in the marginal sea were "inextricably tied" under the rule of *United States* v. *California*.

Calling the conception of ownership of a maritime belt "very immature" in 1845, the United States argued that Texas could not have achieved real ownership of the belt anyhow while a Republic. Said the United States: "At most, the Republic had a potential, but dormant, claim to paramount control and ownership, which a government with national sovereignty might conceivably assert in the future; and with the assumption by the United States of national external sovereignty over Texas that potential claim passed to the Federal Government, to be asserted and vindicated only by, and on behalf of, the United States." The United States dismissed the claim of Texas to a three-league, rather than a three-mile, belt as one which was "very doubtful."

Under this interpretation the controversy over "vacant and unappropriated lands" becomes "irrelevant." Under the terms of Texas' admission and the Constitution, the question was likewise held to be immaterial. If Texas did not have proprietary rights and control of the area as a Republic, as just contended, then the state could not, of course, have rights as a successor. Conceding some control, though not ownership, the state still could not claim ownership as successor, for the "Republic's interest in the marginal sea did not pertain to its internal and domestic sovereignty, to which the State can be said to have succeeded, but only to its national external sovereignty which has passed to the United States." Even if Texas had control and ownership,

[14] See pp. 50–51 above, where the case of *Mann* v. *Tacoma Land Co.*, which the writer believes to be definitive on this point, is discussed.

argued the United States, Texas gave up such rights to the United States on its admission to the Union. This conclusion was based on the "equal footing" clause of the admission resolution: "Since the other States did not, and do not, have ownership of the marginal belt, or the underlying soil, Texas must have relinquished all such rights in order to be 'on an equal footing with the original States in all respects whatever.' " Nor, contended the United States, could it be barred from asserting its rights by the invocation of the doctrines of laches, estoppel, or adverse prescription.[15]

The arguments advanced by both Louisiana and Texas followed in the main the pattern which has been previously discussed.[16] Louisiana, especially, was faced with the problem of distinguishing its case from that of California. Therefore, in addition to defenses similar to those which had been advanced by California, Louisiana went to considerable length to present additional, and, it was contended, different, data. As a first defense, Louisiana argued (1) that the United States did not have fee simple title to the submerged lands off its coast, (2) that the paramount rights and powers of the United States could not include proprietary interest in minerals and other things of value within the territorial limits of Louisiana, and (3) that there had been no assertion by Congress of power and authority over the resources of the Gulf of Mexico, nor any law adopted to authorize their use.

The theory was thus advanced that the United States was in reality seeking nothing more than an advisory opinion.[17] Congress had not acted to take control of these lands, and could in the future even quitclaim them to the states. The solicitor general of the Department of the Interior and the Attorney General of the United States had given opinions subsequent to *United States* v. *California* that the Mineral Leasing Act of 1920 did not carry with it authority for the federal government to administer the area.[18] The United States was arguing abstract principles. The complaint was not definite and could not be; for, in absence of Congressional action, executive officials could not be definitely aware of the nature and extent of their administrative control

[15] These arguments are summarized from United States brief, *Texas* case, 12–17.

[16] Claims by Louisiana, pp. 53–58; claims by Texas, pp. 79–94.

[17] Louisiana brief, 35–38. This point had been developed by California but not to the same degree. The summary of the Louisiana arguments is taken from the Louisiana brief.

[18] See pp. 187–89 for a discussion of these rulings of these national officials and the stipulations entered into by California and the United States.

in the marginal sea. Therefore, argued Louisiana, there was not present a justiciable case or controversy within the meaning of Article III of the Constitution.

As a second defense, Louisiana traced its title to submerged soils through various treaties, cases, and the "equal footing" clause contained in the national resolution admitting the state to the Union. Great emphasis was placed on the case of *New Orleans* v. *United States*,[19] Louisiana arguing that "in that case, as between the parties to this suit [*United States* v. *Louisiana*], it was particularly and finally settled by this Court that the United States did not acquire, but that Louisiana held, 'as an attribute of sovereignty,' proprietary rights in things of that class, which include the bed of the sea. And Louisiana, therefore, urges that the 'doctrine of the Supreme Court in the New Orleans case' is decisive here and should end this suit in its favor."[20] The case of *New Orleans* v. *United States* had been given great weight in *United States* v. *Illinois Central R. Co.*,[21] a case involving the title to the bed of Lake Michigan. The court had there held the title to be in the state or its grantees. Louisiana thus felt justified in placing emphasis on the early *New Orleans* decision. It should be noted, however, that the case did not involve submerged lands in the marginal sea.

Louisiana argued the "equal footing" clause in much the same fashion as had California. Recognizing that some distinction must be made from the *California* case, Louisiana representatives stressed that in the treaty of 11 April 1783 the King of England had relinquished "all claims to the government, proprietary and territorial rights of the same and every part thereof" to the individual states. This treaty declared the boundaries to comprehend "all islands within twenty leagues of any part of the shores of the United States," thus indicating a territorial concept of the marginal sea. Since this treaty was the "supreme law of the land," Louisiana argued that the original thirteen states held title to their submerged soils in the marginal sea, and later states must have a like claim. While the emphasis is perhaps different, the argument on this point is not fundamentally distinguishable from that advanced by California in *United States* v. *California*.

The Louisiana argument was summarized:

---

[19] 10 Pet. 662 (1836).

[20] Louisiana brief, 79. Fourteen pages of the Louisiana brief (pp. 65–79) are devoted to showing that this case is, for all practical purposes, *res judicata* of the issues presented in *United States* v. *Louisiana*.

[21] 154 U.S. 225 (1894).

. . . Louisiana does not argue that the United States, either by the Pollard rule or by some other principle of law, "has lost its paramount rights in the belt" found within the territorial limits of the State. Louisiana has never denied that within the constitutional sphere, the United States has paramount rights and powers over the Gulf of Mexico, like it has over the Mississippi River and other navigable waters leading to the sea. But . . . Louisiana contends that the United States did not originally acquire a title in the resources of the Gulf, except temporarily in trust for the State and its people, and that a decree which would transfer the right to their use and control would be the creation of a new title without constitutional or legal support.[22]

Texas submitted a lengthy and scholarly brief; the noted authorities Roscoe Pound, Joseph Walter Bingham, Manley O. Hudson, and James William Moore were of counsel. Although Attorney General Price Daniel bemoaned the relatively short length of time given for the preparation of the brief,[23] it stands as a competent piece of work, especially in the presentation of the international law of the marginal sea.

While in the main the arguments advanced by Texas paralleled those already considered in Chapter 6, considerable space was devoted to establishing distinctions between the situation of Texas and California. In a memorandum appended to the Texas brief,[24] Charles Cheney Hyde asserted that the fact of Texas independence and assertion of control by the Republic over the submerged soils of the marginal sea very definitely distinguished the Texas situation from that of California. The Texas brief itself developed the point in some detail.

Texas made a great deal out of the necessity for developing the evidence more fully. The state claimed that mixed questions of law and fact were raised by the pleadings; Texas termed the United States' motion as "hypothetical in character." In asking for a judgment based solely on the pleadings, the United States was attempting to foreclose the possibility of Texas' developing its defense, a defense that could be made only through the taking of testimony. "A genuine fact contro-

---

[22] Louisiana brief, 97.

[23] In oral argument before the court, Attorney General Daniel said in speaking of the Texas brief: "Dean Pound told me that the only thing we could do would be to condense this brief a little more. He said Stevenson said of Homer, that he was a great poet because he knew what to leave out. But I reminded him that we did not have as much time as Homer had to work this up." *Proceedings, Oral Transcript*, 42.

[24] Appendix, 12–17. The arguments presented by Texas are summarized at 16–30 of the Texas brief.

versy exists," so that summary judgment on the pleadings would be highly improper. The proper procedure, argued Texas, would be by trial where there would be opportunity to present "controverting testimony."

The state then outlined the nature of its defenses, which it wished to develop more fully if afforded the opportunity. (Texas had previously moved for the appointment of a master; the motion was still pending before the Supreme Court at the time oral argument was held on the motion for judgment by the United States.) Texas traced its alleged ownership of the disputed area through the claims made by the Republic and the annexation resolution,[25] with special reference to the controversy over the Texas public debt and the vacant and unappropriated lands issue. It was rather neatly shown that the United States had been demonstrably inconsistent in that in the *California* case the national government had contended that submerged soils of the marginal seas were included in the phrase "public lands," while in the *Texas* case the national government argued that such soils were not so included. At any rate, Texas wished the opportunity to develop more fully the argument that at the time of admission the state had retained a full proprietary right in the submerged soils of its marginal sea. In fact, Texas argued that the parties who negotiated the annexation treaty in 1845 were in complete agreement that the "equal footing" clause worked to the advantage of the state in the retention of such lands.

The state advanced as defenses the doctrines of prescription and estoppel. Texas asserted, too, that since the Supreme Court in *Toomer* v. *Witsell*[26] had said that state legislation continued operative in the absence of conflicting federal legislation, the state should not be prohibited from exercising its legislative power to "preserve and regulate the exploitation of an important resource" within its borders.

On 5 June 1950 the Supreme Court handed down its decisions in the cases. Justice Jackson disqualified himself as he had in *United States* v. *California;* Justice Clark disqualified himself because the suits against Texas and Louisiana were begun while he was Attorney General. Thus

[25] In a special memorandum Dean Roscoe Pound developed this point of Texas' proprietary claims at some length. Texas brief, Appendix, 1–11.

[26] 334 U.S. 385 (1948). This case arose after *United States* v. *California* and involved the applicability of a South Carolina shrimp fishing regulation in the marginal sea. See pp. 267–70 below, where this case is discussed more fully.

only seven members of the court sat on these two important cases. Although the judgment in both instances was for the United States, the majority was a bare one in the case of *United States* v. *Texas*. Justices Reed, Minton, and Frankfurter dissented; the Texas dispute thus was determined by less than a majority of the court.

Justice Douglas wrote the majority opinion in both cases. For the most part the opinions showed no departure from the path which had been blazed by Mr. Justice Black in *United States* v. *California*. So far as *United States* v. *Louisiana* was concerned, Justice Douglas had only to say that *United States* v. *California* was controlling. *New Orleans* v. *United States* he laid aside with the remark that the waters there involved were inland waters. Then he stated:

> As we pointed out in United States v. California, the issue in this class of litigation does not turn on title or ownership in the conventional sense. California, like the thirteen original colonies, never acquired ownership in the marginal sea. The claim to our three-mile belt was first asserted by the national government. Protection and control of the area are indeed functions of national external sovereignty. . . . The marginal sea is a national, not a state concern. National interests, national responsibilities, national concerns are involved. The problems of commerce, national defense, relations with other powers, war and peace focus there. National rights must therefore be paramount in that area.[27]

Since Louisiana's preadmission or postadmission history did not "make her case stronger than California's," the United States was entitled to the relief prayed for.[28]

United States v. *Texas* was a more difficult nut to crack. It is the contention of the writer, admittedly not capable of proof, that the paramount-powers doctrine expounded by Mr. Justice Black in *United States* v. *California* was deliberately designed to offset the strong arguments on title which Texas was bound to present when litigation would arise between the United States and that state. Had the *California* case been decided in favor of the United States solely on the basis of title, which it conceivably might have been, then the United States would have had little chance to make a similar argument stand up against the infinitely better case which Texas would most certainly present. But a decision which had a basis transcending "mere title" would suffice to erase whatever claims Texas might be able to sustain to the submerged soils under the Gulf of Mexico.

[27] 339 U.S. 699, 704.   [28] *Ibid.*, 705–706.

The tool, this new interpretation of what constituted the paramount powers of the national government, was at hand. Mr. Justice Douglas used it. The opinion is not a lengthy one. After tracing the history of Texas through the annexation resolution, Justice Douglas concluded that no hearing was required to establish the meaning of that resolution. "We are of the view," he stated, "that the 'equal footing' clause of the Joint Resolution admitting Texas to the Union disposes of the present phase of the controversy."[29] Pointing out that the states had been given ownership of soils under inland waters under the rationale that such soils were inseparable from state sovereignty, Justice Douglas held that the "converse situation" must also be true. The "equal footing" clause, he said,

negatives any implied, special limitation of any of the paramount powers of the United States in favor of a State. . . . When Texas came into the Union, she ceased to be an independent nation. She then became a sister State on an "equal footing" with all the other States. That act concededly entailed a relinquishment of some of her sovereignty. The United States then took her place as respects foreign commerce, the waging of war, the making of treaties, defense of the shores, and the like. In external affairs the United States became the sole and exclusive spokesman for the Nation. We hold that as an incident to the transfer of that sovereignty any claim that Texas may have had to the marginal sea was relinquished to the United States.[30]

The hard fact of the matter is that Texas was not admitted to the Union under an "equal footing" clause. The joint resolution of the national Congress providing for annexation,[31] previously noted in Chapter 6, set out two different plans for annexation. Texas was annexed under section 2 of the resolution. That section contained no "equal footing" clause; Texas was not annexed under the terms of section 3, which did contain the "equal footing" clause. The actions which the Texas Congress and Constitutional Convention took were consummated in strict conformity with section 2.[32] It is true that in the final national act of admission of 29 December 1845[33] the term "equal footing" is included. Yet it is possible to argue that this strictly unilateral action was not binding on Texas. Parenthetically, one may add that no requirement of the Constitution binds the Congress to admit new states upon an equal footing with those already members of the

---

[29] 339 U.S. 707, 715.   [30] *Ibid.*, 717–18.   [31] 5 U.S. Stat. 797.
[32] 2 Gammel's *Laws of Texas* 1225, 1228.
[33] 9 U.S. Stat. 108.

Union; it has been noted that the "equal footing" clause originated with the Northwest Ordinance, not with the Constitution.

It is of interest that the Supreme Court, a short time later, revised its assertions on the method of Texas' admission. After Texas, in its petition for rehearing pointed out the errors made by Justice Douglas in his technical usage of the "equal footing" clause and the annexation resolution, the court amended its opinion on 16 October 1950. The court changed the original opinion in four places so as to remove all references to the annexation resolution of 1 March 1845 as containing an "equal footing" clause, and to refer instead to the resolution of admission of 29 December 1845.[34] This amending of the opinion could not correct the error which had been made. Texas had not accepted the "equal footing" phrase; and the unilateral action of the United States could hardly be said to have made it effective, unless one holds that Texas was never a sovereign nation with the right to decide her future status.

Neither does Mr. Justice Douglas show, any more than Justice Black had shown, that paramount national rights as "respects foreign commerce, the waging of war, the making of treaties, defense of the shores, and the like" require that the United States have physical control of the submerged soils of the marginal sea. In these days of aerial warfare, which does not recognize the limitations of a two-dimensional medium for the waging of battle, it would be quite naïve to assume that control of the submerged soils of the marginal sea is more vital to national interests than physical control of the air over the immense industrial complex of, let us say, the city of Detroit. Again, none would deny the paramount power of the United States to establish binding rules of conduct for those operating in the marginal sea, when such binding rules are made in pursuance of national authority; but to say that the grant of power to the national government carries with it what amounts to a cession of territory is, in the opinion of the writer, incorrect constitutional law. The Supreme Court in effect stated that the Constitution, and its protection to individuals, stops at low-water mark. Said Justice Douglas:

[34] For argument on this point, and a bit of a taunt directed in a nice way at the court, see "Defendant's Petition Directed to the Court's Amended Opinion," No. 13 Original, October Term 1950. Texas filed this petition on 31 October 1950. The petition says, at 2–3: "By this action the Court, which had originally recognized that the basis of its decision should be the Annexation Agreement approved by both the United States and Texas, has shifted to a unilateral and purely formal act passed at a later date by the Congress of the United States and never agreed to by Texas." See also 340 U.S. 848.

It is said that there is no necessity for it—that the sovereignty of the sea can be complete and unimpaired no matter if Texas owns the oil underlying it. Yet as pointed out in United States v. State of California, once low-water mark is passed the international domain is reached. *Property rights must then be so subordinated to political rights as in substance to coalesce and unite in the national sovereign.* Today the controversy is over oil. Tomorrow it may be over some other substance or mineral or perhaps the bed of the ocean itself. If the property, whatever it may be, lies seaward of low-water mark, its use, disposition, management, and control involve national interests and national responsibilities. That is the source of national rights in it. Such is the rationale of the *California* decision, which we have applied to Louisiana's case. The same result must be reached here if "equal footing" with the various states is to be achieved. Unless any claim or title which the Republic of Texas had to the marginal sea is subordinated to this full paramount power of the United States on admission, there is or may be in practical effect a subtraction in favor of Texas from the national sovereignty of the United States. Yet neither the original thirteen states . . . nor California nor Louisiana enjoys such an advantage. The "equal footing" clause prevents extension of the sovereignty of a State into a domain of political and sovereign power of the United States from which the other States have been excluded, just as it prevents a contraction of sovereignty . . . which would produce inequality among the States . . . There is no need to take evidence to establish that meaning of "equal footing."[35]

Thus does Justice Douglas dispose of the claims of Texas. "Property rights" must "coalesce and unite in the national sovereign" once low-water mark is reached. Note that the Justice, having reached a conclusion on the one basis, now slips and allows an admission that there may be "property rights" in the marginal sea. If such there be, however, the national government may control them without respect to the limitations imposed by the Constitution. Here is the Sutherland doctrine of inherent powers extended beyond anything that that estimable gentleman would have conceived. The nonownership theory of Congressman Sam Hobbs of Alabama had again been legally vindicated.

The motions of Texas for an order to take testimony and depositions and for the appointment of a special master were denied, and the motion of the United States for judgment was granted.[36] In both the *Texas* and *Louisiana* cases, the court ruled that the parties, or either

35 339 U.S. 707, 719–20. Italics added.
36 *Ibid.,* 720.

of them, could submit before 15 September 1950 the form of the decrees to carry the opinions into effect.[37]

Justice Reed wrote a dissenting opinion in the *Texas* case, with Justice Minton joining him. Justice Frankfurter dissented separately and on different grounds. So far as the case of *Louisiana* was concerned Justice Reed could see no distinction from the *California* case; under the principle of *stare decisis, United States* v. *California* would control. "Texas, however, presents a variation which requires a different result."[38] The fact that Texas as a Republic had the "ownership" of these lands was determinative to Justices Reed and Minton. They could not see how the "equal footing" clause could be applied to strip these lands from Texas. It was an "articulated premise" of the *California* case that the three-mile belt had never belonged to California, and that sovereignty had passed to the United States; so, also, in the *California* case it was held that the thirteen original states had never asserted ownership or dominion over these lands. This was not the case with Texas. Said Justice Reed:

"Equal footing" has heretofore brought to a state the ownership of river beds, but never before has that phrase been interpreted to take away from a newly admitted state property that it had heretofore owned. I see no constitutional requirement that this should be done and I think the Resolution of Annexation left the marginal sea area in Texas. . . .

The argument based on international responsibilities prevailed in the California case because the marginal sea area was staked out by the United States. The argument cannot reasonably be extended to Texas without a holding that Texas ceded that area to the United States.

The necessity for the United States to defend the land and to handle international affairs is not enough to transfer property rights in the marginal sea from Texas to the United States. Federal sovereignty is paramount within national boundaries, but federal ownership depends on taking possession, as the California case holds; on consent, as in the case of places for federal use; or on purchase, as in the case of Alaska or the Territory of Louisiana. The needs of defense and foreign affairs alone cannot transfer ownership of an ocean bed from a state to the Federal Government any more than they could transfer iron ore under uplands from state to federal ownership. National responsibility is no greater in respect to the marginal sea than it is toward every other particle of American territory.[39]

[37] *Ibid.;* 339 U.S. 699, 706.   [38] 339 U.S. 707, 721.
[39] *Ibid.,* 722–23.

The writer would submit that the last sentence of Justice Reed's statement is the true key to the proper consideration of the issues involved in the controversy over ownership and control of the submerged lands.

Mr. Justice Frankfurter, who on occasion has been somewhat verbose, expressed his disagreement with his four brethren of the majority in a short, concise statement:

> Time has not made the reasoning of United States v. State of California . . . more persuasive but the issue there decided is no longer open for me. It is relevant, however, to note that in rejecting California's claim of ownership in the off-shore oil the Court carefully abstained from recognizing such claim of ownership by the United States. . . .
>
> I must leave it to those who deem the reasoning of that decision right to define its scope and apply it, particularly to the historically very different situation of Texas. As is made clear in the opinion of Mr. Justice Reed, the submerged lands now in controversy were part of the domain of Texas when she was on her own. The Court now decides that when Texas entered the Union she lost what she had and the United States acquired it. How that shift came to pass remains for me a puzzle.[40]

Both Texas and Louisiana immediately filed petitions asking for a rehearing. In *United States* v. *Louisiana* a petition for rehearing was denied 16 October 1950,[41] and a motion for leave to file a second petition for rehearing denied 11 December 1950.[42] Two attempts by Texas to get a rehearing were similarly denied by the court.[43]

The Texas petition for rehearing, filed 19 July 1950,[44] is noteworthy. While it appears doubtful that the Texas representatives really expected the court to rehear the case, the petition for rehearing was a) well-documented, neatly reasoned piece of work, very probably calculated to have more political effect than legal weight. Emphasis was placed on the point that the court had erred in its interpretation of the historical facts surrounding the admission of the state and in its refusal to hear evidence in the case.

But the petition will not be remembered for the obvious points stressed for the purpose of securing a rehearing. Rather the worth of the document is found in the memorandum which was attached to it. This "Joint Memorandum in Support of Rehearing in *United States* v. *Texas*" was signed by ten of the most eminent authorities in the field

[40] *Ibid.*, 723–24.   [41] 340 U.S. 856.
[42] 340 U.S. 907. A third attempt was denied 26 February 1951, 340 U.S. 939.
[43] 16 October 1950, 340 U.S. 848; 11 December 1950, 340 U.S. 907.
[44] No. 13 Original, October Term 1949.

of international law: Joseph Walter Bingham, C. John Colombos, Gilbert Gidel, Manley O. Hudson, Charles Cheney Hyde, Hans Kelsen, William E. Masterson, Roscoe Pound, Stefan A. Reisenfeld, and Felipe Sánchez Román. Each of these men prepared, separately, a memorandum for the attorney general of Texas at his request. Each memorandum dealt with the "title to the lands and minerals underlying the Gulf of Mexico within the original boundaries of the State of Texas and the rules of international law applicable thereto." Without collaboration, the substance of the conclusions of each of these experts was that:

1. The Republic of Texas, as an independent nation, had full sovereignty over and ownership of the lands and minerals underlying that portion of the Gulf of Mexico within its original boundaries three leagues from shore. Under international law and under the domestic law adopted by the Republic of Texas, the ownership (*dominium*) of the subjacent soil and minerals was severable from the paramount governmental powers (*imperium*) employed in the original acquisition and in the regulation and control of commerce, navigation, defense, and international relations.

2. The transfer of national sovereignty and governmental powers relating to interstate and foreign commerce, navigation, defense, and international relations from the Republic of Texas to the United States in 1845 did not effect a transfer or relinquishment of the ownership of the lands and minerals above described. International law, as it existed in 1845, did not imply or require a cession of these proprietary rights with a transfer of national sovereignty.

3. The Republic of Texas, upon annexation, did not cede to the United States the ownership of the controverted 2,068,774 acres of lands and minerals within its original boundaries, but specifically retained this ownership under the terms of the agreement between the Republic of Texas and the United States.

4. A contrary position, asserted by the United States 103 years after the international agreement of annexation, creates a dispute as to the meaning of the controlling documents. Under such circumstances either litigant should be entitled to present evidence bearing upon the intention of the contracting parties.

5. Available evidence of the status of international law, reflected by the customs, usages, and practices of nations in 1845 and since that date, will support the foregoing conclusions of fact and law.[45]

---

[45] *Ibid.*, 54–55. William W. Bishop, Jr., did not participate in the preparation of the memorandum because of a lack of time. In a separate statement, he made known his agreement with the position taken by Texas. *Ibid.*, 69. The joint memorandum is reprinted in 3 *Baylor Law Review* (1951), 319–35.

The points just made were then considered in detail in the final product, a joint effort subscribed to by each of the signers. It would most certainly appear that the Texas position, particularly, must have been very strong; otherwise so many recognized experts would hardly have allowed their names to be used in supporting such a position. The joint memorandum is a document of historical and legal worth beyond the case in which it has played a part.

The court handed down its decree in each of the cases on 11 December 1950. With the exception of substituting the name of Texas for that of Louisiana, the two were almost identical,[46] and the form followed was substantially that of *United States* v. *California*. The United States was declared to have been "at all times pertinent hereto, possessed of paramount rights in, and full dominion and power over, the lands, minerals and other things underlying the Gulf of Mexico," out to "twenty-seven marine miles" in the case of Louisiana[47] and "outside of the inland waters" in the case of Texas.[48] In each case the states were declared to have "no title thereto or property interest therein." The words "of proprietorship," which had been part of the decree suggested by the United States in the *California* case, were again omitted.

The original form of the decree proposed by the United States would have required Texas and Louisiana to account for moneys received by them from operators working under state leases subsequent to 23 June 1947, the date of *United States* v. *California*. Although the decrees were opposed *in toto* by both Texas and Louisiana,[49] both states made particular objection to this cut-off date. At the least, Texas and Louisiana felt that the cut-off date should be 16 May 1949, the date when the United States had been given leave to file the complaints; preferably, they wished the date set at 6 June 1950, the date of the decisions. The court, in the decrees, chose 5 June 1950 as the date subsequent to which the states would have to make an accounting of all moneys obtained from oil operations under state leases in the submerged lands.

The decrees enjoined the two states from "carrying on any activities" in the submerged lands areas "for the purpose of taking or removing therefrom any petroleum, gas, or other valuable mineral products,

---

[46] *United States* v. *Texas*, 340 U.S. 900; *United States* v. *Louisiana*, 340 U.S. 899.   [47] 340 U.S. 899.   [48] 340 U.S. 900.
[49] See "Objections to the Decree Proposed by the United States and Memorandum in Support of Objections," No. 13 Original, October Term 1950. This document stating Texas' objections is a technical one, and well done. It is far more complete than that filed by Louisiana.

except under authorization first obtained from the United States." The court then stated that the United States might obtain appropriate injunctive relief upon showing cause for the same.

A pattern somewhat different from that which had been adopted in *United States* v. *California* was established to provide for interim operation of the wells in the Gulf of Mexico. As has been noted, the California situation was complicated by controversy over whether or not particular areas were to be considered as "inland waters" and thus under the control of the state. While such factors were not completely absent so far as Gulf leases were concerned, the question of inland waters as against marginal sea was clearer in most cases. Further, the criticism which had been leveled at the Department of the Interior by men like Harold L. Ickes[50] for its handling of the California stipulations perhaps made the department somewhat more sensitive.

In any event, interim operations in the Gulf of Mexico were not to be conducted under stipulation that the lessees continue to pay the royalty moneys to the state, which in turn would place the royalties in an escrow fund, there to be held until some final disposition could be made. The Attorney General of the United States had held that the Federal Mineral Leasing Act of 1920 was not a sufficient basis for the Department of the Interior to take over administrative authority of oil production in the marginal seas. Still the interim operations were to be more directly controlled by the Department of the Interior, which drew its authority from Executive Order 9633,[51] whereby the President had in 1945 placed the natural resources of the submerged coastal lands under "the jurisdiction and control of the Secretary of the Interior for administrative purposes, pending the enactment of legislation."

In furtherance of this authority, Oscar L. Chapman, Secretary of the Interior, on 11 December 1950 issued a notice covering oil and gas operations in the submerged coastal lands of the Gulf of Mexico.[52] This notice declared that the United States "has paramount rights in, full dominion and power over, and ownership of" these lands. One might inquire as to where, in the face of the numerous actions of the court, Chapman drew his authority to declare ownership.

Operations were to continue under paragraph 2 of the notice. Per-

---

[50] See, e.g., his article in the *New Republic,* 22 May 1950, p. 15.

[51] 10 Fed. Reg. 12305. Under Executive Order 10426, 18 Fed. Reg. 405, dated 16 January 1953, control was transferred to the Secretary of the Navy. See pp. 257–58 below, where this recent action is discussed.

[52] 15 Fed. Reg. 8835.

sons who were operating under state leases could continue to operate for a period of sixty days after 11 December 1950, subject to the payment to the United States of rentals, royalties, and other fees which would have been due the states under state leases, from 11 December to the end of the sixty-day period. Within thirty days from 11 December, the lessees could file with the director of the Bureau of Land Management for permission to continue operations beyond the sixty-day period allowed. Subsequently, 2 February 1951, the sixty-day period originally mentioned was extended another thirty days.[53] A number of further extensions were granted as each newly established cut-off date approached.[54] Finally, in an order dated 26 June 1952, continuance of operations was authorized on an indefinite basis, subject to amendment or revocation on thirty days' notice.[55]

No provision was made, either in the original notice or in the many subsequent extensions, for exploration and geophysical operations in the Gulf or for the letting of new leases. Wells commenced on or before 11 December 1950 could be completed and put in production, but no wells could be started after that date. Needed oil production was lost as a result. The stipulations made in the *California* case are open to criticism, but it is in their favor that no production was lost. The same statement cannot be made of offshore production in the Gulf of Mexico.

As in the case of the submerged lands off the coast of California, the question of which agency really had the authority to administer the oil operations in the marginal sea remained, like Mahomet's coffin, suspended between heaven and hell. The *Texas* and *Louisiana* cases had been decided, but the problems raised by the decisions remained.[56]

[53] 16 Fed. Reg. 1203.
[54] 16 Fed. Reg. 2195; 16 Fed. Reg. 3623; 16 Fed. Reg. 6404; 16 Fed. Reg. 8720; 16 Fed. Reg. 10998; 17 Fed. Reg. 43; 17 Fed. Reg. 2821.
[55] 17 Fed. Reg. 5833.
[56] Evidence of the high feeling in Texas generated by the decision is seen in the action of the lower house of the legislature of that state. On 16 January 1951, a resolution asking the impeachment of Mr. Justice Douglas for his stand in the *Texas* case was approved by a voice vote. A motion to recommit the resolution was defeated on an 88–28 record vote. *New York Times,* 17 January 1951.

13 ·

Quitclaim or Federal Control?

The decision of the Supreme Court in *United States* v. *California* was followed by a period of intense legislative activity on the part of those wishing to return the submerged lands to the status they had held prior to the case. There were introduced in the second session of the Eightieth Congress a great many bills which would have accomplished the same purpose as the quitclaim bill which President Truman had vetoed in 1946.[1] The stimulus to quitclaim was markedly present because of the belief that the Department of Justice was preparing to move against the states of Texas and Louisiana. Further impetus was given to the movement when the complaints against the states were filed and the decisions in *United States* v. *Texas* and *United States* v. *Louisiana* were announced. Starting in January 1948, scores—and the word is used advisedly—of quitclaim measures, were introduced in every session of Congress.[2] Justice Black had recognized that Congressional implemen-

---

[1] See, e.g., H.R. 5531 and H.R. 5660. S. 1988 was introduced by Senator Moore for himself and Senators Knowland, McCarran, Bricker, Hawkes, Butler, Holland, Eastland, Martin, Ellender, Saltonstall, O'Connor, O'Daniel, Downey, Connally, Byrd, Overton, Hickenlooper, Brooks, and Capper.

[2] See, e.g., H.R. 180, 81st Cong., 1st sess.; S. 155, 81st Cong., 1st sess.; S. 1545, 81st Cong., 1st sess.; H.R. 8137, 81st Cong., 2d sess.; H.R. 4484, 82d Cong., 1st sess.; S. 940, 82d Cong., 1st sess. The last named bill was introduced by Senator Holland of Florida for himself and Senators Bricker, Butler of Maryland, Butler of Nebraska, Byrd, Cain, Capehart, Carlson, Connally, Cordon, Duff, Eastland, Ellender, Frear, Hendrickson, Hickenlooper, Jenner, Johnson of Texas, Johnston of South Carolina, Knowland, Long, Malone, Martin, McCarran, McClellan, Mundt, Nixon, O'Connor, Robertson, Saltonstall, Schoeppel, Smathers, Stennis, Taft, and Thye. Senator Holland pointed out at the time of introduction that the bill was favored by these organizations: Council of State Governments,

tation of the decision he was making would be necessary.[3] Even he, however, could not have foreseen the complexity of the problems arising from the submerged lands decisions.

The passage of a quitclaim measure which would restore the control of the submerged soils to the states on a pre-1947 basis is one solution. On the other hand, there are a number of members of Congress who feel that control should properly vest in the United States. Senators and representatives of this persuasion have introduced bills to provide for such control,[4] though these proposals have not been offered in great numbers as have quitclaim measures. The fact that the Federal Mineral Leasing Act of 1920 has been declared to be inapplicable for the purpose of federal control[5] necessitates, many persons feel, the pas-

---

Governors' Conference, National Association of Attorneys General, American Bar Association, National Conference of Mayors, American Association of Port Authorities, National Reclamation Association, National Water Conservation Association, National Institute of Municipal Law Officers (representing 503 cities), and National Association of Secretaries of State. 97 *Congressional Record* 1451–52. The bill was introduced 21 February 1951.

[3] We "cannot and do not assume that Congress, which has constitutional control over Government property, will execute its powers in such way as to bring about injustices to states, their subdivisions, or persons acting pursuant to their permission." 332 U.S. 19, 40.

[4] See, e.g., S. 2165, by Senator Barkley, 80th Cong., 2d sess.; H.R. 5528, by Congressman Lemke, 80th Cong. 2d sess.; and S. 923, by Senator O'Mahoney, 81st Cong., 1st sess. These bills were all introduced at the request of the Departments of Justice and Interior.

[5] See p. 189 above.

By act of 7 August 1947, 30 U.S.C. 352, the Secretary of Interior was authorized to lease for oil and other minerals "acquired lands of the United States" to which the mineral leasing laws had not been extended; but it was provided "that nothing in this chapter is intended, or shall be construed, to apply to or in any manner affect any mineral rights, exploration permits, leases or conveyances nor minerals that are or may be in any tidelands; or submerged lands; or in lands underlying the three-mile zone or belt involved in the case of the United States of America against the State of California now pending on application for rehearing in the Supreme Court of the United States; or in lands underlying such three-mile zone or belt; or the continental shelf, adjacent or littoral to any part of the land within the jurisdiction of the United States of America." It would thus appear that Congress has affirmatively declared that the Mineral Leasing Act of 1920 is not applicable to offshore mineral operations.

There are some persons, like former Senator Burton Wheeler, who represents about a dozen applicants for federal prospecting permits on submerged lands, who feel that the Mineral Leasing Act of 1920 does apply. *Hearings* on S.J. Res. 20 (1951), 248–98. In testimony before the Senate Interior and Insular Affairs Committee, Wheeler was bitterly condemnatory of the rulings of the Attorney General and the solicitor of the Department of the Interior holding the Mineral Leasing Act nonapplicable to offshore lands. See also statement of Harold L. Ickes, *ibid.*, 237, to the same effect but in more colorful language. Ickes had

sage of separate federal legislation before such control can be assumed. Those who favor federal control have introduced, as a matter of strategy designed to split off the support of inland representatives for quitclaim, measures to declare that the states retain ownership and control of their inland waters and the soils beneath them.[6]

The battle between these two points of view was inconclusive through 1952. The fact of the matter was that the advocates of quitclaim in the Congress commanded a substantial majority in both houses; a quitclaim bill could be passed at any time. Such a bill would, however, be subject to a veto by President Truman.[7] The veto possibly could be overridden in the House of Representatives, but it appeared very doubtful that the necessary two-thirds majority for quitclaim could be obtained in the Senate, where the lines were closely drawn.

It was obvious, on the other hand, that bills which would allow national control and administration of the submerged lands in the marginal sea had no chance of passage in either house of the Congress unless quitclaim proponents should allow themselves to be worn down by a process of attrition. No bill calling for complete national control was ever reported out of committee. Neither side was able to force the other to abandon its position, and so long as Truman remained President there was little hope that the admitted Congressional majority for quitclaim could effectuate its point of view.

This impasse was a serious matter, particularly in view of the necessity for full-scale oil production because of the Korean imbroglio, American military and economic commitments abroad, and the almost complete shutoff of Iranian oil production. While the production of oil from the offshore fields in California continued without the loss of a single day's output under the stipulations mentioned in the previous chapter,

---

changed his mind when testifying in 1951, for in *Hearings* on S.J. Res. 48 and H.J. Res. 225 (1946), 11, he had said that the "Mineral Leasing Act of 1920 is not applicable to submerged lands."

[6] For example, S. 2222, by Senator Barkley, 80th Cong., 2d sess.; H.R. 5529, by Congressman Lemke, 80th Cong., 2d sess.; S. 2153, by Senator O'Mahoney, 81st Cong., 1st sess. It should not be necessary to add that the strategy had no greater success between 1948 and 1952 than it had from 1938 to 1939.

[7] Persons close to President Truman indicated that he was adamant in his stand on this point. Thus the then Secretary of the Interior stated that Truman would veto a quitclaim. *New York Times,* 28 April 1949.

J. H. Carmical of the *New York Times,* in the 5 August 1951 issue, indicated that Truman would take this action, as did Congressman Celler (97 *Congressional Record* 9164–65). See pp. 227–28 below, where the Truman veto of 1952 is discussed.

oil operations in the Gulf of Mexico were very spotty after the decisions in the *Louisiana* and *Texas* cases. Geophysical operations were reduced almost to the vanishing point; exploration for new deposits in the Gulf of Mexico well-nigh ceased.[8]

In an effort to remedy the situation, a number of attempts were made to hammer out some compromise acceptable to both sides.[9] None of these attempts showed much promise of success. Two measures by Senator O'Mahoney of Wyoming called for the establishment of arrangements whereby petroleum exploration and production could be carried on in the interim between the court decisions and some final arrangement by Congress.[10] Even these "interim operation" bills did not meet with any great measure of acceptance. Senate Joint Resolution 20 received serious committee consideration as an interim measure in the first session of the Eighty-second Congress, but it was not passed by the Senate. This bill would have legalized all leases granted by the states prior to the Supreme Court decisions. Control would have been vested in the Interior Department with provision made for granting new leases. The bill would have given 37.5 per cent of the royalties to

---

[8] In 1947 there were forty-eight geophysical crews in operation in the Gulf. In April 1951 there were only four, all operating off the coast of Texas. In 1949 twenty-six drilling rigs were operating in this area. The number had dropped to fourteen in late 1950, and in April 1951, there were only five rigs drilling—all off the shore of Louisiana and none off Texas. Testimony of Walter S. Hallanan, president of the Plymouth Oil Company, *Hearings* on S.J. Res. 20 (1951), 75–76. Under the notice issued by the Secretary of the Interior and the decree of the Supreme Court in the *Texas* and *Louisiana* cases, handed down 11 December 1950 and discussed in the previous chapter, no further activities of any kind could be carried on in the submerged lands. Drilling of the five wells under way on that date and production from existing wells could be continued, but no new wells could be started.

The chairman of the Standard Oil Company, R. Gwinn Follis, of San Francisco, said in an interview in New Orleans on 29 November 1951 that the offshore production of crude oil could be doubled in a year and tripled in several years if the dispute over control of the offshore lands were settled. The failure to clarify title "had brought exploration" to a standstill. *New York Times,* 2 December 1951.

[9] Rumors of pending compromise were quite frequent prior to the decision in the *Texas* and *Louisiana* cases. The *Dallas News* of 8 May 1949 indicated that Attorney General Clark had offered Texas a "deal." On 27 July 1949, the *Omaha World Herald* carried the news that a tidelands compromise bill was in the offing as the result of an agreement worked out by Speaker of the House Sam Rayburn and representatives of the Administration and the three states concerned. In a speech before the Texas State Teachers Association, 25 November 1949, Texas Attorney General Price Daniel indicated that these attempts had failed. Nothing of significance ever resulted from them. Daniel personally opposed making any compromise.

[10] S.J. Res. 195, 81st Cong., 2d sess.; S.J. Res. 20, 82d Cong., 1st sess.

the affected states, the remaining royalties going into escrow until final settlement of the matter by Congress.[11]

With those favoring quitclaim in the majority, it was logical that bills supporting that point of view should get farthest along the road toward becoming law. In 1948, after extremely extensive hearings, the Senate Judiciary Subcommittee reported favorably to the full committee Senate Bill 1988, a quitclaim measure.[12] The full committee was not to report the measure to the Senate until 10 June 1948.[13] In the meantime, on 24 March, the House Judiciary Subcommittee approved House Bill 5860, a quitclaim proposal almost identical with Senate Bill 1988. With very little opposition, the House Judiciary Committee gave its approval to the House bill on 16 April 1948. On 30 April the House of Representatives, by a rousing 257–29 vote, passed House Bill 5992, a measure identical with House Bill 5860. In thirty-five of the state delegations not a vote was cast against it, and in no state delegation were the opponents of quitclaim in the majority.

When the House bill went to the Senate, Senator Sheridan Downey of California on 3 May invoked a seldom used rule of the Senate and managed to get the quitclaim measure placed immediately on the calendar rather than having it referred to committee.[14] Senator Downey's

[11] Numerous amendments to the O'Mahoney bill were suggested in committee, most of which would have left the interim control in the hands of the states rather than the federal government.

In a statement to the Senate on 18 January 1951, at the time of introduction, Senator O'Mahoney supported Senate Joint Resolution 20 as being in the interest of national defense in that oil production and exploration in the Gulf of Mexico could get under way again. 97 *Congressional Record* 441–42.

[12] The vote was 2 to 1. Senator Forrest Donnell of Missouri, the dissenting member, waged a lengthy fight against the quitclaim in the hearings. He subjected the witnesses favoring quitclaim to lengthy, and frequently caustic, cross-examination. At times he quarreled with other members over procedure. Much of his questioning was directed toward attempting to prove a link between those favoring quitclaim and the oil companies, particularly a link indicating financial support. Joint *Hearings* on S. 1988 (1948), 192–93, 219, 235–60, 315, 1053, 1063.

When additional hearings were held at Senator Donnell's request on 4 and 5 May 1948, he cross-examined William W. Clary, member of the law firm of O'Melveny and Myers and special assistant to the California attorney general in the *California* case, for ninety pages. *Hearings* on S. 1988 (1948), 1–91.

[13] 94 *Congressional Record* 7682.

[14] The Senator followed the procedure of objecting to further proceedings on H.R. 5992 when it arrived. Acting under the rules, Senate president pro tempore Arthur Vandenberg ordered the measure placed on the calendar, which meant it could be called up for action by any senator. Senator Scott Lucas of Illinois, acting minority leader in the absence of Senator Barkley, served notice that he would move in a short time to take the bill off the calendar and send it to the

action caused harsh words on the Senate floor, and tempers flared. Senator George Aiken of Vermont called Senator Downey's action "one of the most high handed and outrageous procedures ever attempted by any member of Congress."[15] Senator Tobey promised Senator Downey (and the quitclaim advocates) a fight such as the California Senator had never seen, stating that he would use the word "damnedest" if the Senate rules allowed. Slashing at Ed Pauley as a man of "unsavory reputation," Senator Tobey contended that the big oil companies were behind the quitclaim.[16]

The quitclaim measure died on the calendar of the Senate of the Eightieth Congress. Proponents of the quitclaim tried desperately hard to bring the measure to a vote in the Senate before adjournment. They knew they could not possibly muster anything like the 9–1 margin that had been recorded in their favor in the House of Representatives, but they still harbored hopes, at that time, that the President might not veto.[17] Yet the bill was caught in a pincers movement. On the one hand, the Republican leadership of the House was calling for adjournment before the Republican National Convention. On the other hand, there was virtual assurance of time-consuming tactics, if not filibuster, on the part of Republican Senators Tobey and Aiken. As it turned out, Senator Glen Taylor's filibuster on the selective service measure took so much time that the quitclaim could not have been considered anyhow.

Advocates of quitclaim were not so successful in the Eighty-first Congress. Three sets of hearings were held. House Bills 5991 and 5992 were considered by Subcommittee 1 of the House Judiciary Committee. Both these bills were of a compromise character, the former supported halfheartedly by the states, and the latter, though retaining some elements of national control, failing endorsement by the Administration. It was made plain in these hearings that the states continued to favor quitclaim,[18] and the Administration complete national con-

---

Judiciary Committee, an action which could be taken by majority vote. 94 *Congressional Record* 5168–69. The action suggested by Lucas was not, of course, ever taken, since the majority of senators favored quitclaim.

[15] 94 *Congressional Record* 5169.

[16] *Ibid.*, 5169–70.

[17] The point that this hope was ill founded has already been made. Charles B. Degges, Washington correspondent of the *Oakland Tribune,* had reported 16 June 1948 that President Truman "appeared eager to change his mind" following a trip to California where he had been "pressured by Californians." Later statements from those officials close to the President did not bear out Degges' optimism.

[18] See, e.g., testimony of Hall Hammond, attorney general of Maryland and chairman of the Submerged Lands Committee of the National Association of

trol;[19] for all their expressions of co-operation, each side stood by its guns. The bill finally reported to the House of Representatives was House Bill 8137,[20] which, though a special rule provided for its consideration, was not considered by the House during the Eighty-first Congress. House Bill 8137 was a straight quitclaim measure.

The other two sets of hearings in the Eighty-first Congress were held before the Senate Interior and Insular Affairs Committee, one in the first[21] and the other in the second session.[22] Hearings in the first session were conducted on an assortment of Senate bills, including two quitclaim measures;[23] a bill for federal control, introduced by Senator O'Mahoney at the request of the Departments of Justice and Interior;[24] a bill to confirm state title to inland waters, also introduced by the Wyoming Senator at the request of the Departments of Justice and Interior;[25] and a bill introduced by Senator Langer to quitclaim to the states the submerged lands out to a distance of one mile and create a federal waterlands reserve of the remaining lands with the proceeds therefrom going into a fund in aid of education.[26]

Hearings in the second session of the Eighty-first Congress were conducted on Senate Joint Resolution 195, one of the measures introduced by Senator O'Mahoney to cover interim operations in the offshore fields. In most respects this resolution was similar to Senate Joint Resolution 20, providing in effect that state leases would be recognized, that royalties would be paid to the federal government and held in escrow pending final disposition of the status of submerged lands by Congress, and that the Secretary of the Interior would exercise general administrative control during the interim. These hearings covered much the same

Attorneys General, *Hearings* on H.R. 5991 and 5992 (1949), 19–29. Similar expressions of this point of view can be had by glancing at the testimony of any of the various representatives of the states who appeared before the committee.

[19] Testimony of Secretary of the Interior Julius A. Krug, *ibid.*, 166: "H.R. 5992 is not sponsored by the Department of the Interior. The executive branch of the Government stands on the other proposed legislation [for complete national control] dealing with submerged lands. . . ."

[20] 96 *Congressional Record* 7188; H.R. Rept. 2078, 81st Cong.

[21] *Hearings* on S. 155 *et al.* (1949). These hearings were held 4–8 and 10 October 1949.

[22] *Hearings* on S.J. Res. 195 (1950). These hearings were held 14–19 August 1950. [23] S. 155; S. 1545.

[24] S. 923. [25] S. 2153.

[26] S. 1700. Since most of the present petroleum operations off California and Texas are found within this one-mile zone, the bill might have formed a basis for compromise, had either side been in a compromising mood. Actually, the measure was never seriously considered. Petroleum operations off Louisiana are located much beyond the one-mile zone.

ground that had been covered many times before. The two sides refused to alter their positions. Quitclaim proponents were to claim later that quitclaim was not pressed in the Eighty-first Congress because the *Texas* and *Louisiana* cases were pending.[27]

By the end of the first session of the Eighty-second Congress, quitclaim advocates had made considerable progress. Although they had been unsuccessful in getting legislation of any type reported out of the Senate Interior and Insular Affairs Committee, they achieved a victory in the House of Representatives. On 30 July 1951, by a vote of 265 to 109 and 59 not voting,[28] a quitclaim bill was passed. House Bill 4484 had been introduced by Congressman Francis Walter of Pennsylvania and had been reported favorably by the House Committee on the Judiciary. On 27 July 1951, Congressman Lyle of Texas, at the direction of the Rules Committee, called up House Resolution 335, asking its adoption so that the House might resolve itself immediately into the Committee of the Whole House on the State of the Union for the purpose of considering House Bill 4484.[29] Congressman Lyle's action touched off intense debate in the House.

Opponents of quitclaim were well aware that the battle was a losing one for them, but they battled well, airing thoroughly arguments against the state control of offshore lands. They lost the fight to defeat the resolution to resolve the House into a committee of the whole by a vote of 270 to 92 with 71 not voting.[30] Debate in the committee of the whole was relatively lengthy, both sides developing the old, familiar arguments which had been made so many times in committee hearings and in House debates on previous quitclaim measures.[31] Those who fought quitclaim charged that the measure was a "bill for the oil interests,"[32] a "plan to dissipate a great national resource,"[33] a "proposal of the oil lobby,"[34] and a "rape of the judiciary."[35] Congressman

[27] Statement of Congressman Ed Gossett of Texas. 97 *Congressional Record* 9064.
[28] 97 *Congressional Record* 9206. Of the 59 not voting, 32 were paired for the vote on this issue, with 10 operating under general pairs.
[29] *Ibid.*, 9050–51.   [30] *Ibid.*, 9063–64.
[31] *Ibid.*, 9050–9103, 9162–9206.
[32] Congressman Emanuel Celler, *ibid.*, 9062.
[33] Congressman Cleveland Bailey of West Virginia, *ibid.*, 9056. The argument of Congressman Ray Madden of Indiana was built around this same theme. *Ibid.*, 9058–59.
[34] Congressman Bailey, *ibid.*, 9057.
[35] *Ibid.* Representative Robert Ramsay of West Virginia argued that the bill was a "bad bill" because it attempted to set aside decisions of the Supreme Court. *Ibid.*, 9100–9102.

Emanuel Celler of New York charged that the oil companies wanted state ownership because these companies controlled "the processes of State lease making."[36] He labeled as a "snide, mean, contemptible tissue of lies"[37] the argument advanced by the proponents of quitclaim that the decisions of the Supreme Court threatened state ownership of soil under inland waters. Congressman Adolph Sabath of Illinois charged Congressman Leo Allen of Illinois with being interested in the "oil plutocrats."[38] Congressman Claude Bakewell of Missouri, who was the only Republican to sign the minority report of the House Judiciary Committee on House Bill 4484, argued that the legislation was "palpably unconstitutional." He based his reasoning on the fact that Congress was not here disposing of the public lands of the United States, but rather attempting to dispose of its sovereignty; hence there was here no question of title.[39]

Those who favored quitclaim could argue in the full knowledge that when the talking stopped, the measure would pass. Various persons replied at length to the charges made. Many representatives said that applicants for federal leases under the Mineral Leasing Act appeared to have stirred up this controversy in the first place and were now opposing quitclaim because they would lose their chances for speculative profits on lands which they had not spent a penny to develop.[40] Quitclaim was far from being a measure supported by the oil interests; instead, the pressure came from lease applicants seeking to kill the bill.[41]

[36] Congressman Celler, *ibid.*, 9062.

[37] *Ibid.*, 9063. Representative Michael Feighan of Ohio argued that the claim that the national government could take over inland waters under the rule of the Supreme Court in the submerged lands decisions was entirely false. The national government had no such intentions and couldn't if it wanted to, he stated. *Ibid.*, 9070–72.

[38] *Ibid.*, 9052.

[39] *Ibid.*, 9092–93. See pp. 230–33 below, where this point is discussed more fully.

[40] Representative W. R. Poage of Texas called these lease applicants twentieth-century prospectors "who ride Cadillacs, not burros." He referred to former Senator Wheeler, counsel for a group of such applicants, and others who held similar views as a "disreputable group." Congressman Poage said: "No oil lobby is interested in the question of whether the States or the Federal Government owns these lands, except those oil lobbyists who are hopeful of getting something for nothing and they all want the Federal Government to take the property away from those oil companies who have in good faith paid the State for leases." *Ibid.*, 9065–66.

At 9180 is reprinted a letter from one of these promoters who bold-facedly speaks of speculative profits of fantastic size that might be derived on the basis of such leases.

[41] Congressman Francis E. Walter of Pennsylvania, author of House Bill 4484,

The legal arguments were developed at length by many speakers favoring quitclaim.

But argument would avail nothing. The die was cast, and opponents of the measure knew it. They fought a neat delaying action, proposing a series of amendments, each of which was beaten down in turn.[42] They finally saw a motion to recommit, made by Representative Kenneth Keating of New York, defeated.[43] On the actual passage of the bill, Congressman Walter called for the yeas and nays with the result already mentioned. A routine motion to reconsider was laid on the table. Opponents of quitclaim could take some consolation in the fact that they had mustered the largest vote that they had ever been able to obtain in the House of Representatives.

House Bill 4484 was different in some respects from previous quitclaim measures. It confirmed title to offshore soils out to the original boundaries of the states and then declared that the United States controlled the area beyond that point, though the states were given some rights even beyond their constitutional boundaries.[44] It granted au-

---

said that the "only lobbying by oil interests has been against this bill, not for it." No oil companies had approached him in support of the bill. *Ibid.*, 9081. Representative Lloyd Bentsen of Texas stated: "The only oil lobbyists who have contacted me on this issue have favored the federal proposal." *Ibid.*, 9086.

[42] Congressman Celler moved to strike out all but the enacting clause of H.R. 4484 and substitute what was, in effect, the O'Mahoney interim operation bill. *Ibid.*, 9175–77. Representative Carl Hinshaw criticized Celler for including in his amendment a section to protect former Senator Wheeler's clients, a feature not found in the O'Mahoney bill. Hinshaw said Celler's amendment might better have been titled "an amendment for the relief of the clients of Burton K. Wheeler, former Senator of the United States . . . now a Washington Lawyer for those who need influence." *Ibid.*, 9178. The Celler amendment was defeated— ayes, 38; noes, 114. *Ibid.*, 9193.

Representative Clifford Case of New Jersey offered an amendment to limit the extent of submerged lands given to the states to no more than three miles, rather than weigh the claims of states as based on "constitutional provision, statute, or otherwise." *Ibid.*, 9199. It was rejected—ayes, 45; noes, 121. *Ibid.*, 9200.

Other amendments by Representatives Case, Mike Mansfield of Montana, and Eugene McCarthy of Minnesota were defeated. *Ibid.*, 9194, 9202. The Mansfield amendment was, in substance, the "oil for education" amendment which Senator Lister Hill had sponsored in the Senate.

Minor amendments by supporters of the bill were accepted. *Ibid.*, 9203, 9204.

[43] *Ibid.*, 9205–206.

[44] Representative Celler contended in debate that the measure was an open invitation to the states to start extending their boundaries. All they would have to do, he said, would be to base a claim on an old map, a fishing grant, or other type of evidence. He argued at length with Representative J. Frank Wilson, of Texas on this point, Wilson contending that the limit, so far as Texas was

thority to the Secretary of the Interior to lease lands beyond state boundaries, made provision for royalties and rentals, and generally placed under national control the resources of the continental shelf beyond state boundaries. No such provision had been incorporated into previous quitclaim bills which had passed the House. The national-control provisions were part of a strategy to win some supporters of national control over to the acceptance of quitclaim to the limit of traditional state boundaries.

Senator George A. Smathers of Florida, member of the Senate Interior and Insular Affairs Committee, predicted in December 1951 that some sort of coastal lands legislation would be reported to the Senate in 1952, with action possible in February or March.[45] It appears that all members of the committee were agreed that some sort of legislation should be presented, even if the measure reported was Senate Joint Resolution 20, the interim operation bill. The measure could then be amended by quitclaim proponents on the floor to a form substantially that of House Bill 4484, if the Senate Interior and Insular Affairs Committee refused to report House Bill 4484.

This procedure was used in pushing the quitclaim bill through the Senate during the second session of the Eighty-second Congress. On 27 February 1952, Senate Majority Leader Ernest McFarland of Arizona moved to proceed to the consideration of Senate Joint Resolution

---

concerned, was three leagues. Celler saw no reason why the states could not go on extending boundaries right out to the edge of the continental shelf, thus depriving the United States of areas supposedly guaranteed it by the bill. *Ibid.,* 9164.

The writer is inclined to think that the Congressman from New York had a point. The bill should have spelled out more exactly the extent of the offshore areas being quitclaimed to the states and those remaining under federal jurisdiction and control. The writer would suggest that Congress might perform a real service by passing a resolution similar to Part I of House Joint Resolution 209 introduced by Congressman Carl Hinshaw of California in the first session of the Eighty-second Congress. Part I of that resolution would have defined such terms as "high seas," "territorial waters," "tidelands," "submerged lands," and "inland waters." Regardless of what type of legislation is ultimately passed by Congress, it would be well to state precisely the meaning of these words. The definitions need not be those accepted in international law, but the words should be given a common meaning so that both sides would utilize a common terminology, regardless of what their ultimate objective might be.

[45] *Florida Times Union*, 28 December 1951. Senator Smathers favored what he called a "middle of the road approach." He would fix the responsibility of the states at their originally declared boundary lines. The writer would suggest that this is hardly a "middle of the road" attitude, although those advocating turning over the continental shelf to the states might deem it so.

20. Senator O'Mahoney of Wyoming objected, for he wished to consider Senate Bill 49, which was a bill for the admission of Hawaii to the Union.[46] His objection was the first in a series which were raised to the consideration of legislation dealing with the submerged lands. On occasion, both sides resorted to delaying tactics as one or the other group sought to press a temporary advantage.

There is no reason to restate here the arguments which had been advanced so frequently before. The legislation technically under consideration was the resolution to provide for interim control of the controverted lands; yet all the members of the Senate must have known that eventually a quitclaim would be voted. Senators Spessard Holland of Florida and Russell Long of Louisiana took the brunt of the battle for the advocates of quitclaim with assists from Senators Knowland of California, Smathers of Florida, and others similarly inclined. Senator O'Mahoney quarterbacked the campaign for the antiquitclaim forces, with help from Senators Anderson of New Mexico, Murray of Montana, Lehman of New York, and Hill of Alabama. Approximately one-half the Senate membership spoke at one time or another, but most of the appearances were merely made in order that the individual senator might be "on the record."

On 3 March 1952, Senator Hill sent to the desk his "oil for education" plan, which he intended to propose as an amendment to Senate Joint Resolution 20. This measure was cosponsored by eighteen other senators.[47] On this same day, Senate routine was enlivened by an ex-

---

[46] 98 *Congressional Record* 1563–64. Senate Joint Resolution 20 was the measure for interim operation of the wells and drilling operations in the marginal sea; administration of the interim bill was to be lodged in the Department of the Interior. All references to Volume 98 of the *Congressional Record,* the volume dealing with the second session of the Eighty-second Congress, are to the daily issues of the *Record.* The permanent volumes were not yet available at the time this manuscript went to press. The pagination of the daily issues and the final volumes differs considerably. Members of Congress have also been known to tone down their more flamboyant utterances in the permanent volume.

[47] *Ibid.,* 1727. The amendment provided that royalties from the offshore petroleum operations would be paid into the federal treasury and used for educational purposes. The cosponsors were Douglas, Morse, Benton, Tobey, Neely, Sparkman, Kefauver, Chávez, Humphrey, Hennings, Lehman, Murray, Gillette, Langer, Aiken, Moody, Fulbright, and Case. Both the *Washington Post* and the *New York Times* supported the measure editorially. For a fuller explanation of the amendment in Senator Hill's own words, see 204 *Harper's Magazine* (March 1952), 28–31. Limited hearings had been held on the idea in February 1952. *Hearings* before the Senate Committee on Interior and Insular Affairs, on amendment to S.J. Res. 20, intended to be proposed by Mr. Hill, 82d Cong., 2d sess. (1952). See also Richard L. Strout, "Deep Sea Billions for Education," *Christian Science Monitor,* 11 January 1952.

change during which Senators Long and Connally of Texas accused Senator Knowland, among others, of running a roadblock on the tidelands legislation in order to force consideration of the admission of Hawaii and to force reconsideration of the Alaskan admission question.[48] Action on the latter territory had been defeated by a narrow margin a few days before. Finally, Senator Knowland moved that Senate Joint Resolution 20 be tabled.[49] Because of parliamentary confusion, four roll-call votes were necessary before the Senate finally voted to consider Senate Joint Resolution 20.[50] Senator McFarland then asked unanimous consideration to limit debate, a request which got nowhere as each side accused the other of "dragging its feet."[51] After much wrangling, the Arizona Senator agreed that he would not try for such an agreement for at least a day or so.[52]

Debate swirled and eddied in desultory fashion during the next few days. Senator O'Mahoney carried much of the burden to start with, predicting (1) that President Truman would veto any quitclaim,[53] (2) that a quitclaim would never become law, and (3) that a president would never be elected who would sign such a measure.[54] On 7 March the Wyoming solon submitted an amendment he intended to propose which would have renounced any and all federal claims under inland navigable waters and which would have recognized any rights already granted by the states for the construction of docks, piers, jetties, groins, reclaimed land, etc., which jutted into the coastal areas.[55]

On 26 March debate became more heated with charges and countercharges of pressure from oil interests being aired. Significantly, Senator O'Mahoney made public admission of a fact well known to those conversant with the controversy when he stated that there were oil com-

---

[48] 98 *Congressional Record* 1739–41. [49] *Ibid.*, 1747.
[50] *Ibid.*, 1749. [51] *Ibid.*, 1750–52.
[52] *Ibid.*, 1762. [53] *Ibid.*, 1831.
[54] *Ibid.*, 1906. In the latter case, the Senator from Wyoming proved himself a poor prophet.
[55] *Ibid.*, 1986. The amendment was substantially Senate Bill 1540 and is reprinted *ibid.*, 2111. The major difference was that the measure included a specific quitclaim to submerged soils out to the international boundary in the Great Lakes; Senate Bill 1540 did not. Senator Holland, on 11 March, made a telling point in reference to this amendment. He stated as his belief that the amendment constituted a manifestation that the fight was "paying off." For the first time, an inland waters quitclaim measure had included the Great Lakes. Further, Holland contended, the fact that O'Mahoney's amendment recognized rights to structures and reclaimed land in the marginal sea dramatized the fact that the advocates of national control were being forced to recognize that rights in the marginal seas had developed prior to the Supreme Court decisions. *Ibid.*, 2111–13.

panies on both sides of the fight over Senate Joint Resolution 20.[56] Senator Holland on this day sent to the desk his substitute amendment, which was substantially House Bill 4484. The quitclaim under his measure would extend out only to a state's constitutionally defined boundaries, *i.e.*, three leagues in the case of Texas and the west coast of Florida, three miles in the case of a state constitution setting such a boundary, or three miles in a case where a state's constitution set no boundaries in the marginal sea.[57]

Finally, on 27 March, a unanimous-consent agreement was reached for 2 April.[58] Some rather hot words were flung in the course of the day before the agreement was reached. Senator Murray called the quit-claim an "act of usurpation of the people's rights never before experienced in the history of our country."[59] Senator Langer of North Dakota quoted Harold Ickes as characterizing the quitclaim as a "filch" and the "biggest steal in American History—maybe in all history."[60] Senator Blair Moody of Michigan said of quitclaim that here "is a scheme that makes Tea Pot Dome look like a conservation project."[61]

Further discussion took place again on 1 April, but the end had to come. After debate under time limitations on 2 April, the vote was taken on the Hill amendment, which Senator Holland called a "defensive measure growing out of the desperate effort" to prevent quit-claim.[62] Senator Holland moved to lay the Hill amendment on the table, and Senator Hill requested a roll-call vote. The result showed yeas 47, nays 36, with 13 not voting and 6 senators paired.[63] Of the 47 yea votes, 20 were Democrat and 27 were Republican. Of the nay votes, 26 were Democrat and 10 were Republican. Seven Republicans and 6 Democrats did not vote. The result of this vote showed clearly that the quitclaim advocates were in solid control.

The vote was followed by another period of debate, productive only of a firm statement by Senator Holland that his amendment quit-claimed only out to the constitutionally established boundaries of a state or to the three-mile limit if there were no state constitutional provision. The vote on the Holland substitute bill counted yeas 50, nays 34, 12 not voting, and 2 senators paired.[64] On third reading, there was little change in the line-up, even though Senator O'Mahoney made it clear the President would veto the bill.[65] There were yeas 50, nays 35, with

---

[56] *Ibid.*, 2925.
[57] *Ibid.*, 2929. The amendment is reprinted *ibid.*, 2931–32.
[58] *Ibid.*, 3094.   [59] *Ibid.*, 3038.   [60] *Ibid.*, 3053.
[61] *Ibid.*, 3077.   [62] *Ibid.*, 3383.   [63] *Ibid.*, 3391–92.
[64] *Ibid.*, 3413.   [65] *Ibid.*, 3414–15.

11 not voting and 2 senators paired.[66] After much delay, the quitclaim had passed.

The voting line-up on the final tally is interesting. There were an equal number of Democrats and Republicans voting yea. Eleven Republicans and 24 Democrats voted nay. Of the 11 not voting, 8 were Republicans and 3 were Democrats. Of this group, it was announced that Duff, Brewster, Lodge, Dirksen, Smith (N.J.), and Thye would have voted yea had they been present. Butler and Kefauver were paired.

The bill then went over to the House, where the terms of the Holland measure were stricken and House Bill 4484, the original House bill, substituted in its place. In conference committee, agreement was reached, however, that the Senate bill should be the one to be submitted for passage.[67] The House acted and approved the conference version of 15 May 1952 by a roll-call vote of 247 (95 Democrats, 152 Republicans) to 89 (70 Democrats, 18 Republicans, 1 Independent).[68] There was no roll call in the Senate; the measure was passed by a voice vote on 16 May.[69]

Back in April of 1952, I. E. Smoot, postmaster at Salt Lake City, had stated following an interview with the President that Truman was prepared to veto a quitclaim. Five hours after Smoot's announcement, the President categorically denied having made any such statement.[70] On 17 May, however, the President made his stand amply clear in a speech delivered to the national convention banquet of the Americans for Democratic Action. His language was not particularly circumspect as he spoke of the oil lobbies wanting "us to turn that vast treasure over to a handful of states, where the powerful private oil interests hope to exploit it to suit themselves." He spoke of "corruption" and of "robbery in broad daylight—and on a colossal scale." It was his view that he would be protecting "the people's interest" by vetoing the measure.[71] President Truman exercised his power of veto on 29 May, on the grounds that the bill would give a "precious national heritage" to a few fortunate states. He stated that he was willing to compromise on the issue. The compromise to which he referred was the national control bill which would have returned 37.5 per cent of the royalties from the national operations to the littoral states concerned. He invited Congress to pass specific legislation guaranteeing state rights in inland navigable

[66] *Ibid.*, 3416.
[67] See Senator O'Mahoney's explanation of the conference committee's activities. *Ibid.*, 5392.   [68] *Ibid.*, 5338.   [69] *Ibid.*, 5393.
[70] *Florida Times Union*, 15 April 1952. The dispatch was from United Press.
[71] *New York Times*, 18 May 1952.

waters and protecting claims to piers, breakwaters, reclaimed lands, and other structures. He went on record as favoring the "oil for education" measure proposed by Senator Hill. The general tone of the message was unbelievably conciliatory after his stormy speech of a few evenings previous.[72] Needless to say, the advocates of quitclaim were not mollified.

The next few weeks were marked by speculation on whether or not an attempt would be made to override the veto. Advocates of quitclaim were fairly certain of the possibilities in the House of Representatives, but the Senate lines were narrowly drawn. Day after day, the issue was held from coming to a vote. Drew Pearson, in his customary spectacular manner, reported that the oil lobbies were working at fever pitch to get enough Senate votes to override the veto. In his column of 7 June, he reported that the vote was due the following Tuesday and that some senators who had voted against quitclaim were "going to be out of town on business" at the time of the vote.[73]

Tuesday came and went, with no vote. Quitclaim advocates received a jolt on 28 June when Senator Kem, who had not voted on the measure originally, announced that he would vote to sustain the veto. Senator Holland, however, indicated that he had not given up hope. Senator O'Mahoney stated that he was certain there were not enough votes to override and that the measure would not even be called up.[74] The Senator from Wyoming was correct. The quitclaim advocates never mustered the necessary two-thirds majority and therefore never forced the issue. The question of sustaining or overriding the veto did not come to a vote.

The tidelands oil issue was now a red-hot political potato. President Truman had served notice in his speech to the Americans for Democratic Action of the use he intended the Democratic party to make of the issue. He well knew that many of his statements in both speech and

[72] 98 *Congressional Record* 6351–53. Marquis Childs, in his column of 4 June 1952, called the veto message a "potent political document." He predicted the President's veto would be sustained.
[73] He reported Duff, Lodge, Smith (N.J.), and Thye as "doubtful." It has already been shown that these were on record as favoring quitclaim, though they had not voted on 2 April.
[74] *Florida Times Union,* 29 June 1952. Senator Smathers of Florida had predicted on 20 June that the veto would be sustained. In a very neat piece of political strategy, he announced that if a federal control bill were brought out again he would sponsor an amendment to apply the "oil for education" idea to all leases on public lands. Some of the inland senators who had voted for the Hill amendment might well have been placed in extremely embarrassing positions had Smathers' proposal ever gone beyond the discussion stage.

veto message were capable of political use in a campaign year. There was now no doubt that the issue, though a minor one, had excellent political potentialities.

Even during the period of the presidential primaries, attention was paid to the controversy. Senator Richard Russell, running against Estes Kefauver in the Florida popularity contest, announced himself in favor of quitclaim. Senator Russell won, though the tidelands issue was of no great importance in the victory. Senator Kefauver, on the other hand, came out foursquare for the "oil for education" amendment. He announced his support of President Truman's veto. Despite that position, his delegates still scored an overwhelming primary victory in California against a slate of delegates solidly pledged to quitclaim. At this stage in the development of the political picture, at least, it began to look as though the tidelands issue was not one about which the average man was very much excited.

On the other hand, Raymond Moley had predicted as early as January 1952 that. Texas was "debatable territory" and might go Republican because of the decisions in the tidelands and educational segregation cases. Moley calculated that Truman could not carry the state again, nor could Chief Justice Fred Vinson, should he be the nominee of the Democratic party. Moley marked Governor Allan Shivers of Texas as the man to watch, a prediction adequately borne out by the events which transpired at the Democratic National Convention and during the presidential campaign.[75]

The tidelands oil issue was certainly of some importance during the 1952 campaign, if only because the attitudes of the candidates on the the subject reflected somewhat the philosophies of the two men concerned—Dwight D. Eisenhower and Adlai Stevenson. There is no way by which an adequate assessment of the part played by the tidelands issue can be made in terms of the actual shift of votes to the General because of his stand.

The unequivocal position of General Eisenhower favoring quitclaim and the equally categorical stand of Governor Stevenson opposing such a measure had at least a nominal effect in Texas. In that state the weight of the extremely potent political organization of the personable Governor Shivers was thrown solidly behind Eisenhower. It may be recalled that the Texas Governor did not announce his support of the General until after Governor Stevenson had let it be known that he

[75] Column of 3 January 1952. The reader may not agree with Moley's philosophy, but the column of this date is a masterpiece of analysis of the Texas situation.

would continue, if elected President, to follow the position taken by President Truman. To the extent that Governor Stevenson's pronouncement influenced Governor Shivers to cast his lot with Eisenhower, it is possible to say that the tidelands issue played its part. None would deny that the Shivers organization carried the state for the General.

The controversy was of less importance in Louisiana, though the large Republican vote polled there may have resulted, in small part, from the stand taken by General Eisenhower on the question. Again, a Democratic governor supported the Republican candidate. Governor Kennon of Louisiana opposed Stevenson on the tidelands issue. The organization of Governor Kennon, however, did not have nearly so much power as that of Governor Shivers in Texas.

It is the opinion of the writer that the tidelands issue was of little importance in California. At least there is available no evidence to support the view that it ranked significantly in the minds of the voters there.

The two candidates gave adequate attention in their campaigns to the issue of ownership of submerged soils. The public statements made by the two aspirants for the highest office in the land served to highlight as never before the fundamental issues involved in the quarrel over rights to these soils. It would be no exaggeration to say that the American people generally became aware of the issue for the first time in 1952.

In 1939 the issue was first raised as to whether or not quitclaim legislation would be constitutional. At that time, Leslie C. McNemar had contended that a resolution suggested by former Representative Dockweiler, which would have accomplished the same ends as the quitclaim measures proposed in the Seventy-ninth, Eightieth, Eighty-first, and Eighty-second Congresses, was unconstitutional because Congress could not sever from the United States any power granted it by the Constitution.[76] In 1951, as has been seen, Congressman Claude Bakewell advanced the same objection, arguing that Congress was not disposing of property of the United States but rather attempting to dispose of the sovereignty of the national government.[77]

Although most proponents of quitclaim have paid little attention to the argument, the question is worthy of more consideration than has

[76] *Hearings* on S.J. Res. 83 and 92 (1939), 431–32. See p. 152 n. above, where this point was raised.
[77] P. 221.

been accorded it. Quitclaim advocates have assumed that the statement of Justice Black concluding the *California* case[78] is determinative of the matter and an open invitation for Congress to pass regulatory legislation—or quitclaim. Too, in speaking of the nonapplicability of prescription and similar doctrines, Black had stated: "Assuming that Government agents could by conduct, short of a congressional surrender of title or interest, preclude the Government from asserting its legal rights, we cannot say it has done so here."[79] Here again, it would appear, is an intimation that Congress could, if it so willed, quitclaim "property rights" in the offshore lands.

Now if the maritime belt is "territory" of the United States, none can deny that Congress may dispose of it as it wishes. In that regard there was at least one important precedent for the type of action contemplated by House Bill 4484. In 1947 the United States Supreme Court had before it the case of *United States* v. *Wyoming*.[80] The national government had brought an action for an accounting and an injunction against Wyoming and the Ohio Oil Company, holder of an oil lease from the state. The lease had been issued by Wyoming in the belief that the state held title to certain land as a result of a grant at the time of admission on 10 July 1890. The court held, however, that this parcel of land could not have passed to the state until an official survey had been made, an action not taken until 27 July 1916. By proclamation of 5 December 1915, the President had included the land in a petroleum reserve. Hence, the national government held title to the land which the state had thought for fifty-seven years it owned.

In a drive spearheaded by Senator O'Mahoney, Congress "reversed" the decision of the Supreme Court in short order. On 2 July 1948 it passed an act directing the Secretary of the Interior to convey the land in question to the state of Wyoming.[81] Thus, to use the phrase of those opposing the quitclaim of the submerged lands in the marginal sea to the littoral states, the national government "gave away" property of the nation to a single state.

But the land at issue here was plainly "territory" of the United States,

[78] "We cannot and do not assume that Congress, which has constitutional control over Government property, will execute its powers in such way as to bring about injustices. . . ." 332 U.S. 19, 40.

[79] *Ibid.*, 39.

[80] 331 U.S. 440.

[81] 62 U.S. Stat. 1233. For a complete discussion of this case, see *Hearings* on S. 155 *et al.* (1949), 42–55. Pertinent documents in the Wyoming land dispute are reprinted at 44–51. The issue of ownership had arisen about twenty years before and had been in and out of courts and Congress.

held to be so by court decision. In the case of offshore lands, the court steadfastly refused to recognize a proprietary concept in the decrees which followed the submerged lands decisions. One may argue that there were present no questions of title but rather issues of external sovereignty, which Congress may not abdicate. Although this non-territorial concept of the marginal sea may be poor international law, it is at present good municipal law—so long as the court's decisions stand. One may argue further whether or not a decision of the present Congress quitclaiming to the states the area in question may not be revoked by a future Congress. How can the present Congress bind a future Congress in this regard, if the argument just made be sound?

It is the opinion of the writer that a quitclaim measure is constitutional, though not so obviously so as to preclude argument. Proponents of quitclaim should study well the submerged lands decisions, the arguments advanced by Leslie C. McNemar, and the various statements of Congressman Sam Hobbs advancing his nonownership theory, for the writer ventures to predict that any quitclaim legislation will be tested for constitutionality in the courts.[82]

Practically, one may say that future Congresses would not lightly disturb or disestablish rights proclaimed by the present one. Further, many

[82] The writer is not prepared to prophesy how such an action would be brought. The assertion may safely be made that such an action would not be brought by Secretary of the Interior Douglas McKay or Attorney General Herbert Brownell. One possibility might be an action brought by a private person seeking a mineral lease outside the boundary set by a quitclaim, the boundary being in dispute.

On 25 February 1953, Senator Clinton Anderson of New Mexico indicated in testimony before the Senate Interior and Insular Affairs Committee that the action to test constitutionality of quitclaim would be brought by an "interior state." United Press dispatch of that date. Former Senator Burton K. Wheeler argued that the interior states had a "moral and legal right" to protest to the Supreme Court. See comment in *Labor,* 7 March 1953, supporting the stand taken by Anderson and Wheeler.

At the date this work went to press the transcripts of the committee hearings were not available. The writer has no way of judging the efficacy of the arguments presented. He ventures to suggest, however, that there are serious legal impediments to be overcome before an interior state would have standing in court to attack the quitclaim. Is the interest of an interior state in the offshore areas greater than that involved in many federal grant-in-aid programs? See *Massachusetts* v. *Mellon,* 262 U.S. 447 (1923), where a state was held not to have standing to contest the validity of a federal grant-in-aid.

Robert Allen reported in his column of 14 March 1953 that plans were being drawn by Governor Dennis Roberts of Rhode Island, acting in concert with J. Howard McGrath, Philip Perlman, and United States Senator Theodore Green, to have this state take the lead in such an action. See 99 *Congressional Record* 2040–41 (16 March 1953), for correspondence on the subject between Senator Green and Governor Roberts.

laws passed by the national legislature in effect "bind" future sessions of that body, even though not legally. More important, however, the writer takes the view that a quitclaim measure is actually two actions: (1) a declaration that title is "established," and (2) a declaration that the title is then "confirmed" in the states. In line with the numerous decisions previously cited,[83] the first action is a political one and not subject to review by the courts. The second then becomes a disposition of territory which Congress may constitutionally make. Add to this line of reasoning the statements of Justice Black and the argument becomes compelling that Congress may, indeed, constitutionally quitclaim.[84]

[83] See pp. 116–17, 142, and 172–73 above.

[84] Solicitor General Philip Perlman intimated in 1949 that Congress could pass a quitclaim bill, though he would disagree with the policy. *Hearings* on H.R. 5991 and 5992 (1949), 196. Secretary of the Interior Oscar Chapman stated that the right of Congress in this regard was "obvious." *Hearings* on S.J. Res. 195 (1950), 214–15.

But Perlman had become more equivocal two years later. In answer to a question asked by Senator Guy Cordon of Oregon, the Solicitor General stated that it was "very doubtful" that Congress could dispose of the submerged lands. Again, Perlman said: "But my own opinion is there is considerable doubt as to whether the United States, retaining sovereignty over the area, could quitclaim for any consideration the things which come to it by reason of national external sovereignty." *Hearings* on S.J. Res. 20 (1951), 38, 49.

Under severe questioning, Perlman qualified his statements somewhat, removing some of the absolute quality from his position: "But the question as to the exploration of the mineral resources, the question as to the disposition of them, I think it is always open for Congress to determine. And no matter what legislation is passed here on the subject . . . Congress can still legislate with respect to the area." *Ibid.*, 71. Congressman J. M. Combs of Texas then asked Perlman whether Congress could decide that the states involved had a right to take and use and appropriate the oil "by whatever title or law you might see." In answer the Solicitor General said "Yes." *Ibid.*, 73. Following this line of reasoning, Congress may not quitclaim "title," for it has none, but it may dispose of the mineral resources as it sees fit, choosing to allow the states to do so as a matter of policy. It is difficult to see any grounds for unconstitutionality in such an action. The states would merely be administrative agencies effectuating a national policy declared by Congress. The legislative body thus chooses to vest control in the states rather than the Interior Department. Both quitclaim measures passed by Congress contained language to this effect, placed there as a hedge against the possibility of the quitclaim portions being unconstitutional.

Quitclaim legislation offered in 1953 was similarly drawn in very careful fashion to provide for state "administration" should the quitclaim itself be held invalid. See S.J. Res. 13, 83d Cong., 1st sess., introduced by Senator Holland of Florida and thirty-nine other senators. This resolution is reprinted in 99 *Congressional Record* 287–88 (9 January 1953).

The 1950 *Texas* and *Louisiana* cases received extensive coverage from the press. Behind the scenes of Congressional hearings and judicial brilliance, officials of the states concerned gathered quietly with representatives of the national government and worked to bring some sort of temporary order out of chaos. Somehow, even without the guidance of Congressional act, machinery had to be contrived to keep the situation an orderly one. Additionally, in the *California* case, efforts had to be made to delineate, if possible, the inland waters from the marginal-sea areas.

Mention has been made in Chapter 11 of the stipulations which were worked out between the Attorney General of the United States and the the Secretary of the Interior on the one hand and the representatives of California on the other. Damage to equipment, loss from seepage, and the general shortage of petroleum products in an emergency situation demanded that the wells be kept in operation, regardless of the final decision as to which wells were to remain under state control and which under federal. Accordingly, two stipulations were made, one affecting the line of demarcation between inland waters and the open sea and the other dealing with oil and gas operations in the offshore fields. Both stated that nothing contained therein should be "deemed in any way to abridge the power or jurisdiction of the Supreme Court." The stipulations were to run until 30 September 1948.[85] The stipulation dealing with administrative control of offshore operations provided that the state of California should segregate and hold in escrow the royalties collected, reporting the amount quarterly to the Secretary of the Interior. New leases could be negotiated by the state with the approval of the Secretary of the Interior. This stipulation was extended on 28 July 1948[86] and again on 2 August 1949.[87] The agreement was again extended on 21 August 1950, but this time provision was made for the payment to the Treasurer of the United States of the moneys collected from royalties. It was specified that the Treasurer was to hold the royalty payments in a segregated account. Further, because of the costs of administration, the state lands commissioner of California was authorized to spend not in excess of twelve thousand dollars per month from revenues in the fund which had accrued prior to 1 October 1950, to defray expenses. The Secretary of the Interior was authorized to reimburse the Geological Survey and other Interior agencies up to

---

[85] Summarized from a letter from Attorney General Clark to President Truman, 30 October 1947. Reprinted in *Hearings* on S.J. Res. 195 (1951), 239–40. Copies of the two stipulations are found *ibid.*, 21–24.

[86] A copy is found *ibid.*, 24–25.   [87] A copy is found *ibid.*, 25–26.

the amount of fifty thousand dollars for their expenses after 30 September 1950.[88] In effect, the national government was saying, "Let us hold the money awhile."

Under this arrangement, it was stated in 1951, without dissent, that not a single day's oil production had been lost since 23 June 1947 in the California offshore fields.[89] Production from California "state" lands leased for oil production was proceeding at an annual rate of fifteen and one-quarter million barrels in 1951; in 1943 production from state lands had been seven and one-quarter million barrels yearly. Under the stipulations, an average of six new authorizations to drill were being granted each month. On 31 December 1949 there were 407 wells on California leases; on 31 December 1950 there were 483.[90] Not one of these new authorizations was vetoed by the Secretary of the Interior; each met his approval.[91]

These are the stipulations which Ickes attacked so bitterly. In his weekly comments in the *New Republic* he frequently discussed various aspects of the coastal lands problems and on a number of occasions called attention to what he felt was collusion between officials of the state of California and the federal government to circumvent the decision of the Supreme Court. Thus he referred to the "extraordinary and revolutionary" record in the *California* case.[92] Ickes stated in 1951:

I . . . say that the stipulations entered into between those two officers of the Federal Government [the Attorney General and the Secretary of the Interior] and the attorney general of the State of California, constitutes nothing less than a contempt of the Supreme Court of the United States. It conferred or attempted to confer upon the attorney general of California power which, even if these two executive officials of the Federal Government could grant it, he could not legally exercise it. . . .

This whole thing has been as obscure and messed up a public issue as anything with which I have ever had any connection.[93]

[88] A copy of this stipulation is found *ibid.*, 347–49. California impounded twenty-seven million dollars during the period it was charged with holding royalty money in escrow.

[89] Testimony of Everett W. Mattoon, assistant attorney general of California, *Hearings* on S.J. Res. 20 (1951), 120.

[90] Testimony of Rufus W. Putnam, executive officer, California State Lands Commission, *ibid.*, 142.

[91] The statement was made by Mattoon without contradiction by any of the representatives of the national government. *Ibid.*, 121.

[92] *New Republic*, 22 May 1950, p. 15.

[93] *Hearings* on S.J. Res. 20 (1951), 236. Ickes called the Attorney General of the United States and the Secretary of the Interior derelict in their duty for not applying the Mineral Leasing Act of 1920 rather than operating under the stipu-

Ickes attempted to file suggestions with the Supreme Court calling attention to his thoughts on the stipulations; the court denied the motion.[94]

But condemnation or not, the agreement with California continued in force. Administration of the operations in that area was, indeed, conducted in a queer sort of Alice in Wonderland atmosphere where royalties were impounded by first one unit of government and then the other, the two governments working in harmony and yet wondering how long the uneasy truce might last.

As noted in Chapter 12, the pattern of arrangements worked out in California was not continued in the Texas and Louisiana situations. Perhaps the acid comments of Ickes had their effect. Solicitor General Perlman indicated that no such machinery was needed in Texas because the problem of delineating inland waters from open sea was not a difficult one. In the case of Louisiana, he indicated that informal relationships had been established. A line had been established, and the Interior Department advised prospective lessees where the national government had no claim or would make none. Further, Perlman did not want to establish a stipulation pattern with those states anyhow, because of the difficulty experienced with California, not in the administration of the actual leasing and production operations, but in drawing the line of demarcation between inland waters and open sea.[95]

The real problem in California was not the stipulation involving administration; it was the question of demarcating the boundary line between what areas were state and what were national. On 29 January 1948 the Department of Justice asked the Supreme Court to rule spe-

lations. It was his contention that since the Mineral Leasing Act was the only instrument available, the Secretary of the Interior should have made use of it. In his newspaper column of 13 February 1948 he shouted: ". . . what good is a paper title, if government officials occupy their time trying to devise a plan by which they can divest the country of this title, without the people knowing what is happening?" Yet in 1946, Ickes had stated categorically that the Federal Mineral Leasing Act could not be applied to submerged lands. *Hearings* on S.J. Res. 48 and H.J. Res. 225 (1946), 11.

Former Senator Burton Wheeler contended that the stipulations were "not worth the paper they were written on" and "absolutely void." He condemned those whom he called trespassers under leases granted under the stipulations. Wheeler, who represented applicants for leases under the Mineral Leasing Act of 1920, contended that leases should be granted his clients. *Hearings* on S.J. Res. 20 (1951), 272, 274.

[94] 339 U.S. 975 (1950).

[95] *Hearings* on S.J. Res. 20 (1951), 41–42. In the *Hearings* on S.J. Res. 195 (1950), 36 ff., Texas Attorney General Price Daniel argued that the pattern established by the California stipulations should be followed in the enactment of any interim legislation by the Congress.

cifically that the United States controlled three areas, rich in oil, off the California coast. This was the first action to be brought in an effort to delineate the inland waters from the "areas below low-water mark to the three-mile limit in the open sea."

The three areas affected were the Santa Barbara Channel, part of San Pedro Bay, and that part of the coast from San Pedro Bay to Newport Bay, in which were located over three hundred offshore producing wells. In regard to the first area, California contended that because there were islands which were a part of California located off the coast, the waters were inland waters. The national government argued that the area was open sea, coming under the scope of the ruling in *United States* v. *California*. In the case of San Pedro Bay, both parties agreed that it was an inland water area, but the Justice Department asked that the line of demarcation be placed a considerable distance farther east and inland than that line claimed by California. In regard to the third area, the national government noted that the state considered this a part of San Pedro Bay; the national government contended, however, that it was open sea and asked the court so to decide. The claims of the United States included lands adjacent to the important Elwood field north of Santa Barbara, the area encompassing the producing and probably producing field at the city of Long Beach, and the area east to the city of Huntington Beach.

On 21 June 1948 the Supreme Court ordered that a special master be appointed to take evidence on these conflicting claims, a suggestion which had been made by California. The court denied the state's request that the entire boundary be fixed from Mexico to Oregon and ordered the special master to make inquiry and hold hearings, if necessary, to determine what particular portions of the boundary called for "precise determination and adjudication." The special master was authorized to recommend to the court the procedure to be followed in determining "the precise boundary of such segments."[96] On 3 July 1948, D. Lawrence Groner, retired federal judge of considerable reputation and experience in the field of marine and coastal legal procedure, was appointed as special master under the formal order issued by the court on 21 June. The hearings, which Justice Black had stated in the original opinion would probably be necessary, were about to commence.

After nine months, Judge Groner was forced to resign because of ill health, and William H. Davis was appointed as his successor. Judge Davis proceeded with the reference and filed a report on the limited

---

[96] 334 U.S. 855.

scope of the reference on 27 June 1949.[97] California had claimed before the special master that 104 additional areas should be set out for boundary determination, but the report added only four to the three originally requested by the United States. On the same day, the court then ordered the special master to "proceed with all convenient speed" to consider, with respect to the seven areas set out: (1) simplification of issues, (2) statements of the issues, and (3) the nature and forms of evidence proposed to be submitted.[98] This second reference was submitted 4 June 1951.[99]

On 3 December 1951 a third reference was made to Davis.[100] In this reference the Supreme Court for the first time ordered the master to take evidence and submit "recommended answers" to specific questions involving demarcation of the boundary, "with a view toward securing from this Court an order for his further guidance in applying the proper principles of law to the seven coastal segments enumerated in groups I and II of his Masters Report of May 31, 1949." Hearings were held on this third reference and completed in June 1952. Although the master had filed his report with the Supreme Court late in 1952, the court had taken no announced action on it at the time of writing. Action on the third reference would not terminate the litigation, for one side or the other would undoubtedly object to the master's report.

Some indication of the tremendous complexities of the situation are apparent in this brief summary of the operations of the special master. A total of over four years were consumed in disposing of the preliminaries to the real hearing. Add to the seven areas which were slated for eventual decision the many other areas where adjudication would be necessary, and it is little wonder that Judge Manley Hudson commented in 1948 that the Supreme Court "has opened a Pandora's box from which germinating influences may spring to upset acquired titles and established procedures all along our coast."[101]

---

[97] 337 U.S. 952.   [98] *Ibid.*

[99] 341 U.S. 946. An order directing each of the parties to advance $3,134.82 to the special master as their share of expenses and services rendered by him was entered 21 November 1949. 338 U.S. 889. A second order allowing compensation and expenses was entered 26 November 1951. 342 U.S. 884. Justice Douglas dissented for reasons which do not appear.

[100] 342 U.S. 891. Justices Jackson and Clark took no part. Justice Black was of the opinion that the case should be set for argument with a view to narrowing the issues upon which evidence was to be heard.

[101] Joint *Hearings* on S. 1988 (1948), 237.

While the politicians and the lawyers battled out the issue of rights in the maritime belt, many journalists and commentators followed their arguments and antics with interest.

As might be expected, Harold L. Ickes was in the forefront of those writers supporting the federal claims, quick to take umbrage at any suggestion that the federal right be in any way infringed.[102] Marquis Childs opposed the quitclaim and advocated federal control.[103] Senator O'Mahoney turned journalist and distributed a column through the North American Newspaper Alliance in which he attempted to reassure the inland states that the national government had no designs on inland waters.[104] Drew Pearson castigated the "oil lobbyists" seeking to "win the wealthy submerged oil lands" off the shores of Texas, Louisiana, and California.[105] He accused the oil lobby of trying to prove that it didn't exist,[106] and was forced to retract statements made respecting the giving of committee proxies by members of the Interior and Insular Affairs Committee in order to "get votes for the oil companies."[107] Robert S. Allen condemned the "interests trying to wrest control of the great Texas tideland oil resources from the federal government."[108]

Only a few newspapers entered the fray on the side of Ickes, Childs, Pearson, and Allen. In the Midwest, the *St. Louis Post-Dispatch* was active in its opposition to quitclaim; Senator Donnell drew much of his ammunition for cross-examination of quitclaim advocates in the 1948 hearings from editorials and articles appearing in that journal.[109] In the

[102] Citations have already been given to some of his *New Republic* articles and newspaper columns. See his article, "Save the Tidelands," in *Frontier,* September 1951. Ickes was bitterly attacked. See, e.g., speech by former Congressman John S. Gibson, reprinted in 97 *Congressional Record* 11924–25. The speech was originally delivered 5 March 1946.

[103] Though opposing quitclaim, Childs confidently predicted in his column of 25 February 1948 that such action would occur.

[104] Published 16 September 1951.

[105] Col. of 26 July 1951.

[106] Col. of 30 September 1951.

[107] The charge was made in his column of 24 May 1951. Senator Long took time on the Senate floor to set the record straight. 97 *Congressional Record* 5884. Pearson retracted his statement in part in his column of 2 June 1951.

[108] Allen used a letter written by Congressman W. R. Poage of Texas to the writer as a basis for attack on the Texas representative, intimating that the lawmaker was a tool of those interests. The column appeared 4 December 1950. Allen used language which made it appear that the writer had given him the letter. Actually, Congressman Poage had had the letter mimeographed and had given it to the press following his return from a trip to Europe.

[109] See, e.g., his cross-examination of Robert Kenny, former attorney general of California, *Hearings* on S. 1988 (1948), 294 ff.

East, the *Washington Post* was most active in fighting for national control and administration of the offshore areas. The writer would rate it as probably the most energetic paper in the nation among those standing in opposition to quitclaim. Numerous articles and editorials on the subject appeared in its columns. The *Christian Science Monitor* called the decision of the Supreme Court in the *Texas* and *Louisiana* cases the "better answer." It alleged editorially: "Signs have abounded from the beginning that the states abutting these submarine bonanzas are under too much pressure from the oil producers and from the stake their own hard-pressed budgets have in oil royalties to be counted on to protect the stake the other 45 states have in the sinews of national defense."[110] The *New York Times* contended editorially that the national interest should prevail over the financial interests of a few states, and has advocated federal control as more effective than state control.[111]

Of the columnists favoring quitclaim, Raymond Moley was perhaps the most noted. Upon the filing of the complaints against Texas and Louisiana, he said that the "integrity of millions of private transactions is imperiled by governmental dishonesty," and stated that it was to be hoped that Congress might "move to stop this dubious seizure."[112] He spoke of the submerged lands decisions as "opening property to seizure," and twice used his nationally distributed column to point out the imperative necessity of quitclaim action by Congress.[113] Allen Duckworth of the *Dallas Morning News* wrote what was probably the most controversial series of articles. Published under the general title of "The Big Grab," these articles traced the submerged lands controversy from its inception and charged Ickes with the responsibility of initiating the affair. The articles were rabidly pro-Texas, espousing the state point of view on ownership of the offshore areas.[114]

[110] 10 June 1950.

[111] 23 April 1950, 7 June 1950, 27 October 1950, 8 April 1951. Editorial comment favoring federal control has ranged from the highly respected *New York Times, Christian Science Monitor, Washington Post,* and *St. Louis Post-Dispatch* to the less respected George Seldes with his *In Fact.* In the 24 May 1948 issue, Seldes called the quitclaim measure a "piece of public plunder" and stated that in its treatment of the tidelands issue the press had "ignored one of the most fantastic pieces of greed and corruption on record."

[112] Column of 16 December 1949.

[113] Columns of 2 July 1950, 18 August 1950, and 25 March 1951. The decisions of the court in the *Texas* and *Louisiana* cases are criticized in his column of 16 June 1950.

[114] *Dallas Morning News,* 4–12 March 1951. On 29 March 1951, the *News* reprinted a column by Ickes attacking Duckworth's articles as "shameless lies" and Duckworth himself as a "man who has no regard for journalistic ethics." The *Dallas Morning News* he labeled as the "daily prevaricator." The Duck-

Arthur Krock, of "exclusive presidential interview" fame, can hardly be classified definitely as belonging to one camp or the other. The noted *New York Times* columnist wrote a number of articles dealing with the *Texas* and *Louisiana* cases.[115] They were straightforward, factual, and educational. So far as the writer has been able to determine, no other columnist attempted to do what Krock did—present the facts to the public in simple, understandable fashion without the customary propaganda trappings. While some other columnists were screaming invective, he was presenting basic material. It would be difficult to read into his columns a belief in either point of view.

The number of newspapers favoring quitclaim was far greater than the number in the group opposing such a measure. The *Dallas Morning News,* the *Austin American,* and the *Fort Worth Star-Telegram* were especially active in Texas; needless to say, the newspapers of that state lined up almost unanimously for state control of offshore areas. In Louisiana, the New Orleans *Times-Picayune* and the *New Orleans States* took the lead. In California, the *Oakland Tribune* was most active, with the *Los Angeles Times* and the *San Francisco Chronicle* also lending their support. There were other papers, though not nearly so active, in practically every state of the Union that expressed their belief that title to the coastal lands should be confirmed in the states.[116] Periodicals, such as the *Saturday Evening Post,* announced in favor of the states' position. There can be no argument that the states' position had the best of it in terms of newspaper and periodical support.

It is not the job of the writer in a work of this type to assess the relative worth of newspaper and columnist comment. The controversy over the submerged lands resulted in the dissemination of a good deal of vitriolic comment by persons representing both positions. Both sides indulged in the spreading of half-truths and the use of propaganda devices calculated to sway the public mind. One group has called for the nation to rise against the "power-mad bureaucrats" while the other has inveighed against the "plutocratic oil lobbyists seeking to plunder the national domain." It has been, the writer contends, for the most part a case of the pot calling the kettle black. That the writer happens

worth columns were reprinted in many of the leading newspapers of the country, among them the *Los Angeles Times,* the *Kansas City Star,* the *Miami Herald,* the *Minneapolis Star and Tribune,* the *San Francisco Chronicle,* the *St. Louis Globe Democrat,* the *Atlanta Journal,* the *Baltimore Sun,* the *Nashville Banner,* the New Orleans *Times-Picayune,* and the *Galveston News.*

[115] *New York Times,* 30 May; 4, 8, and 13 June; 13 July 1950.

[116] See, e.g., editorials of the *Florida Times Union,* 31 May, 15 October, and 12 November 1952.

to believe the decisions in the submerged lands cases were incorrect as a matter of law does not prevent him from recognizing that there have been phases of the activities of zealots for the state point of view which have led to journalistic excesses. A similar statement can be made with assurance in the case of those individuals who have attempted to convey the opposite point of view.

Reference to any of the numerous hearings which have been held by Congressional committees or to the numerous publications, articles, or speeches of those who favor quitclaim inevitably turns up a large number of allusions to the part played by so-called "speculators" or "promoters." The series of articles by Allen Duckworth in the *Dallas Morning News* was given over in considerable part to the charge that the entire controversy over rights to oil in the submerged lands arose as a result of the agitation of this group.

Harold L. Ickes did not make any secret of the fact that his change in attitude toward ownership of the submerged soils in the marginal sea came about after talks with applicants for leases under the Mineral Leasing Act of 1920. He so expressed himself in a letter to the writer,[117] and he was equally frank in his statements before the committees of Congress.[118] After having talked to a number of these lease applicants, he finally concluded

. . . that while I would not presume to pass on the law to determine whether or not the Federal Government had title, or the State Governments, there was enough doubt so that the courts, which after all are our tribunals to decide what the law is, should have a chance to pass upon the question.

It was on that basis, and on that basis alone, that I thought that the whole subject matter should go to the Federal courts for decision. I had no predilection one way or the other; I was not for any claimant nor was I against any claimant. I wanted the law determined and then I would be able to follow the law.[119]

To this extent, the charge is correct that persons seeking to acquire leases under the Federal Mineral Leasing Act of 1920 were responsible for stirring up the entire issue in the first place.

[117] Dated 29 November 1947.
[118] Joint *Hearings* on S. 1988 (1948), 1118–24, 1128, 1132–34; *Hearings* on S.J. Res. 20 (1951), 235, 244.
[119] *Hearings* on S.J. Res. 20 (1951), 235.

Names of some of the persons seeking these leases are found over and over again in the hearings: Robert E. Lee Jordan, Deryl Mayhew, Uel T. McMurry, I. E. Smoot, Joseph Cunningham, and a number of others. Many are properly classified as legitimate businessmen. There are others, however, who did not file their lease applications until after oil had been discovered. With the filing of the lease, some of these persons then sold shares of stock in their companies, on the strength of a remote possibility that their claims might some day be vindicated. One operator spoke in a promotion letter of the possibility of getting a federal lease as being

. . . a most magnificent gamble in that all existing law is on our side and the high stakes involved are all out of proportion to the risk of losing. Even a compromise with respect to back royalties will result in tremendous sums becoming available to the Shore-Line stockholders from the prolific production of oil from the Huntington Beach field alone, not to mention the potential value of other acreage under application and assignment.

A rare speculative opportunity, contingent solely upon a legal question, would perhaps most accurately describe this matter. If the permits are granted, oil companies will offer fabulous sums either for the stock or for operating agreements or leases bearing handsome royalties; if they are not granted, the stock will not be worth a dime. There you have it in a nutshell. Nobody should invest in an issue of this character unless they can afford to lose what they invest. . . . Cash requirements . . . make it necessary to dispose of a few hundred shares at this time.[120]

This was Robert F. Purvis, a stockholder of the Shore-Line Oil Company, writing. The Shore-Line Oil Company's total assets consisted of lease applications filed under the Mineral Leasing Act of 1920; the company had never put down a single well anywhere.[121]

In 1934, Joseph Cunningham, "good friend" of Robert F. Purvis, and others had filed on ten thousand acres of submerged lands.[122] The writer has discussed in Chapter 8 the attitude of the Department of the Interior at that time. The applications were first turned down but were

[120] The letter was written 10 February 1950. It was reprinted in 97 *Congressional Record* 9180.

[121] Statement of Congressman Carl Hinshaw of California, 97 *Congressional Record* 9179. So far as can be discovered, Representative Hinshaw's statement that Shore-Line had not sunk wells was not disputed. Congressman Hinshaw has been particularly active in carrying on the legislative battle to secure quitclaim of submerged offshore soils to the littoral states.

[122] The words are those of Purvis in his letter reprinted in 97 *Congressional Record* 9179, 9180.

later held in abeyance by the then Secretary of the Interior Harold
Ickes. By the late 1940's, former Senator Burton Wheeler came into the
picture as counsel for some of these lease applicants. He appeared in
1951 to attempt to get a clause, which would protect the interests of
his clients, inserted in a bill providing for interim operations in the
offshore fields.[123] At that time he castigated the oil lobbies and painted
his clients as "little prospectors" relying upon the good faith of the
federal government to protect the "rights" they had acquired by filing
applications on these lands. Yet it is no problem to show that some of
the lease applications were filed on lands where there was already oil
production or a good chance of production.

As counsel for Deryl Mayhew, Wheeler also filed a test case, a suit
in the nature of a mandamus and for a declaratory judgment, in January 1948. Judge Charles F. McLaughlin of the United States District
Court for the District of Columbia held on 16 March 1951 that the
time was not ripe for judicial action because the Supreme Court,
through its special master, still retained jurisdiction over the disputed
area in question. The suit instituted by Mayhew was therefore held in
abeyance.[124] A number of similar suits were also held in abeyance.

One such action, however, was allowed to go to trial because a few
of the parcels of land involved were admittedly in the marginal sea
and not in inland waters.[125] There was therefore no reason to hold the
case in abeyance pending a final disposition of any future master's report. Some action in the case had been contemplated by the end of
1952, but at the time of writing no decision had been handed down.

One of the strangest attempts to "muscle in" on oil-productive areas
in the offshore fields involved the manipulation of land scrip, scrip
issued for the most part to soldiers in lieu of a cash bonus.[126] Since most

---

[123] Testimony, *Hearings* on S.J. Res. 20 (1951), 248–98.

[124] *Mayhew* v. *Krug,* Civil Action 411–48, U.S. District Court for the District
of Columbia. The memorandum of Judge McLaughlin is reprinted in *Hearings*
on S.J. Res. 20 (1951), 501–503.

It should be noted that Wheeler represented only a few of the total number of
persons who have filed for such leases. His clients were "early filers." It was
argued that they were protected under technical amendments later added to the
Mineral Leasing Act of 1920. In the absolutely correct sense of the word, they
were seeking prospecting permits rather than leases. See Wheeler's testimony,
Hearings on S.J. Res. 20 (1951), 285.

[125] *Justheim* v. *Chapman,* Civil Action 4172–49, U.S. District Court for the
District of Columbia. Signal Oil and Gas Company and the Southwest Exploration Company intervened as defendants in this suit.

[126] See pp. 50–51 above, where the case of *Mann* v. *Tacoma Land Co.,*
involving Valentine scrip, was discussed.

of these issues of scrip took place in the middle nineteenth century, it would be presumed that the scrip had long since been redeemed for public land of the United States, the purpose for which it was issued. E. L. Cord, onetime manufacturer of the fabulous front-wheel drive Cord automobile, and ten associates managed to find and buy a goodly amount of scrip, reportedly expending one million dollars in the process. They then proceeded to file applications on Gulf of Mexico and California offshore lands to the extent of 4,138 acres. Cord very shrewdly spotted his share of the scrip, which totaled 1,932 acres, around in the Gulf of Mexico. He bunched some of his scrip in one-acre parcels around 34 producing wells with a production, in February 1951, of approximately eleven thousand barrels per day.[127] Secretary of the Interior Chapman refused on 21 November 1951 to exchange the lands requested for the scrip on the grounds that the tracts which were sought were not "public lands." The scrip was redeemable only for "public lands available for settlement."[128] Cord indicated that he and his associates would go to court over the issue, though the writer has not been able to discover whether such an action ever occurred.

The applicants for federal leases represent a fringe group in the controversy.[129] Generally favorable to federal control, they naturally have fought interim legislation guaranteeing the leases issued by state authority. They have bitterly opposed quitclaim measures. They have sought the right to take over rich productive areas, frequently on the strength of claims filed after an area was a producing one. For the most part, their arguments have not been taken seriously; until former Sen-

[127] *New York Times,* 22 November 1951.

[128] Secretary Chapman based his action on an opinion by Mastin G. White, solicitor of the Department of the Interior. The opinion is No. M–36084, dated 25 June 1951. The opinion ruled that the lands sought were not in the category of "public lands" to which scrip could be applied, that the scrip could not be applied against mineral lands, and that the lands applied for had not been surveyed and were not capable of being surveyed. Lands bought with the scrip could be only "surveyed lands or lands subject to survey."

[129] One of the queerest incidents of the entire controversy was the filing in the Supreme Court on 16 April 1951 of a suit on behalf of twenty-one bands of California Mission Indians. The petition to intervene in *United States* v. *California* on their behalf was filed by Norman M. Littell, who contended that for over five hundred years much of the area of the maritime belt had been rightfully owned by these Indians. His brief has historical worth. The argument was most ingenious. He outlined an interesting story, tracing title back to pre-Spanish occupation days. His petition was not allowed. 334 U.S. 825 (1948). Littell, whose name appears occasionally in the controversy, thus introduced another factor.

ator Wheeler entered the picture, one could say their point of view was well-nigh ignored. They remain today a sort of ubiquitous group, always around and ever hopeful that somehow their claims will receive credence.

14 ·

The New Doctrine of Paramount Powers

More than seven thousand pages of testimony has been taken to date in upwards of a dozen Congressional committee hearings which have been held on the submerged lands issue. Extensive hearings were completed during the first session of the Eighty-third Congress. Hundreds of pages of the *Congressional Record* have been devoted to the arguments of the parties on the question. The Supreme Court is, at the date of this writing, in the throes of trying to discover a satisfactory formula for delimiting the inland waters from the marginal-sea areas off the coast of California.

Journalists have been grinding out extensive material pro and con on the dispute. Coverage of the issue was extensive in the 1952 presidential campaign. The question of tidelands policy became one which was argued by the ordinary citizen. The controversy has excited the attention of legal scholars, and numerous articles have been written on the myriad phases of the controversy.[1] While Congress and many

[1] Typical of such articles or comments are the following: John J. Wiecks, "Submerged Coastal Lands—Who Has Title?" 3 *Intramural Law Review* (1947), 44–52; Max Weingarten, "Submerged Lands: Conflicting Claims of the Federal Government and States to Title in the Bed of the Ocean," 35 *California Law Review* (1947), 605–608; "The Tidelands Case, United States v. State of Texas," 12 *Texas Bar Journal* (1949), 113–14, 137–40; "American Bar Association Urges S. 1988 for State Titles to Tidelands," 34 *American Bar Association Journal* (1948), 279–80; "The Approaching Federal Threat to Massachusetts Land Titles," 34 *Massachusetts Law Quarterly* (1949), 33–44; "Conflicting State and Federal Claims of Title in Submerged Lands of the Continental Shelf," 56 *Yale Law Journal* (1947), 356–70; John P. Woodley, "Federal Rights to Tidelands," 8 *Louisiana Law Review* (1948), 578–88; W. P. Keeton, "Federal and State Claims to Submerged Soils under Coastal Waters," 25 *Texas Law Review* (1947), 262–74; "The Federal Threat to Massachusetts Land Titles," 33 *Massachusetts Law Quarterly* (1948), 47–65; Tom C. Clark, "National Sovereignty

journalists have focused attention on the immediate problems involved in the control of oil production and title in the submerged soils, other persons, particularly those in the legal profession, have been looking further ahead in terms of the possible future applications of the doctrines which the Supreme Court expounded in the submerged lands cases.

Regardless of quitclaim, the doctrine of "paramount powers" and the use to which Justices Black and Douglas put it will have far-reaching effects, for its application cannot be limited to the mere question

---

and Dominion over Lands Underlying the Ocean," 27 *Texas Law Review* (1948), 140–57; John E. Thomason, "United States v. California: Paramount Rights of the Federal Government in Submerged Coastal Lands," 26 *Texas Law Review* (1948), 304–12; "The Muniments of Title of Massachusetts to Her Submerged Lands," 35 *Massachusetts Law Quarterly* (1950), 1–62; Price Daniel, "Texas' Title to Submerged Lands," 1 *Baylor Law Review* (1949), 237–47; M. J. Richard, "Tidelands and Riparian Rights in Florida," 3 *Miami Law Quarterly* (1949), 339–64; Julius F. Parker, "Problems in Florida and Other Coastal States Caused by the California Tidelands Decision," 1 *Florida Law Review* (1948), 44–60; Elton M. Hyder, Jr., "United States v. California," 19 *Mississippi Law Journal* (1948), 265–90; H. W. Briggs, "Jurisdiction over the Sea Bed and Subsoil beyond Territorial Waters," 45 *American Journal of International Law* (1951), 338–42; R. S. Trigg, "National Sovereignty over Maritime Resources," 99 *University of Pennsylvania Law Review* (1950), 82–97; John Hanna, "Submerged Lands Cases," 3 *Stanford Law Review* (1951), 193–219; Richard Wait, "Supplementary History of Title of Massachusetts to Submerged Sea Lands," 36 *Massachusetts Law Quarterly* (1951), 17–26; James Munro, "The Supreme Court and the Marginal Sea," 4 *Wyoming Law Journal* (1950), 181–91; "Equal Footing and the Marginal Sea," 19 *University of Kansas City Law Review* (1950), 66–71; and E. J. Sullivan, "The Tidelands Question," 3 *Wyoming Law Journal* (1948), 10–20. This list is not a complete one but is meant to be representative.

Of forty-three articles in legal journals which the writer covered, forty are critical of the court's decisions. In the above list, the article by Justice Tom C. Clark and the article by James Munro support the position of the court.

For two pertinent articles written from the standpoint of the geographer, see S. Whittemore Boggs, "Delimitation of the Territorial Sea," 24 *American Journal of International Law* (1930), 541–55; "Delimitation of Seaward Areas under National Jurisdiction," 45 *American Journal of International Law* (1951), 240–66.

For specific law review comment on the *Texas* and *Louisiana* cases, see 15 *Albany Law Review* (1951), 85–97; 13 *Georgia Bar Journal* (1950), 103–104; 99 *University of Pennsylvania Law Review* (1950), 259–60; 24 *Temple Law Quarterly* (1951), 377–80; 21 *Tennessee Law Review* (1951) 676–78; and 36 *Virginia Law Review* (1950), 806–10.

For particularly extensive coverage, the writer would recommend two items: Robert E. Hardwicke, Carl Illig, and C. Perry Patterson, "The Constitution and the Continental Shelf," 26 *Texas Law Review* (1948), 398–439, and "The Texas Tidelands Case: A Symposium," 3 *Baylor Law Review* (1951), 115–266. Among participants in the latter effort were Dean Roscoe Pound and Charles Cheney Hyde.

of oil in the marginal sea. Numerous additional problems will be, and some have already been, raised; the decisions have set off a chain reaction. It is the purpose here to examine in greater detail the doctrine of paramount rights as expounded by Justices Black and Douglas and to see its applicability in other problem areas.

It will be remembered that Justice Black very carefully refrained from any declaration that the United States held *title* in the maritime belt, and it has been demonstrated that that view was reaffirmed in the decrees which the Supreme Court issued following the decisions in the cases. Although Justice Black, in his rather jumbled opinion, did not explain the matter, there may be good reason why he refrained from such a statement. The general rule in American constitutional law is that grants of power to the national government do not confer thereby any territory. The applicable rule was stated by Chief Justice Marshall in *United States* v. *Bevans*:

> Can the cession of all cases of admiralty and maritime jurisdiction be construed into a cession of the waters on which those cases may arise?
> This is a question on which the Court is incapable of feeling a doubt. The article which describes the judicial power of the United States is not intended for the cession of territory, or of general jurisdiction. It is obviously designed for other purposes. It is in the 8th section of the 2nd article,[2] we are to look for cessions of territory and of exclusive jurisdiction. . . . It is observable that the power of exclusive legislation (which is jurisdiction) is united with the cession of territory, which is to be the free act of the states.[3]

Although this particular case related to admiralty and maritime jurisdiction, the rule is equally applicable to all powers exercised by the national government. The control over external sovereignty held by the national government was the basis for Justice Black's paramount-powers pronouncement. Under the paramount-powers doctrine, however, no territorial acquisition could be made by the national government unless and until Congress acted to annex. It would seem that Justice Black, had he cared to do so, could have cleared up much of the apprehension which the opinion has caused. There is no title to lands in the maritime belt because the Congress has never annexed the

---

[2] The typographical error occurs in the report. What is obviously meant is the eighth section of the first article.

[3] 3 Wheat. 336, 388 (1818). See also *Corfield* v. *Coryell,* 6 Fed. Cases No. 3230, pp. 546, 551 (1823): "But this grant [to regulate commerce] contains no cession, either express or implied, of territory, or of public or private property."

zone. Justice Black thus followed the line of reasoning of Congress-man Hobbs' "nonownership" theory.

Justice Black did not base his opinion primarily upon a distinction between inland and ocean waters, but rather on a differentiation be-tween internal and external sovereignty. The delegated powers of the national government relate to internal power and authority; they are correspondingly subject to the limitations of just compensation in their exercise. The doctrine of paramount rights, it has been previously shown, relates to external power and authority and cannot, therefore, be placed in the same category as the delegated powers.

Here is the really significant aspect of the opinion. This is the con-tribution Justice Black has made to American constitutional law, a contribution fully as important and possibly more far-reaching in its effects than Justice Sutherland's famed inherent-powers doctrine, to which the paramount-powers principle bears more than a superficial relationship. Justice Black nowhere made direct reference to Justice Sutherland's "inherent powers"; but it is obvious that the two ideas are cut from the same cloth, though one may argue whether Sutherland's idea applies in the marginal belt if the belt is *property*.

Mr. Justice Sutherland had argued in 1936 in *United States* v. *Cur-tiss-Wright Export Corp.*[4] that there was a fundamental distinction between the powers exercised by the national government over domestic as contrasted with foreign affairs. "The two classes of powers are differ-ent," he declared, "both in respect of their origin and their nature. The broad statement that the federal government can exercise no powers except those specifically enumerated in the Constitution, and such im-plied powers as are necessary to carry into effect the enumerated powers, is categorically true only in respect of our internal affairs."[5] This fol-lowed, according to Sutherland's line of reasoning, because the states had never possessed powers in international affairs; therefore the enumerated powers could relate only to the conduct of internal affairs. Powers of external sovereignty passed directly from Great Britain to the states in a collective, not an individual, capacity.

It results that the investment of the federal government with the powers of external sovereignty did not depend upon the affirmative grants of the Constitution. The powers to declare and wage war, to conclude peace, to make treaties, to maintain diplomatic relations with other sovereignties, if they had never been mentioned in the Constitution, would have vested in the federal government as necessary concomitants of nationality. . . .

4 299 U.S. 304.   5 *Ibid.*, 315–16.

As a member of the family of nations the right and power of the United States in that field are equal to the right and power of the other members of the international family. Otherwise the United States is not completely sovereign.[6]

Basically, then, Sutherland's contribution is to the effect that the national government has, in the general field of international affairs, powers simply because it is a government, an entity admittedly a member of the family of nations. These powers accrue to it solely in that capacity and are not subject to any concept of federalism with its historic differentiation between delegated and reserved powers. The powers of the United States in international affairs are not subject to the limitations present when the Congress exercises an enumerated power.

Justice Black, in postulating his paramount-rights doctrine, spoke of the protection of the three-mile belt as a "function of national *external* sovereignty."[7] When the national government assumed control over foreign relations, it thereby assumed responsibility for the protection and maintenance of the integrity of the states as against possible foreign aggression. The states, with the adoption of the Constitution, were no longer in a position, if they ever had been, to protect themselves from encroachment. In order to discharge this function adequately, according to Mr. Justice Black, it is necessary that the national government, as a function of external sovereignty, be able to exercise paramount control, without limitation, when and where necessary in the maritime belt. Indeed, if one considers Justice Black's great emphasis on the fact that the maritime belt is ownerless, only the Congress could annex it. Since the Supreme Court does not have the power to annex the area, the advocacy of the paramount-rights doctrine appears to be the only method whereby the court could declare national rights.

In *United States* v. *California,* Justice Black was blazing a new judicial trail which his brother Douglas could follow in the *Texas* and *Louisiana* decisions. It is axiomatic for Justice Black that, as "a nation with all the attributes of sovereignty, the United States is vested with

---

[6] *Ibid.,* 318. See pp. 29–31 above, where Justice Sutherland's historical analysis in the *Curtiss-Wright* case is criticized. Justice Sutherland took the same point of view in *United States* v. *Belmont et al.,* 301 U.S. 324, 331 (1937): "Plainly, the external powers of the United States are to be exercised without regard to state laws or policies; . . . complete power over international affairs is in the national government." See also the opinion of Justice Douglas to the same effect in *United States* v. *Pink,* 315 U.S. 203, 229, 233–34 (1942).

[7] 332 U.S. 19, 34. Italics added.

all the powers of government necessary to maintain an effective control of international relations."[8] He would agree that the "sovereign power of a nation in its foreign intercourse is subject to no constitutional restraint."[9]

The paramount-rights doctrine has been used in the submerged lands cases to obtain for the United States what amounts to all the aspects of ownership of an area, without the necessity for any formal Congressional declaration of annexation.[10] What further applications of the doctrine are possible? What are its limitations?

There have been numerous contentions advanced that the rulings in the submerged lands cases have destroyed, through the application of the doctrine of paramount powers, something that was basic in the American federal system. In its request for a rehearing, California contended that "if the need of the National Government for oil in order to perform its constitutional powers is to determine the question of ownership or the right to 'appropriate' such oil for its own use, then a similar need for coal, iron, uranium, food or any other commodity will *ipso facto* vest in the Federal Government the right to take such property without payment of just compensation."[11] It is to be recalled that Mr. Justice Reed took much this same point of view in dissenting in *United States* v. *Texas.*[12]

The argument was thus advanced that under the paramount-rights doctrine the United States might take for its use, without compensation, any commodity. The national government would need only to show that the commodity and its use would bear some relationship to one of the delegated powers: national defense, commerce, or admiralty and maritime jurisdiction, for example. The paramount-rights doctrine would thus be "extended" inland, allowing the national government

[8] *Burnet* v. *Brooks,* 288 U.S. 378, 396 (1933).
[9] Argument of Coxe for plaintiff in error, *Pollard* v. *Hagan,* 3 How. 212, 217 (1845).
[10] If one combines a Presidential proclamation, such as the one made by President Truman in 1945 covering the continental shelf, with the doctrine of paramount rights, it would appear that the President now has an additional tool in the field of international relations. Without the necessity of waiting for a dissident, recalcitrant, or quiescent Congress, the President may extend the authority of the United States. Such an extension might bear a direct relationship to the safety of the nation—or it might be a tool in aid of the destruction of the fundamental principles upon which the nation has been built.
[11] California petition for rehearing, 11.
[12] 339 U.S. 707, 723.

to exercise an authority which would be utterly alien to the whole American conception of government.

While there is some ground for the type of apprehension expressed by California, Justice Reed, and the legal profession generally, it would appear that such a construction of the submerged lands opinions ignores to some extent the basic rationale of the doctrine of paramount rights. The distinction is one between internal and external sovereignty; and paramount rights, as used by Justice Black, depend upon external sovereignty. How then is it possible, even within the framework of Black's imprecise opinion, to hold that the doctrine of paramount rights may be extended inland to deprive persons of property without compensation? Especially as applied, let us say, to iron ore in the Mesabi Range in Minnesota, the argument of California lacks complete validity.

But what of the possible application of the new doctrine of paramount powers to lands under inland waters? Particular, and to some extent justifiable, concern has been exhibited by the states over the possibility that the submerged lands decisions might serve as a lever for the eventual reversal of the line of cases which currently are authority for the titles which the states hold to the soils of inland navigable waters. The states argued that the older decisions were predicated, not upon the fact that the waters concerned were "inland," but rather that such waters were "navigable." The fact that the Court refused to accept that criterion and distinguished these earlier cases, particularly *Pollard v. Hagan,* on the ground that there was a difference between "inland" waters and waters covered by the complaint of the United States might mean that a future application of the paramount-powers doctrine could be made to destroy state title under inland, but navigable, waters.

The bald fact of the matter is that the fears of the states stemmed not so much from the words of the court in the *California, Texas,* and *Louisiana* cases as they did from the disquieting actions of executive officials of the national government and of the Supreme Court itself. The controversy was initiated by Secretary of the Interior Harold L. Ickes, who reversed a previous long-standing rule to which he himself had adhered in order to bring the issue out into the open.[13] To that time, there is no proof that any officer of the national government had attempted to assert proprietary authority over the coastal lands.

The states had always been aware that the title which they held, and which they had granted or leased to individuals in the soils of navigable waters, was qualified by the undoubted rights which the United States

[13] See pp. 128–35 above.

held over navigation, interstate commerce, and defense. Yet to 1947 no question of title involving soils under navigable waters had been raised that had not been settled by the courts in favor of the states. With the spectacle of Ickes' reversal of policy squarely before them, could the states be blamed for not accepting wholeheartedly the assurances of national representatives given in 1951 and 1952 that no future attempt would be made to declare paramount authority over inland waters?

The Department of Justice had contributed to the feeling of unrest. In the United States brief in the *California* case the national government called the rule of *Pollard* v. *Hagan* and similar cases "unsound."[14] While the United States did not ask that these cases be overruled (it suggested that the cases be reaffirmed and "clarified"), the Department of Justice did ask that the "unsound rule" of those cases not be extended to the marginal sea. Was the adjective "unsound" a harbinger of some future attempt to upset the title of the states to inland waters?

The Supreme Court itself must assume a share of responsibility for the feeling of the states. The fact that the court chose to state, in its final order and decree in the *California* case, that the representatives of the United States "purported" to bind the United States to the stipulations made between the United States and California[15] caused concern. After all, one stipulation exempted the Bays of San Francisco, San Diego, and San Pedro, declaring them inland waters. The stipulation was a mere statement of existing fact; and though the exact extent of the waters in question might be disputed, there could be absolutely no doubt that a portion or all of these bays were properly classified as "inland." When the court, therefore, seemingly voiced disapproval of the stipulations, the states, justifiably or not, worried lest the court have in the back of its collective mind a possible reversal of the inland waters cases.

Additionally, the Supreme Court did not, in acting in any of the three cases or on the petitions for rehearing, distinguish or mention the apparent contradiction of the coastal lands decisions to *United States* v. *Chandler-Dunbar Water Co.*[16] and similar decisions where the waters in question constituted an international boundary. Where is the distinction between a river which is an international boundary and the marginal-sea zone? The state, under the submerged lands decisions, held title to the bed of the former but not the latter. Was the *Chandler-*

---

[14] P. 11.
[15] 332 U.S. 804 (1947). The stipulations were discussed by the writer briefly in Chapter 11 and in greater detail in Chapter 13.
[16] 209 U.S. 447 (1908).

Dunbar decision overruled by implication? Perhaps the paramount-powers doctrine could be extended to cover first the bed of a river which is an international boundary, and later the beds of inland lakes and rivers which are not international boundaries. The fears of the states might be groundless so far as many of the arguments advanced by them were concerned; the writer will submit that so long as the status of the *Chandler-Dunbar* case and cases involving the Great Lakes remain unclarified, there is a genuine cause to wonder if, indeed, there is not a remote possibility of turning the paramount-powers doctrine to the task of overturning titles to inland waters.

Some credence is lent to the fears of the states in this regard by virtue of recent action in what is known as the *Santa Margarita River Case*. The United States purchased the Rancho Santa Margarita some ten years ago, and established a Marine Corps training base, Camp Pendleton. Early in 1951, the Department of Justice filed a complaint with the District Court for the Southern District of California asking that "this court quiet the title of the United States of America in and to its rights to the use of water in the Santa Margarita River, and that it adjudge, declare, and determine that all of the rights of the United States of America in and to the Santa Margarita River are paramount to the rights of the defendants herein named.[17] Estimates as to the number of "defendants" varied from ten to sixteen thousand.[18] Each of the defendants was or is being served with process. Water is life in the Fallbrook area of San Diego, California, just as it is in many locations of the Southwest. The action of the United States therefore stirred up a very large hornet's nest.

The use of the word "paramount" in the complaint was immediately construed by some persons as an attempt to extend to inland waters the paramount-rights doctrine of the submerged lands cases.[19] The

[17] The complaint is reprinted in part in 97 *Congressional Record* 7582.

[18] Congressman Patrick J. Hillings of California used the ten thousand figure, a number which seems close to the mark. 97 *Congressional Record* 4186, Appendix. Congressman Edwin E. Willis of Louisiana used the figure sixteen thousand and Congressman Samuel W. Yorty of California the figure fourteen thousand. 97 *Congressional Record* 7582, 9191.

[19] Congressman Willis of Louisiana expressed this point of view: "The purpose of the suit appears to be to broaden the paramount doctrine of the tidelands decision of the Supreme Court so as to apply to inland streams. . . ." 97 *Congressional Record* 7582. See also *Hearings* before a Special Subcommittee on Irrigation and Reclamation of the House Committee on Interior and Insular Affairs, on Santa Margarita Water Rights Controversy, 82d Cong., 1st sess. (1951), 6, 8, 13, 28–29, 59–61, 113–16; *Hearings* before a Subcommittee of the Senate Committee on Interior and Insular Affairs on H.R. 5368 and S. 2809, 82d Cong., 2d sess. (1952), 13–14, 61–65, 123–24.

Department of Justice took the position that the United States was not asserting sovereign rights, but the rights of a proprietor bordering an inland stream and that it was asserting only those rights which had been vested in the previous titleholder as against the rights claimed by the many upstream owners.[20] Thus the word "paramount" with respect to the litigation over riparian rights was, as Congressman Francis Walter of Pennsylvania put it, a "word of art that is causing a lot of apprehension needlessly."[21] Whether the apprehension was "needless" or not, it did arise as a result of the Santa Margarita controversy. So important did the Santa Margarita controversy loom in the minds of Congress that the appropriation act covering the Justice Department for fiscal year 1952–53 prohibited that agency from using any funds to prosecute the suit. The comptroller general ruled that the prohibition extended to the Navy Department as well.[22] The dispute provided added ammunition for those who contended that the national government was attempting to move inland under its "new" doctrine of paramount rights.

In June of 1952 another incident occurred which further raised the fears and anger of quitclaim supporters. Truman Felt, Washington correspondent for the *Florida Times Union*, reported in that paper on 10 June 1952 that Senator Holland had uncovered a plan whereby Secretary of the Interior Chapman intended to take over administration of the marginal-sea oil production, even though the Federal Mineral Leasing Act did not apply. Over a year previously General Services Administrator Jess Larson had signed and executed an order turning over the tidelands oil areas to the Interior Department as "surplus government property." Attorney General J. Howard McGrath and

[20] Expression of this idea was given by Congressman Michael Feighan of Ohio. 97 *Congressional Record* 9169–70. A. Devitt Vanech, Assistant Attorney General of the United States, said in testifying before Subcommittee No. 1 of the House Judiciary Committee that the word had been used because decisions of the California Supreme Court on the subject of riparian rights had used it. Testimony reprinted in 97 *Congressional Record* 4186–87, Appendix.

[21] 97 *Congressional Record* 4186, Appendix. Congressman Yorty of California could not accept this interpretation. He contended that the United States was trying to assert in its complaint a claim which would act to upset the law of water rights along the entire stream course. The United States was not trying to assert "mere proprietary rights," but sovereign rights. 97 *Congressional Record* 9191.

[22] For a brief, factual, unbiased account of this dispute see Kimmis Hendrick, "Congress Action Suspends California Water Rights Case," *Christian Science Monitor*, 17 September 1952. See also 99 *Congressional Record* 428 (2 February 1953), Appendix, for correspondence of the comptroller general relating to illegal expenditures by the Navy Department in the Santa Margarita dispute.

Solicitor General Perlman refused their assent, however. When James P. McGranery took over, he signed the order on 6 June 1952, after telling Senator Holland forty-eight hours before signing that he had no personal knowledge of the issues involved. The *Times Union* of 13 June credited Senator Holland with blocking the scheme, for President Truman dropped the idea after it was brought to light. Secretary Chapman gave Congress a blanket assurance that he would wait legislation before acting.[23] Needless to say, the incident did not reassure those who believed in the rights of the states.

Truman added further fuel to the fire with his Executive Order 10426,[24] which was issued 16 January 1953. This order created the continental shelf as a naval petroleum reserve and placed the area under the jurisdiction of the Secretary of the Navy. While the order apparently was a sweeping one, in reality the *status quo* was not substantially disturbed. Section 2 of the order expressly exempted from Navy control the offshore California zones operating under stipulation of the United States Attorney General and the attorney general

---

[23] There had been other indications in 1951 that the Department of the Interior was searching for authority which would allow it to administer the offshore petroleum operations. Senator Holland was not the first member of Congress to point out this fact. On 7 November 1951, Senator Tom Connally of Texas sent a telegram to Secretary of the Interior Oscar Chapman in which he protested against taking over the "tidelands oil by executive order or otherwise." The Senator contended that for the Interior Department to administer these lands without Congressional sanction would be a "tragic invasion of the rights of Congress." He called such contemplated action "official misconduct" and threatened impeachment proceedings if Chapman went through with any such plan. A copy of the telegram was supplied the author by Senator Connally.

On 16 November 1951, Secretary of the Interior Chapman answered the telegram by denying any intent on the part of the federal government to "seize" the lands. The Secretary contended that all actions taken to date had been made known to Congress. Further, he stated that "Congress ought to legislate expressly with respect to this problem by giving the executive branch specific guidance on the complicated problems which arise in this field." The Secretary closed by emphasizing the importance of oil production to the Korean War and said that no decision to proceed "under any existing provision of the law" had been made. A copy of the Secretary's letter was supplied the author by Senator Connally.

Senator Connally's action was, of course, known to the members of Congress at the time Senator Holland broke his story in 1952. The contratemps between Connally and Chapman had been reported in the *New York Times,* 17 and 21 November 1951.

[24] 18 Fed. Reg. 405. It is reported that Attorney General McGranery told Truman that the President was without legal power to create the offshore submerged lands as a petroleum reserve. McGranery contended that petroleum reserves could be created only from "public lands." The submerged soils did not come in that category. 99 *Congressional Record* 788, Appendix (18 February 1953).

of California. Section 3(a) provided that operations in the Gulf of
Mexico should be transferred to the administrative control of the Secretary of the Navy, but that he should conduct his supervisory activities
under the notice, as amended.[25] Operations in the Gulf, it will be
recalled, have been conducted under this notice which was promulgated
following the *Texas* and *Louisiana* cases. Section 3(c) of the Truman
order did give the Secretary of the Navy power to change the notice,
but President Eisenhower's administration gave no indication that
such an action would be taken.

Thus no offshore submerged land area presently under state lease was
in any substantial way affected by Truman's action. Areas of the continental shelf not presently under state lease were brought under the
control of the Secretary of the Navy. It is assumed by the writer, though
the order did not say so, that the Secretary of the Navy is subject
to the regular statutory provisions for the administration of naval petroleum reserves in his control of these broad expanses, other than those
areas under state lease. Statutory provisions on this topic (34 U.S.C.
§524) require a joint resolution of Congress before oil production can
commence in a naval oil reserve. It would appear improbable, therefore, that the power granted the Secretary of the Navy in President
Truman's order has much substance to it.

The order was issued for political purposes. As a measure designed
to gain time for the proponents of national control and as a tactic for
harassing the incoming Eisenhower administration, the action was
masterfully conceived and executed. The timing was most adroit. True,
the action evoked criticism from many persons who felt that it was not
in the American spirit of "fair play." Yet as a political maneuver, the
order may have served to delay quitclaim legislation at least a short
time, while the resulting legal snarl is unraveled. The order is easily
superseded by a quitclaim resolution passed by the Congress. As a
practical matter, the order will not long stand.

Representatives of California, Texas, and Louisiana made the most
of these and similar incidents in order to swing the representatives of
inland states to quitclaim.[26] The writer would not intimate that their

[25] 15 Fed. Reg. 8835. See pp. 211–12 above.
[26] The writer would call attention to three typical publications which are
based on arguments of this nature. Former California Attorney General Fred N.
Howser was the author of *This Can Happen to Any State* (San Francisco,
Williams Printing Co., 1948). This pamphlet is full of statements predicting dire
calamities if Congress should not pass quitclaim legislation. It is interspersed with
enough provable facts to give the entire pamphlet an air of authenticity. Some
six thousand copies were printed at a cost to the "general fund" of the state of

fears are entirely groundless. Court decisions have all too frequently been expanded far beyond their original meaning. But it is difficult, in the face of the reasoning which underlies Justice Black's exposition of the paramount-powers doctrine to see how title to inland waters could be seriously threatened. Black stated clearly that California "has a qualified ownership of lands under inland navigable waters such as rivers, harbors, and even tidelands down to the low-water mark."[27]

California of about two thousand dollars. Copies were placed in the hands of all Congressmen. The project was financed, according to Howser, entirely by California; no organization made any outside contribution. Senator Forrest Donnell bitterly attacked Howser and the pamphlet as an affront to the integrity of the Supreme Court. *Hearings* on S. 1988 (1948), 198–99, 204–44.

Former California Senator Sheridan Downey is the author of a popular treatment entitled *Truth About the Tidelands* (San Francisco, Publisher's Service, 1948). This seventy-one-page effort is bitterly critical of Ickes and the Supreme Court.

The National Association of Attorneys General has published the most accurate and authoritative work among the material properly classified as "biased." Entitled *Every State Has Submerged Lands* (1951), it is less flashy than Downey's work. It is far more solid in content and contains very few incorrect statements. It does not, however, tell the complete story in all cases. The writer would classify this effort as a perfectly proper one with a very few exceptions. The right to present a point of view is not to be condemned. This the National Association of Attorneys General has done in restrained fashion.

Former Senator Burton Wheeler referred to these and similar publications as "the most vicious things I have ever seen." Again he said: "I think it is reprehensible, the propaganda that has been gotten out by some of the oil companies and by some of the States in the vicious attacks which have been made upon the Supreme Court. In all history, I have never seen as vicious an attack as has been made upon the Supreme Court of the United States." *Hearings* on S.J. Res. 20 (1951), 249. Wheeler's speech, aside from the fact that it is inaccurate, falls in the same category into which he was trying to place the expressions of those who sought to express a point of view contrary to his.

The remarks of Justice Brewer may appropriately be quoted at this point: "It is a mistake to suppose that the Supreme Court is either honored or helped by being spoken of as beyond criticism. On the contrary, the life and character of the justices should be the objects of constant watchfulness by all, and its judgments subject to the freest criticism. The time is past in the history of the world when any living man or body of men can be set on a pedestal and decorated with a halo. True, many criticisms may be, like their authors, devoid of good taste, but better all sorts of criticism than no criticism at all. The moving waters are full of life and health; only in the still waters is stagnation and death." 15 Nat. Corp. Rep. 849 (1898).

[27] 332 U.S. 19, 30. While the court did not state in so many words in what fashion it was using the word "qualified," it is of interest to note that the cases which are cited in a footnote to the statement deal with the incidental takings of property beneath the soils of inland navigable waters in instances where the national government was exercising its undoubted rights to regulate commerce. The cases cited were *United States* v. *Commodore Park*, 324 U.S. 386 (1945); *Scranton* v. *Wheeler*, 179 U.S. 141 (1900); and *Stockton* v. *Baltimore & N.Y. R. Co.*, 32 F. 9 (1887).

He distinguished between internal and external sovereignty, and under this reasoning the corresponding distinction between inland waters and those of the open sea takes on form and substance. To say that the ruling prejudices the title to soils under inland navigable waters may be a good selling point to whip a quiescent Congress to quitclaim action, but the opinion is not being read correctly, if the writer has interpreted Justice Black's decision aright. On the other hand, the writer does not subscribe to the point of view of those who hold that the idea of the United States' trying to wrest title to inland waters from the states is ridiculous and that the oil interests are using it as a scarehead to cover their own evil motives. The interests of the states in the controverted lands were great enough that no "oil lobby" stimulus was needed to move them to action.

The point at which justifiable concern does arise is when questions are raised as to whether or not particular waters fall within or without the rule of the Supreme Court. Justice Black stated that there was no reason why the Court could not later, if necessary, have "more detailed hearings in order to determine with greater definiteness particular segments" of the marginal-sea belt.[28] Again, when he spoke of improvements already made in submerged areas, he said that "we cannot know how many of these improvements are within and how many without the boundary of the marginal sea which can later be accurately defined."[29] Justice Black could not have foreseen clearly at the time the number of hearings and the complex nature of proceedings that would be necessary. He could not have foreseen clearly the grave questions raised and clouds cast on title as the result of his decision.

The court is faced, at the very least, with the making of innumerable decisions in regard to peripheral areas.[30] The court eventually will be

---

[28] 332 U.S. 19, 26.

[29] *Ibid.*, 40. Why should the Justice have spoken so unless he contemplated a distinction between inland waters and marginal-sea areas?

[30] Even the simple question of determining the location of low-water mark offers its little complications. Thus the court has said that inasmuch as the United States Coast and Geodetic Survey defines "mean high water at any place" as "the average height of all the high waters at that place over a considerable period of time," and finds that "from theoretical considerations of an astronomical character, there should be a periodic variation in the rise of water above sea level" and that, "in order to ascertain mean high-tide line with requisite certainty in fixing the boundary of valuable tidelands, . . . an average of 18.6 years should be determined as near as possible." *Borax Consolidated* v. *Los Angeles,* 296 U.S. 10, 26–27 (1935).

This is the rule for determining high-tide line. Can it also be used for the determination of low-tide line? If so, imagine the difficulties involved from a technical point in determining its location for the coast line of the United States.

forced, of necessity, to decide what constitutes a "true bay," for bays, it would appear, presently come under the inland water rule.[31] The United States, in its brief before the special master in the *California* case, advanced the formula that a bay more than ten miles wide at its mouth did not constitute "inland waters." Would so-called "historic bays" be considered as bays for the purpose of applying the inland waters rule?[32] What of lands which have been filled in to make a harbor in what was formerly the open sea? Would the Supreme Court accept as determinative the decisions of lower federal and state courts holding such bays as Monterey Bay,[33] San Pedro Bay,[34] and Santa Monica Bay[35] to be true bays? To take but one example, the United

---

And this is perhaps the simplest calculation that will have to be made among the many problems that will be presented.

[31] *Smith* v. *Maryland,* 18 How. 71 (1855); *McCready* v. *Virginia,* 94 U.S. 391 (1877); *United States* v. *Mission Rock Co.,* 189 U.S. 391 (1903). The court did not, it is true, hold these bays to be "inland waters." Rather it found the waters "navigable" and hence held the beds to be the property of the states concerned.

[32] The question of "historic bays" has been a vexing one in international law. Delaware Bay and Chesapeake Bay, though the distance across their mouths is greater than six nautical miles, are considered true bays. George Grafton Wilson, *Handbook of International Law,* 104–107; John Bassett Moore, *A Digest of International Law,* 735–42.

[33] *Ocean Industries, Inc.* v. *Greene,* 15 F. 2d 862 (1926). The company attempted to operate a floating fish-reduction plant in Monterey Bay. The California Fish and Game Commission took action to stop the operations, which were illegal under the law of California. The District Court for the Northern District of California held that Monterey Bay was a true bay and a part of the "territory" of California; the ruling was based on the fact that, even though the headlands of the bay are more than six miles apart, the constitution of the state of California and the actions of its officers had been sufficient to bring the bay under the jurisdiction and control of the state.

[34] *United States* v. *Carrillo,* 13 F. Supp. 121 (1935). Carrillo and others had hijacked the *Monte Carlo,* a gambling ship, as she lay anchored in San Pedro Bay. The defendants were on trial under four separate counts alleging that they conspired to commit acts of piracy and to rob and plunder, and that they did commit those acts. The court held that it had jurisdiction to try the counts charging plundering and attacking a vessel with intent to plunder, but that it lacked jurisdiction on the counts charging piracy on the high seas and breaking and entering a vessel. The court relied on the "historic" aspect to prove that San Pedro Bay was a true bay. The *Monte Carlo* was not, therefore, on the high seas, and a charge of piracy on the high seas could not be sustained.

[35] *People* v. *Stralla,* 14 Cal. 2d 617 (1939). This case dealt with one of the attempts of "Admiral Tony" Stralla to operate gambling ships off the coast of California. The defendant attempted to operate in Santa Monica Bay, and was, he argued, operating on the high seas and could not be subjected, therefore, to the jurisdiction of the state. The court held that Santa Monica Bay was a true bay, that he was not operating on the high seas, and that he was amenable to the jurisdiction of the court.

See also *Galveston* v. *Menard,* 23 Tex. 349 (1859), holding that Galveston

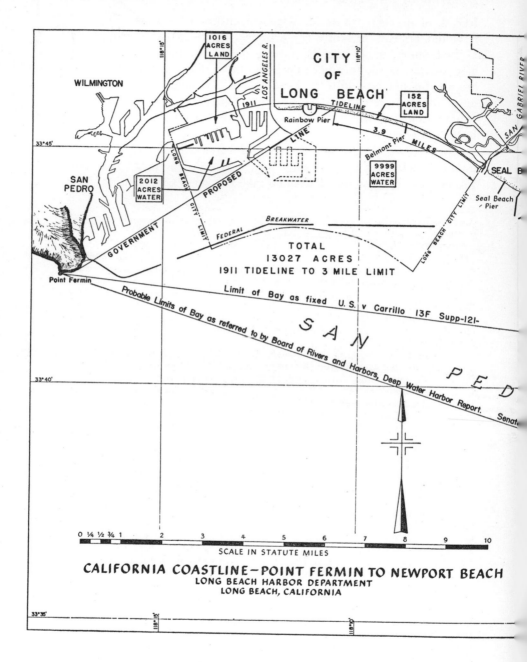

CALIFORNIA COASTLINE—POINT FERMIN TO NEWPORT BEACH
LONG BEACH HARBOR DEPARTMENT
LONG BEACH, CALIFORNIA

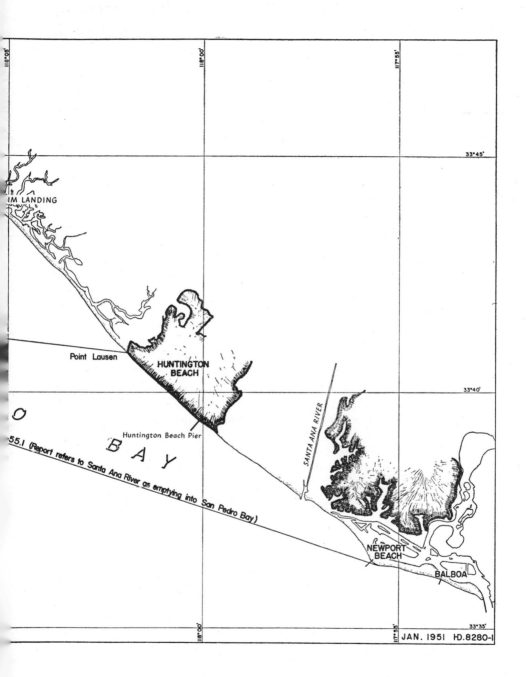

33°45'

IM LANDING

Point Lausen

HUNTINGTON
BEACH

O

B A Y

Huntington Beach Pier

55.1 (Report refers to Santa Ana River as emptying into San Pedro Bay)

SANTA ANA RIVER

33°40'

NEWPORT
BEACH

BALBOA

33°35'

JAN. 1951 H.D. 8280-I

States has already given indications that it does not intend to be bound by the limits of San Pedro Bay as laid down by the federal court in *United States* v. *Carrillo.*[36] The line proposed by the Department of Justice before the special master[37] would place only 2,012 acres of water and 1,016 acres of reclaimed land under the control of the city of Long Beach; the line proposed runs well within the federal breakwater and cuts off 75 or 80 per cent of the present city limits in San Pedro Bay. The line established in *United States* v. *Carrillo* runs from Point Fermin to Point Lausen; if this line were to be determinative, an additional 9,847 acres of water would remain in city control.[38] The United States refuses to be bound by the decisions of its own courts. Multiply this single example by x number of others and it is possible to foresee enough business to keep the courts and special masters appointed by them busy for years.

The picture is further complicated by the recent decision of the International Court of Justice in *United Kingdom* v. *Norway.*[39] The International Court held valid a 1935 Norwegian decree which reserved an exclusive fisheries zone four miles wide as measured from the *skjaergaard,* or chain of some 120,000 rocky islands lying off the Norwegian mainland. The decision has its portents for the hearings to delineate boundaries in California. Should the United States try to place the boundary too close inshore, the resulting three-mile limit would, in international law, be also similarly restricted. If the United States places the line too far out, valuable oil resources will be left in the hands of the states. Further, there are islands off the coastal areas in question, Santa Catalina being one of the most famous. Drawing the boundary on the basis suggested originally by the United States would have resulted in this island's being outside American territorial waters.

Exactly how much of the harbor development of the nation falls

---

Bay is a true bay and that the former Republic of Texas held the submerged soils thereunder to do with as it saw fit. The case is a state case and declares ownership out to three leagues.

[36] 13 F. Supp. 121 (1935). See n. 34, this chapter.

[37] See pp. 236–38 above, for a discussion of the procedure being followed in handling this question of separating inland waters from the waters of the marginal sea.

[38] For the particular situation of the city of Long Beach see testimony of Representative Clyde Doyle of California, *Hearings* on S.J. Res. 20 (1951), 104–14, and testimony of Irving M. Smith, Long Beach city attorney, *ibid.,* 147–68. The writer was shocked at how far inland the government proposed to move the line of San Pedro Bay. See the map on the preceding page.

[39] International Court of Justice, 18 December 1951.

under the rule of the *California, Texas,* and *Louisiana* cases it is presently impossible to say. In 1939 it was estimated that in the larger ports of the nation $1,125,000,000 had been spent in reclaiming and developing submerged lands.[40] Undoubtedly some of these lands are now in an "open sea" category. Port authorities are worried,[41] and they have a right to be. Title to any improvement in the open sea or in an area where the exact status cannot be further determined except by judicial action is definitely clouded if not extinguished by the ruling in the submerged lands cases. In these zones, harbor development and development for other purposes must come to a halt, for capital cannot be induced to venture where the title to land is not good. Justice Black rationalized this state of affairs by saying that this "great national question is not dependent upon what expenses may have been incurred upon mistaken assumptions."[42] This is poor comfort for present and prospective investors.

Of equal complexity is the issue of the exercise of state police power in the marginal-sea areas. How far may a state now go in regulating and policing of the offshore waters? Have the submerged lands decisions changed the basic premise upon which state authority was previously predicated? The answers to the questions are not simple ones; from a practical standpoint, they are of the greatest importance to all the coastal states.

Take, for example, the question of the general regulation of coastal fisheries. Chief Justice Fuller in *Louisiana* v. *Mississippi* said that the "maritime belt is that part of the sea which, in contradistinction to the open sea, is under the sway of the riparian States which can exclusively reserve the fishery within their respective maritime belts for their own citizens, whether fish, or pearls, or amber, or other products of the sea."[43] It has been held that the states own the fish within these waters, insofar as they are capable of ownership.[44] The state has a proprietary

[40] Brief of the American Association of Port Authorities, *Hearings* on S.J. Res. 83 and 92 (1939), 231.
[41] Such is the point of view taken by Leander Shelley, general counsel of the Port of New York Authority and chairman of the Law and Legislation Committee, American Association of Port Authorities, in testimony in joint *Hearings* on S. 1988 (1948), 882–912.
[42] 332 U.S. 19, 40.
[43] 202 U.S. 1, 52 (1906).
[44] *Bayside Fish Flour Co.* v. *Gentry,* 297 U.S. 422 (1936); *Van Camp Sea Food Co.* v. *Department of Natural Resources,* 30 F. 2d 111 (1929); *Bayside Fish Flour Co.* v. *Zellerbach,* 124 Cal. App. 564 (1932), and cases therein cited.

interest in these fish and may enact regulations for their protection,[45] even to the extent of discriminating against out-of-state residents in allowing the products of the fisheries to be taken.[46] The state may enact regulations to protect the sponges under the waters of the marginal sea, and these regulations have been upheld by the courts.[47]

As one looks over these decisions in regard to fisheries and their control, he cannot but be impressed by one fact. The basis for the courts' holdings was that these fish were the property of the state, insofar as there could be property in them. The regulations which the courts have allowed have been predicated upon that basic idea. Of more importance to the discussion, the cases have dealt for the most part with incidents which have occurred within the area of the marginal sea. What, then, can be the status of these decisions in the light of the paramount-powers doctrine?

To the extent that regulation of fisheries in the marginal sea was

[45] The three cases cited in n. 44 dealt with California regulation of fish-reduction plants. These plants were taking sardines and converting them to fish flour and fertilizer in violation of state law. In *Bayside Fish Flour Co.* v. *Gentry* the Supreme Court, Justice Sutherland speaking, upheld the regulation of fish-reduction plants, even as applied to sardines taken outside the three-mile limit.

In *Mirkovich* v. *Milnor,* 34 F. Supp. 409 (1940), the constitutionality of a California statute designed to put floating canneries, operating outside the three-mile limit, out of business was upheld. The act did not operate on an individual catching fish outside the three-mile limit and delivering them to a floating cannery outside that limit, until he had to put in at a California port for fuel and repairs. Then he could be picked up and prosecuted. The state could validly regulate the taking of fish outside its limits in order to protect the fisheries within its limits. The court said at 411: "And to the extent that [the statute] affects any exportation of fish taken from the waters of the state, its action is fully justified on the principle that a state is the owner of its fisheries for the benefit of its citizens and can impose any condition on the taking and use, after taking, of fish within its waters, reasonably necessary for the conservation of its fisheries and the beneficial use of its own citizens." See also *Santa Cruz Oil Corp.* v. *Milnor,* 55 Cal. App. 2d 56 (1942), for a similar decision on a different section of the general statute designed to prevent the operation of floating canneries.

The state may regulate the size of nets which may be used in fishing in the three-mile zone. *In re Marincovich,* 48 Cal. App. 474 (1920). It may likewise set closed seasons on types of fish, determine areas which may be fished, and even regulate in what fashion fish may be taken from the marginal sea. *Suttori* v. *Peckham,* 48 Cal. App. 88 (1920).

[46] *Smith* v. *Maryland,* 18 How. 71 (1855); *McCready* v. *Virginia,* 94 U.S. 391 (1877); *Manchester* v. *Massachusetts,* 139 U.S. 240 (1891); *Corfield* v. *Coryell,* 6 Fed. Cases No. 3230, p. 546 (1823); *Borsage* v. *State,* 23 Ala. App. 18 (1929); *State* v. *Ruvido,* 137 Me. 102 (1940).

[47] *The Abby Dodge,* 223 U.S. 166 (1912); *Lipscomb* v. *Gialourakis,* 101 Fla. 113 (1931); *Pope* v. *Blanton,* 10 F. Supp. 18 (1935). In *The Abby Dodge,* at 174, the court said that the right of the state in fish and sponges in the marginal sea was a "property right."

based on the ownership of the fish found therein, it would appear that these decisions no longer hold. If the state cannot hold title to oil, a natural resource found in the marginal sea, the state cannot be said to hold title, under any system of logic, to any other natural resources of the area. To make this statement, however, is not to say that regulation of fisheries could not still be valid. Two doctrines might apply. The first is drawn from cases such as *Bayside Fish Flour Co.* v. *Gentry,*[48] *Mirkovich* v. *Milnor,*[49] and *Santa Cruz Oil Corp.* v. *Milnor.*[50] These cases held that the taking of fish outside the three-mile limit, admittedly beyond any possible jurisdiction of the state of California insofar as the act of taking was concerned, could be regulated by indirection in order to protect the fish within California waters. Although the *California, Texas,* and *Louisiana* decisions destroy any doctrine of proprietary interest in the fish in the three-mile zone, state police regulations within the area might still be valid as constituting a protection for the fisheries in inland navigable waters—bays, harbors, straits, etc.

The second doctrine is of more general applicability. A state police regulation of fisheries in the marginal sea may be justified so long as the Congress passes no regulation which would contravene it. The power of the state must, perforce, end where that of the national government begins in such a case. In the absence of Congressional legislation, the state may regulate. The doctrine expressed in *Gilman* v. *Philadelphia*[51] is generally applicable here: until the dormant power of Congress is utilized and made effective through legislation, the reserved powers of the states are plenary. Such a doctrine would have a sound practical basis.

The fishing interests, as a matter of fact, were quick to seize on *United States* v. *California* as a possible means of escape from state control. The first case in which an attempt was made to utilize the ruling was brought by fishing interests. In the case of *Toomer* v. *Witsell*[52] suit was brought against the South Carolina State Board of Fisheries to enjoin enforcement of a statute which prohibited shrimp fishing in inland waters and which set a twenty-five-dollar fee for residents of South Carolina fishing in the three-mile zone of the marginal sea while levying a twenty-five-hundred-dollar fee on nonresident boats fishing in the same area, with a maximum of one hundred nonresident licenses being issued. Certain taxes were imposed on shrimp taken in the three-mile zone, and there were penalty provisions. Toomer and

[48] 297 U.S. 422 (1936).
[50] 55 Cal. App. 2d 56 (1942).
[52] 73 F. Supp. 371 (1947).

[49] 34 F. Supp. 409 (1940).
[51] 3 Wall. 713 (1866).

others fished for shrimp in the three-mile zone off North and South Carolina, Georgia, and Florida. The fishing occurred only in and beyond the three-mile zone, not in inland waters. Toomer sought an injunction to prevent enforcement of the South Carolina statute, alleging that South Carolina did not have jurisdiction over the three-mile zone under the ruling in *United States* v. *California* and hence could not levy the tax or assess a penalty for nonconformance. The court took jurisdiction under the rule of diverse citizenship.

Judge Parker, speaking for the three-judge federal district court, denied the request for an injunction and held that the intent of *United States* v. *California* was not to overrule the long line of fisheries decisions. The question of overruling such decisions he left specifically to the Supreme Court. Since the United States had asserted its paramount rights only over oil, the state might exercise police power over the maritime belt to control fishing therein.

A writ of certiorari was taken to the United States Supreme Court, which noted probable jurisdiction.[53] The case was argued in January 1948, and the decision was handed down on 7 June 1948.[54] Chief Justice Vinson wrote the opinion, affirming in part and reversing in part. The state act taxing green shrimp taken in the marginal belt at one-eighth of a cent per pound was held valid. The requirement, however, that out-of-state residents pay a license fee one hundred times as great as state residents was struck down as abridging the privileges and immunities clause of Article IV, section 2, of the Constitution. The requirement that owners of shrimp boats fishing in the maritime belt off South Carolina dock at a South Carolina port to unload, pack, and stamp their catch was held violative of the commerce clause of the Constitution. Justice Frankfurter, joined by Justice Jackson, concurred, except that he would have struck down the licensing provision as violative of the commerce rather than the privileges and immunities clause.

The importance of the case of *Toomer* v. *Witsell* does not lie in the validity or invalidity of particular sections of the South Carolina statutes. It is in the premise made by the Chief Justice that the import of the case is found:

Since the present case evinces no conflict between South Carolina's regulatory scheme and any assertion of federal power, the District Court properly concluded that the State has sufficient interests in the shrimp

[53] 332 U.S. 830 (1947).   [54] 334 U.S. 385.

fishery within three miles of its coast so that it may exercise its police power to protect and regulate that fishery.

It does not follow from the existence of power to regulate, however, that such power need not be exercised within the confines of generally applicable Constitutional limitations. In the view we take, the heart of this case is whether South Carolina's admitted power has been so exercised.[55]

Basically, South Carolina could regulate the fisheries in the three-mile zone, barring the assertion of paramount national power, but such regulation must conform to "generally applicable Constitutional limitations." It was on this last basis that the two provisions of the South Carolina law were invalidated.

The majority opinion rejects specifically the concept of fish in the three-mile zone as "property."[56] It operates on the second of the bases discussed previously by the writer. There is even a possibility that the Supreme Court, through its refusal to hold valid the requirement that shrimp boats fishing in South Carolina's marginal-sea waters dock at South Carolina ports, may have thereby cast some question on the type of indirect regulation held valid in *Mirkovich* v. *Milnor*.[57] While the opinion attempts to distinguish the instant case from *McCready* v. *Virginia*,[58] there is some question, too, whether the court has not made it more difficult for the states to regulate fisheries. By striking down the higher out-of-state license fee, the court opened the issue of just how much higher a nonresident fee can be than a resident fee and still not incur the court's wrath expressed through the invocation of the privileges and immunities clause. Further, how is the state to collect the one-eighth of a cent per pound tax on green shrimp taken in the waters of the marginal sea if there be no requirement that out-of-state boats dock at state ports? The answer, probably, is an increased number of state patrol boats. Practically, the enforcement of the law is made more difficult.

So far as the regulation of fisheries is concerned, it can be argued that the Congress has given positive approval to the principle of state regulation. On 24 July 1947, a month after the decision in *United*

[55] *Ibid.*, 393–94.

[56] Chief Justice Vinson said: "The whole ownership theory, in fact, is now generally regarded as but a fiction expressive in legal shorthand of the importance to its people that a State have power to preserve and regulate the exploitation of an important resource." *Ibid.*, 402.

[57] Discussed in n. 45, this chapter.

[58] See Chief Justice Vinson's discussion. 334 U.S. 385, 400–403.

States v. *California,* the President signed a resolution approving the Pacific Marine Fisheries Compact.[59] This compact was entered into by the states of California, Washington, and Oregon for the development and protection of the "areas of the Pacific Ocean." It is entirely within the power of Congress to grant positive authority to the states to regulate the fisheries in the three-mile zone. By sanctioning a compact for that very purpose, it would seem that the Congress has taken this step in the Pacific area.

The over-all problem of fisheries regulation under state police power remains, however. The case of *Toomer* v. *Witsell* has provided the basis: The states may regulate in the absence of an assertion of paramount national authority, but such regulations must conform to the general restrictions placed on the states by the national Constitution.

Other types of state police regulation in the three-mile zone could be easily rationalized so as not to conflict with the rule of the submerged lands decisions. A simple regulation such as that of New York City which prohibits a boat from coming within one thousand feet of a bathing beach undoubtedly would be upheld.[60] Harbor regulations would not be disturbed, for decisions have already held valid such regulations where they have not been in conflict with the commerce power.[61] State control over such items as kelp would remain in effect until the federal government asserted a superior right. The state could still remove sand and gravel from the marginal-sea area until the federal government chose to assert paramount rights to the materials.[62] From a practical point of view, however, there will be no development along these lines in the absence of national legislation confirming rights

---

[59] 61 U.S. Stat. 419.

[60] In *People* v. *Reilly,* 14 N.Y.S. 2d 589 (1939), a conviction for violation of this city ordinance was upheld. At 595, the court said: "To the State may be traced and from the State has been derived the title to the land now vested in the City of New York." Since New York held title to the bathing beach and waters out to the three-mile limit, the city could validly regulate the waters. Why the court chose to base its reasoning on the proprietary concept rather than on the more obvious and less complicated one of simple police power regulations is not evident in the opinion. It should be noted that while the decision would remain the same under *United States* v. *California* the basis of the reasoning would have to be altered.

[61] *The W. H. Beaman,* 45 F. 125 (1891).

[62] The state would not, however, be able to take the sand and gravel in the marginal sea upon the basis of ownership. Such taking could only be on sufferance of the federal government. Thus such cases as *State* v. *Stewart,* 184 Miss. 202 (1936), allowing the state to assume jurisdiction and control over the taking of sand and gravel from the marginal sea because the state "owned" the three-mile zone would no longer have legal effect.

to those operating in the areas, either through quitclaim or by complete national control. Capital will not take the risk of having its investments in such commodities lost without notice or compensation.

There is likewise the possibility that, in removing products such as sand and gravel, the operators may lay themselves open to claims for damages by the national government. Though damages were not asked and will not be exacted of the oil companies operating in the California, Texas, and Louisiana submerged lands, persons interested in extracting other products from the soils of the marginal sea will now be on their guard. One unfortunate effect of these decisions is that, for the time being at least, no person can venture into activities relating to products in the marginal sea. Thus, further explorations for oil and other minerals, projects for reclaiming land, and recovery of sand and gravel and similar products—all now await clarification of status before further development can be risked.

Certain types of concurrent criminal jurisdiction are not disturbed by the rulings in the *California, Texas*, and *Louisiana* cases. The statement in *Murray* v. *Hildreth*[63] still stands as good law: "As between nations, there is concurrent jurisdiction in foreign waters; and, as between the United States and the several states, there is no reason why the jurisdiction over crimes within the three-mile limit could not be made concurrent, as has usually been done in the punishment of offenses committed in violation of both federal and state law."

The general problem of state taxation of physical assets in the marginal-sea areas promises to be a problem even more difficult of solution. The decisions in the submerged lands cases have removed from the states the power to exact royalties for the production of oil. The state may still, as has been shown, exact license fees under certain circumstances, as for fishery rights. Can it also levy a property tax against, let us say, a pier built out into the open sea? Or is the rule now that the state may tax only that portion of the pier extending down to low-water mark? May the owner escape taxation on the remainder of the improvement?[64] Admittedly, the income from such an operation may

---

[63] 61 F. 2d 483, 485 (1932). The case involved a prosecution for murder committed alongside a rumrunner two hundred feet off the Florida coast. The defendant contended that the district court had no jurisdiction, that only the Florida courts could try him. The district court held, however, that there was concurrent jurisdiction in such a case. See also *Miller* v. *United States*, 88 F. 2d 102 (1937).

[64] Constitutionally the national government may not levy a direct tax, unless apportioned according to population. May the national government levy a property tax on such a pier, not apportioning it? The land area does not belong

be taxed by the state of which the owner is resident. But what of the property tax on the pier?

It is a problem for which there is no ready answer. Logically, if the states own no land below low-water mark out to the three-mile limit in the open sea, it follows that there can be no direct property tax assessed on improvements in that area. Resort might be had to other forms of taxation to accomplish the same purpose, but the direct tax itself, as utilized by certain California and Texas counties on oil rigs below low-water mark, is no longer justifiable. In *People ex rel. Mexican Tel. Co.* v. *State Tax Commission*[65] the state tax and method of assessing it on a telephone cable from low-water mark out to the three-mile limit was upheld. The case tells very little, however, for the question of jurisdiction and ownership of the three-mile zone was not argued. There were gratuitous statements that the state owned all the land within the three-mile belt, but the case turned on an argument by the company that since it had a franchise from the national government it was a federal instrumentality and therefore immune from state taxation. Of more importance, no one disputed state ownership of the three-mile zone at that date. It is difficult to say to what extent a lack of power to assess property taxes in the marginal sea will affect the tax structures of the states or their municipal subdivisions because of the great difficulty of determining which improvements or portions of improvements are actually below low-water mark.[66]

The *California, Texas,* and *Louisiana* cases have raised a great many problems which demand immediate solutions. While it may be true that the doctrine of paramount powers expounded in these decisions is not applicable to lands under inland waters, there is still cause for concern in the clouding of titles of areas which are not clearly within or

---

to any state, and the area is one where ordinary constitutional limitations do not apply.

[65] 219 N.Y. App. Dec. 401 (1927). In *Carnasion* v. *Paul*, 53 So. 2d 304 (Fla. 1951), a tax levied by Volusia County, Florida, on a steel and concrete pier extending out into the Atlantic Ocean was contested on the ground that *United States* v. *California* had removed the county's power to tax. The Florida Supreme Court held the tax valid, on the ground that the exercise of the taxing power did not infringe the paramount rights of the United States in the area.

[66] In 1937, in two lower federal court cases, it was held that the United States could tax income derived from oil operations in what were then thought to be state "owned" submerged lands. A portion of the income in these cases was derived from below low-water mark in the open sea. *Bankline Oil Co.* v. *Commissioner*, 90 F. 2d 899; affirmed on appeal 303 U.S. 362 (1938); *Spalding* v.

sea. Dean Roscoe Pound has been especially critical of this phase of the court's opinion.[2] Just why the expropriation of petroleum in the marginal sea may be justified because of the nation's position in international affairs while the government seizure of steel mills is invalid in a period of emergency,[3] it is somewhat difficult to rationalize. The writer believes that the court made its theory of internal-external relationships abundantly clear, but the writer fails to see the justification in American constitutional law for thus propounding the theory. Further, in utilizing the paramount-powers doctrine, the court has opened up unnecessarily new possibilities for the extension of national power. The doctrine ignores the settled principles of American federalism with its basis of delegated and reserved powers and posits a concept of governmental power not subject to constitutional limitation.

4. The court erred in adopting the nonownership concept of the marginal sea.[4] The nonownership theory has little status, except among a small group of continental jurists, in international law. Further, the concept as applied to coastal areas of the United States is fraught with dangerous possibilities, especially if the base line were to be drawn too far inland in an effort to place the maximum amount of known oil production under federal control. Moving the base line inland would cut down dangerously the area of national authority vis-à-vis other nations.

5. The nonownership dogma ignored the accomplished fact that the marginal-sea areas, correctly or incorrectly, had been incorporated into the declared land areas of many of the states. County and municipal boundaries extended out to the state's declared boundaries, and property taxes were assessed and collected on improvements made under state or local grant in the offshore areas.

6. The court erred in treating the states of California, Texas, and Louisiana as it would have treated a private litigant against which suit had been brought by the United States. While prescription, laches, and estoppel cannot run against the sovereign, the court should have recognized that the long-continued policies of the political branches created, at the minimum, a presumption of validity to the claims of the states. Certainly any rights which the states may have held transcended

[2] 3 *Baylor Law Review* (1951), 120 ff.
[3] *Youngstown Sheet and Tube Co.* v. *Sawyer,* 343 U.S. 579 (1952).
[4] This point of view is stressed in the "Joint Memorandum in Support of Rehearing," signed by ten of the world's leading international lawyers. The joint memorandum is found in the Texas petition for rehearing, No. 13 Original, October Term 1949, pp. 54 ff. The memorandum was filed 19 July 1950 and is discussed above, pp. 208–10.

those which a person might have claimed. The states are integral and indestructible parts of the federal system, and the relationship between the national government and the states is undeniably different from that between the national government and a private citizen of the United States.

Congress has acted in the past to correct inequities arising from court decisions. Congress should act to correct the inequities resulting from the submerged lands opinions. Congress has the constitutional power to do so. The writer holds no brief for the excessive and sometimes well-nigh slanderous propaganda used by both sides; such materials should be recognized as elements of any dispute of this nature. The situation now demands a solution and not words. A quitclaim of the disputed areas is indicated as the best and most practical answer available. Further, the quitclaim does no violence to the theory and long practice of American federalism. For 150 years the offshore lands occupied the status which they would again assume under quitclaim.

By April 1953, when this volume was in page proof, it was apparent that a bill quitclaiming the submerged offshore soils to the historic boundaries of the littoral states would be passed by the Congress. Some advocates of state control, such as Senator Russell Long of Louisiana and Senator Price Daniel of Texas, had planned to include legislation on the continental shelf in the bill quitclaiming submerged lands to historic limits. Agreement was reached, however, to deal with the two areas in separate legislation, a policy undoubtedly influenced by the acknowledged fact that attempts to give to the littoral states income from the continental shelf outside historic limits would jeopardize the chance of passage of the entire measure.

In March 1953 a quitclaim bill was pushed successfully through the House of Representatives over violent but numerically unavailing opposition. The margin was a substantial one, 285 to 108, a margin greater than that by which the 1951 quitclaim had passed the House. The bill as passed provided for national control seaward of the historic boundaries. This House measure closely paralleled the recommendations made earlier in this chapter by the writer.

Passage of a similar bill in the Senate is virtually guaranteed. Senators Anderson of New Mexico, Lehman of New York, Douglas of Illinois, and others are, at the time of this writing, arguing at length against the measure. While a full-scale filibuster has not yet developed, it seems likely that the advocates of national control will adopt such a tactic. In the end, however, the bill will pass and will be approved by the President.

A quitclaim to historic boundaries comports, the writer contends, with legal principles and precedent. History will deal kindly with this action. It is difficult to see how, in calmer times, a restoration of rights to a previously long-existent status will be called a "land grab." There will remain unsettled, however, the question of the continental shelf. Should the advocates of quitclaim, knowing their power, seek to force through a bill to extend state boundaries beyond constitutional limits far out in this area, history may record the event unfavorably. In this circumstance the battle for "principle under law" may be judged to have turned into one of "profit at any cost."

Quitclaim to historic boundaries will not mean, therefore, that the last gun has been fired in the "tidelands controversy." Legislation dealing with the continental shelf will come before the Eighty-third Congress; the writer would not hazard a prophecy on its possible fate. Further, attempts will be made to test the constitutionality of quitclaim out to historic boundaries. The dispute will continue in the public eye for yet some time.

Here then is a case study in American federalism—the genesis, the life, and the possible future status of one controversy in the long history of attempts to demarcate the line which separates state and national power. As has been the case with many opinions of the court, the narrow holding of the tribunal will be regarded in the future as relatively unimportant. A quitclaim will not affect the basis of the court's decision as a possible precedent for some as yet unforeseen future situation. The doctrine of paramount rights which the court enunciated was used in 1947 and 1950 to draw in a little darker outline the boundary which must constantly be shaped in the American federal system.

Appendix

Appendix

CONGRESSIONAL HEARINGS ON CONTROL OF SUBMERGED LANDS IN THE MARGINAL SEA

Hearings before the House Judiciary Committee on S.J. Res. 208, 75th Cong., 3d sess. (1938). Cited as *Hearings* on S.J. Res. 208 (1938).

Hearings before Subcommittee No. 4 of the House Judiciary Committee on H.J. Res. 176 and 181, 76th Cong., 1st sess. (1939). Cited as · *Hearings* on H.J. Res. 176 and 181 (1939).

Hearings before the Senate Committee on Public Lands and Surveys on S.J. Res. 83 and 92, 76th Cong., 1st sess. (1939). Cited as *Hearings* on S.J. Res. 83 and 92 (1939).

Joint *Hearings* before the House Judiciary Committee and a Special Subcommittee of the Senate Judiciary Committee on H.J. Res. 118 *et al.*, 79th Cong., 1st sess. (1945). Cited as *Hearings* on H.J. Res. 118 *et al.* (1945).

Hearings before the Senate Judiciary Committee on S.J. Res. 48 and H.J. Res. 225, 79th Cong., 2d sess. (1946). Cited as *Hearings* on S.J. Res. 48 and H.J. Res. 225 (1946).

Joint *Hearings* before the Committees on the Judiciary, Congress of the United States, on S. 1988 and similar House bills, 80th Cong., 2d sess. (1948). Cited as joint *Hearings* on S. 1988 (1948).

Hearings before a Subcommittee of the Senate Judiciary Committee on S. 1988 and similar House bills, 80th Cong., 2d sess. (1948). Cited as *Hearings* on S. 1988. (1948).

Hearings before the Senate Committee on Interior and Insular Affairs on S. 155 *et al.*, 81st Cong., 1st sess. (1949). Cited as *Hearings* on S. 155 *et al.* (1949).

Hearings before Subcommittee No. 1 of the House Judiciary Committee on H.R. 5991 and 5992, 81st Cong., 1st sess. (1949). Cited as *Hearings* on H.R. 5991 and 5992 (1949).

Hearings before the Senate Committee on Interior and Insular Affairs on S.J. Res. 195, 81st Cong., 2d sess. (1950). Cited as *Hearings* on S.J. Res. 195 (1950).

Hearings before the Senate Committee on Interior and Insular Affairs on S.J. Res. 20, 82d Cong., 1st sess. (1951). Cited as *Hearings* on S.J. Res. 20 (1951). This set of hearings includes the record of committee conferences with the executive departments on Senate Bill 940, which were held a month after the original hearings. These conferences are sometimes listed as separate hearings.

Hearings before the Senate Committee on Interior and Insular Affairs on the Hill amendment to S.J. Res. 20, 82d Cong., 2d sess. (1952). Cited as *Hearings* on the Hill amendment (1952).

Hearings before Subcommittee No. 1 of the House Judiciary Committee on H.R. 2948 and similar bills, 83d Cong., 1st sess. (1953).

Hearings before the Senate Committee on Interior and Insular Affairs on S.J. Res. 13 and other bills, 83d Cong., 1st sess. (1953).

NOTE: The last two hearings are not cited in the text of this work, for they were not published until after the volume was in page proof. Little that was new or startling transpired at the 1953 hearings.

Table of Cases

Table of Cases

Abby Dodge, The, 223 U.S. 166 (1912) 99, 176–77, 266

Alaska Gold Recovery Co. *v.* Northern M. & T. Co., 7 Alaska
386 (1926) 99

Alaska Pacific Fisheries *v.* United States, 248 U.S. 78 (1918) . 99, 130

Amaya *v.* Stanolind Oil and Gas Co., 62 F. Supp. 181 (1945) . . 92

American Insurance Co. *v.* Canter, 1 Pet. 511 (1828) 96

Ann, The, Fed. Cases No. 397 (1812) 23

Anna, The, 165 Eng. Rep. 809, 5 C. Rob. 373 (1805) 12

Apollon, The, 9 Wheat. 362 (1824) 23

Appelby *v.* City of New York, 271 U.S. 364 (1926) . . . 28, 30, 31

Armour & Co. *v.* Newport, 110 Atl. 645 (R.I. 1920) 18, 31

Arnold *v.* Mundy, 1 Halst. 1 (N.J.L. 1821) 27, 37

Attorney General for British Columbia *v.* Attorney General for
Canada, [1914] A.C. 153 16

Attorney General *v.* Chambers, 43 Eng. Rep. 486 (1854) 14

Attorney General *v.* Hanmer, 4 Jur. N.S. 751 (1858) 14

Attorney General *v.* Parmenter, 147 Eng. Rep. 345 (1811) . . . 14

Bacon *v.* Walker, 204 U.S. 311 (1907) 101

Baer *v.* Moran Brothers, 153 U.S. 287 (1894) 38, 51

Bagnell *v.* Broderick, 13 Pet. 436 (1839) 96

Bailey and Fulgham *v.* United States, 62 Ct. Cl. 77
(1926) 39–40, 41, 111, 113

Balzac *v.* Porto Rico, 258 U.S. 298 (1922) 96

Bankline Oil Co. *v.* Commissioner, 90 F. 2d 899, 303 U.S. 362
(1938) 272

Barker *v.* Bates, 13 Pick. 255 (Mass. 1832) 37

Barney *v.* Keokuk, 94 U.S. 324 (1876) 49, 51, 52

Bayside Fish Flour Co. *v.* Gentry, 297 U.S. 422 (1936)   76, 265, 266, 267
Bayside Fish Flour Co. *v.* Zellerbach, 124 Cal. App. 564 (1932)   76, 265
Beaman, The W. H., see *W. H. Beaman*
Beard *v.* Federy, 3 Wall. 478 (1866) 59, 61
Beecher *v.* Wetherby, 95 U.S. 517 (1877) 96
Benest *v.* Pipon, 12 Eng. Rep. 243 (1829) 13
Blundell *v.* Catterall, 106 Eng. Rep. 1190, 5 B. & Ald. 268 (1821) . 13
Bodi *v.* Winous Point Shooting Club, 57 Ohio St. 226 (1897) . . 50
Bolsa Land Co. *v.* Burdick, 151 Cal. 254 (1907) 75
Boone *v.* Kingsbury, 206 Cal. 148 (1928) 68–69, 75
Borax Consolidated *v.* Los Angeles, 296 U.S. 10 (1935) . 6, 50, 52, 260
Borsage *v.* State, 23 Ala. App. 18 (1928) 52, 266
Bowlby *v.* Shively, 22 Ore. 410 (1892) 50
Brewer-Elliott Oil Co. *v.* United States, 260 U.S. 77 (1922) . . . 51
Broward *v.* Mabry, 50 So. 826 (Fla. 1909) 33, 50
Broward *v.* Sledge, 50 So. 831 (Fla. 1909) 33
Browne *v.* Kennedy, 5 Har. & J. 195 (Md. 1821) 27
Brown *v.* Spillman, 155 U.S. 665 (1895) 69
Buford *v.* Houtz, 133 U.S. 320 (1890) 61, 62, 100
Bulstrode *v.* Hall and Stephens, 82 Eng. Rep. 1024, 1 Sid.
    148 (1674) 12, 13
Burnet *v.* Brooks, 288 U.S. 378 (1933) 252

Cardwell *v.* American Bridge Co., 113 U.S. 205 (1885) 50
Carnasion *v.* Paul, 53 So. 2d 304 (Fla. 1951) 272
Carr *v.* Kingsbury, 111 Cal. App. 165 (1931) 38, 68
Cathcart *v.* Robinson, 5 Pet. 264 (1831) 27
Chappell *v.* Waterworth, 155 U.S. 102 (1894) 40
Churchill Co. *v.* Kingsbury, 178 Cal. 554 (1918) 62
Church *v.* Hubbart, 2 Cranch 187 (1804) 23, 38
Coburn *v.* San Mateo County, 75 F. 520 (1896) 62
Commonwealth *v.* Alger, 7 Cush. 53 (Mass. 1851) 27, 30, 37
Commonwealth *v.* Boston Terminal Co., 185 Mass. 281 (1904) . . 34
Commonwealth *v.* Charleston, 1 Pick. 179 (Mass. 1822) 28
Commonwealth *v.* Manchester, 152 Mass. 230 (1890) 33, 37
Commonwealth *v.* Roxbury, 9 Gray 451 (Mass. 1857) . 18, 27, 29, 37
Cook *v.* Cook, 342 U.S. 126 (1951) 175
Cooper, *In re*, 143 U.S. 472 (1892) 116, 142, 173
Corfield *v.* Coryell, 6 Fed. Cases 546 (1823) . . . 36, 37, 249, 266
County of St. Clair *v.* Lovingston, 23 Wall. 46 (1874) 30, 36
Coyle *v.* Smith, 221 U.S. 559 (1911) 44
Cummings *v.* Kingsbury, 111 Cal. App. 763 (1931) 68
Cunard Steamship Co. *v.* Mellon, 262 U.S. 100 (1923) 24
Cunningham, Joseph, *In re*, 55 I.D. 1 (1934) 74, 131

Darbee and Immel Oyster and Land Co. *v.* Pacific Oyster Co.,
150 Cal. 392 (1907) 76
Dean *v.* San Diego, 275 F. 228 (1921) 50, 62
De Fortuyn, The, Marsden's *Admiralty Cases* 175 (1760) . . . 12
Doran *v.* Central Pacific R. Co., 24 Cal. 246 (1864) 100
Dorr *v.* United States, 195 U.S. 138 (1904) 96
Dunham *v.* Lamphere, 3 Gray 268 (Mass. 1856) . . . 24, 33, 37, 52
Dunn *v.* Ickes, 115 F. 2d 36 (1940) 135
Dwelle *v.* Wilson, 14 Ohio Cir. Ct. R. 551 (1897) 50

Economy Light and Power Co. *v.* United States, 256 U.S. 113 (1921) 44
Ervien *v.* United States, 251 U.S. 41 (1919) 44
Escanaba & Lake Michigan Transportation Co. *v.* Chicago,
107 U.S. 678 (1882) 49
Ex parte . . . . *see* name of party

Farry *v.* King, 120 Cal. App. 118 (1932) 68
Feisthamel *v.* Kingsbury, 111 Cal. App. 762 (1931) 68
Fitzhardinge *v.* Purcell . . . . . *see* Lord Fitzhardinge *v.* Purcell
Fleming *v.* Page, 9 How. 602 (1850) 95
Fort Leavenworth R. Co. *v.* Lowe, 114 U.S. 525 (1885) 36
Foster *v.* Neilson, 2 Pet. 253 (1829) 96
Francis *v.* Ocean Insurance Co., 6 Cow. 404 (N.Y. 1826) . . . 21
Freed *v.* Miami Beach Pier Corp., 112 So. 841 (Fla. 1927) . . 50, 124
Free Fishers of Whitstable *v.* Gann, 144 Eng. Rep. 1003 (1865) . 14
Furman *v.* City of New York, 7 N.Y. Super. Ct. 16 (1851) . . . 27

Galveston *v.* Mann, 135 Tex. 319 (1940) 91
Galveston *v.* Menard, 23 Tex. 349 (1859) 91, 261
Gann *v.* Free Fishers of Whitstable, 11 Eng. Rep. 1305 (1865) . . 13
General Iron Screw Collier Co. *v.* Schurmans, 70 Eng. Rep. 712
(1860) 15
Gillam *v.* United States, 27 F. 2d 296 (1924) 21
Gillespie *v.* Nebraska, 28 L.D. 124 (1899) 130
Gilman *v.* Philadelphia, 3 Wall. 713 (1866) 267
Goodtitle *v.* Kibbe, 9 How. 471 (1850) 47, 97
Gorham *v.* Alkali Works, 27 So. 2d 299 (La. 1946) 57
Gough *v.* Bell, 2 Zab. 441 (N.J.L. 1850) 27, 37
Greenleaf Lumber Co. *v.* Garrison, 237 U.S. 251 (1915) . . 40, 111

Harcourt *v.* Gaillard, 12 Wheat. 523 (1827) 35
Hardin *v.* Jordan, 140 U.S. 371 (1891) 128
Hardin *v.* Shedd, 190 U.S. 508 (1903) 50, 51
Hawkins Point Lighthouse Case, 39 F. 77 (1889) 40, 41, 111

Heine *v.* Roth, 2 Alaska 416 (1905) 98
Heydenfeldt *v.* Daney Gold Mining Co., 93 U.S. 634 (1876) . . 96
Hicks *v.* Bell, 3 Cal. 219 (1853) 62
Hihn Co. *v.* City of Santa Cruz, 170 Cal. 436 (1915) 62
Hinman *v.* Warren, 6 Ore. 408 (1876) 50
Hogg *v.* Beerman, 41 Ohio St. 91 (1884) 25
Humboldt Manufacturers' Association *v.* Christopherson, 73 F.
   239 (1896) 24
Hungaria, The, 41 F. 109 (1889) 25

Illinois Central R. Co. *v.* Illinois, 146 U.S. 387
   (1892) 30, 50, 53, 186, 200
In re . . . . *see* name of party

Johnson *v.* Barret, 82 Eng. Rep. 887 (1646) 12, 13
Johnson *v.* McIntosh, 8 Wheat. 543 (1823) 96
Jones *v.* United States, 137 U.S. 202 (1890) 173
Joyner *v.* Kingsbury, 97 Cal. App. 17 (1929), 111 Cal. App.
   764 (1931) 68
Justheim *v.* Chapman, Civil Action 4172–49, U.S.D.C. for
   D.C. (1949) 244

Kaiser Wilhelm der Grosse, The, 175 F. 215 (1909) 21
Kasson, James, *In re,* 13 L.D. 299 (1891) 130
Kelley *v.* Kingsbury, 210 Cal. 37 (1930) 68
King *v.* Smith, 2 Doug. 441 (1780) 14
Knight *v.* United Land Association, 142 U.S. 161 (1891) . . 50, 61
Kohl *v.* United States, 91 U.S. 367 (1876) 36

Leda, The, Swa. Adm. 40 (1856) 14
Lewis Blue Point Oyster Co. *v.* Briggs, 229 U.S. 82
   (1913) 40, 41, 111, 113
Lipscomb *v.* Gialourakis, 133 So. 104 (Fla. 1931) . . . 50, 52, 266
Logan, James W., *In re,* 29 L.D. 395 (1900) 99, 130
Long Beach *v.* Marshall, 11 Cal. 2d 609 (1938) 73, 75
Los Angeles *v.* San Pedro, etc., R. Co., 182 Cal. 652 (1920) . . . 62
Lord Advocate *v.* Clyde Trustees, 19 Rettie 174 (Court of
   Sessions, 1891) 14
Lord Advocate *v.* Wemyss, [1900] A. C. 48 14
Lord Fitzhardinge *v.* Purcell, [1908] 2 Ch. 139 14
Louisiana *v.* Mississippi, 202 U.S. 1 (1906) 52, 176, 265
Lux *v.* Haggin, 69 Cal. 255 (1886) 50

McCardle, *Ex parte,* 7 Wall. 506 (1869) 153
McCloskey *v.* Pacific Coast Co., 160 F. 794 (1908) 99
McCready *v.* Virginia, 94 U.S. 391 (1877) . 32, 37, 53, 261, 266, 269
M'Ilvaine *v.* Coxe's Lessee, 4 Cranch 209 (1809) 33
Maggart *v.* Kingsbury, 111 Cal. App. 765 (1931) 68
Manchester *v.* Massachusetts, 139 U.S. 240
   (1891) 29, 33, 37, 39, 176, 266
Mann *v.* Tacoma Land Co., 153 U.S. 273 (1894) . 50–51, 98, 198, 244
Marianna Flora, The, 11 Wheat. 1 (1826) 23
Marincovich, *In re,* 48 Cal. App. 474 (1920) 65, 76, 266
Martin, Jesse C., *In re,* 32 L.D. (1903) 99
Martin *v.* Waddell, 16 Pet. 345 (1842) 13, 27, 29, 30, 33, 46
Massachusetts *v.* Mellon, 262 U.S. 447 (1923) 232
Massachusetts *v.* New York, 271 U.S. 65 (1926) 30, 53, 185
Mayhew *v.* Krug, Civil Action 411–48, U.S.D.C. for D.C. (1948) 244
Merryman *v.* Bourne, 9 Wall. 592 (1896) 59
Middleton *v.* La Compagnie Generale Transatlantique, 100
   F. 866 (1900) 20
Miller *v.* Stockburger, 12 Cal. 2d 440 (1938) 74
Miller *v.* United States, 88 F. 2d 102 (1937) 271
Mirkovich *v.* Milnor, 34 F. Supp. 409 (1940) . . . 77, 266, 267, 269
Missouri *v.* Holland, 252 U.S. 416 (1920) 174
Mobile *v.* Emmanuel, 1 How. 95 (1843) 45
Mobile *v.* Eslava, 16 Pet. 234 (1842) 45
Mobile *v.* Hallett, 16 Pet. 261 (1842) 45
Moore *v.* Smaw, 17 Cal. 199 (1861) 61, 62
Morton *v.* Nebraska, 21 Wall. 660 (1874) 61, 100
Mumford *v.* Wardell, 6 Wall. 423 (1867) 30, 49
Murphy *v.* Ryan, Ir. R. 2 C.L. 143 (1868) 14
Murray *v.* Hildreth, 61 F. 2d 483 (1932) 271

Narragansett Real Estate Co. *v.* Mackenzie, 82 Atl. 804 (R.I. 1912) 28
Newhall *v.* Sanger, 92 U.S. 761 (1875) 50
New Orleans *v.* United States, 10 Pet. 662 (1836) 200, 203
New York, N.H. & H.R. Co. *v.* Morgan, 56 Atl. 179 (R.I. 1903) . 28

Oakland *v.* Buteau, 219 Cal. 745 (1934) 75
Oakland *v.* Oakland Water Front Co., 118 Cal. 160 (1897) . . . 75
Ocean Industries *v.* Greene, 15 F. 2d 862 (1926) 77, 261
Ormerod *v.* New York, etc., R. Co., 13 F. 370 (1882) 40

Pacific Coast Dairy *v.* Department of Agriculture, 318 U.S.
   285 (1943) 4

Paladini *v.* Superior Court, 178 Cal. 369 (1918) 76
Parkinson *v.* Bracken, 39 Am. Dec. 296 (Wis. 1842) 96
Penhallow *v.* Doane, 3 Dall. 54 (1795) 30
People *ex rel.* Mexican Telegraph Co. *v.* State Tax Commission,
   220 N.Y.S. 8 (1927) 52, 272
People *v.* Kirk, 162 Ill. 138 (1896) 50
People *v.* Monterey Fish Products Co., 195 Cal. 548 (1925) . . . 76
People *v.* N.Y. & Staten Island Ferry Co., 68 N.Y. 71 (1876) . 28, 32
People *v.* Reilly, 14 N.Y.S. 2d 589 (1939) 33, 52, 270
People *v.* Silberwood, 67 N.W. 1087 (Mich. 1896) 50
People *v.* Stafford Packing Co., 193 Cal. 719 (1924) 76
People *v.* Stralla, 14 Cal. 2d 617 (1939) 261
People *v.* Trinity Church, 22 N.Y. 44 (1860) 30, 32
People *v.* Truckee Lumber Co., 116 Cal. 397 (1897) 76
Philadelphia *v.* Scott, 81 Pa. 80 (1876) 28
Phoedovius, *In re,* 177 Cal. 238 (1918) 76
Pollard's Lessee *v.* Hagan, 3 How. 212
   (1845)   36, 44–48, 49, 56, 96, 130, 170–71, 175–76, 178, 252, 253, 254
Pollard *v.* Files, 2 How. 591 (1844) 45
Pollard *v.* Kibbe, 14 Pet. 353 (1840) 45
Pope *v.* Blanton, 10 F. Supp. 18 (1935) 266
Port of Seattle *v.* Oregon & Washington R. Co., 255 U.S. 56
   (1921) 41, 50

Queen *v.* Keyn, L.R .2 Exch. Div. 63 (1876) . . 15–17, 25, 172, 278

Red Star Olga Fishing Station, *In re,* 26 L.D. 533 (1898) . . 99, 130
Rex *v.* Forty-nine Casks of Brandy, 166 Eng. Rep. 401 (1836) . . 12
Rhode Island *v.* Massachusetts, 12 Pet. 657 (1838) 33
Rogers *v.* Jones, 1 Wend. 237 (1828) 28
Ross *v.* Burkhard Co., 90 Cal. App. 201 (1928) 52
Royal Fishery of Banne, Case of the, 80 Eng. Rep. 540, Davis
   55 (1674) 12, 13

San Francisco *v.* LeRoy, 138 U.S. 656 (1891) 62
San Pedro, etc., R. Co., *v.* Hamilton, 161 Cal. 610 (1911) . . . 6, 38
Santa Cruz Oil Corp. *v.* Milnor, 55 Cal. App. 2d 56 (1942) 77, 266, 267
Scott *v.* Lattig, 227 U.S. 229 (1913) 50
Scranton *v.* Wheeler, 179 U.S. 141 (1900) 40, 259
Secretary of State for India *v.* Chelikani Rama Rao, 43
   Indian App. 192 (1916) 17
Sherrer *v.* Sherrer, 334 U.S. 343 (1948) 175
Shively *v.* Bowlby, 152 U.S. 1 (1894) . 27, 28, 30, 33, 37, 47, 49, 52, 97
Shively *v.* Welch, 10 Sawyer 136 (Ore. 1884) 50

Silas Mason Co. *v.* Tax Commission, 302 U.S. 186 (1937) . . . 50
Simons *v.* French, 25 Conn. 346 (1856) 28
Skiriotes *v.* Florida, 313 U.S. 69 (1941) 100, 177
Smith *v.* Maryland, 18 How. 71 (1855) 32, 34, 37, 261, 266
Soult *v.* L'Africaine, 22 Fed. Cases 805 (1804) 22
Spalding *v.* United States. 17 F. Supp. 957, 97 F. 2d 701,
  305 U.S. 644 (1938) 272
State *v.* Black River Phosphate Co., 32 Fla. 82 (1893) . . 27, 33, 50
State *v.* Bradford, 121 Tex. 515 (1932) 91
State *v.* Capdeville, 146 La. 94 (1919) 50
State *v.* Delesdenier, 7 Tex. 76 (1851) 91
State *v.* Jadwin, 85 S.W. 490 (Tex. 1904) 91
State *v.* Pollock, 239 Pac. 8 (Wash. 1925) 24, 52
State *v.* Ruvido, 137 Me. 102 (1940) 24
State *v.* Stewart, 184 Miss. 202 (1936) 270
Stearns *v.* Minnesota, 179 U.S. 223 (1900) 44
Stephenson *v.* Wood, 119 Tex. 564 (1931) 90
Stevens *v.* Paterson & Newark R. Co., 34 N.J.L. 532 (1870) . . . 28
Stockton *v.* Baltimore & N.Y. R. Co., 32 F. 9 (1887) . . . 111, 259
Stone *v.* Los Angeles, 114 Cal. App. 192 (1931) 74
Suttori *v.* Peckham, 48 Cal. App. 88 (1920) 52, 76, 266

Texas *v.* White, 7 Wall. 700 (1869) 94
Tinicum Fishing Co. *v.* Hartley, 61 Pa. 21 (1869) 18
Toomer *v.* Witsell, 334 U.S. 385 (1948) 202, 267–70
Twee Gebroeders, The, 165 Eng. Rep. 422, 3 C. Rob. 162 (1800) . 12

United Kingdom *v.* Norway, International Court of Justice
  (18 December 1951) 19, 264
United States *ex rel.* Jordan *v.* Ickes, 55 F. Supp. 875, 143 F.
  2d. 152 (1944) 135
United States *v.* Arredondo, 6 Pet. 691 (1832) 96
United States *v.* Ashton, 170 F. 509 (1909) 50
United States *v.* Belmont, 301 U.S. 324 (1937) 251
United States *v.* Bevans, 3 Wheat. 336 (1818) 32, 36, 249
United States *v.* Brewer-Elliott Oil and Gas Co., 249 F.
  609 (1918) 126–27
United States *v.* California, 332 U.S. 19 (1947) . . . . *see* Index
United States *v.* Carrillo, 13 F. Supp. 121 (1935) 261, 264
United States *v.* Castillero, 2 Black 17 (1862) 96
United States *v.* Chandler-Dunbar Water Co., 209 U.S.
  447 (1908) 53, 183, 185, 254–55, 278
United States *v.* Cohen Grocery Co., 255 U.S. 81 (1920) 41

United States *v.* Commodore Park, 324 U.S. 386 (1945) 259
United States *v.* Cook, 19 Wall. 591 (1873) 96
United States *v.* Coronado Beach Co., 255 U.S. 472 (1921) . . 50, 61
United States *v.* Curtiss-Wright, 299 U.S. 304 (1936) . . 30, 250–51
United States *v.* Gettysburg R. Co., 160 U.S. 668 (1896) 36
United States *v.* Holt Bank, 270 U.S. 49 (1926) 96
United States *v.* Louisiana, 339 U.S. 699 (1950) . . . . *see* Index
United States *v.* McIntosh, 2 F. Supp. 244 (1932) 41
United States *v.* Mission Rock Co., 189 U.S. 391 (1903) . 50, 192, 261
United States *v.* Newark Meadows Improvement Co.,
   173 F. 426 (1909) 24, 32
United States *v.* New River Collieries Co., 262 U.S. 341 (1923) . . 41
United States *v.* Pacific Western Oil Corp., U.S.D.C. for
   Southern District of California
   (filed 1945) . . . 123, 133, 137, 138, 142, 144, 145, 146, 151, 161
United States *v.* Pink, 315 U.S. 203 (1942) 251
United States *v.* San Pedro & Cañon del Agua Co., 17 Pac.
   337 (N.M. 1888) 62
United States *v.* Smiley, 27 Fed. Cases 1132 (1864) 20
United States *v.* Smith, Fed. Cases No. 16337 (1816) 21
United States *v.* Southeastern Underwriters, 322 U.S. 533 (1944) 153
United States *v.* Standard Oil Co., 21 F. Supp. 645 (1937) . . . 100
United States *v.* Standard Oil Co., 332 U.S. 301 (1947) 181
United States *v.* Sweet, 245 U.S. 563 (1918) 61, 100
United States *v.* Texas, 339 U.S. 707 (1950) . . . . . *see* Index
United States *v. The James G. Swan,* 50 F. 108 (1892) . . 116, 142
United States *v. The Kodiak,* 53 F. 126 (1892) . . . 116, 117, 142
United States *v.* Utah, 283 U.S. 64 (1931) 51, 52
United States *v.* Wyoming, 331 U.S. 440 (1947) 231–32

Van Camp Sea Food Co. *v.* Department of Natural Resources,
   30 F. 2d 111 (1929) 76, 265

Wainwright *v.* McCullough, 63 Pa. 66 (1869) 28
Ward *v.* Mulford, 32 Cal. 365 (1867) 130
Weber *v.* Board of Harbor Commissioners, 18 Wall. 57 (1873) 28, 49, 62
Western Pacific R. Co. *v.* Southern Pacific R. Co., 151 F. 376 (1907) 75
Weston *v.* Sampson, 8 Cush. 347 (Mass. 1851) 18, 27, 31, 37
W. H. Beaman, The, 45 F. 125 (1891) 270
Williams *v.* North Carolina, 325 U.S. 226 (1944) 175
Wilson *v.* Shaw, 204 U.S. 24 (1906) 116, 142
Withers *v.* Buckley, 20 How. 84 (1857) 47
Workman *v.* Boone, 280 U.S. 517 (1929) 68

Table of Cases 297

Work *v.* Louisiana, 269 U.S. 250 (1925) 61
Wright *v.* Seymour, 69 Cal. 122 (1886) 50, 62

Youngstown Sheet and Tube Co. *v.* Sawyer, 343 U.S.
  579 (1952) 41, 279

Zug *v.* Commonwealth, 70 Pa. 138 (1871) 28

Index

Index

Admiralty and maritime jurisdiction of national government as distinct from property rights: 32, 249

Admission of states: *see* "equal footing"

Adverse possession, doctrine of: argued in *California* case, 178–79; argued in *Texas* and *Louisiana* cases, 199

Aiken, Senator George: 218

Allen, Congressman Leo: 221

Allen, Robert S., columns cited: 232 n., 239

Allred, James V., testimony of: 118, 119, 123

American Association of Port Authorities, favors 1945 quitclaim: 151

Anderson, Senator Clinton: 224; predicts court test of quitclaim, 232 n.

Angell, Joseph, quoted: 11, 31

Articles of Confederation: status of states under, 29–31; ownership of land by central government under, 35–36, 43–44

Bailey, Congressman Cleveland, quoted: 220

Baker, Rex G., testimony of: 90

Bakewell, Congressman Claude, argues constitutionality of quitclaim: 221, 230

Barkley, Alben, opposes quitclaim: 156

Bay, difficulty of determining what constitutes: 261–65; *see also* historic bays

Bentsen, Congressman Lloyd, quoted: 222 n.

Biddle, Francis: files *Pacific Western* suit, 137; quoted, 146; reasons of, for filing *Pacific Western* suit, 160–61

Biesemeier, Commander Harold, testimony of: 112, 114

Bingham, Joseph Walter: cited, 21 n.; supports Texas petition for rehearing, 209

Bishop, William W., supports Texas petition for rehearing: 209 n.

Black, Justice Hugo: and *Queen* v. *Keyn*, 17 n.; and territorial concept of marginal sea, 26; opinion of, in *California* case, 167–80; dicta of, relating to possible quitclaim quoted, 231; refuses to declare title, 249–50; distinguishes between external and internal sovereignty, 250–51, 253, 260; intimates further

301

302 *Index*

hearings a necessity in determining boundaries of marginal belt, 260

Blanton, Thomas L.: views of, on "equal footing" concept, 49; testimony of, 109

Brandeis, Justice Louis D., quoted: 41

Brewer, Justice David J.: limits extent of "public lands," 98; quoted on criticism of Supreme Court, 259 n.

Brewster, Senator Owen: 227

Brooks, Congressman Overton, testimony of: 150

Brownell, Herbert: 232 n.

Buchanan, James, denies effect of three-league boundary in international law: 82

Buettner, Philip, testimony of: 108 n.

Burroughs, Sir John, cited: 9 n.

Butler, Senator Hugh: 227

Bynkershoek, states rule for control of marginal sea: 9

Calhoun, John C., favors annexation of Texas: 84

California: claims of, to soils under marginal sea, 59–78; problems of, in regulating offshore oil production, 66–74; statistics on value of other products and development in offshore areas of, 75–77 nn.; files answer to complaint, 162–63; contentions of, in case against, 165–66; importance of tidelands issue in, in 1952 presidential election, 229; continues offshore production under stipulations, 235; has difficulty determining seaward boundary after *California* case, 236–38; see also *United States* v. *California*

California Senate Committee to Investigate the Abstraction of Oil and Gas from State Lands: discusses P.E. Strip, 70 n.; condemns handling of offshore leases, 71–72

Callis, Serjeant Robert, cited: 10

Calvo, cited: 25 n.

"Cannon shot" rule: 9; recognized by British courts, 12, 19–20, 23 n.; used by Randolph in opinion as Attorney General, 127; see also three-mile limit

"Capture theory": 69

Case, Congressman Clifford P.: 222 n.

"Case or controversy": *California* case held to present, 168; argued in *Louisiana* and *Texas* cases, 199–200

Catron, Justice John, dissents in *Pollard* v. *Hagan:* 47–48

Celler, Congressman Emanuel: quoted, 220, 221; actions criticized, 222 n.

Chambers, Frank, testimony of: 108, 114

Chapman, Oscar L.: issues notice on Gulf petroleum operations, 211–12; attitude on quitclaim noted, 233 n.; denies use of land scrip for Gulf of Mexico submerged lands, 245; in dispute with Connally, 257 n.

Childs, Marquis, columns cited: 228 n., 239

Chitty, Joseph, cited: 11 n.

Clark, Tom: substitutes action against California for *Pacific Western* suit, 138, 161; gives reasons for acting against California, 162; states opinion on inapplicability of Mineral Leasing Act of 1920 to submerged lands, 189; views *California* case as declaring national ownership, 193 n., 196 n.; admits suit to be filed against Texas and Louisiana, 196; disqualifies self in *Texas* and *Louisiana* cases, 202; letter to Truman cited, 234

Clary, William W.: testimony of, 67; prepares list of prospecting permits denied by General Land Office,

131–32 n.; letter on Littell incident cited, 160 n.; states reasons for not arguing paramount-powers theory, 167

Clay, Henry, opposes annexation of Texas: 84

Clements, F. W., testimony of: 130

Colombos, C. John, supports Texas petition for rehearing: 209

Colonial charters, and grants in the marginal sea: 17–18

Combs, Congressman J. M.: testimony of, 82; questions Perlman, 233 n.

Commerce clause, use of, to press national claims: 39–41

Congress of the United States: admits Louisiana, 55–56; admits California, 60–66; admits Texas, 83, 88; policy of, toward submerged lands prior to World War II, 95–121; attempts quitclaim in 1945, 144–58; makes later quitclaim attempts, 212–33

Connally, Senator Tom: 225; testimony of, 115; comments on attempt to single out California, 118; condemns Interior Department plan to take over submerged lands, 257 n.

Continental shelf: Truman proclamation on, 141–43; Truman order creating naval petroleum reserve of, 257–58; *see also* Gulf of Mexico, marginal sea

Cord, E. L., offers land scrip for Gulf of Mexico submerged lands: 244–45

Cordon, Senator Guy: 233 n.

Cornwall Arbitration: 15

Criminal jurisdiction in marginal sea: 271; *see also* police power

Cunningham, Joseph: testimony of, 71 n.; seeks federal prospecting permit, 74–75; federal prospecting

permit refused, 131–32; applicant for federal lease, 243–44

Cushing, Caleb, opinion of, as Attorney General quoted: 126

Daniel, Price: testimony of, 80, 88, 89, 91; comments on *California* case, 195; opposes compromise, 216 n.

Davis, Judge William H.: appointed special master in *California* case, 237; references made to, 237–38

Dean, Ezra, favors annexation of Texas: 84

DeLacy, Hugh, statement of, cited: 147

Digges, Thomas, cited: 10

Dirksen, Senator Everett: 227

Dockweiler, Thomas A. J.: testimony of, 71, 106; suggests quitclaim in 1939, 145

Doherty, Daniel J., testimony of: 116, 116 n.

Donnell, Senator Forrest: opposes quitclaim, 156; and connection with *St. Louis Post-Dispatch*, 239; attacks publication written by Howser, 259 n.

Douglas, Justice William O.: 238 n.; opinions of, in *Texas* and *Louisiana* cases, 203–207; resolution asking impeachment of, passed by Texas house, 212 n.

Downey, Senator Sheridan: 217; publication of, noted, 259 n.

Doyle, Congressman Clyde, testimony of: 133 n.

Duckworth, Allen, columns cited: 240

Duff, Senator James H.: 227, 228 n.

Edelstein, Harry W., testimony of: 124

Editorial comment: *see* journalistic comment

Eisenhower, Dwight, takes stand on tidelands: 229–30

Elliot, Fred C., testimony of: 131 n.

Eminent domain, defined by Justice McKinley: 45–46 n.

Estoppel, doctrine of: argued in *California* case, 178–79; argued in *Texas* case, 202

"Equal footing": admission of states on, generally, 43–44; explained in *Pollard* v. *Hagan,* 44–48; idea of *Pollard* case followed in subsequent decisions, 49 n.; claim of Louisiana based on, 55–56; claim of California based on, 62–64; problem of, in case of Texas, 87–88; position of national government on, in *California* case, 164; argued by national government against Texas, 198–99; argued by Louisiana, 200; argued by Texas, 202; considered in Douglas' opinion in *Texas* case, 204–205; considered by Reed in dissent, 207–208

Fairchild, R. W., testimony of: 109, 113, 118

Fallbrook controversy: see *Santa Margarita River Case*

Fauchille, Paul, cited: 22 n.

Federal Mineral Leasing Act of 1920: as basis for California act, 67; not applicable below high-water mark, 74, 154 n., 189, 211; returns under, 89; filings under, denied, 131 n.; table of filings made under, 134 n.; applicability of, to submerged lands argued, 214 n.; attempts to apply provisions of, to submerged soils, 242–46

Feighan, Congressman Michael: 221

Felt, Truman, column cited: 256–57

Fenn, Percy Thomas, cited: 7, 10

Fenwick, Charles G., cited: 7, 19

Fisheries: regulation of, by California,

75–77; regulation of, by Texas, 90; problem of control of, after tidelands cases, 265–70

Franconia decision: 15 n.; see *Queen* v. *Keyn* in Table of Cases

Frankfurter, Justice Felix: 268; dissents in *California* case, 180–81; dissents in *Texas* case, 208

Freed, Hirsh, testimony of: 150

Fulbright, Senator J. William, opposes quitclaim: 156

Fuller, Chief Justice Melville, opinion of, in *Louisiana* v. *Mississippi* quoted: 265

Fulton, Thomas Wemyss, cited: 8 n., 9 n., 22

Gadsden Treaty: 83

Galiani, proposes fixed range for cannon: 9

Galveston Bay: 261 n.

General Services Administration, plan of, to take over administration of submerged lands bared: 256–57

Gentili, on property concept of marginal sea: 22

Gibson, Congressman John S.: 239

Gidel, Gilbert, supports Texas petition for rehearing: 209

Giles, Bascom: testimony of, 80, 82; comments on *California* case, 195

Gilman, Warren, testimony of: 44 n., 124

Gossett, Congressman Ed: 196, 220

Governors' Conference, memorializes Congress favoring quitclaim: 187

Gray, Justice Horace, corrects dicta of *Pollard* case: 96–97

Greaves, H. R. G., quoted: 29

Green, Senator Theodore: 232 n.

Grisbadarna Arbitration: 23

Groner, Judge D. Lawrence, appointed special master in *California* case: 237

Grotius: cited, 9; on property concept in marginal sea, 22

Guadalupe Hidalgo, Treaty of: 60–62, 82–83

Gulf of Mexico: extent of petroleum operations in, 53–54, 57–58, 79–80, 89–90; administrative provision made for petroleum production in, after *Texas* and *Louisiana* cases, 211–12; effect of *Texas* and *Louisiana* cases on exploration in, 216 n.; *see also* continental shelf

Hale, Lord Chief Justice, propounds theory of Crown ownership of marginal sea: 10, 11 n.

Hall, William E., cited and quoted: 7, 8, 11, 20 n., 22

Hammond, Hall, testimony of: 218 n.

Harbor development: value of, in California, 75 n.; affected by tidelands cases, 264–65

Havenner, Congressman Frank R., testimony of: 76 n.

Heckendorf, Percy C., testimony of: 76 n.

Hendrick, Kimmis, column cited: 256 n.

High-water mark, defined: 260 n.

Hill, Senator Lister, sponsors "oil for education" amendment: 224, 228

Hillings, Congressman Patrick J.: 255 n.

Hinshaw, Congressman Carl: quoted, 222 n.; introduces resolution to define "tidelands" and other terms, 223 n.

Historic bays: 34; question of what constitutes, 261–64

Hobbs, Congressman Sam: 232, 275; introduces coastal lands legislation, 103; proponent of nonownership theory, 107–109, 110, 154, 206; attempts resolution aimed solely at California, 117; on constitutionality

of quitclaim, 152 n.; opposes quitclaim, 155–56

Holland, Senator Spessard: leads quitclaim battle, 224, 225 n., 226; introduces 1953 Senate quitclaim legislation, 233 n.; bares scheme of General Services Administration to take over control of submerged lands, 256–57

Holmes, Justice Oliver Wendell, ruling of, in *Chandler-Dunbar* case: 183, 185

Howser, Fred N.: files California petition for rehearing, 182; asks legislation by Congress, 193; publication by, noted, 258 n.

Hudson, Judge Manley O.: 201; opinion of, on reservation of marginal-sea lands quoted, 51 n.; views of, on state ownership of offshore soils, 177 n.; supports Texas petition for rehearing, 209; opinion of, on *California* case quoted, 238

Hudson, Raymond, attorney for lease applicants, states position: 152–53

Hughes, Chief Justice Charles Evans, comments on *The Abby Dodge:* 100

Hurst, Sir Cecil, cited: 11

Hyde, Charles Cheney: 201; cited, 23 n.; supports Texas petition for rehearing, 209

Ickes, Harold L.: 253; raises novel legal point on Texas claim, 93 n.; persuades Nye to introduce legislation, 101; charges Navy mismanagement of oil reserves, 106–107; letter to Olin S. Proctor quoted, 128–29; denies federal prospecting permits in offshore soils, 131–32; changes mind on state ownership, 132–35; criticizes attorneys general for entering dispute, 135–36; part of, in Ritter-Chapin incident, 136 n.; quarrels with Pauley, 137–41; letter of, to writer quoted, 147;

testifies on quitclaim, 153; says Mineral Leasing Act of 1920 inapplicable to submerged lands, 189 n.; criticizes California stipulations, 211, 235–36; changes mind on applicability of Mineral Leasing Act to submerged soils, 214 n., 242; columns cited, 239; replies to Duckworth, 240 n.

Ingersoll, J. R., opposes annexation of Texas: 84

Inherent powers, relation of, to paramount-powers doctrine: 250–51

Inland waters, status of, under paramount-powers doctrine: 253–60

Interior, Department of: favors Nye and Hobbs resolutions, 122; policy of, on submerged lands prior to 1947, 128–41, 157; negotiates stipulations with California, 187; takes over interim Gulf petroleum operations, 211–12

Jackson, Andrew, recognizes Texas' independence: 81

Jackson, Justice Robert: 238 n., 268; disqualifies self in *Texas* and *Louisiana* cases, 202

Jessup, Philip Caryl, cited: 19

Jester, Beauford H., testimony of: 79

Johnson, Harry R., testimony of: 106

Johnson, Senator Hiram: testimony of, 76 n.; criticizes Nye, 117 n.

Jordan, Robert E. Lee: seeks federal prospecting permit, 74–75; opposes 1945 quitclaim, 154; petition of, to intervene in *California* case denied, 191; applicant for federal lease, 243

Journalistic comment on the dispute: 239–42

Judd, Orrin, testimony of: 149, 153

Justice, Department of: favors Nye and Hobbs resolutions, 122; policy of, on submerged lands prior to

1947, 125–28, 141, 157; attacked by attorneys general, 149–50; issues notice of filing of *Pacific Western* action, 159–60; files complaint against California, 162; arguments of, in *California* case, 164–65, 169–80 *passim;* negotiates stipulations with California, 187–88; files complaint against Texas and Louisiana, 196; arguments of, in *Texas* and *Louisiana* cases, 197–99; asks court to declare national control of three offshore California areas, 237; contributes to unrest after *California* case, 254; files complaint in *Santa Margarita River Case,* 255

Keating, Congressman Kenneth: 222

Keech, Richmond B., testimony of: 149 n., 151

Keenan, Robert B., presents case for federal lease applicants: 115

Keeton, W. Page, cited and quoted: 113, 178, 192 n.

Kefauver, Senator Estes: 227; uses tidelands issue in 1952 presidential primary, 229

Kelp: production of, regulated by California, 76–77; Congress aware of possible productive potential of, 99

Kelsen, Hans, supports Texas petition for rehearing: 209

Kem, Senator James P.: 228

Kennon, Governor Robert F.: 230

Kenny, Robert: testimony of, 148, 150, 151, 153; condemns filing of *Pacific Western* suit, 159–60, 161

King, Samuel A., testimony of: 70, 109

Knowland, Senator William F.: 224, 225

Krock, Arthur, columns cited: 241

Krug, Julius A., testimony of: 219 n.

Laches, doctrine of: argued in *California* case, 178–79; argued in *Texas* and *Louisiana* cases, 199

LaFollette, Congressman Robert M., Jr., opposes quitclaim: 156

Land scrip, use of, in tidelands dispute: 244–45

Langer, Senator William: introduces quitclaim legislation, 219; quoted, 226

Larson, Jess: 256

Legal periodicals, articles on tidelands controversy in: 247 n.

Lehman, Senator Herbert H: 224

Lindley, Curtiss H.: quoted, 51; on Spanish mineral law, 61

Littell, Norman M.: discusses Biddle's action in filing *Pacific Western* suit, 160–61; asks leave to file brief *amicus curiae* in *California* case, 191–92; files petition to intervene in *California* case on behalf of bands of Mission Indians, 245 n.

Lodge, Senator Henry Cabot, Jr.: 227, 228 n.

Long, Senator Russell: 224, 225; forces Pearson retraction, 239 n.

Long Beach: leases its offshore lands, 73–74; gets royalty returns from offshore operations, 74 n.; receives permission to construct pier, 124; plans of, for harbor development adopted by Congress, 125 n.; position of, as a result of *California* case, 264

Loret, Joseph A.: cited, 20 n., 44 n.; testimony of, 115, 118

Los Angeles: exchanges submerged lands with national government: 125–26

Louisiana: claims of, to soils under marginal sea, 53–58; importance of tidelands issue in, in 1952 presidential election, 230; does not follow pattern of California stipulations, 236; see also *United States v. Louisiana*

Louisiana Purchase: 54–55

Low-water mark, necessity for definition of: 260 n.

Lucas, Senator Scott: 217 n.

Lyle, Congressman John E.: 220

McCarran, Senator Pat: 146

McCarthy, Congressman Eugene: 222 n.

McCorvey, Gessner, testimony of: 151

McCraw, William, testimony of: 113

McFarland, Senator Ernest: 223, 225

McFarland, H. C., opinion of, quoted: 130

McGranery, James P.: 257

McGrath, J. Howard: 232 n., 256

McKay, Douglas: 232 n.

McKinley, Justice John, opinion of, in *Pollard* v. *Hagan:* 44–47

McMurry, Uel T., applicant for federal lease: 243

McNemar, Leslie C.: gives views on three-mile belt, 37–38; cited, 39 n., 41; discusses "equal footing" concept, 48; defines "public domain," 51 n.; argues United States never granted away mineral rights, 63; testimony of, 103, 116, 117; argues for petroleum reserve, 105; adopts Hobbs' theory, 108 n.; says Fifth Amendment not applicable below low-water mark, 110–11; sees need for Congressional declaration, 114; on constitutionality of quitclaim, 152 n., 230, 232

Madden, Congressman Ray: 220 n.

Mansfield, Congressman Mike: 222 n.

Marginal sea: development of territorial concept of, in international law, 7–9, 19–26; defined, 9 n.; development of territorial concept of, in British law, 10–19; minority view on property concept in, 24–25; claims of original states to lands under, 27–42; claims of later states to lands under, 43–53; claims of Louisiana to lands under, 53–58; claims of California to lands under, 59–78; claims of Texas to lands under, 79–94; position of national government on, in *California* case, 164; Black on, 170–72; territorial character of, supported by Texas petition for rehearing, 209–10; constitutionality of quitclaim of, assessed, 230–33; difficulty of determining boundary lines in, after *California* case, 236–38; Black's refusal to declare title in, 249–51; concept of property in, 274

Marshall, Chief Justice John: 23; opinion of, in *United States* v. *Bevans,* 32; rule of, on relation of grant of power to cession of territory, 249

Masterson, William E.: cited, 21; supports Texas petition for rehearing, 209

Mattison, Walter J., testimony of: 151

Mattoon, Everett W., testimony of: 67, 235

Mayhew, Deryl: applicant for federal lease, 243; files test case, 244

Mershon, Stephen Lyon, cited: 23

Miami Beach, receives permission to construct pier: 124

Michener, Congressman Earl: 107, 108 n.

Mineral Leasing Act of 1920: *see* Federal Mineral Leasing Act of 1920

Minton, Justice Sherman, dissent in *Texas* case: 207

Mitchell, William D., opinion of, as Attorney General cited: 126

Moley, Raymond, columns cited: 229, 240

Monterey Bay: 261

Moody, Senator Blair: 226

Moore, James William: 201

Mouton, M. W., cited: 9

Murray, Senator James: 224, 226

National Association of Attorneys General: supports state ownership, 118; activities of, criticized by Ickes, 135–36; supports 1945 quitclaim, 148–49; files brief *amicus curiae* in *California* case, 149; files brief *amicus curiae* asking rehearing in *California* case, 186; publication of, noted, 259 n.

National Resources Committee, stresses need for national control of offshore soils: 103–104

Naval petroleum reserves: location of, 106 n.; mismanaged, 106–107; created in continental shelf, 257–58

Navigable waters: state ownership of soils under, summarized, 52–53; attitude of Congress toward land under, 95–99, 101; emphasis placed on, in *California* case, 165–66; distinction developed between inland water and open sea, 175–76, 178; rights of states to ownership of submerged soils related to rights in, 275

Navy Department: stresses need for conservation and national control of offshore fields, 104–107; location of oil reserves, 106 n.; criticized for mismanagement of reserves, 106–107; argues national defense power, 110–13; favors Nye and Hobbs resolutions, 122; policy of, on submerged lands, 125 n., 141, 157; continental shelf placed under control of, 257–58

Newspaper comment: *see* journalistic comment

Nicholson, George F., testimony of: 119

Nonownership theory: advanced by Hobbs, 107–109, 110; adopted by court in *California* case, 169; stated in tidelands cases, 275; criticized, 279

Northwest Ordinance: 36; and the "equal footing" clause, 43 n.

Norwegian Fisheries case: 19 n., 21 n., 264

Nye, Senator Gerald P.: 275; introduces coastal lands bills, 101–103

O'Connor, Congressman James F.: 103, 114

Offshore drilling: *see* petroleum production in offshore areas

"Oil for education" amendment: action on, in House, 222; action on, in Senate, 224, 226; favored by Truman, 228; favored by writer if applied seaward of historic state boundaries, 277

Oil lobby: 119 n., 220, 221, 222 n., 226, 227, 260

Olson, Culbert L., condemns handling of offshore leases: 71–72

Olson Committee: *see* California Senate Committee to Investigate the Abstraction of Oil and Gas from State Lands

O'Mahoney, Senator Joseph: 216, 219, 224, 225, 227 n., 228; spearheads drive for federal quitclaim of Wyoming lands, 231–32

Oppenheim, L., cited: 23 n.

Orn, Clayton L., testimony of: 90

Ortolan, cited: 25

Pacific Marine Fisheries Compact: 269–70

Paramount powers: not argued in *California* case, 166–67; Black develops concept of, 173–75; possi-

bility advanced for use of, in *California* case, 203; doctrine of, stated in *Louisiana* case, 203; doctrine of, stated in *Texas* case, 205–206; problems under, discussed and evaluated, 247–73; doctrine summarized, 275–76

Parker, Judge John J., opinion of, in *Toomer* v. *Witsell:* 268

Parks, George B., cited: 70–71 n.

Pauley, Edwin W., quarrels with Ickes: 137–41

Pearson, Drew, columns cited: 228, 239

Pebbles, Harold A., testimony of: 148

Perlman, Philip B.: 232 n.; declares stipulations in effect, 193; attitude of, on quitclaim, 233 n.

"P.E. Strip": 70

Petroleum production in offshore areas: cost of, 58, 89–90; off California, 66–67; aided by slant-drilling, 70–71, 72 n., 89; Texas potential, 79–80; *see also* royalties, rentals, and bonuses

Poage, Congressman W. R.: 239; quoted, 221 n.

Police power (state): Black concedes authority to exercise, in marginal sea, 175, 178; and regulation of fisheries, 265–70; general regulation of marginal waters, 270–71; taxation, 271–72; *see also* criminal jurisdiction

Polk, James Knox, favors annexation of Texas: 84

Porterie, Gaston, testimony of: 119

Pound, Roscoe: 201, 279; supports Texas petition for rehearing, 209

Prescription, doctrine of: argued in *California* case, 178–79, 183; argued in *Texas* case, 202; Black quoted on nonapplicability of, in *California* case, 231

Presidential campaign of 1952, tidelands issue in: 228–30

Preston, E. J., opposes 1945 quitclaim: 148, 154

Proctor, Olin S., denied permit: 128–
29

Public lands of the United States:
defined, 50, 51; tidelands not included in, 50–51; lands beneath
navigable waters not included in,
64; Congress controls, 96; Congress
reserves minerals in, 100

Purvis, Robert F., letter of, quoted:
243

Putnam, Rufus W., testimony of: 66,
235

Pyles, Ernie, testimony of: 66, 67

Quitclaim legislation: attempted in
1945, 144–58; attempts at compromise on, 216–17; passes House in
Eightieth Congress and dies in Senate, 217–18; attempted in Eighty-
first Congress, 218–20; attempted
in Eighty-second Congress, 220–
27; Truman's 1952 veto of, 227–
28; constitutionality of, 230–33;
writer's proposals on, 276–78

Randolph, Edmund, opinion of, as
Attorney General quoted: 127–28

Reed, Justice Stanley F.: dissents in
California case, 181; dissents in
Texas case, 207–208, 252, 253

Res judicata, doctrine of, argued by
Louisiana: 199–200

Riesenfeld, Stefan A.: cited, 20 n.;
supports Texas petition for rehearing, 209

Roberts, Governor Dennis: 232 n.

Rolph, Governor James, Jr., attempts
to compromise California offshore
petroleum situation: 71

Royalties, rentals, and bonuses for oil
operations in marginal-sea soils:

of Louisiana, 53, 57–58; of California, 67, 71, 73; of Long Beach,
74 n.; of Texas, 79–80, 89

"Rum treaties": 21

Russell, Senator Richard, announces
in favor of quitclaim: 229

Sabath, Congressman Adolph: 221

Sánchez Román, Felipe, supports
Texas petition for rehearing: 209

San Ildefonso, Treaty of: 54–55

San Pedro Bay: 261, 264

Santa Catalina Island: 264

Santa Margarita River Case: 255–56

Santa Monica Bay: 261

Sargent, John G., opinions of, as
Attorney General quoted: 125

Sawyer, E. W., letter of, on Oakland
"gang": 119–20 n.

Selden, cited: 9–10

Seldes, George: 240 n.

Sellers, Grover, testimony of: 150

Several fishery, defined: 13 n.

Shelley, Leander, testimony of: 134–
35, 151, 265

Shivers, Governor Allan: testimony
of, 80; marked by Moley as the
man to watch, 229; carries Texas
for Eisenhower, 229–30

Shore-Line Oil Company: 243

Slant-drilling: *see* petroleum production in offshore areas

Smathers, Senator George A.: 224,
228 n.; predicts passage of 1952
quitclaim by Congress, 223

Smith, Senator H. Alexander: 227

Smith, Irving, testimony of, on value
of Long Beach harbor improvements: 75 n.

Smoot, I. E.: 227; applicant for
federal lease, 243

Soule, Senator Pierre, argues "equal
footing": 63–64

Spanish mineral law, rights to precious minerals under: 61

Staples, Abram, testimony of: 151

Stevenson, Adlai, takes stand on tidelands: 229–30

Stipulations: negotiated in *California* case, 186–88; argued in *Texas* and *Louisiana* cases, 199; pattern of *California* case not followed in Gulf area, 211–12; extended and amended, 234–35; attacked by Ickes, 235–36

Stockburger, Arlin R., charged with incompetence: 72

Story, Justice Joseph: 23

Stuart, Captain H. A., argues for petroleum reserve: 105–106

Stuart, Robert A., testimony of: 89 n., 109, 115, 116, 119, 124

Submerged lands: *see* marginal sea, three-mile limit

Summerland oil field, discovered: 66

Sumners, Congressman Hatton W.: 102, 145, 146

Sutherland, Justice George: opinion of, in *United States* v. *Curtiss-Wright* criticized, 30–31; states doctrine of inherent powers, 250; opinion of, cited, 266 n.

Swamp Land Grants Act: 130–31

Taney, Chief Justice Roger, ruling of, in *Martin* v. *Waddell:* 46

Taxation, by state of physical assets in marginal sea: 271–72

Teague, Congressman Olin, testimony of: 89

Territorial waters: *see* marginal sea, three-mile limit

Territorial Waters Jurisdiction Act: 16–17

Texas: claims of, to soils under marginal sea, 79–94; procedure on annexation of, 83–88; provisions for leasing offshore lands of, 88–89;

conveys submerged lands to United States, 93; "equal footing" in admission of, discussed by Douglas, 204–205; importance of tidelands in 1952 presidential election in, 229–30; does not follow pattern of California stipulations, 236; see also *United States* v. *Texas*

Three-mile limit: attitude of British courts on, 14–19, 22; difficulty of agreement on, 19–21; opinion of Leslie McNemar on, 37–38; Louisiana tries to extend, 57; Buchanan assures Britain on extension of, in Gulf of Mexico, 82; Texas tries to extend, 88 n.; position of national government on, in *California* case, 164; Black concedes police power in, 175, 178; *see also* "cannon shot" rule

Thye, Senator Edward J.: 228 n.

Tidelands: technically defined, 6, 38; not included in public lands, 50–51; as technically defined held owned by state, 52

Tidelands cases: see *United States* v. *California, United States* v. *Texas, United States* v. *Louisiana*

Tobey, Senator Charles W., opposes quitclaim: 156, 218

Tolan, Congressman John W.: 102

Trammell, George W., testimony of: 74 n., 106, 119

Transcontinental Treaty: 80

Treaty of Paris: 29

Truett, Laurence A., testimony of: 116, 118

Truman, Harry S.: orders Clark to act against California, 138, 161; supports Pauley against Ickes, 139–40; issues continental-shelf proclamation, 141–43; vetoes quitclaim, 156–57; comments on *California* case, 195 n.; vetoes 1952 quitclaim, 227–28; makes quitclaim 1952 campaign issue, 228–29; issues order creating continental shelf naval petroleum reserve, 257–58

Truscott, Frank F., testimony of: 151

United Landowners Association: 120 n.

United States v. *California:* complaint filed in, 162; answer filed in, 162–63; contentions of national government in, 164–65; contentions of California in, 165–66; arguments in, based on title, 166–67; opinion of Black in, 167–80; dissents in, 180–81; petition filed for rehearing in, 182–85; incompatibility of, with *Chandler-Dunbar* case, 185; stipulations negotiated in, 186–88; order and decree proposed and promulgated in, 190–94; difficulty of demarcating boundary in, 236–38; opinion in, 278–80

United States v. *Louisiana:* complaint filed in, 196–97; Louisiana arguments in, 199–201; opinion in, 203, 278–80; petitions filed for rehearing in, 208; decree in, 210–11; administrative provision for petroleum production made in, 211–12

United States v. *Texas:* complaint filed in, 196–97; national government's arguments stated in, 197–99; Texas arguments stated in, 201–202; opinion in, 203–207, 278–80; dissents in, 207–208; petitions for rehearing filed in, 208–10; decree in, 210–11; administrative provision for petroleum production made in, 211–12

Valentine scrip: 50 n.

Van Devanter, Justice Willis, defines "territory": 24

Vanech, A. Devitt: 256 n.

Vattel, on property concept of marginal sea: 22

Vinson, Chief Justice Fred N., opinion of, in *Toomer* v. *Witsell:* 268–69

Voorhis, Congressman Jerry, opposes quitclaim: 155

Walker, Orin DeMotte, attorney for Jordan: 148, 154

Walsh, Senator Thomas J.: 103

Walter, Congressman Francis: 220, 221, 222; quoted on Santa Margarita dispute, 256

War Department, policy of, on submerged lands prior to 1947: 123–25

Warren, Governor Earl, testimony of: 72, 106, 116, 118, 119

Webster, Daniel, argues "equal footing": 63–64

Wheeler, Burton: represents federal mineral lease applicants, 214 n., 244, 246; actions of, on behalf of lease applicants criticized, 221 n., 222 n.; predicts court test for quitclaim, 232 n.; attacks California stipulations, 236 n.; condemns criticism of Supreme Court, 259 n.

Whipstocking: *see* petroleum production in offshore areas

White, Mastin G.: opinion of, on inapplicability of Mineral Leasing Act of 1920 to submerged lands cited, 189 n.; opinion of, on use of land scrip for submerged soils cited, 245 n.

Willis, Congressman Edwin E.: 255 n.

Wilson, George Grafton, cited: 19

Wilson, Congressman J. Frank: 222 n.

Yorty, Congressman Samuel W.: 255 n., 256 n.

J. S. TOLE